Contributions to Finance and Accounting

The book series 'Contributions to Finance and Accounting' features the latest research from research areas like financial management, investment, capital markets, financial institutions, FinTech and financial innovation, accounting methods and standards, reporting, and corporate governance, among others. Books published in this series are primarily monographs and edited volumes that present new research results, both theoretical and empirical, on a clearly defined topic. All books are published in print and digital formats and disseminated globally. This book series is indexed in Scopus.

Ahmet Akusta · Musa Gün
Editors

Financial Frontiers in Energy Markets

Policy Frameworks, Risk Management, and Investment Strategies in a Global Context

Springer

Editors
Ahmet Akusta
Konya Technical University
Konya, Türkiye

Musa Gün
Recep Tayyip Erdoğan University
Rize, Türkiye

ISSN 2730-6038 ISSN 2730-6046 (electronic)
Contributions to Finance and Accounting
ISBN 978-3-032-16737-8 ISBN 978-3-032-16738-5 (eBook)
https://doi.org/10.1007/978-3-032-16738-5

This Springer imprint is published by the registered company Springer Nature Switzerland AG
The registered company address is: Gewerbestrasse 11, 6330 Cham, Switzerland

Preface

The accelerating transformation of global energy systems has profoundly reshaped the landscape of finance, investment, and policy. In this context, *Financial Frontiers in Energy Markets: Policy Frameworks, Risk Management, and Investment Strategies in a Global Context* offers an integrated perspective on the evolving nexus between finance and energy. This book brings together studies that explore the dynamic intersection of energy and finance across multiple regions, technologies, and methodological perspectives. The chapters collectively demonstrate that energy is no longer only a production factor but a critical financial asset class, influencing global stability, sustainability, and economic resilience.

The central aim of the volume is to analyze how financial risks, policy frameworks, and investment strategies interact to shape both conventional and renewable energy markets. It provides a comprehensive analytical framework linking market volatility, regulation, and technological innovation to financial performance and transition pathways. The volume begins with theoretical and structural insights into the financialization of energy markets, followed by empirical examinations of volatility transmission, geopolitical uncertainty, and the macroeconomic implications of oil price dynamics. Studies focusing on Saudi supply behavior, Chinese demand, and institutional quality in energy security offer a deeper understanding of how global and regional forces interact in shaping risks.

Subsequent chapters examine renewable energy investments under economic globalization, sustainability challenges in the Western Balkans, and energy use patterns in BRICS economies. Empirical evidence from OECD countries provides a detailed assessment of CO_2 emission determinants, while analyses of Islamic Development Bank projects reveal the growing role of ethical and inclusive financing mechanisms in the clean energy transition.

In line with Springer's focus on practical relevance and academic rigor, the book highlights financial innovation and regulatory transformation as key drivers of the energy transition. Employing econometric, machine learning, and bibliometric methods, the authors investigate carbon risk pricing, green bond development, and technological advances such as blockchain and artificial intelligence in energy trade.

Real-world evidence illustrates how investors, regulators, and policymakers can navigate risks and seize opportunities in a volatile global environment. The final chapters discuss electricity market liberalization and strategies to alleviate energy poverty—emphasizing that equitable access to energy remains central to sustainable development. By combining theoretical insights, empirical evidence, and policy relevance, this volume serves as an essential resource for researchers, students, practitioners, and policymakers seeking to understand financial innovation in the global energy transition.

Konya, Türkiye Ahmet Akusta
Rize, Türkiye Musa Gün

Acknowledgments

The authors would like to thank their families for their patience, understanding, and constant encouragement throughout the preparation of this book. Their unwavering support was instrumental in making this work a reality.

The authors also gratefully acknowledge the valuable contributions of the reviewers, whose insightful comments and suggestions greatly improved the quality, coherence, and presentation of the chapters.

Finally, sincere thanks are extended to the Springer editorial team for their professional guidance, editorial assistance, and commitment throughout the publication process. Their collaboration and attention to detail ensured that this volume reached its final form with the highest academic and production standards.

Ahmet Akusta
Musa Gün

About This Book

This book explores the multifaceted relationship between energy markets and finance through original studies addressing volatility, investment, innovation, and sustainability. Covering diverse contexts from OECD and BRICS countries to the Western Balkans, Latin America, and Sub-Saharan Africa, the chapters examine energy price dynamics, renewable investment, CO_2 emissions, and geopolitical risks. Using advanced econometric, machine learning, and bibliometric approaches, the authors analyze topics such as carbon risk pricing, green and Islamic finance, blockchain, and artificial intelligence in energy trade. The book also highlights policy challenges related to decarbonization, electricity market liberalization, and energy poverty, offering an integrated view of how financial systems can foster sustainable and resilient energy transitions.

The target audience and potential users of this book include:

- Researchers and academics working on energy economics, finance, and sustainability
- Policymakers and regulators designing energy and climate policy frameworks
- Professionals and analysts in financial institutions, energy companies, and investment funds
- Graduate students and practitioners seeking to understand financial risk, innovation, and transition strategies in global energy markets.

Contents

About the Editors

Ahmet Akusta is a Lecturer in the Department of Business Administration at Konya Technical University, Türkiye. He holds a Ph.D. in Business Administration from Necmettin Erbakan University, where his doctoral research focused on forecasting Bitcoin price volatility using machine learning techniques. He earned his first master's degree in International Business from Marmara University and a second in Business Administration from Necmettin Erbakan University, specializing in dividend policy and ownership structure in emerging markets. His teaching and research interests include machine learning applications in finance, ESG-based profitability analysis, risk parity optimization, and volatility modeling. Dr. Akusta has contributed to numerous international journals and conferences in the fields of financial technology and energy finance.

Musa Gün is an Associate Professor of Finance at Recep Tayyip Erdoğan University, Türkiye. He received his Ph.D. in Finance from Istanbul University and holds a master's degree in Financial Economics from Doğuş University. He began his academic career as a Research Assistant at Recep Tayyip Erdoğan University after professional experience in the banking and auditing sectors. His research primarily focuses on asset pricing models, market anomalies, credit risk management, investment valuation, and financial technologies. Dr. Gün has published extensively in leading academic journals and has served as a reviewer and session chair at several international conferences.

The editors bring a combination of expertise in financial economics, energy markets, and quantitative modeling, reflecting a shared interest in the intersection of finance, technology, and sustainability. Their academic backgrounds and interdisciplinary research perspectives have guided the development of *Financial Frontiers in Energy Markets: Policy Frameworks, Risk Management, and Investment Strategies in a Global Context*, ensuring both scholarly rigor and practical relevance.

Energy Markets and Financial Systems: Dynamics, Financialization, and Volatility Transmission

Gökhan Berk Özbek and Ewelina Idziak

Abstract This study provides a comprehensive perspective on energy markets, the process of financialization, and their interaction with financial markets. In this context, the financialization process of energy markets has been examined from a historical perspective, the increasing importance and role of energy in the global economy have been explored, and the structures and actors within energy markets have been elaborated. In addition to the theoretical framework, the relationship between energy markets and financial markets has been investigated in the context of volatility spillover dynamics. To this end, the MSCI World Index has been selected to represent global stock markets, and the S&P GSCI Energy Index to represent global energy markets. The three-year period between July 2022 and June 2025, during which significant global developments occurred both in macroeconomic and geopolitical terms, has been selected as the analysis window. As the econometric method, the Bivariate BEKK-GARCH model has been employed. According to the empirical findings, bidirectional contagion effects have been detected between stock markets and energy markets. Although sudden shocks in energy markets initially create a hedge effect on stock markets in the short term, persistent long-term volatility in energy markets has been found to increase volatility in stock markets. On the other hand, shocks originating from stock markets were found to intensify volatility in energy markets in the short run, yet this contagion transforms into a stabilizing role in the long term.

Keywords Energy markets · Crude oil · Natural gas · Electricity · Energy-finance nexus · BEKK-GARCH

G. B. Özbek (✉)
Harmancık Vocational School, Bursa Uludağ University, Bursa, Türkiye
e-mail: gbozbek@uludag.edu.tr

E. Idziak
Kazimierz Wielki University, Bydgoszcz, Poland
e-mail: ewelina.idziak@ukw.edu.pl

A. Akusta and M. Gün (eds.), *Financial Frontiers in Energy Markets*, Contributions to Finance and Accounting, https://doi.org/10.1007/978-3-032-16738-5_1

1 Introduction

Throughout history, humankind's most significant breakthroughs have been achieved through the ability to control energy and transform it for various purposes. This process, which began with the harnessing and direction of natural energy sources such as fire, water, and wind, has today reached the level of controlling atomic energy. In doing so, humanity has not only managed to dominate its environment but has also succeeded in building great civilizations. (Harari, 2014). Energy, which lies at the foundation of all human life cycles, has gradually become one of the most essential components of the modern global economy. In critical areas such as industrialization, transportation, communication and technological advancement, energy is indispensable for achieving sustainable growth. It functions as the invisible heart of national economies.

In the post-World War II era, a global economic structure increasingly dependent on oil began to emerge as a result of rapid growth and industrialization efforts worldwide. Under the Bretton Woods system, energy prices remained relatively stable for an extended period. During this phase, energy was regarded as a stable industrial input and had not yet evolved into an instrument of financial speculation.

The 1970s marked a period in which the global economy was forced to completely reassess its approach to energy resources. The first major macroeconomic shift occurred with the collapse of the Bretton Woods system. In early 1971, the U.S, whose dollar liabilities exceeded its gold reserves by more than fivefold, unilaterally suspended the dollar's convertibility into gold on August 15, 1971, thereby initiating the global transition to a floating exchange rate regime. Subsequently, on October 6, 1973, the Yom Kippur War broke out, triggering a crisis that would deeply affect the industries and economies of Western countries. In response to the war, the Organization of the Petroleum Exporting Countries (OPEC) imposed an embargo on Western nations supporting Israel. This sudden and sharp increase in oil prices created a shock effect in Western industrial sectors, where rising production costs paved the way for high inflation. Alongside inflation, many economies entered into simultaneous recessions, resulting in a widespread stagflation spiral. Even before the effects of the first oil shock had subsided, the 1979 Iranian Revolution and the subsequent Iran-Iraq War caused a significant contraction in oil supply, once again pushing the global economy into recession. Notably, the price of crude oil per barrel rose from $3.35 in January 1970 to $32.50 by the end of the decade (Hammes & Wills, 2005). This dramatic increase had profound impacts across the global economy. These developments revealed that energy could no longer be considered merely as an industrial input; rather, it had become directly associated with global financial stability (or fragility).

The lessons drawn from the energy crises of the 1970s, combined with the momentum gained by financial liberalization movements in the 1980s, laid the foundation for treating energy as a financial instrument. Various exchanges standardized futures contracts on oil and natural gas, enabling energy to be used for financial purposes such as hedging, arbitrage, and speculation. During the 1990s, the acceleration of developments in derivative markets led to a significant diversification of energy-related derivative instruments. In the post-millennium era, China's rapid and sustained economic growth led to a sharp increase in global energy demand, which in turn contributed to a considerable rise in energy prices. The global financial crisis had a profound impact on energy markets as well, reaffirming the interconnectedness between financial and energy markets (Joo et al., 2020; Lahmiri, 2017). The period following the 2015 Paris Agreement constitutes another critical historical milestone for energy markets. From this point onward, the energy-finance nexus began to be prioritized through the lens of sustainability. Renewable energy investments, carbon markets, and green bonds have emerged as prominent new financial instruments. The Paris Agreement initiated a global energy transition process, which necessitates substantial investments for the transformation of the fossil fuel industry toward renewable energy and low-carbon technologies (Peake & Ekins, 2017). This imperative has led to a gradual shift in the role of energy, from being a classically financialized commodity toward becoming a central component of sustainable finance. On the other hand, various geopolitical tensions around the world during this period (such as the Russia-Ukraine war) have sparked debates on energy security and on how scenarios of failing to ensure such security may affect global financial stability (Henderson, 2024; Nguyen et al., 2024).

This section will provide a detailed examination of the role of energy in the global economy, the process of its financialization, the structure of energy markets, and the key market participants. In addition, an econometric application will be presented to analyze the interaction between energy and the financial system.

2 Energy at the Core of Global Change

Although the dynamics of economic growth were traditionally examined within the framework of conventional production functions that focused on labor and capital, the profound geopolitical developments of the 1970s, whose consequences reverberated throughout the global economy, led to a growing body of literature investigating the impact of energy on economic growth.

Subsequent empirical studies have shed more light on the dimensions of the relationship between energy and economic growth, making it increasingly evident that energy is not merely a production input but a vital component of sustainable growth. In particular, the disruptive effects of the 1973 and 1979 oil shocks on the global economy, how they undermined economic growth and generated significant macroeconomic uncertainties, highlighted the centrality of energy in economic analysis.

Early influential studies in this field focused on the United States. Kraft and Kraft (1978), using U.S. data from the 1947–1974 period, found a unidirectional causality running from gross national product (GNP) to gross energy consumption. However, this result was quickly challenged by Akarca and Long (1980), who showed that a mere two-year adjustment in the sample period led to drastically different findings, suggesting that the previously identified causality was driven solely by that short timeframe and was not representative of the broader relationship. Their findings indicated no causality in either direction for the remaining period. Later, Yu and Hwang (1984) produced results consistent with those of Akarca and Long (1980), reinforcing the skepticism toward the earlier unidirectional claim. Nevertheless, as both studies emphasized, the post-1970 period marked a turning point in the energy–growth nexus, introducing considerable outliers and structural shifts into the empirical analysis. Indeed, Abosedra and Baghestani (1989) obtained empirical findings that support the results of Kraft and Kraft (1978) by extending the sample period starting from 1947 to different endpoints such as 1972, 1974, 1979, and 1987.

Subsequent studies conducted in the following years revealed that the results could vary significantly depending on both the country examined and the specific time periods considered (Cheng, 1995; Erol & Yu, 1987; Huang et al., 2008; Hwang & Gum, 1991; Lee & Chang, 2007; Soytas & Sari, 2003; Yu & Choi, 1985). The importance of correctly identifying this relationship for individual countries lies in its implications for sound policy-making. For instance, in a country where energy consumption has a significant impact on economic growth, energy conservation policies may have considerably adverse effects on the economy. When studies focusing particularly on the post-1970s period are examined, the existence of a long-run relationship between energy and economic growth becomes prominent. Especially in frontier and emerging economies, the growth hypothesis, which posits that energy consumption drives economic growth, has gained considerable empirical support (see Ahmad et al., 2020; Ozturk, 2010 for more details).

Fluctuations in energy prices have the potential to evolve from a micro-level impact at the firm level into a macroeconomic phenomenon within a short period of time. Increases in the prices of energy resources such as oil and natural gas directly lead to rising production costs in industrial sectors that rely heavily on these inputs. This situation gives rise to cost-push inflation and, unlike demand-pull inflation, results in reduced investment due to the higher cost of production. Consequently, employment contracts, unemployment rises, and ultimately, the recessionary spiral deepens. The oil shocks of 1973 and 1979 represent the clearest examples of this phenomenon (Mork & Hall, 1980). The simultaneous occurrence of high inflation and high unemployment during this period led to the questioning of the classical Phillips Curve and gave rise to the concept of stagflation. In this regard, energy prices play a critical role in shaping the high-inflationary trajectories that countries may experience (Thoresen, 1983).

On the other hand, energy is not only a fundamental input for economic activities but also one of the most strategic components of international political economy. While fluctuations in energy prices have the potential to affect microeconomic variables, such as household savings, corporate costs, profitability, and macroeconomic indicators, such as growth rates, inflation, and the current account balance, they also lie at the core of national security strategies of states. Indeed, the Middle East and its vast petroleum reserves have attracted the intense attention of global powers and international capital since the early twentieth century. Particularly for the U.S.,

Middle Eastern oil resources have long been a fundamental determinant of its foreign policy. A key turning point in this trajectory occurred in February 1945, when President Franklin D. Roosevelt hosted Saudi Arabia's founding King Abdulaziz Ibn Saud aboard the USS Quincy warship anchored in Egypt. As a result of the discussions and agreements reached during this meeting, Saudi Arabia agreed to become a supplier of affordably priced oil to Western markets in exchange for U.S. military and political protection. From that moment on, developments in the Middle East became a central focus of U.S. foreign policy. Over the years, the deepening dependence of the U.S. on oil imports from the region rendered this interest into a strategic obsession (Jones, 2012). Beginning in the early twenty-first century, China's surging participation in regional oil demand further elevated the geopolitical significance of the region's reserves (Salameh, 2003). These developments also served as the primary driver behind the increasing global capital inflows and foreign investment interest directed toward the Gulf countries. In light of these geopolitical dynamics, the intersection between energy and the financial system has gained even greater importance. This is because energy prices are shaped not only by supply–demand fundamentals, but also by political uncertainties and perceptions of global risk. One of the most striking examples of this geopolitical dimension has recently been witnessed in the context of Russia's natural gas resources and their implications for the European Union's energy security.

3 The Financialization of Energy

Energy markets have ceased to function solely as traditional commodity markets governed by classical supply and demand dynamics, particularly as a result of the 1973 and 1979 oil shocks, as well as the financial liberalization waves that gained momentum after the 1980s. These developments increasingly attracted the attention of financial investors. In addition to investors' appetite for speculation, the adoption of floating exchange rate regimes following the collapse of the Bretton Woods system also contributed to a surge in commodity price volatility. Consequently, a growing need for hedging strategies emerged within commodity markets. Within this evolving context, crude oil and other energy sources began to be perceived as strategic tools within the portfolios of global investors.

Since the early 2000s, energy commodities, particularly oil and natural gas, have increasingly begun to behave like financial assets. In parallel with this transformation, financial actors such as commodity index traders (CITs), commodity trading advisers, and hedge funds have become more active and dominant in these markets. The key distinction between these actors and traditional commodity traders lies in the fact that they are not directly exposed to the physical commodities in their commercial activities (Goldstein & Yang, 2022). As a result, the spillover effects of futures markets on spot markets have attracted growing interest in the literature (Kim & Lim, 2019; Kumar Mahalik et al., 2014; Magkonis & Tsouknidis, 2017; Ren et al., 2025). Since the early 2000s, there has been a substantial inflow of funds into commodity

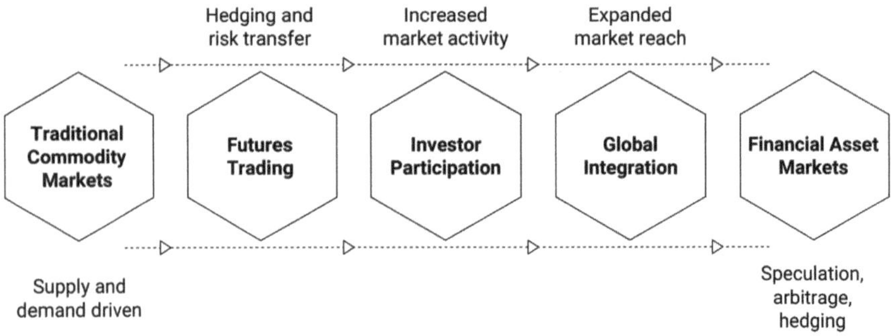

Fig. 1 Financialization process of energy. *Source* Authors' compilation, created using the Napkin application

markets, particularly through investor-led funds (Hamilton & Wu, 2015). One of the main drivers behind this surge in capital flows was the sharp decline experienced in stock markets at the beginning of the 2000s (Ding et al., 2021). By 2008, a significant increase in commodity price volatility had been observed. This development was attributed by many finance and commodity experts to excessive speculation in futures markets, which was argued to have substantially contributed to rising energy costs (Cheng & Xiong, 2014).

Another notable area of interest in the literature concerns the integration between energy prices and stock markets. A substantial number of studies in this field provide evidence supporting a negative relationship between energy prices and stock market performance (Ahmed & Sarkodie, 2021; Elian & Kisswani, 2018; Gurrib, 2018; Maghyereh & Al-Kandari, 2007; Stoupos & Kiohos, 2021). Ultimately, the financialization of energy has created both opportunities (such as the emergence of new investment instruments) and risks (such as the amplification of financial crises through energy price shocks) for investors. Figure 1 provides a visual summary of the financialization process of energy.

4 Market Structures and Key Actors

Crude oil is the most liquid commodity market in the world, with daily contract volumes reaching hundreds of billions of dollars in financial markets. Crude oil prices are based on key benchmarks, primarily West Texas Intermediate (WTI), Brent, and Oman. WTI is generally lighter and has a lower sulfur content compared to Brent, which, in principle, makes it more expensive (Hammoudeh et al., 2008). However, actual market behavior does not always align with this expectation. In particular, since April 2011, Brent has consistently traded at a premium to WTI, and the widening of this spread has raised questions regarding such significant price differences in a commodity that is priced globally despite spatial distinctions. Due to the global arbitrage mechanism, it is generally expected that such price behavior would exhibit cointegration and convergence. Nevertheless, factors such as transportation costs, tariffs, and differences in quality are also influential and should not be overlooked in explaining this divergence (Mann & Sephton, 2016). In addition, structural factors such as natural disasters in the U.S. and refinery outages have also contributed to the widening of the spread in favor of Brent (Hammoudeh et al., 2008). As a result, these benchmark prices constitute the basis for pricing both physical delivery contracts and futures contracts. Crude oil futures traded in financial markets have, over time, deepened the interaction between oil prices and global macroeconomic indicators. On the other hand, the significant increase in speculative activity in the futures markets over the years has drawn various criticisms (Juvenal & Petrella, 2015). One such criticism is that speculative movements distort the price discovery function in spot markets, leading to excessive price fluctuations and undermining the statistically sound relationship that should exist between oil inventories and oil prices. Another criticism is that, due to the growing dominance of financial actors with speculative motives over commodity users in the price mechanism, the hedging functions of futures markets are no longer being effectively fulfilled (Fattouh et al., 2013).

However, there are also opposing views suggesting that financial actors do not have a significant impact on the determination of spot prices. According to these arguments, the main source of this misconception arises from comparing the trading volume of futures contracts (covering deliveries spread over extended periods) with the quantity of physical oil produced on a single day. In reality, when dates are properly aligned, the volume of futures contracts corresponds to only a fraction of the physical production realized on that specific day (Ripple, 2008). This view is grounded in the assumption that speculators in the futures markets are predominantly non-commercial investors, that is, they are not directly involved in the production or consumption of crude oil. As a result, these futures contracts are typically settled in cash rather than through physical delivery. Consequently, as the contract approaches maturity, a convergence toward the spot price is expected, which implies that these futures transactions do not exert a significant influence on spot prices (Smith, 2009).

This view asserts that prices cannot deviate from the fundamentals of supply and demand. Accordingly, the focus shifts toward a long-standing cartel: the Organization of the Petroleum Exporting Countries (OPEC). Established in 1960, OPEC gained a dominant role in the global energy landscape, particularly during the 1973 oil crisis, and has significantly influenced developments in the world economy. Today, OPEC member countries account for over 50% of global crude oil exports and possess more than 70% of the world's proven oil reserves. In this respect, OPEC is considered the most influential market actor in terms of its ability to steer prices through production quotas and supply cuts (Bentzen, 2007; Smith, 2009). Nevertheless, two other major factors that can also shape price levels are the output of non-OPEC producers and global demand, which is driven by economic growth dynamics (Gately, 1984).

Another important energy resource, natural gas, remained for many years a commodity heavily dependent on pipeline infrastructure. This reliance kept pricing largely regional over extended periods. The main benchmarks used in natural gas pricing have been Henry Hub, Title Transfer Facility (TTF), Japan-Korea Marker (JKM), National Balancing Point (NBP), and Alberta Energy Company (AECO). In global trade, natural gas contracts were traditionally structured as long-term agreements indexed to oil prices. However, the natural gas market underwent a profound transformation with the advent of Liquefied Natural Gas (LNG). Especially since 2016, LNG markets have experienced substantial growth, which has driven natural gas markets to evolve toward a more global and spot-based structure. The share of traditional oil-indexed long-term contracts has declined, while spot and hub-based pricing mechanisms have risen sharply. This has accelerated the shift toward gas-on-gas (GOG) pricing and contributed to a growing global integration and convergence of gas prices (Fulwood, 2024; Heather, 2024).

In recent years, the global gas markets have experienced highly turbulent periods. Initially, the COVID-19 pandemic led to a significant decline in global demand, resulting in a period where supply substantially exceeded demand. However, following the exit from the pandemic, a major demand surge occurred in 2021. The Russia-Ukraine war in 2022 further exacerbated the crisis, pushing demand well beyond available supply (Heather, 2023). During this period, U.S. LNG exports to Europe also increased. This has further elevated the importance of the International Gas Union's (IGU) missions and activities, which are aimed at strengthening the role of natural gas in the global energy balance, promoting its sustainable use, supporting the development of technology and infrastructure, and fostering international cooperation in energy security.

Electricity, however, exhibits a distinct characteristic compared to other energy commodities, which is the necessity of being produced and consumed simultaneously, meaning it cannot be stored. This unique feature has led to electricity remaining under the regulation of large state-owned enterprises (electric utilities) for an extended period, as these utilities controlled the entire chain of production, transmission, and distribution (Karthikeyan et al., 2013). However, starting particularly from the 1990s, this vertically integrated structure began to evolve into an open market system, which is a transformation driven by the aim of enhancing economic efficiency. The deregulation movements and the emergence of competition-based systems ultimately led to the establishment of electricity markets. In this new system, electricity generation shifted from a centralized model under public authority to a competitive free-market environment dominated by private companies (Albadi & El-Saadany, 2008; Ventosa et al., 2005). Following the establishment of the first electricity exchanges in the U.K. and the Scandinavian countries during the 1990s, numerous competitive electricity markets began operating in subsequent years across other European countries, as well as in the U.S. and Australia (Mayer & Trück, 2018).

Renewable energy has added truly transformative dimensions to energy markets and industry, particularly over the past quarter-century. Although renewable energy sources initially entered the market in a non-competitive position due to their high entry costs, over the years they have become increasingly widespread, primarily thanks to government incentives and subsidies. This expansion has been further accelerated by rapid technological advancement, ultimately turning renewable energy into a global phenomenon (Gross et al., 2003). From this point onward, the shift toward renewable energy has also contributed to the development of consumer sensitivity in this regard. This trend has made it essential to clearly distinguish whether the source of energy is renewable or based on conventional production. In Europe, Guarantee of Origin (GO) systems have been established in line with EU Directives 2001/77/EC and 2009/28/EC to certify the renewable origin of electricity production. In the U.S., a similar structure is implemented through Renewable Energy Certificates (RECs). These certificates have evolved into an additional source of income for companies and a green portfolio instrument for investors (Holzapfel et al., 2024; Hulshof et al., 2019).

On the other hand, carbon markets, which came to the forefront with the Kyoto Protocol, have gained significant importance with the Paris Agreement. Through the EU Emissions Trading System (EU ETS), a "cap-and-trade" mechanism has been established, whereby an upper limit (cap) is imposed on emissions to reduce the environmental impact of carbon emissions (Meadows et al., 2019). This system is significantly effective in reducing greenhouse gas emissions (Bayer & Aklin, 2020; Ellerman et al., 2016). Nevertheless, debates persist regarding the possibility that the system may create a disparity in competitive advantage between companies subject to regulation and those that are not, as well as its potential adverse effects on national economic systems. However, empirical research has revealed that these regulations tend to generate value for firms and that the impact on the loss of competitiveness is statistically insignificant (Chan et al., 2013; Joltreau & Sommerfeld, 2019).

5 Revisiting the Energy–Finance Nexus

At this stage of the chapter, the relationship between energy markets and financial markets will be examined in the context of risk transmission. In doing so, the analysis will provide an up-to-date perspective on the financialization of energy and, more specifically, generate empirical evidence on the propagation effects of shocks between stock markets and energy markets, enabling meaningful policy implications to be derived.

5.1 Data and Methodology

The variables used in the study are defined as the MSCI World Index and the S&P GSCI Energy Index, thereby enabling the analysis to incorporate indicators with strong representativeness for both global energy and global stock markets. The study employs daily closing prices (USD) for the variables. Only the trading days on which both indices are concurrently available are included in the analysis. The selected research period spans three years, from June 30, 2022, to June 30, 2025. This timeframe allows for the inclusion of major shocks such as the Russia–Ukraine war, OPEC decisions, and global inflation on the energy markets side; and FED interest rate hikes, global financial instability, and the banking crisis on the stock markets side. The data were obtained from Investing.com and incorporated into the analysis after computing their natural logarithmic differences. To examine the volatility spillover dynamics between the variables, the bivariate (full) BEKK-GARCH model (Engle & Kroner, 1995) is employed. The BEKK-GARCH(1,1) specification is used for lag length selection.

$$Q_t = CC\prime + A\varepsilon_{t-1}\varepsilon\prime_{t-1}A\prime + BQ_{t-1}B\prime \tag{1}$$

Equation 1 defines the full BEKK-GARCH(1,1) model used to estimate the conditional variance–covariance matrix Q_t of two financial return series. Here, C is a triangular matrix ensuring positive definiteness, while A and B are fully parameterized square matrices that capture short-term shock effects and the persistence of volatility across markets, including cross-market spillovers. The residual vector ε_{t-1} introduces new information into the system.

5.2 *Unveiling Market Shocks: The Data Behind Energy-Finance Volatility*

Table 1 presents the descriptive statistics and unit root test results for the variables. To examine the stationarity of the time series, the Augmented Dickey-Fuller (ADF) test (Dickey & Fuller, 1979, 1981) and the Phillips-Perron (PP) test (Phillips & Perron, 1988) were employed. For the ADF test, the optimal lag lengths were selected based on the Schwarz Information Criterion. In the PP test, the spectral estimation method was specified as the Bartlett kernel, while the optimal bandwidth was determined using the Newey-West method.

When Table 1 is examined, it is observed that the average return of the stock markets was positive during the period, while the average return of the energy markets was negative. The standard deviation of the energy markets throughout the period was also approximately twice as high as that of the stock markets. Regarding the unit root test results, both variables were found to be stationary at the level.

Table 1 Descriptive statistics and unit root test results

Variables	Mean	Max	Min	Std. Dev	Median	ADF (Intercept&Trend)	PP (Intercept&Trend)
MSCI World	0.0005	0.0608	−0.0595	0.0094	0.0006	−24.9887(0)*	−24.8848(13)*
S&P GSCI Energy	−0.0006	0.0594	−0.0824	0.0187	0.0004	−25.3970(0)*	−26.0366(19)*

Note Values in parentheses indicate lag lengths (for ADF test) and bandwidths (for PP test). The symbols * denote 1% significance levels

Table 2 Bivariate BEKK-GARCH results

Variables				ARCHLM(1)
MSCI World				0.0986*
S&P GSCI Energy				0.0967*
Model	$A_{(1,2)}$	$A_{(2,1)}$	$B_{(1,2)}$	$B_{(2,1)}$
MSCI World & S&P GSCI Energy	−0.4507*	0.1374*	0.4660*	−0.1496*

Note The symbols * denote 1% significance levels

In order to test the presence of ARCH effects in the time series, an ARCH-LM pre-test was initially conducted. According to the test results presented in Table 2, ARCH effects are present in the variables. Subsequently, a bivariate BEKK-GARCH test was performed, and the findings are reported in the continuation of Table 2.

When the BEKK-GARCH results are examined, it is observed that there exists bidirectional risk transmission between the variables, both in the short and long term. According to the empirical findings, sudden shocks in the energy markets initially exhibit a hedging effect on stock markets. However, the persistent volatility in energy markets transforms into a contagion effect on stock markets in the long run. Conversely, abrupt shocks originating from stock markets increase volatility in energy markets in the short term. Yet, in the long term, the persistent volatility in stock markets turns into a transmission that absorbs volatility in energy markets. When the coefficients are analyzed, it is seen that the risk transmission from energy markets to stock markets is stronger (in terms of both ARCH and GARCH effects) compared to the transmission from stock markets to energy markets.

6 Conclusion

Given the long-term financialization process of energy markets, institutional transformations, the structural evolution of market mechanisms, the increasingly critical role of energy in the global economy, and the deepening interaction between energy and financial markets, it is clear that energy can no longer be considered merely an industrial commodity. Within the scope of this chapter, which outlines the transition of energy from a production input to a complex financial asset, the current relationship between energy markets and stock markets has also been examined. The empirical findings reveal a bidirectional volatility transmission between the markets. Although shocks in energy markets initially provide a hedging effect on stock markets, the persistence of volatility is believed to spread into stock markets through rising production costs, inflationary pressures, and altered growth expectations. On the other hand, shocks in stock markets caused by global uncertainties and economic depressions are thought to create contagion in energy markets due to anticipated impacts on demand; however, in the long run, the effect of financial shocks is believed to be absorbed within energy markets, which are more directly tied to real

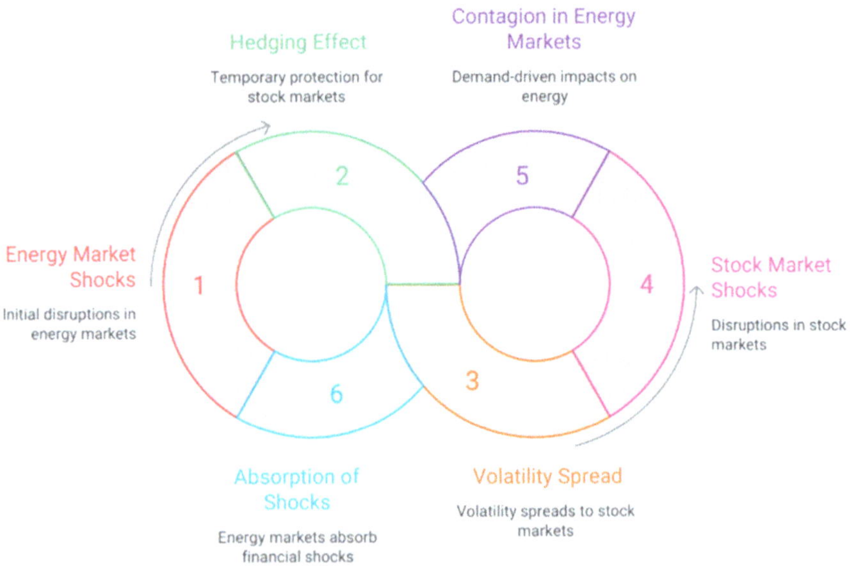

Fig. 2 Volatility transmission cycle. *Source* Authors' compilation, created using the Napkin application

production and consumption. The empirical findings are additionally illustrated in Fig. 2.

It is evident that energy markets will undergo significant transformations in the near future in line with renewable energy expansion and net-zero carbon targets. Nevertheless, the potential impacts of ongoing global geopolitical uncertainties on energy markets are also likely to remain persistent. In this context, the continued and up-to-date examination of the evolution of energy markets, their role in the global economy, and their interactions with financial markets is of critical importance for policymakers, producers, investors, and all households.

References

Abosedra, S., & Baghestani, H. (1989). New evidence on the causal relationship between United States energy consumption and gross national product. *The Journal of Energy and Development, 14*(2), 285–292. https://www.jstor.org/stable/24807939

Ahmad, N., Aghdam, R. F., Butt, I., & Naveed, A. (2020). Citation-based systematic literature review of energy-growth nexus: An overview of the field and content analysis of the top 50 influential papers. *Energy Economics, 86*, Article 104642. https://doi.org/10.1016/j.eneco.2019.104642

Ahmed, M. Y., & Sarkodie, S. A. (2021). Counterfactual shock in energy commodities affects stock market dynamics: Evidence from the United States. *Resources Policy, 72*, Article 102083. https://doi.org/10.1016/j.resourpol.2021.102083

Akarca, A. T., & Long, T. V. (1980). On the relationship between energy and GNP: a reexamination. *The Journal of Energy and Development, 5*(2), 326–331. https://www.jstor.org/stable/24806899

Albadi, M. H., & El-Saadany, E. F. (2008). A summary of demand response in electricity markets. *Electric Power Systems Research, 78*(11), 1989–1996. https://doi.org/10.1016/j.epsr.2008.04.002

Bayer, P., & Aklin, M. (2020). The European Union emissions trading system reduced CO2 emissions despite low prices. *Proceedings of the National Academy of Sciences, 117*(16), 8804–8812. https://doi.org/10.1073/pnas.1918128117

Bentzen, J. (2007). Does OPEC influence crude oil prices? Testing for co-movements and causality between regional crude oil prices. *Applied Economics, 39*(11), 1375–1385. https://doi.org/10.1080/00036840600606344

Chan, H. S. R., Li, S., & Zhang, F. (2013). Firm competitiveness and the European Union emissions trading scheme. *Energy Policy, 63*, 1056–1064. https://doi.org/10.1016/j.enpol.2013.09.032

Cheng, B. S. (1995). An investigation of cointegration and causality between energy consumption and economic growth. *Journal of Energy and Development, 21*, 73.

Cheng, I. H., & Xiong, W. (2014). Financialization of commodity markets. *Annual Review of Financial Economics, 6*(1), 419–441. https://doi.org/10.1146/annurev-financial-110613-034432

Dickey, D. A., & Fuller, W. A. (1979). Distribution of the estimators for autoregressive time series with a unit root. *Journal of the American Statistical Association, 74*(1), 427–431. https://doi.org/10.1080/01621459.1979.10482531

Dickey, D. A., & Fuller, W. A. (1981). Likelihood ratio tests for autoregressive time series with a unit root. *Econometrica, 49*, 1057–1072. https://doi.org/10.2307/1912517

Ding, S., Cui, T., Zheng, D., & Du, M. (2021). The effects of commodity financialization on commodity market volatility. *Resources Policy, 73*, Article 102220. https://doi.org/10.1016/j.resourpol.2021.102220

Elian, M. I., & Kisswani, K. M. (2018). Oil price changes and stock market returns: Cointegration evidence from emerging market. *Economic Change and Restructuring, 51*(4), 317–337. https://doi.org/10.1007/s10644-016-9199-5

Ellerman, A. D., Marcantonini, C., & Zaklan, A. (2016). The European Union emissions trading system: Ten years and counting. *Review of Environmental Economics and Policy., 10*(1), 89–107. https://doi.org/10.1093/reep/rev014

Engle, R. F., & Kroner, K. F. (1995). Multivariate simultaneous generalized ARCH. *Econometric Theory, 11*(1), 122–150. https://doi.org/10.1017/S0266466600009063

Erol, U., & Yu, E. S. (1987). On the causal relationship between energy and income for industrialized countries. *The Journal of Energy and Development, 13*(1), 113–122. https://www.jstor.org/stable/24807616

Fattouh, B., Kilian, L., & Mahadeva, L. (2013). The role of speculation in oil markets: What have we learned so far? *The Energy Journal, 34*(3), 7–33. https://doi.org/10.5547/01956574.34.3.2

Fulwood, M. (2024). *What drives international gas prices in competitive markets? Four fallacies and a hypothesis* (No. 195). OIES Paper: NG. The Oxford Institute for Energy Studies, Oxford, UK.

Gately, D. (1984). A ten-year retrospective: OPEC and the world oil market. *Journal of Economic Literature, 22*(3), 1100–1114. https://www.jstor.org/stable/2725308

Goldstein, I., & Yang, L. (2022). Commodity financialization and information transmission. *The Journal of Finance, 77*(5), 2613–2667. https://doi.org/10.1111/jofi.13165

Gross, R., Leach, M., & Bauen, A. (2003). Progress in renewable energy. *Environment International, 29*(1), 105–122. https://doi.org/10.1016/S0160-4120(02)00130-7

Gurrib, I. (2018). Can an energy futures index predict US stock market index movements? *International Journal of Energy Economics and Policy, 8*(5), 230–240.

Hamilton, J. D., & Wu, J. C. (2015). Effects of index-fund investing on commodity futures prices. *International Economic Review, 56*(1), 187–205. https://doi.org/10.1111/iere.12099

Hammes, D., & Wills, D. (2005). Black gold: The end of Bretton Woods and the oil-price shocks of the 1970s. *The Independent Review, 9*(4), 501–511. https://www.jstor.org/stable/24562081

Hammoudeh, S. M., Ewing, B. T., & Thompson, M. A. (2008). Threshold cointegration analysis of crude oil benchmarks. *The Energy Journal, 29*(4), 79–96. https://doi.org/10.5547/ISSN0195-6574-EJ-Vol29-No4-

Harari, Y. N. (2014). *Sapiens: A Brief History of Humankind*. Random House.

Heather, P. (2023). *European traded gas hubs: Their continued relevance* (No. 183). OIES Paper: NG. The Oxford Institute for Energy Studies, Oxford, UK.

Heather, P. (2024). *European traded gas hubs: The markets have rebalanced* (No. 192). OIES Paper: NG. The Oxford Institute for Energy Studies, Oxford, UK.

Henderson, J. (2024). The impact of the Russia-Ukraine war on global gas markets. *Current Sustainable/renewable Energy Reports, 11*(1), 1–9. https://doi.org/10.1007/s40518-024-00232-x

Holzapfel, P. K., Bánk, J., Bach, V., & Finkbeiner, M. (2024). Relevance of guarantees of origin for Europe's renewable energy targets. *Renewable and Sustainable Energy Reviews, 205*, Article 114850. https://doi.org/10.1016/j.rser.2024.114850

Huang, B. N., Hwang, M. J., & Yang, C. W. (2008). Causal relationship between energy consumption and GDP growth revisited: A dynamic panel data approach. *Ecological Economics, 67*(1), 41–54. https://doi.org/10.1016/j.ecolecon.2007.11.006

Hulshof, D., Jepma, C., & Mulder, M. (2019). Performance of markets for European renewable energy certificates. *Energy Policy, 128*, 697–710. https://doi.org/10.1016/j.enpol.2019.01.051

Hwang, D. B., & Gum, B. (1991). The causal relationship between energy and GNP: The case of Taiwan. *The Journal of Energy and Development, 16*(2), 219–226. https://www.jstor.org/stable/24807960

Joltreau, E., & Sommerfeld, K. (2019). Why does emissions trading under the EU Emissions Trading System (ETS) not affect firms' competitiveness? Empirical findings from the literature. *Climate Policy, 19*(4), 453–471. https://doi.org/10.1080/14693062.2018.1502145

Jones, T. C. (2012). America, oil, and war in the Middle East. *The Journal of American History, 99*(1), 208–218. https://doi.org/10.1093/jahist/jas045

Joo, K., Suh, J. H., Lee, D., & Ahn, K. (2020). Impact of the global financial crisis on the crude oil market. *Energy Strategy Reviews, 30*, Article 100516. https://doi.org/10.1016/j.esr.2020.100516

Juvenal, L., & Petrella, I. (2015). Speculation in the oil market. *Journal of Applied Econometrics, 30*(4), 621–649. https://doi.org/10.1002/jae.2388

Karthikeyan, S. P., Raglend, I. J., & Kothari, D. P. (2013). A review on market power in deregulated electricity market. *International Journal of Electrical Power & Energy Systems, 48*, 139–147. https://doi.org/10.1016/j.ijepes.2012.11.024

Kim, K., & Lim, S. (2019). Price discovery and volatility spillover in spot and futures markets: Evidences from steel-related commodities in China. *Applied Economics Letters, 26*(5), 351–357. https://doi.org/10.1080/13504851.2018.1478385

Kraft, J., & Kraft, A. (1978). On the relationship between energy and GNP. *The Journal of Energy and Development, 3*(2), 401–403. https://www.jstor.org/stable/24806805

Kumar Mahalik, M., Acharya, D., & Suresh Babu, M. (2014). Price discovery and volatility spillovers in futures and spot commodity markets: Some Indian evidence. *Journal of Advances in Management Research, 11*(2), 211–226. https://doi.org/10.1108/JAMR-09-2012-0039

Lahmiri, S. (2017). A study on chaos in crude oil markets before and after 2008 international financial crisis. *Physica a: Statistical Mechanics and Its Applications, 466*, 389–395. https://doi.org/10.1016/j.physa.2016.09.031

Lee, C. C., & Chang, C. P. (2007). Energy consumption and GDP revisited: A panel analysis of developed and developing countries. *Energy Economics, 29*(6), 1206–1223. https://doi.org/10.1016/j.eneco.2007.01.001

Maghyereh, A., & Al-Kandari, A. (2007). Oil prices and stock markets in GCC countries: New evidence from nonlinear cointegration analysis. *Managerial Finance, 33*(7), 449–460. https://doi.org/10.1108/03074350710753735

Magkonis, G., & Tsouknidis, D. A. (2017). Dynamic spillover effects across petroleum spot and futures volatilities, trading volume and open interest. *International Review of Financial Analysis, 52*, 104–118. https://doi.org/10.1016/j.irfa.2017.05.005

Mann, J., & Sephton, P. (2016). Global relationships across crude oil benchmarks. *Journal of Commodity Markets, 2*(1), 1–5. https://doi.org/10.1016/j.jcomm.2016.04.002

Mayer, K., & Trück, S. (2018). Electricity markets around the world. *Journal of Commodity Markets, 9*, 77–100. https://doi.org/10.1016/j.jcomm.2018.02.001

Meadows, D., Vis, P., & Zapfel, P. (2019). The EU emissions trading system. In J. Delbeke, & P. Vis (Eds.), *Towards a climate-neutral Europe: Curbing the trend* (pp. 66–94). Routledge. https://doi.org/10.4324/9789276082569

Mork, K. A., & Hall, D. E. (1980). Energy prices, inflation, and recession, 1974–1975. *The Energy Journal, 1*(3), 31–63. https://doi.org/10.5547/ISSN0195-6574-EJ-Vol1-No3-2

Nguyen, H. H., Van Nguyen, P., & Ngo, V. M. (2024). Energy security and the shift to renewable resources: The case of Russia-Ukraine war. *The Extractive Industries and Society, 17*, Article 101442. https://doi.org/10.1016/j.exis.2024.101442

Ozturk, I. (2010). A literature survey on energy–growth nexus. *Energy Policy, 38*(1), 340–349. https://doi.org/10.1016/j.enpol.2009.09.024

Peake, S., & Ekins, P. (2017). Exploring the financial and investment implications of the Paris Agreement. *Climate Policy, 17*(7), 832–852. https://doi.org/10.1080/14693062.2016.1258633

Phillips, P. C., & Perron, P. (1988). Testing for A unit root in time series regression. *Biometrika, 75*(2), 335–346. https://doi.org/10.1093/biomet/75.2.335

Ren, X., Xiao, S., Zhang, W., & Sun, X. (2025). Tail risk spillover of commodity futures markets. *Accounting & Finance, 65*(1), 109–141. https://doi.org/10.1111/acfi.13321

Ripple, R. D. (2008). Futures trading: What is excessive? *Oil and Gas Journal, 106*(22), 24.

Salameh, M. G. (2003). Quest for Middle East oil: The US versus the Asia-Pacific region. *Energy Policy, 31*(11), 1085–1091. https://doi.org/10.1016/S0301-4215(02)00215-X

Smith, J. L. (2009). World oil: Market or mayhem? *Journal of Economic Perspectives, 23*(3), 145–164. https://doi.org/10.1257/jep.23.3.145

Soytas, U., & Sari, R. (2003). Energy consumption and GDP: Causality relationship in G-7 countries and emerging markets. *Energy Economics, 25*(1), 33–37. https://doi.org/10.1016/S0140-9883(02)00009-9

Stoupos, N., & Kiohos, A. (2021). Energy commodities and advanced stock markets: A post-crisis approach. *Resources Policy, 70*, Article 101887. https://doi.org/10.1016/j.resourpol.2020.101887

Thoresen, P. E. (1983). Inflation controlled by energy prices. *Energy Economics, 5*(3), 202–206. https://doi.org/10.1016/0140-9883(83)90062-2

Ventosa, M., Baıllo, A., Ramos, A., & Rivier, M. (2005). Electricity market modeling trends. *Energy Policy, 33*(7), 897–913. https://doi.org/10.1016/j.enpol.2003.10.013

Yu, E. S. H., & Choi, J. Y. (1985). The causal relationship between energy and GNP: An international comparison. *The Journal of Energy and Development, 10*(2), 249–272. https://www.jstor.org/stable/24807818

Yu, E. S. H., & Hwang, B. K. (1984). The relationship between energy and GNP: Further results. *Energy Economics, 6*(3), 186–190. https://doi.org/10.1016/0140-9883(84)90015-X

Theoretical Foundations of Energy Finance: A Multidimensional Framework

Ahmet Akusta and Musa Gün

Abstract Energy has moved beyond its traditional role as a factor of production to become a central arena of financial activity, connecting global markets, investment practices, and policy design. This chapter reviews the conceptual and theoretical foundations of the energy–finance nexus, highlighting how financialization, systemic risks, and emerging green and digital finance mechanisms shape both market behavior and institutional responses. By drawing on neoclassical, Keynesian, behavioral, and complexity-based traditions, it develops a multidimensional framework that integrates economic, financial, technological, and political perspectives. The review shows that financialization tends to heighten volatility and market interconnectedness, while crises intensify the transmission of shocks across energy, carbon, and financial systems. Climate, geopolitical, and policy risks compound these vulnerabilities, influencing investment behavior, risk management, and governance structures. At the same time, green finance instruments, ESG investing, carbon markets, and digital platforms are beginning to transform the financial architecture that underpins the energy transition—although their effectiveness depends critically on consistent policy, strong governance, and inclusive frameworks. This synthesis demonstrates that the energy transition is inseparable from a financial transition. Effective policy design, risk mitigation, and equitable capital allocation are critical to aligning investment with sustainability objectives. By integrating theoretical perspectives and policy considerations, this chapter offers a roadmap for understanding the energy–finance nexus and informs future research and policymaking in the evolving global energy landscape.

Keywords Energy–Finance nexus · Financialization of energy · Sustainable finance · Systemic risk and uncertainty · Energy transition

---

A. Akusta
Konya Technical University, Konya, Türkiye
e-mail: aakusta@ktun.edu.tr

M. Gün (✉)
Recep Tayyip Erdogan University, Rize, Türkiye
e-mail: musa.gun@erdogan.edu.tr

A. Akusta and M. Gün (eds.), *Financial Frontiers in Energy Markets*, Contributions to Finance and Accounting, https://doi.org/10.1007/978-3-032-16738-5_2

1 Introduction

Energy has always been central to economic growth, from the Industrial Revolution to today's globalized economy. Traditionally understood as a production input, energy has evolved into more than a physical commodity: over the last four decades, it has become a financialized asset class. This transformation has redefined its role in global markets, positioning energy as both a driver of economic activity and a key financial frontier that expands the scope of investment, risk management, and regulatory debates (Filippov, 2024; Heffron et al., 2021).

The emergence of energy finance as a distinct field reflects this paradigm shift. It examines the interplay between energy markets, financial institutions, policy environments, and behavioral factors (Rabbani et al., 2025). As these linkages deepen, shocks in one domain increasingly spill over into others, raising concerns for systemic stability. This reinforces the idea that energy finance should not be regarded merely as a branch of commodity finance, but as an independent area of inquiry that requires a robust theoretical basis.

A major driver of this transformation has been the financialization of energy commodities. Since the mid-2000s, institutional investors and hedge funds have played an expanding role in energy markets, fundamentally altering trading behavior (Brogaard et al., 2019). Commercial motives have increasingly given way to speculative positioning, with hedge fund strategies contributing to heightened price volatility and occasional extremes (Koch, 2014). Investor sentiment also plays a central role in transmitting shocks between energy and financial markets. These developments coincide with a broader economic orientation toward short-term horizons, which sits uneasily with the long-term, capital-intensive character of energy investments.

Building on this process, the literature highlights the emergence of a tightly integrated carbon–energy–finance system, characterized by strong return and volatility spillovers (Cao et al., 2022; Liu & Yan, 2024). Such spillovers become especially pronounced during crises such as the COVID-19 pandemic and the Russia–Ukraine conflict, when contagion effects spread across markets and amplify systemic risks. Although financial participation has brought liquidity, it has also tied energy markets more closely to the economic system, making them more vulnerable to systemic shocks.

At the same time, new financial frontiers are emerging. Technological innovations such as blockchain and digital finance promise to decentralize and reshape energy trading and investment (Zhang et al., 2025). Green and sustainable finance instruments, such as green bonds and climate portfolios, have emerged as the springboard for financing the global energy transition (Kim & Lee, 2021; Metawa et al., 2023). In addition, geopolitical risk and policy uncertainty play a significant role in renewable energy financing and cross-border investments, as national strategies are the determining factors for the global flows of capital (Shao et al., 2024). Taken together, these dynamics position energy finance at the intersection of markets, technology, and governance. Such considerations suggest that a multidimensional view is necessary. The researchers propose several frontier areas that scrutinize the relationship between fintech and renewables, such as the potential influence of fintech in renewable energy, regulatory regime ideal design, renewables financing in developing countries, private–public capital cooperation, and the relevance to sustainable development goals (Xia & Fatema, 2025). Such a perspective offers a richer understanding of energy as a financial frontier by linking financial, technological, institutional, and policy dimensions.

In sum, energy has progressed from a factor of production to a key financial asset that drives global markets. How financial markets shape price behavior, transmit risks during crises, and interact with technological, environmental, and geopolitical shifts illustrates how far the field has evolved. This introduction chapter lays the groundwork for the main contribution of this book, which is the construction of a multi-dimensional theory of energy finance, filling a gap in the literature and proposing a basis for further research and policy making.

The remainder of this chapter is structured as follows. Section 2 provides a historical and conceptual overview of the energy–finance nexus. Section 3 reviews theoretical perspectives on energy market dynamics. Section 4 examines the mechanisms and implications of financialization. In Section 5, we analyze how risks cascade across energy and financial markets, generating systemic vulnerabilities that necessitate improved risk management. Section 6 discusses the role of the energy transition in reshaping financial paradigms. Finally, the last section concludes the study by offering a general evaluation of the work.

2 Conceptualizing the Energy–Finance Nexus

The linkages among energy consumption, financial development, and economic growth have been widely studied, though findings remain mixed (Mahi et al., 2020). The energy–finance nexus carries significant implications at both national and global scales. Rising financialization, combined with the rapid transition to renewable energy, has intensified these interconnections, producing a complex system that requires an integrated analytical approach. Mapping the building blocks of this nexus—its channels, mechanisms, and drivers of change—is therefore essential.

This chapter conceptualizes the nexus along three dimensions. Economically, it reflects the interaction of energy supply and demand with growth, inflation, and macroeconomic stability. Financially, it concerns the treatment of energy commodities as investment assets, with implications for risk transfer and portfolio diversification. Politically and environmentally, it encompasses policy frameworks, sustainability imperatives, and climate dynamics that increasingly guide the flow of capital and technology. Evidence on these linkages is diverse. In ASEAN-5 economies, studies suggest a long-run co-movement among energy consumption, financial development, and growth (Mahi et al., 2020). In capital markets, oil price shocks have been linked to equity movements, with positive effects on GCC stock markets from supply shocks (Ziadat & McMillan, 2022), and in the U.S., oil demand shocks associated with larger corporate payouts (Wong & Hasan, 2021).

Beyond traditional market relationships, sustainability introduces new layers of complexity. Green and clean finance are increasingly deployed to reconcile energy use with environmental objectives. For instance, Belt and Road studies suggest that green finance supports energy efficiency and ecological integration (Tu et al., 2021). The emerging "carbon–energy–finance" system, encompassing carbon allowances across equity and bond markets, further illustrates the growing interdependence of seemingly distinct asset classes.

These dynamics operate through multiple mechanisms, ranging from commodity financialization and risk transfer to investment allocation, green and digital finance, and regulatory oversight. In Table 1, these primary mechanisms are summarized.

Together, these mechanisms determine the integration channels. Financialization has made commodity prices more sensitive to global capital flows (Boubakri et al., 2019). Risk transmission has become particularly acute during crises, as interactions between energy and carbon markets fuel volatility (Liu et al., 2023). Access to finance is another key determinant: well-developed financial systems can accelerate renewable energy investment, whereas weak institutions and policy uncertainty can impede it (Isah et al., 2023). Innovations in green and digital finance are directing capital toward sustainable projects, while policy and regulation continue to shape institutional incentives and risk exposures.

Crises, geopolitical tensions, and policy uncertainty amplify these dynamics. The COVID-19 pandemic, for example, disrupted European gas futures and heightened risk sentiment. Exchange rates and energy commodities have shown stronger

Table 1 Primary mechanisms of the energy–finance nexus

Mechanism	Description	Key References
Financialization of Commodities	Integration of energy into global finance, influencing price volatility and exchange rate dynamics	Boubakri et al. (2019)
Risk Transmission and Spillover	Crisis-induced volatility spillovers between energy and financial markets ("energy contagion")	Liu et al. (2023)
Capital Allocation and Investment	The role of financial systems in funding energy projects is hindered by uncertainty or weak financing	Isah et al. (2023)
Green and Digital Finance	Innovative instruments (green bonds, Fintech) supporting renewables and sustainability	Rabbani et al. (2025); Tu et al. (2021); Ma et al. (2024)
Policy and Regulatory Frameworks	Government Incentives and Regulations Shaping Energy–Finance Interactions	Nelson et al. (2019)

co-movement under policy uncertainty and geopolitical shocks (Gbadega & Sun, 2022). Meanwhile, countries with strong financial institutions are better positioned to support renewable investment and innovation, particularly when backed by stable policy frameworks.

The implications are far-reaching. Investors face changing hedging and diversification opportunities, as correlations between energy and financial markets shift with crises. Policymakers must ensure coherence, as energy development influences demand patterns with direct environmental consequences. Resource-exporting economies, in particular, face both opportunities to leverage energy for growth and risks associated with volatility and financial instability, including the challenge of avoiding resource-curse dynamics (Jena & Chaturvedi, 2025).

Overall, the energy–finance nexus represents a hybrid system of market, policy, and structural drivers. Understanding its complexity requires an interdisciplinary approach that integrates economic, financial, political, and environmental perspectives. This theoretical foundation is developed further in the following sections.

3 Theoretical Perspectives on Energy Market Dynamics

Contemporary energy markets can only be grasped through an extensive dialogue with theories that explain the formation of energy prices, the investment decisions of economic actors, and the transformation of entire energy systems. And no single model adequately captures the multifaceted world of energy finance, fraught with competing economic, political, and psychological forces. On the other hand, instead of focusing on distinct traditions in the development of their disciplines, research rationally combines these four types of approaches (i.e., rationalistic, institutional, behavioral, systemic) due to the interdisciplinary nature of analyzing the discipline.

The neoclassical economic framework is usually used as a groundwork. It connects variability of energy prices and choices of allocation through supply–demand balances, rational expectations, and optimization in the face of scarcity. Applications include the measurement of the rebound effect in industrial energy use (Li et al., 2019) or the investigation of how factor market distortions and technological innovation influence electricity consumption. But empirical studies raise questions about the method's limitations. Energy investment behavior is an area that has not been well explained by neoclassical models, as it is influenced by social norms, personal values, and organizational routines (März, 2018). Moreover, profit rates in U.S. manufacturing deviate from the expected trend toward convergence (Joffe, 2024), revealing a disconnect between theoretical notions of efficiency and the realities shaped by institutional and behavioral factors.

Keynesian frameworks provide alternative insights. Post-Keynesian theory conceptualizes inflation as a conflict phenomenon, with rising energy costs triggering corporate mark-ups and wage pressures. Hein (2024) argues that recent inflationary episodes stem from distributional struggles rather than neutral market adjustments, highlighting the role of coordinated income, fiscal, and monetary policies.

New Keynesian approaches, operationalized through dynamic stochastic general equilibrium (NK-DSGE) models, analyze macroeconomic fragility in oil-exporting economies. Amiri et al. (2021) demonstrate that oil price shocks lead to monetary expansion, inflation, and exchange rate depreciation, whereas sovereign wealth funds serve as buffers. Together, these perspectives reveal how institutional mediation and macroeconomic rigidities constrain market adjustment, challenging the adequacy of equilibrium models.

Behavioral finance adds another dimension by emphasizing bounded rationality, sentiment, and herding behavior. Evidence from green energy and clean technology stocks shows persistent analyst over-optimism between 1992 and 2016 (Liu et al., 2025). Investor mood, proxied by music preferences, has been linked to fluctuations in energy stock returns and volatility. Case-based research further illustrates how corporate restructuring and demerger events can shape investor sentiment, influencing financial decision-making under uncertainty (Vaishali et al., 2024). Research on European corporate capital structures finds relative independence among energy firms, reflecting their need for stable and individualized financing (Golubić et al., 2025). Additionally, volatility indicators such as the VIX and SKEW highlight the sector's vulnerability to uncertainty (Mariné-Osorio & González-Núñez, 2024). These studies demonstrate that energy finance is shaped as much by psychology as by fundamentals.

Complexity theory advances the analysis by framing energy markets as adaptive systems characterized by feedback loops and emergent behavior. System dynamics models assess biofuel policies, weighing environmental, economic, and food security outcomes simultaneously. Water-energy-food nexus models illuminate hydropower development in China, showing how ecological and social constraints shape outcomes (Sun et al., 2021). Network-based approaches map embodied energy flows across provinces (Gao et al., 2018), while complex adaptive system frameworks simulate interactions among generation units to optimize power system design (Suo et al., 2023). These perspectives capture the non-linear, multi-actor evolution of energy systems beyond static equilibrium.

A comparative overview (see Table 2) highlights the distinct contributions of each framework.

This comparative evidence highlights that each paradigm sheds light on distinct facets of energy markets. Neoclassical models formalize efficiency analysis but abstract from social context; Keynesian approaches highlight institutional mediation and macroeconomic fragility; behavioral finance exposes the role of biases and emotions; and complexity theory captures adaptive, systemic interactions.

The convergence of these insights suggests the need for a hybrid framework. By incorporating rationalist efficiency models, Keynesian institutional analysis, behavioral attention to cognition and emotion, and complexity-oriented systems modeling into their research apparatus, scholars and practitioners can better understand the changing and shifting nature of global energy finance. Multidimensional synthesis of this kind not only adds explanatory force but also enhances our ability to design policies and investments that are responsive to uncertainty, interdependence, and systemic change.

Table 2 Comparison of theoretical perspectives on energy market dynamics

Dimension	Neoclassical economics	Post-/New Keynesian	Behavioral finance	Complexity theory
Core Assumptions	Rational optimization; equilibrium tendencies	Distributional conflict; uncertainty; institutional constraints	Bounded rationality; psychological biases; sentiment effects	Interacting agents; feedback loops; emergent behavior
Key Mechanisms	Price signals: market-clearing	Mark-up pricing; fiscal & monetary policy; SWFs as buffers	Overconfidence; herding; fear & uncertainty	System feedback: adaptive interactions
Applications	Rebound modeling (Li et al., 2019); innovation & electricity	Conflict inflation (Hein, 2024); DSGE oil shocks (Amiri et al., 2021)	Green stock optimism (Liu et al., 2025); sentiment & volatility	Biofuels & hydropower (Sun et al., 2021); energy networks (Gao et al., 2018)

4 Financialization of Energy Markets: Mechanisms and Implications

Over the last half century, energy markets have experienced a dramatic expansion of financialization, with commodities no longer merely physical goods but functioning as traded financial instruments. Hedge funds, investment banks, and large institutional investors have entered the markets for raw energy materials, changing how prices are determined. Unsurprisingly, energy prices are no longer purely a function of fundamental supply and demand but rather of financial speculation, investor sentiment, and global risk appetite. This transformation has been both driven and enabled by financial derivatives—such as futures, options, and swaps—which are designed to transfer risk, diversify portfolios, and facilitate speculation.

Financialization refers to the integration of energy commodities into the wider financial system. With futures contracts becoming increasingly attractive to institutional investors, energy has emerged as a core component of diversified portfolios, heightening its interdependence with other asset classes. Consequently, volatility in energy prices often reflects not only real economic shocks but also financial shocks originating in equity markets and changes in investor risk tolerance. News-driven sentiment similarly exerts measurable influence on crude oil futures, with textual and media-based indicators proving informative for volatility forecasts (Chen et al., 2021; Pan et al., 2024). While some studies highlight the destabilizing potential of financialization, including the emergence of speculative bubbles and price deviations from fundamentals (Khan et al., 2022), others stress the regulatory implications, advocating closer supervision of highly financialized markets.

The mechanisms driving financialization are multifaceted. Derivatives trading, particularly in futures and options, is central to risk management yet also channels speculative behavior (Martínez & Torró, 2018). Speculators and hedgers exert nonlinear effects on prices, with returns primarily reflecting risk premiums rather than superior forecasting ability (Merkoulova, 2020). Commodity index investments have grown rapidly, strengthening co-movements between energy futures and financial assets, particularly in the aftermath of global crises such as 2008–09 (Liu et al., 2020). Sentiment-driven factors, such as investor fear captured by the Oil Volatility Index, now exert a significant influence on market outcomes. These developments underscore the extent to which financial actors, incentives, and instruments now shape the form and function of energy markets.

The impact of financialization has been both far-reaching and heterogeneous. Price dynamics have become more volatile, characterized by sudden jumps, speculative bubbles, and time-varying correlations—especially during periods of systemic stress (Khan et al., 2022). Market integration and co-movement between energy commodities and other financial assets have intensified, particularly during global economic shocks and pandemics, which affect portfolio diversification and risk management strategies. Price discovery functions have been partially disrupted, with structural breaks evident between spot and futures markets. However, new trading venues, such as the Shanghai crude oil futures, show progressive consolidation of pricing capabilities (Su & Lin, 2024).

Hedging effectiveness has also been affected. Therefore, managing spark spread risk through futures remains challenging, and corporate risk management practices have adapted to the new levels of volatility (He & Chen, 2025). At the same time, financialized energy prices affect the real economy in several ways, including sectors such as biofuels, investment activities, and firm-level financialization strategies (Guo & Tanaka, 2025). In summary, while financialization may create opportunities in terms of liquidity and risk-taking, it also poses significant risks. These include high volatility, speculation, bubbles, and closer links between energy and financial markets.

Overall, the financialization of energy markets represents a significant structural shift with wide-ranging implications. The interplay of derivatives, speculative activity, and institutional investment has embedded energy markets more deeply within the global financial system, altering volatility patterns, market integration, and price discovery mechanisms. For investors, this has complicated diversification strategies, while for policymakers and regulators, it has raised concerns over systemic fragility and the design of safeguards that preserve liquidity without amplifying instability. In this sense, understanding financialization is not merely an academic exercise but a practical requirement for navigating today's energy markets and developing sound policy responses.

5 Risk, Uncertainty, and Systemic Vulnerabilities

Energy markets now operate within an environment of overlapping uncertainties: geopolitical tensions, climate risks, technological change, and financial speculation. The increasing integration of energy with the broader economy has amplified channels of risk transmission, generating systemic vulnerabilities within global financial networks. Because shocks in one area reverberate rapidly across others, both investors and policymakers must remain vigilant.

Three broad categories of risk dominate the literature: climate risk, geopolitical risk, and policy-related uncertainty. Climate risk is typically divided into physical and transition risks. Physical risks stem from extreme weather events and other environmental shocks that can damage infrastructure, disrupt supply chains, and reduce productivity. Empirical evidence suggests that firms in less climate-exposed regions often enjoy stronger financial performance, whereas events such as droughts or heatwaves have been linked to weaker stock returns for U.S. energy firms (Bauri et al., 2025; Ewald et al., 2024; Kim et al., 2024). Transition risks, by contrast, arise from the reallocation of capital and business models required to achieve a low-carbon economy. Investors increasingly embed carbon-related risks into asset valuations, with European carbon allowances and climate policy indices serving as widely used proxies (Broeders et al., 2023).

Geopolitical risk represents another persistent source of disruption. It encompasses both active events, such as armed conflicts, and perceived threats, such as diplomatic tensions, each of which exerts distinct influences on energy markets (He & Sun, 2024). These risks have proven to be major drivers of price volatility and systemic spillovers. The Russia–Ukraine war, for example, vividly demonstrated how geopolitical conflict can intensify interdependencies between energy and financial systems, triggering global reverberations (Ahmed & Sohag, 2025).

Policy and economic uncertainty also shape the energy–finance nexus. The Economic Policy Uncertainty Index reflects volatility in fiscal, monetary, and regulatory frameworks that affect spillovers across carbon, energy, and financial markets. Similarly, climate policy uncertainty has become a critical factor influencing energy prices, with differentiated impacts across oil, coal, and natural gas markets (Zhao et al., 2025).

The risks associated with these exposures must be quantified in a sophisticated way. Climate and transition risk is then commonly quantified through climate vulnerability indices, carbon allowance returns, and text-based machine learning models (Song et al., 2025). Geopolitical risks are often assessed using news-based indices that allow for disaggregating threats from actions (He & Sun, 2024). Systemic risk can be estimated via the Vector Autoregressive-based, network spillover techniques, and metrics investigating the role of Conditional Value-at-Risk and Marginal Expected Shortfall, which analyze not only each component's contribution but also its risk connectivity channels (Tiwari et al., 2021; Zhang & Li, 2021).

These risks are transmitted through several means. Price volatility spillovers, such as those that propagate shocks from oil or gas to equity and currency markets, are evident, and policy uncertainty has an impact on both investors' attitudes and market correlations. Corporate exposure to climate risk and carbon significantly shape the ideal gap as they affect the leverage decision, which in turn affects financial flexibility, directly connecting environmental risks to firm performance (Song et al., 2025). Additionally, speculative factors in emerging assets (such as cryptocurrencies) can increase the risk of shifts in energy financing following a bubble burst (Ji et al., 2022).

Climate, geopolitical, and policy risks interact with one another, creating a complex risk landscape. One-off events can have multiple impacts, creating feedback loops that jeopardize energy transition and financial stability goals. The evidence highlights the importance of a systemic risk view in which crises are not only interconnected but also non-linear.

Finally, the energy-finance interaction is characterized by an inescapable degree of uncertainty and systemic fragility. While this dimension of risk has long been recognized by researchers and policymakers seeking to understand how energy markets can be managed in a way that supports (or even utilizes) the social function of finance, until relatively recently, it has been largely unmeasured and poorly understood by the financial sector, and hence poorly managed. Anticipating and managing such systemic risks is increasingly essential to building resilience in the global energy–finance landscape.

6 Energy Transition and the Evolution of Financial Paradigms

The global energy transition represents one of the largest reallocations of capital in modern history. Shifting from a fossil-fuel-based economy toward one dominated by low-carbon and renewable sources requires massive long-term investment in infrastructure, technologies, and institutional change (Hall et al., 2018). This shift places significant pressure on traditional financial systems, which were designed to evaluate fossil fuel projects rather than renewable or low-carbon investments. Financing the transition has therefore become a dynamic domain in its own right, giving rise to new instruments, markets, and investment philosophies capable of mobilizing capital at the scale required.

The co-evolution of financial and energy systems is most visible in the rapid development of new financial instruments. Renewable energy projects often involve high upfront costs and uncertain payoffs, making conventional financing insufficient (Egli et al., 2018). In response, a wide array of de-risking tools has emerged, ranging from green bonds and targeted credit lines to dedicated funds. Green bonds, in particular, have become a cornerstone of climate finance, channeling capital into solar, wind, and other clean energy projects. Green credit schemes have been associated with measurable reductions in corporate emissions. At the same time, digital financial technologies—including crowdfunding platforms and blockchain-based trading systems—are opening new channels for capital flows, diversifying funding sources, and improving transparency (Bassi et al., 2025; Zheng et al., 2025). Recent evidence also highlights how financial inclusion and digitalization jointly promote clean energy portfolios by reducing financing barriers and enhancing inclusive growth (Ramzan et al., 2024). Development and public banks also continue to play a central role by mitigating risk and mobilizing private finance, particularly in emerging economies.

Investment philosophies are being revolutionized alongside the new instruments. The growing emphasis on Environmental, Social, and Governance (ESG) factors reflects how non-financial considerations have become integral to investors' decision-making processes. In acknowledging climate risks as financial risks, ESG investing reframes how corporate valuations and responsibilities are accounted for in the energy sector (Foley et al., 2024). High ESG performance is increasingly viewed as a proxy for resilience and long-term strategic capability, and renewable energy companies are proving to be appealing options for institutional investors. There is substantial evidence demonstrating a positive relationship between ESG commitments and the financial performance of companies in developed markets (Pinheiro et al., 2024), but questions continue to arise regarding differences in greenwashing and reporting practices. The growth of ESG-branded assets highlights another critical tension: ensuring that these instruments deliver genuine sustainability outcomes rather than serving as vehicles for reputational signaling. The effectiveness of green finance depends on clear standards, robust governance, and transparency. Without these safeguards, the credibility of the financial system in driving the energy transition may be undermined.

A further component of the changing financial landscape is the emergence of carbon markets. These markets socialize the idea that carbon emissions have a cost, establishing climate policy as part of economic actions. Carbon markets work by establishing tradable allowances, offering firms a clear incentive to take steps to reduce emissions and make low-carbon alternatives more competitive (Guesmi et al., 2024). Sectoral evidence further supports the strategic role of carbon markets in aligning industry-level contributions with Paris Agreement commitments (Rossetto, 2023). But the value of these sorts of mechanisms depends on policy stability. Instability in carbon prices, often stemming from regulatory uncertainty, not only erodes investor confidence but also impacts green finance and energy markets more generally (Uddin et al., 2025). Nonetheless, evidence increasingly suggests that carbon markets and green finance are mutually reinforcing. Robust carbon pricing creates demand for green financial products, while the growth of green financial instruments can support the development and liquidity of carbon trading systems.

The multiple channels through which finance shapes the energy transition can be grouped into a set of paradigmatic mechanisms. Green finance mobilizes capital directly, ESG investing redefines corporate value, carbon markets use pricing incentives to shift behavior, and digital finance expands participation and efficiency. These mechanisms interact dynamically and are summarized in Table 3.

Despite their promise, these paradigms are not evolving uniformly worldwide. Developed economies tend to exhibit more advanced ecosystems for green finance and ESG investment, yet still face challenges related to investor hesitancy and policy

Table 3 Key financial channels of the energy transition

Financial paradigm	Primary mechanism	Example application in energy transition	Key references
Green Finance	Direct Capital Allocation	Green bonds fund solar and wind farms; green credit supports corporate technological upgrades	Wang and Li (2024); Lee et al. (2024)
ESG Investing	Risk and Value Re-evaluation	Funds divest from fossil fuels and reallocate to renewables with strong sustainability scores	Foley et al. (2024); Pinheiro et al. (2024)
Carbon Markets	Price-Based Incentivization	Rising carbon prices increase coal costs, making renewable energy sources more competitive	Uddin et al. (2025); Guesmi et al. (2024)
Digital Finance & Fintech	Accessibility and Efficiency	Crowdfunding enables community solar ownership; blockchain enhances transparent energy trading	Zheng et al. (2025); Bassi et al. (2025)

uncertainty. In contrast, many emerging economies where international development finance is critical to supporting energy transitions are characterized by relatively underdeveloped financial markets, weak regulatory environments, and high perceived risks (Causevic et al., 2022). The Brazilian example demonstrates that state-led financial institutions can effectively mobilize investment, while Nigeria highlights the obstacles stemming from policy uncertainty and dependence on external financing sources (Isah et al., 2023). China is a hybrid country, with rapidly developing green finance inputs and state-led coordination, but challenges in implementing planning initiatives on the ground, regional tensions, and growing gaps between environmental and economic priorities (Lee et al., 2024).

Collectively, these developments, which point to a reality about the world's energy transition, have no chance unless finance also undergoes a profound shift. Green finance, ESG strategies, carbon markets, and digital platforms have shifted from the periphery to the mainstream, transforming how capital is justified, how risks are priced, and how incentives are aligned with sustainability goals. Yet these mechanisms remain fragile, relying on consistent policy support, strong institutional quality, and transparent governance. Ultimately, the success of the energy transition hinges not only on mobilizing capital but on ensuring that finance operates in a way that is inclusive, efficient, and compatible with the long-term objectives of climate resilience and sustainable development.

7 Conclusion

This chapter seeks to delineate the financial contours of emerging energy geographies by proposing a multidimensional framework that traces their expanding linkages with global capital markets. The discussion begins with an examination of how energy has evolved into a financial frontier—an arena where the conventional logic of commodity production intersects with risk transmission, capital allocation, and policy design. Building on this foundation, the chapter surveys a range of theoretical perspectives—from neoclassical and Keynesian economics to behavioral finance and complexity theory—that illuminate the diverse yet interconnected forces shaping market dynamics. The overarching claim is that the energy–finance nexus should not be understood merely as the intersection of two separate domains, but rather as a co-evolving system characterized by structural complexity, thereby necessitating an interdisciplinary approach.

The synthesis of findings highlights several established insights. First, financial development plays a decisive role in influencing both energy consumption and environmental outcomes, although the direction and magnitude of its effects differ across contexts and income levels (Annor et al., 2025). While finance can accelerate investment flows into renewable energy, weak governance structures may equally allow it to reinforce carbon-intensive lock-ins. Second, the process of energy transition is inseparable from an accompanying financial transition. Instruments such as green bonds and ESG-based strategies constitute essential mechanisms for reallocating capital toward low-carbon investment priorities (Joshipura et al., 2025). Third, technological advances in digital finance—including FinTech, artificial intelligence, and blockchain are reshaping the architecture of energy finance by improving efficiency in risk management and financial inclusion, while simultaneously generating new forms of regulatory risk (Labaran & Masood, 2025). Finally, systemic risks persist across the energy–finance interface: volatility, geopolitical shocks, and climate-related disruptions continue to propagate through borders and across asset classes, underscoring the need for constant vigilance.

Nonetheless, important questions remain unresolved. The optimal policy mix for simultaneously de-risking renewable energy investments and ensuring distributive equity remains contested. Furthermore, the persistent lack of conceptual clarity surrounding ESG and green finance continues to fragment both scholarly research and practical application. Addressing these gaps is essential if financial systems are to effectively support a sustainable energy transition. The management of systemic risk at the nexus of geopolitics, finance, and the energy trilemma also requires further research. Moreover, Justice and equity dimensions—in particular, financial access and governance quality- are important to the reduction of energy poverty and facilitating a just transition.

The agenda ahead is both scholarly and practical. Research must deepen interdisciplinary integration, refine advanced methods such as artificial intelligence and network analysis, and generate context-specific insights tailored to national and regional conditions. Policymakers, in turn, must create stable governance frameworks, catalyze green finance, enhance transparency through digital tools, and prioritize inclusive strategies to distribute the benefits of the energy transition equitably.

The financial system sits at the very heart of the global energy transformation. By fostering an integrated and nuanced understanding of the energy-finance nexus, this book has aimed to provide a conceptual map for navigating the turbulence of systemic change. The challenges ahead are immense, but so too are the opportunities for building a more sustainable and resilient future.

References

Ahmed, F., & Sohag, K. (2025). Spillover effects of separated oil price shocks on regional financial stress amidst Russia-Ukraine and global geopolitical tensions: A novel GVAR approach. *Eurasian Economic Review, 15*, 593–639. https://doi.org/10.1007/s40822-025-00329-8

Amiri, H., Sayadi, M., & Mamipour, S. (2021). Oil price shocks and macroeconomic outcomes; fresh evidences from a scenario-based NK-DSGE analysis for oil-exporting countries. *Resources Policy, 74*, Article 102262. https://doi.org/10.1016/j.resourpol.2021.102262

Annor, L. D. J., Robaina, M., & Vieira, E. (2025). Financial development, inclusive growth, and environmental quality: emerging markets perspective. *Environment, Development & Sustainability, 27*(3). https://doi.org/10.1007/s10668-023-04198-6

Mariné-Osorio, F. J., & González-Núñez, J. C. (2024). Fear and uncertainty in the principal stocks of the S&P500. *Revista mexicana de economía y finanzas, 19*(4). https://doi.org/10.21919/remef.v19i4.1069

Liu, Y., Wang, M., & Yang, X. (2025). Earnings optimism in green stocks. *Journal of Sustainable Finance & Investment, 15*(2), 319–341. https://doi.org/10.1080/20430795.2024.2389152

Golubić, Z. L., Pecina, E., & Orlović, Z. (2025). Exploring herding in capital structure choices: Insights from developed European economies. *Journal of Corporate Accounting & Finance, 36*(3), 378–393. https://doi.org/10.1002/jcaf.22789

Bassi, E., Lustenberger, M., & Letina, S. (2025). Blockchain-based voluntary carbon market: Strategic insights into network structure. *Frontiers in Blockchain, 8*, 1603695. https://doi.org/10.3389/fbloc.2025.1603695

Bauri, S., Mondal, A., & Fatma, U. (2025). Impact of climate risk on financial performance–evidence from select energy companies from select G-20 countries. *International Journal of Energy Sector Management, 19*(2), 241–268. https://doi.org/10.1108/IJESM-11-2023-0018

Boubakri, S., Guillaumin, C., & Silanine, A. (2019). Non-linear relationship between real commodity price volatility and real effective exchange rate: The case of commodity-exporting countries. *Journal of Macroeconomics, 60*, 212–228. https://doi.org/10.1016/j.jmacro.2019.02.004

Broeders, D., Schouten, B., Tiems, I., & Verhoeven, N. (2023). Pricing of climate transition risks across different financial markets. *Journal of Risk Management in Financial Institutions, 16*(2), 102–115. https://doi.org/10.69554/PEJU2948

Brogaard, J., Ringgenberg, M. C., & Sovich, D. (2019). The economic impact of index investing. *The Review of Financial Studies, 32*(9), 3461–3499. https://doi.org/10.1093/rfs/hhy129

Cao, G., Xie, F., & Ling, M. (2022). Spillover effects in Chinese carbon, energy and financial markets. *International Finance, 25*(3), 320–342. https://doi.org/10.1111/infi.12417

Causevic, A., Avdic, S., Padegimas, B., & Macura, B. (2022). Analysis of international public funding flows for the environment, climate change, and sustainability: The case of Bosnia and

Herzegovina. *Energy, Sustainability and Society, 12*(1), 34. https://doi.org/10.1186/s13705-022-00359-z

Chen, Z., Liang, C., & Umar, M. (2021). Is investor sentiment stronger than VIX and uncertainty indices in predicting energy volatility? *Resources Policy, 74*, Article 102391. https://doi.org/10.1016/j.resourpol.2021.102391

Egli, F., Steffen, B., & Schmidt, T. S. (2018). A dynamic analysis of financing conditions for renewable energy technologies. *Nature Energy, 3*(12), 1084–1092. https://doi.org/10.1038/s41560-018-0277-y

Ewald, C. O., Huang, C., & Ren, Y. (2024). On the effects of physical climate risks on the Chinese energy sector. *Journal of Risk and Financial Management, 17*(10), 458. https://doi.org/10.3390/jrfm17100458

Filippov, S. P. (2024). Transition to a carbon neutral economy: Opportunities and limitations. *Current Challenges. Thermal Engineering, 71*(1), 1–11. https://doi.org/10.1134/S0040601524010038

Foley, A. M., Heffron, R. J., Al Kez, D., Del Rio, D. D. F., McInerney, C., & Welfle, A. (2024). Restoring trust in ESG investing through the adoption of just transition ethics. *Renewable and Sustainable Energy Reviews, 199*, Article 114557. https://doi.org/10.1016/j.rser.2024.114557

Gao, C., Su, B., Sun, M., Zhang, X., & Zhang, Z. (2018). Interprovincial transfer of embodied primary energy in China: A complex network approach. *Applied Energy, 215*, 792–807. https://doi.org/10.1016/j.apenergy.2018.02.075

Gbadega, P. A., & Sun, Y. (2022). Centralized peer-to-peer transactive energy market approach in a prosumer-centric residential smart grid environment. *Energy Reports, 8*, 105–116. https://doi.org/10.1016/j.egyr.2022.10.080

Guesmi, K., Mohammed, K. S., & Tiwari, S. (2024). Green horizons: Enabling the energy transition through climate change policies. *International Review of Economics & Finance, 94*, Article 103409. https://doi.org/10.1016/j.iref.2024.103409

Guo, J., & Tanaka, T. (2025). The influence of US biofuel production and global energy prices on local food prices in Latin American countries: A time-varying analysis. *Biofuels, Bioproducts and Biorefining*. https://doi.org/10.1002/bbb.2781

Hall, S., Roelich, K. E., Davis, M. E., & Holstenkamp, L. (2018). Finance and justice in low-carbon energy transitions. *Applied Energy, 222*, 772–780. https://doi.org/10.1016/j.apenergy.2018.04.007

He, F., Chen, L., Hao, J., & Chang, D. (2025). Futures trading and corporate financialization: A quasi-natural experiment from the launch of China's crude oil futures. *Journal of Futures Markets*. https://doi.org/10.1002/fut.22584

He, Z., & Sun, H. (2024). The time-varying and asymmetric impacts of oil price shocks on geopolitical risk. *International Review of Economics & Finance, 91*, 942–957. https://doi.org/10.1016/j.iref.2024.01.036

Heffron, R. J. A., Connor, R., Crossley, P. J., Mayor, V. L. I., Talus, K., & Tomain, J. P. (2021). The identification and impact of justice risks to commercial risks in the energy sector: Post COVID-19 and for the energy transition. *Journal of Energy & Natural Resources Law, 39*(4), 373–396. https://doi.org/10.1080/02646811.2021.1874148

Hein, E. (2024). Inflation is always and everywhere… a conflict phenomenon: Post-Keynesian inflation theory and energy price driven conflict inflation, distribution, demand and employment. *European Journal of Economics and Economic Policies, 21*(2), 202–231. https://doi.org/10.4337/ejeep.2024.0135

Isah, A., Dioha, M. O., Debnath, R., Abraham-Dukuma, M. C., & Butu, H. M. (2023). Financing renewable energy: Policy insights from Brazil and Nigeria. *Energy, Sustainability and Society, 13*(1), 2. https://doi.org/10.1186/s13705-022-00379-9

Jena, L. P., & Chaturvedi, A. (2025). Renewable energy financing in the Pacific Island Countries. *Energy for Sustainable Development, 85*, Article 101642. https://doi.org/10.1016/j.esd.2024.101642

Ji, Q., Ripple, R. D., Zhang, D., & Zhao, Y. (2022). Cryptocurrency bubble on the systemic risk in global energy companies. *The Energy Journal, 43*(1_suppl), 1–24. https://doi.org/10.5547/01956574.43.SI1.qiji

Joffe, M. (2024). Profit rate dynamics in US manufacturing. *International Review of Applied Economics, 38*(1–2), 194–223. https://doi.org/10.1080/02692171.2022.2154917

Joshipura, M., Nasrallah, N., & Kedia, N. (2025). Green and climate finance for sustainability: Hybrid review and framework development. *Business Strategy and the Environment, 34*(3), 3618–3634. https://doi.org/10.1002/bse.4173

Khan, K., Su, C. W., & Khurshid, A. (2022). Do booms and busts identify bubbles in energy prices? *Resources Policy, 76*, Article 102556. https://doi.org/10.1016/j.resourpol.2022.102556

Kim, J. W., & Lee, J. S. (2021). Greening energy finance of multilateral development banks: Review of the world bank's energy project investment (1985–2019). *Energies, 14*(9), 2648. https://doi.org/10.3390/en14092648

Kim, S., Jeon, J., & Kim, H. (2024). Drought and energy stock markets in the United States. *Environmental Research Letters, 19*(9), Article 094012. https://doi.org/10.1088/1748-9326/ad61ff

Koch, N. T. (2014). Tail events: A new approach to understanding extreme energy commodity prices. *Energy Economics, 42*, 250–258. https://doi.org/10.1016/j.eneco.2014.02.015

Labaran, M. J., & Masood, T. (2025). Technological frontiers: Addressing renewable energy supply chain and sustainability challenges. *Discover Sustainability, 6*(1), 100. https://doi.org/10.1007/s43621-025-00909-3

Lee, C. C., Li, J., & Wang, F. (2024). The role of green finance in the construction of new energy system: Evidence from China. *Energy Economics, 139*, Article 107878. https://doi.org/10.1016/j.eneco.2024.107878

Li, G., Sun, J., & Wang, Z. (2019). Exploring the energy consumption rebound effect of industrial enterprises in the Beijing–Tianjin–Hebei region. *Energy Efficiency, 12*(4), 1007–1026. https://doi.org/10.1007/s12053-018-9743-4

Liu, J., Hu, Y., Yan, L. Z., & Chang, C. P. (2023). Volatility spillover and hedging strategies between the European carbon emissions and energy markets. *Energy Strategy Reviews, 46*, Article 101058. https://doi.org/10.1016/j.esr.2023.101058

Liu, P., Vedenov, D., & Power, G. J. (2020). Commodity financialization and sector ETFs: Evidence from crude oil futures. *Research in International Business and Finance, 51*, Article 101109. https://doi.org/10.1016/j.ribaf.2019.101109

Liu, Y., & Yan, B. (2024). Spillover effects of carbon, energy, and stock markets considering economic policy uncertainty. *Journal of Economics and Finance, 48*(3), 563–591. https://doi.org/10.1007/s12197-024-09665-y

Ma, C. Q., Lei, Y. T., Ren, Y. S., Chen, X. Q., Wang, Y. R., & Narayan, S. (2024). Systematic analysis of the blockchain in the energy sector: Trends, issues, and future directions. *Telecommunications Policy, 48*(2), Article 102677. https://doi.org/10.1016/j.telpol.2023.102677

Mahi, M., Phoong, S. W., Ismail, I., & Isa, C. R. (2020). Energy–finance–growth nexus in ASEAN-5 countries: An ARDL bounds test approach. *Sustainability, 12*(1), 5. https://doi.org/10.3390/su12010005

Martínez, B., & Torró, H. (2018). Hedging spark spread risk with futures. *Energy Policy, 113*, 731–746. https://doi.org/10.1016/j.enpol.2017.11.038

März, S. (2018). Beyond economics—understanding the decision-making of German small private landlords in terms of energy efficiency investment. *Energy Efficiency, 11*(7), 1721–1743. https://doi.org/10.1007/s12053-017-9567-7

Merkoulova, Y. (2020). Predictive abilities of speculators in energy markets. *Journal of Futures Markets, 40*(5), 804–815. https://doi.org/10.1002/fut.22058

Metawa, N., Boujlil, R., & Alsunbul, S. (2023). Fraud-free green finance: Using deep learning to preserve the integrity of financial statements for enhanced capital market sustainability. *International Journal of Energy Economics and Policy, 13*(6), 570–579. https://doi.org/10.32479/ijeep.15197

Nelson, T., Pascoe, O., Calais, P., Mitchell, L., & McNeill, J. (2019). Efficient integration of climate and energy policy in Australia's National Electricity Market. *Economic Analysis and Policy, 64*, 178–193. https://doi.org/10.1016/j.eap.2019.08.001

Pan, Z., Zhong, H., Wang, Y., & Huang, J. (2024). Forecasting oil futures returns with news. *Energy Economics, 134*, Article 107606. https://doi.org/10.1016/j.eneco.2024.107606

Pinheiro, A. B., Panza, G. B., Berhorst, N. L., Toaldo, A. M. M., & Segatto, A. P. (2024). Exploring the relationship among ESG, innovation, and economic and financial performance: Evidence from the energy sector. *International Journal of Energy Sector Management, 18*(3), 500–516. https://doi.org/10.1108/IJESM-02-2023-0008

Rabbani, M. R., Kiran, M., & Shaikh, Z. H. (2025). Financing the future: insights into sustainable energy investments through scientific mapping and meta-analysis. *SN Business & Economics, 5*(7), 183. https://doi.org/10.1007/s43621-024-00788-0

Ramzan, M., HongXing, Y., Abbas, Q., & Fatima, S. (2024). Do financial inclusion, inclusive digitalization and growth promote clean energy portfolio? *Clean Technologies and Environmental Policy, 26*(8), 2687–2705. https://doi.org/10.1007/s10098-023-02722-w

Rossetto, D. (2023). The relative importance of carbon markets to the waste management sector's future contribution to climate change commitments under the Paris Agreement: Insights from Australia. *Carbon Neutrality, 2*(1), 25. https://doi.org/10.1007/s43979-023-00063-7

Shao, H., Wang, Y., Lee, C.-C., & Wen, H. (2024). How does political stability affect renewable energy finance? *International Evidence. Energy, 293*, Article 133829. https://doi.org/10.1016/j.energy.2024.133829

Song, Y., Lu, L., Liu, J., Zhou, J., Wang, X., & Li, F. (2025). A study of the factors contributing to the impact of climate risks on corporate performance in China's energy sector. *Sustainability, 17*(11), 5139. https://doi.org/10.3390/su17115139

Su, T., & Lin, B. (2024). Reassessing the information transmission and pricing influence of Shanghai crude oil futures: A time-varying perspective. *Energy Economics, 140*, Article 107977. https://doi.org/10.1016/j.eneco.2024.107977

Sun, L., Niu, D., Wang, K., & Xu, X. (2021). Sustainable development pathways of hydropower in China: Interdisciplinary qualitative analysis and scenario-based system dynamics quantitative modeling. *Journal of Cleaner Production, 287*, Article 125528. https://doi.org/10.1016/j.jclepro.2020.125528

Suo, X., Zhao, S., Ma, Y., & Dong, L. (2023). Multi-type power generation planning method for power systems based on complex adaptive system theory. *IET Renewable Power Generation, 17*(8), 1899–1911. https://doi.org/10.1049/rpg2.12732

Tiwari, A. K., Pathak, R., DasGupta, R., & Sadorsky, P. (2021). Modelling dependence and systemic risk between oil prices and BSE sectoral indices using stochastic copula and CoVar. *ΔCoVar and MES Approaches. Applied Economics, 53*(58), 6770–6788. https://doi.org/10.1080/00036846.2021.1949430

Tu, C. A., Chien, F., Hussein, M. A., RAMLI MM, Y. A. N. T. O., S. PSI, M. S., Iqbal, S., & Bilal, A. R. (2021). Estimating role of green financing on energy security, economic and environmental integration of BRI member countries. *The Singapore Economic Review*, 1–19. https://doi.org/10.1142/S0217590821500193

Uddin, M. A., Chang, B. H., Aldawsari, S. H., & Li, R. (2025). The interplay between green finance, policy uncertainty and carbon market volatility: A time frequency approach. *Sustainability, 17*(3), 1198. https://doi.org/10.3390/su17031198

Vaishali, Gupta, S., & Kumar, R. (2024). Navigating the financial frontier: A case of investment decision-making in the wake of Reliance Industries Limited's demerger. *Emerald Emerging Markets Case Studies*, 1–24. https://doi.org/10.1108/EEMCS-01-2024-0005

Wang, K. H., & Li, S. M. (2024). Green bonds and carbon prices: A dynamic relationship revealed. *Environment, Development and Sustainability*, 1–24. https://doi.org/10.1007/s10668-024-05651-w

Wong, J. B., & Hasan, M. M. (2021). Oil shocks and corporate payouts. *Energy Economics, 99*, Article 105315. https://doi.org/10.1016/j.eneco.2021.105315

Xia, L., & Fatema, N. (2025). Energy finance, digital financial inclusion, accountability and sustainable development: Evidence from BRICS. *Humanities and Social Sciences Communications, 12*(1), 245. https://doi.org/10.1057/s41599-025-05410-w

Zhang, S., Li, X., & Shi, D. (2025). How does digital finance affect energy consumption in China? Empirical evidence from China. *Environment, Development and Sustainability, 27*(5), 10719–10735. https://doi.org/10.1007/s10668-023-04329-z

Zhang, Q., & Li, F. (2021). From systematic risk to systemic risk: Analysis over day-ahead market operation under high renewable penetration by CoVaR and marginal CoVaR. *IEEE Transactions on Sustainable Energy, 12*(2), 761–771. https://doi.org/10.1109/TSTE.2020.3015497

Zhao, L., Li, Y., & Yang, G. (2025). Effects of climate policy uncertainty on energy markets: Insights from the BEKK-GARCH model. *Applied Economics Letters,* 1–6. https://doi.org/10.1080/13504851.2025.2454529

Zheng, H., Li, D., & Cai, J. (2025). Driving green innovation: The impact of digital finance on China's transition to clean energy. *Energy, 318*, Article 134760. https://doi.org/10.1016/j.energy.2025.134760

Ziadat, S. A., & McMillan, D. G. (2022). Oil-stock nexus: The role of oil shocks for GCC markets. *Studies in Economics and Finance, 39*(5), 801–818. https://doi.org/10.1108/SEF-12-2021-0529

Volatility and Geopolitical Uncertainty in Oil Pricing: Empirical Insights from Major Global Shocks

İbrahim Gündüz

Abstract This study aims to understand the impact of volatility in oil prices and uncertainty in the global world on global energy prices. In order to achieve this aim, we will focus on the changes taking place in the oil market. Oil, which has taken an important place in global production and consumption for many years, still preserves its importance in different sectors of the world. This effect has serious consequences all over the world in economic, social, political, etc. areas. In this study, two different methods will be used jointly. The first method is "case study analysis", which involves the analysis of different events in different periods, while the second method is time-based "time series analysis", which highlights the changes over time. The results of the study show that the behavior of oil prices cannot be clarified only by the logic of supply and demand balance, which is put forward in the classical sense. The study indicated that political crises and global oil supply and demand insufficiency have longer-term effects on oil prices. It has been witnessed that these situations have significantly increased both the oil price and the volatility in the oil price. As a result of the analysis, three conclusions were reached. First, the volatility of oil markets varies depending on the source of the risk. Secondly, when evaluated in terms of oil prices, global health crises can have more devastating effects than even geopolitical conflicts. Thirdly, uncertainty is a crucial variable in analyses of oil prices. Considering the persistence of uncertainty and its impact on energy security together is of critical importance in analyzing oil prices and oil markets. Studies that do not take these issues into account have the potential to produce seriously deceptive results in terms of both accuracy and validity. As a result, future policies will need to take into account systemic risks, diversify supply channels, and be prepared for crises not only arising from political developments but also from global health shocks and financial shocks.

Keywords COVID-19 · Cumulative abnormal returns (CAR) · Energy security · Geopolitical risk · Oil price volatility · Speculation

İ. Gündüz (✉)
Duzce University, Düzce, Türkiye
e-mail: ibrahimgunduz@duzce.edu.tr

A. Akusta and M. Gün (eds.), *Financial Frontiers in Energy Markets*, Contributions to Finance and Accounting, https://doi.org/10.1007/978-3-032-16738-5_3

1 Introduction

Oil has been used since ancient times. However, with the industrial revolution, there has been a significant increase in the use of oil both in the industrial and domestic fields. Due to this increase, oil has become one of the most important commodities of the modern economy. The case that oil is so important both in the industrial field and at the social level is due to the fact that it contains many different valuable industrial raw materials. This effect increases the use of both crude oil and the products obtained as a result of refining fact that oil is so important both in the industrial field and at the social level is due to the fact that itional resource.

The chemical structure of oil comes to the fore in making it so important both in the industrial field and social level. Due to this structure of crude oil, both crude oil and refined products have a wide range of uses. There are many different valuable industrial raw materials in the crude oil content. These raw materials are subjected to refining processes, and various industrial raw materials are obtained. This structure of crude oil, both crude oil and refined products, has a wide range of uses. There are many different valuable industrial raw materials in the crude oil content. These raw materials are subjected to refining processes, and various industrial raw materials are obtained. Due to this function, the field of use of petroleum is expanding.

Volatility is an important framework in oil pricing. Volatility refers to the variability in the price of a good, product, or service. Volatility is frequently used by researchers. The chemical structure of oil affects its price. Due to its chemical properties, oil is highly flammable. Therefore, oil requires more sensitive transportation and storage conditions compared to other commodities. The security risk of oil makes its prices more susceptible to various threats. So, high security risk leads to high volatility. The high volatility in oil prices not only aggravates the decision-making processes of policymakers. It also creates an unpredictable economic environment for actors in financial and commodity markets. The effects of volatility in oil prices influence many sectors on a national and global scale. Therefore, volatility in oil prices is not only an economic issue but a multidimensional risk area that encompasses geopolitical, environmental, and social dimensions (Kang et al., 2017).

After the 2000s, individuals, institutions, states, and international organizations have faced unprecedented risks. This environment, full of crises, undoubtedly influences oil prices as well. The main factors impacting oil prices are listed as: geopolitical variables, financial speculations, and basic economic indicators. Geopolitical risks and tensions often lead to sharp and short-term shocks in oil prices, while speculative behavior frustrates economic systems in the long term, causing large price volatility. These persistent effects contribute to ongoing volatility in oil markets.

Global disasters also have considerable effects on oil price volatility. Such crises can be caused by natural events such as earthquakes, floods, or volcanic eruptions, or by epidemics affecting humans and wildlife. For example, epidemics that have become more often after 2000 have had measurable effects on oil prices. However, the COVID-19 pandemic, which started in China in 2020 and spread all over the world, has had much deeper effects than previous outbreaks. This is because the pandemic has caused unprecedented loss of life and severely disrupted daily life around the world. Widespread quarantine and economic slowdowns have caused a dramatic drop in oil demand, leading to rapid filling of storage capacity and heavy financial losses for oil-exporting countries. At one point, oil prices dropped to a "negative" price, meaning that producers had to pay buyers to get rid of excess oil. This period has led to the beginning of a historically rare period in the oil markets. The supply surplus and price effects during this period were estimated to be about seven times greater than those of the global financial crisis of 2008 (Hoang et al., 2021). A similar shock happened during the Russian invasion of Ukraine in 2022, again due to risks to supply security (Mbah & Wasum, 2022).

This section will discuss the factors that affect oil prices within the framework of the combination of volatility, politics, speculation, and market fundamentals. The discussion is based on three key events that have disrupted the global oil markets. These are: Russia's annexation of Crimea, the COVID-19 pandemic, and the Russia-Ukraine war. As a result of comparing these events, it will be made to shown which effects disappear in a short time and which ones are permanent. Many studies have shown that even short-term shocks in oil prices can have long-term effects. This section provides examples that confirm this situation.

2 Literature Review

2.1 The Concept of Volatility and its Importance in Energy Markets

Nowadays, oil has become an indispensable part of life, extending from individual consumers to corporate users. The use of oil in many sectors in both raw and refined forms takes it beyond being a one-way energy source. Therefore, volatility or fluctuations in oil prices have the potential to seriously influence a wide range of actors, from individuals to states. Uncertainties and risks related to oil increase volatility by directly affecting oil prices. These volatilities are measured by different micro and macro indicators. The term "volatility", which is widely used in the literature, is used to describe such uncertainties. The term "volatility" is also used to describe how prices often move in unexpected ways. This notion also includes different sides of market behavior, such as prices returning to the average, making sudden jumps, or entering a completely new form (Kang et al., 2017).

Researchers use different econometric tools for understanding price designs.. "The GARCH model " is an important model that shows the change in volatility in oil markets over time. The results in the GARC model show that uncertainties last longer during periods of crisis. According to the GARCH model, negative news is more effective than positive news. According to this model, market volatility is not lost soon. According to the GARCH model, market volatilities persist for a long time after the first shock (Kang et al., 2017). The "ARMA" and "ARIMA" models represent the structure and persistence of price volatility over time. Different techniques are used in the "ARMA" and "ARIMA" models. Thus, different changes are understood more clearly (Möst & Keles, 2010).

Nowadays, the concept of volatility has changed with structural changes and policy innovations. The concept of clean energy caused an increase in carbon prices. Thus, new uncertainties appeared in energy markets. There is a relationship between oil price volatility and low-carbon financial capital. This creates a more confusing and interconnected risk structure. The level of relationship between decarbonization markets and the financial system is starting to develop. Additionally, with the volatility in carbon prices, it has spread to financial markets. Thus, carbon futures have been linked to green investments. (He et al., 2025). Also, some studies show that volatilities in oil prices influence companies' emissions and profitability, so fossil fuel markets and carbon pricing systems work mutually (Lu et al., 2024). Some researchers say that uncertainty in oil prices volatilizes carbon prices, increasing policy and market instability. (Li et al., 2023). In this regard, environmental policies, technological innovations, and emission trading become important elements that redefine the causes of volatility in energy markets (Wang et al., Wang et al., 2024). Carbon prices reflect market expectations and reliability in climate policies, enabling the transition of uncertainty to oil-related financial instruments.

2.2 Geopolitical Risk: Conceptualization and Measurement

Geopolitical risks play a critical role among the factors shaping oil prices. In political and economic studies, geopolitics is defined as the influence of the geographical location of a region or border on policy-making (Sharma et al., 2025). Given the combustible nature of oil and the variety in its transportation and storage methods, geopolitical risks directly affect oil prices. These risks include conflicts, wars, low-intensity tensions, threats, and the possibility of escalation into armed conflict (Barro, & Urs'ua, J., 2012).

Different methods have been developed to consider the impact of geopolitical risks on energy prices. One of the most popular methods is the text-based Geopolitical Risk Index (GPR), which is based on newspapers, magazines, and reports. This method analyzes tendencies from written sources rather than numerical data, and such data are often referred to as "paper-based" evidence (Blondeel et al., 2021). These indicators show volatility trends related to geopolitical risks and provide data-based answers to the following questions: How do oil prices react during periods of increased geopolitical risk? Will volatility increase or decrease? These indicators also help to explain regime changes by showing during which period the uncertainty in the oil markets arose (Kang et al., 2017). However, regime changes vary by country and institution. The effects of geopolitical risks are not the same everywhere; for example, price increases in oil-dependent countries have stronger economic effects than in countries that diversify their energy sources (Bradshaw & Sander, 2021).

Policy discussions show the impact of geopolitical tensions on carbon markets. Lu et al. (2024) showed that during crisis periods, carbon prices volatilities more volatile as investors are uncertain about energy demand and new regulations. According to Li et al. (2024) stated that political shocks cause the oil and carbon markets to move together, increasing uncertainty and making price forecasting difficult. This situation shows that conflicts today affect both the energy system and the related markets.

The transition to clean energy has created new types of geopolitical risks. According to Wang et al. (Wang, Ren, & Li, 2024), green technologies, carbon trading, and state-led investment plans have changed the way politics and energy markets influence each other. Today, market volatility is no longer driven strictly by supply issues; it is also driven by tightly interconnected financial systems, institutions, and climate policies.

2.3 Fundamental Indicators: Supply–Demand, Production, Inventories, and OPEC Decisions

Apart from politics and speculation, basic economic factors also influence oil prices. These factors include the amount of oil produced and consumed, the size of global inventories, and decisions made by OPEC. On the demand side, oil consumption is of great importance. Although most discussions focus on supply, it is usually the stable structure of demand that determines the amount of production. When demand decreases, companies cannot stop production immediately, which quickly leads to an oversupply and lower prices.

On the supply side, both local and global conditions affect oil prices. Wars and unrest in producing countries generally increase prices. Problems in large producers such as Saudi Arabia and the USA increase this effect, while problems in small producers do not affect the market much. Large oil reserves stabilize the market, while small reserves drive up prices.

OPEC plays a critical role in regulating and monitoring the oil market and prices. OPEC was established to provide a balance between supply and demand. The organization aims to maintain price stability and protect the interests of both exporters and importers. OPEC aims to maintain price stability and prevent unexpected price shocks by adjusting production quotas. OPEC's decisions and statements play an important role in maintaining balance in the global oil market.

3 Methodology

This study will use case analysis and time series analysis to deal with the volatility in oil prices. The main reason for using these methods is that the reactions of oil prices to geopolitical shocks and global disruptions are thought to be handled more accurately with these methods.. The study will use case analysis and time-based analysis. The reason for using time-based analysis is to show the short-term and long-term volatility of oil prices against events that develop at a global level and the reasons for these.

Oil is given different names in the literature, taking into account its structure, the region where it is extracted, or the region where it is traded. For example, Crude oil, WTI oil or Brent oil, etc. To ensure the consistency of the analyses in the study and ensure that the study is based on the right argument. The analysis will be done using "Brent Oil" data, which is the most used oil type in the world.

Oil price data is collected from provable and constantly updated institutional databases, including the Monthly Releases of the US Energy Information Administration (EIA), the World Bank, and OPEC. The data set in the study was prepared by taking three basic criteria into consideration. Firstly, data that are effective in determining oil prices and shared by internationally reliable institutions as open access. Thus, the reliability of the study seeks maximization. Secondly, each time series in the study was standardized and included in the analyses. In this way, it tried to ensure the measurement consistency and time consistency of the study. All these methods done in order to contribute to the comparability of time data. Thirdly, in the variable selection in the model used in the study, a method was applied to reveal the effects of geopolitical crises and economic shocks on the oil market. This will promote a better understanding of the effects that behavioral indicators (variables) have on the oil market.

3.1 Case Study Design

In the event study design, the period under consideration covers daily closing prices of oil for several days before and after Russia's invasion of Ukraine on February 24, 2022. The day of the invasion is designated as the event day ($\tau = 0$). Based on the analysis and the collected data, logarithmic returns of oil prices were calculated. These data are compared with "normal return" data to obtain (AR) Abnormal Returns and to deepen the analysis. In the study, it will be understood whether stock market and financial asset prices experience a permanent or temporary volatility after major events that develop in the global order. To achieve this goal, Cumulative Abnormal Returns (CAR) and Standardized Cumulative Abnormal Returns (SCAR) methods will be used. Abnormal Volatility (AV) and Cumulative Abnormal Volatility (CAV) measurement methods are added to determine the corrections in the oil price and to strengthen the study. These indicators helped analyze the development process of uncertainty in the days following the crisis. In this regard, it was also tried to shed light on how the oil market reacts to geopolitical shocks.

"Time series" analysis was used to support other methods in the study. In this analysis, events that occurred at a global level, such as wars, crises, and conflicts, were compared with events that previously occurred at a global level, such as pandemics, financial crises, etc. Russia's annexation of Crimea in 2014 and the

COVID-19 pandemic. In this context, the uncertainty waves in time, "six-month rolling volatility," have been used to understand how long it lasts and how strong it is. The main purpose of this analysis method is to compare the time frame of market instability and market size in different crisis periods according to various factors. These factors include geopolitical tensions, global pandemics, and structural economic changes. This method will help to understand and compare the pricing behavior of oil and the volatility in oil prices under different shocks.

3.2 Dataset

This study is based on the analysis of three major events that took place between 2014–2022. The Case in 2014 is considered to be a "supply-driven" development that started with the collapse in oil prices that shaped production strategies and revealed structural weaknesses in the global market. The COVID-19 pandemic has led to a process in which the uncertainty caused by the lack of demand in the energy sector has spread to many financial areas. The third period includes a geopolitical break process in which Russia's invasion of Ukraine damaged energy security, and this situation triggered a permanent change in price dynamics and volatility. The case analysis aims to compare three different factors affecting oil prices (supply, demand, and geopolitical factors) in an analytical framework. So the scientific aspect of the study will become stronger.

"The Brent oil price" was taken as a basis in order to accurately present the clarity and comparability of the data and analyses in the study. Analyses regarding the Brent oil price and oil prices, and price volatility will be conducted. Brent oil is determined as the reference data source because it is easily accessible in the global market and has deep liquidity in the financial field. The data set is limited to Brent oil. This helps to prevent deficiencies and errors that may arise from different oil indices. Oil price data is drawn from open and verifiable sources, including the US Energy Information Administration (EIA), the World Bank, and OPEC's Monthly Oil Market Reports. This method cross-checked to ensure consistency and reliability in the data.

The use of analyses related to the carbon market and research related to the energy transition in an integrated method will deepen the content of the study and make its predictions even stronger. In this way, the methodological strength and depth of the study will be increased. This perspective will contribute to the understanding of the relationship between traditional energy markets and low-carbon policies and to the presentation of this relationship. This comprehensive perspective also helps to study the transformations in energy management. At the same time, in order to contribute to the understanding of long-term sustainability, security targets and volatility observed in the oil market are compared, and the accuracy of the results of the analyses in the study is also checked. Eventually, the study aims to contribute to the literature in this field by analyzing concepts such as geopolitical energy, environmental economics, and financial uncertainty in the evolving green transition period in market processes.

4 Analysis and Findings

4.1 Event Study Results: The 2022 Russia–Ukraine Conflict

The analysis begins with an examination of the effects of Russia's attack on Ukraine in 2022 on oil prices. To understand this intervention by Russia in Ukraine, we also need to look at the events that took place between these two countries in 2014. Indeed, analyzing the developments in the oil market after the Russian annexation in 2014 will help expand the scope of the event in 2022, depending on the time, and will help to understand the effects of wars on oil prices. Evaluating these two developments together, originating from Russia, will help compare the effects of short-term geopolitical shocks and long-term and permanent reactions (Table 1).

It shows that the war that started in 2022 did not only trigger a short-term fluctuation in oil prices. It also shows that this war has caused a constant transformation in the formation of oil prices and oil volatility behaviors.

The data in the table shows that the cumulative abnormal return (CAR) values from the event window remain positive. In addition, it is observed that oil prices continue to increase even after the initial shock of the first incident has passed. After the war, oil prices recalibrated due to the actions of market participants and institutions. With this situation, the market's reaction to the war developed gradually. The results of this model show that changes in the market are not random volatilities but deviations from the normal functioning of the market. This is supported by positive and statistically significant SCAR values. Abnormal return persistence (The AR post) values support these findings. Returns after the start of the war diverged significantly from zero. This has proven that the performance of the oil market does not conform to typical patterns of understanding. Post-event returns diverged meaningfully from zero, signaling that market performance in the aftermath of the invasion departed from typical patterns. In fact, prices did not return to their previous levels after this process; due to increasing geopolitical uncertainties, the market has adapted to new conditions and entered a structural change process.

Volatility indicators follow a similar path. Both the cumulative abnormal volatility (CAV) and the standardized CAV (SCAV) values were in the positive area after the sudden event period. This proves that the uncertainty situation has become an established feature of investor expectations. Therefore, it is possible to state that the impact of the conflict extends beyond price levels and affects the perception of risk and its value.

All these evaluations support the fact that global energy markets are sensitive to geopolitical disruptions or risks. Therefore, the Russia-Ukraine war has not only intensified short-term price movements. It has also paved the way for a longer-term stabilization of volatility regimes in oilrefore, the Russia-Ukraine war has not only intensified short-term price movements. It has also paved the way for longer-term stability and security.

Table 1 Brent Crude Oil Prices During the Russia–Ukraine Conflict (February 14–28, 2022)

Date	Price	Return (log)	Abnormal Return (AR)	Cumulative Abnormal Return (CAR)	Abnormal Volatility (AV)	Cumulative Abnormal Volatility (CAV)	Relative Day (τ)	Interval
2022-02-14	93.5	0.022497	0.023388	0.023388	0.000119	0.000119	−10	Pre
2022-02-15	90.21	−0.035821	−0.03493	−0.011542	0.000896	0.001015	−9	Pre
2022-02-16	91.83	0.017799	0.01869	0.007147	−7.1e-05	0.000944	−8	Pre
2022-02-17	90.04	−0.019685	−0.018794	−0.011647	0.0	0.000944	−7	Pre
2022-02-18	90.21	0.001886	0.002777	−0.00887	−0.000384	0.000561	−6	Pre
2022-02-20	91.62	0.015509	0.0164	0.00753	−0.000147	0.000414	−4	Pre
2022-02-21	92.65	0.011179	0.01207	0.0196	−0.000262	0.000152	−3	Pre
2022-02-22	91.91	−0.008019	−0.007128	0.012472	−0.000323	−0.000171	−2	Pre
2022-02-23	90.69	−0.013363	−0.012472	−0.0	−0.000209	−0.00038	−1	Pre
2022-02-24	90.94	0.002753	0.003644	0.003644	−0.00038	−0.00076	0	Event
2022-02-25	89.89	−0.011613	−0.010722	−0.007079	−0.000252	−0.001012	1	Post
2022-02-28	93.5	0.039375	0.040266	0.033187	0.001163	0.000151	4	Post

4.2 Comparative Analysis of Global Shocks (2014–2022)

Russia's declaration of war on Ukraine in 2022 led to a more than short-term price increase in oil prices. This period sparked a permanent change in oil market behavior. Adjustments in oil prices and volatility have extended well beyond the immediate aftermath of the war. This suggests that the market response will result in a deeper structural rebalancing rather than a short-lived reaction.

Cumulative Abnormal Returns (CAR) remained positive throughout the entire event window. This indicates that prices continued to increase in the days following the initial shock. In addition, it has been observed that oil prices did not stabilize after the war. On the contrary, it has been observed that the market has gradually internalized geopolitical uncertainty and has taken on a structure in which this uncertainty is the new normal. The persistence of positive Standardized CAR (SCAR) values indicates that the deviations are statistically significant and have moved outside the normal volatility range. This supports the view that a new pricing regime has emerged in oil pricing.

At the same time, the Abnormal returns (after AR) are also sharply different from zero. This indicates that oil prices rose beyond the event date at the same time, and the abnormal returns (after AR) are also sharply different from zero. This indicates that oil prices rose beyond the event date. This constant difference means that the value of oil is constant.

The volatility in oil prices in the 2014–2022 period reveals the economic and geopolitical vulnerabilities of global energy markets. In Fig. 1, the yellow line representing monthly oil prices is seen to have fallen sharply from levels above $ 100 to below $ 50 after the 2014 Oil Price Collapse, in other words, the event indicated by the red dashed line.. The underlying causes of this collapse are closely linked to the rise in oil production and the resulting supply surplus, combined with OPEC's refusal to respond positively to calls for production cuts. Indeed, after Russia intervened in Crimea in 2014, oil prices briefly spiked above USD 100 due to heightened uncertainty. However, as oil supply continued to grow and supply chains remained undisrupted, the downward trend in prices was reinforced. Although a partial recovery in prices was observed after 2016 in line with increasing global demand, the yellow line never displayed a sustained upward trajectory.

4.3 Volatility Dynamics and Structural Uncertainty

It is important to determine the behavior of volatility in the oil market and prices. It helps to understand the events that develop in the oil markets and the reasons behind the events in times of uncertainty. Volatility more clearly and accurately shows the intensity and persistence of market reactions to shocks, as opposed to short-term price changes. This structure of volatility helps to reveal how investors adjust their expectations and re-evaluate risk over time. Therefore, volatility in the global energy

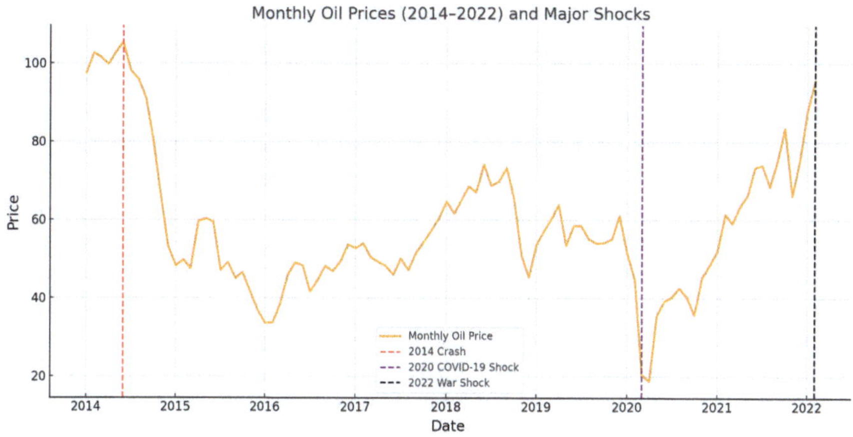

Fig. 1 Oil Price Dynamics under Major Global Shocks (2014–2022)

system represents a much stronger and more functional structure than a financial measurement. Volatility reflects the way the market absorbs geopolitical tensions, policy transitions, and large-scale disruptions such as the COVID-19 pandemic.

This subsection has been created to describe these dynamics. A six-month rolling window approach is applied to track the evolution of volatility in the oil market over time. This technique made it possible to track successive waves of uncertainty and observe how they strengthened or weakened in response to major global developments between 2014 and 2022. As shown in Fig. 2, the results exhibit distinct and recurring patterns associated with supply shocks, demand curtailments, and geopolitical crises. However, the data also show the persistent structural vulnerability of international oil markets.

Fig. 2 Six-Month Rolling Volatility of Monthly Oil Returns (2014–2022)

Figure 2 shows the rolling six-month volatility of monthly oil returns from 2014 to 2022. It also includes how uncertainty in oil markets evolved in response to successive global shocks. The yellow line in Fig. 2 reflects the fluctuation traces, the price level itself over time, but also the market size, volatility. This measure is particularly valuable because it reveals how energy markets react not only to shifts in prices but also to changes in risk perception and expectations about future stability. The first major disruption, marked by the red dashed line, corresponds to the 2014 oil price collapse. During this episode, prices fell sharply from above USD 100 to below USD 50 per barrelyet volatility rose only moderately. This muted reaction supports that markets initially interpreted the downturn as cyclical rather than structural, underestimating the long-term consequences of the shift in supply conditions and the growing role of non-OPEC producers.

The six-month rolling volatility of monthly oil returns from 2014 to 2022 shows how uncertainty in oil markets evolved in response to successive global shocks. The yellow line in the figure traces volatility, reflecting not the price level itself but the magnitude of market volatility over time. This measure is particularly valuable because it reveals how energy markets react not only to shifts in prices but also to changes in risk perception and expectations about future stability.

The first major disruption, marked by the red dashed line, corresponds to the 2014 oil price collapse. During this episode, prices fell sharply—from above USD 100 to below USD 50 per barrel, yet volatility rose only moderately. This muted reaction implies that markets initially interpreted the downturn as cyclical rather than structural, underestimating the long-term consequences of the shift in supply conditions and the growing role of non-OPEC producers.

5 Conclusion

This study was prepared to analyze, with data, how oil markets responded to supply, demand, and geopolitical shocks over the last decade. The results of the research show that oil prices are shaped not only by economic and political developments, but also by global health crises. For example, the COVID-19 pandemic in 2020 pushed oil prices to unprecedented levels. During this period, oil demand also fell to historic lows. However, Russia's annexation of Crimea in 2014 caused a short-term supply shortage. During this period, there was no similar drop in oil prices like the COVID-19 period. Indeed, wars and geopolitical tensions have a tendency to lead to sharp but short-term increases in the volatility of oil prices. However, it seems that global health events such as the COVID-19 pandemic have revealed a much longer-term phase of instability in the volatility of oil prices. The reason for this outcome is that the pandemic has left a deeper and more lasting mark on market confidence by reshaping human behavior, investor sentiment, and policy responses, beyond its economic impact.

The study shows that comparing major global shocks can yield very different results depending on the broader contexts of similar crises. For example, two cases originating from Russia support this judgment. In fact, the drop in oil prices after the intervention in 2014 and the rise in oil prices after the intervention in 2022 support this inference. The global economic environment in the years when the cases developed was effective in producing such different results. The oil price behavior in 2014 was influenced by developments such as excessive supply conditions, internal divisions within OPEC, the rapid expansion of shale gas production in the US, etc. These developments increased the pressure on the oil price. These developments caused oil prices to fall. However, by 2022, oil prices had risen due to the ongoing uncertainty and anxiety following the pandemic. The persistence of positive Cumulative Abnormal Return (CAR) and Cumulative Abnormal Volatility (CAV) values in the post-2022 period supports the assumption that investors no longer see the Russia-Ukraine war as a temporary disruption, but as a permanent regime change. This transformation in views on the oil market also reinforced the long-standing geopolitical coldness between Russia and the West and the changes in risk perception following the pandemic.

After the comparative case analysis, three main conclusions were reached. Firstly, each shock has its own unique character. For example, the reason for the decline in oil prices in 2014 was the existence of a supply-driven period that triggered the low prices period. During the COVID-19 pandemic in 2020, there was an unprecedented decline in oil demand, which caused a collapse in oil prices. However, after this period, oil prices gradually began to recover. After the Russian attack in 2022, global energy security concerns have intensified, both with the steps taken by Russia and the new measures announced by other countries against Russia. This situation has led to a continuous increase in prices and has also created permanent volatility in oil prices. Second, the type of vulnerability varies with the nature of the disruption. Geopolitical shocks continue to be the strongest and most persistent drivers of oil price movements. However, it should not be forgotten that social and behavioral disorders that arise due to the impact of global crises, such as pandemics, may invalidate traditional economic mechanisms and understanding. Thirdly, the persistent uncertainty following COVID-19 has highlighted the need for adaptive frameworks, flexible pricing systems, and tighter coordination between fiscal and energy policies by governments. This has led to the questioning of traditional policy models.

The results of the study also provide important outputs for decision makers. For example, it highlights the importance of the necessity of integrating geopolitical risk management into long-term energy strategies. In reality, the permanent positive CAR and CAV values observed in the oil market in the period after the Russian invasion in 2022 show that the markets have now structurally internalized geopolitical shocks rather than temporary risks. Therefore, decision makers must produce policies taking this change into account.. Governments should also diversify energy sources and transportation routes, strengthen regional partnerships, and accelerate the adoption of renewable energy to reduce systemic vulnerabilities and develop policies in this context. Additionally, the pandemic period has revealed the vulnerability of demand-driven policies.

The evolution of oil price volatility in 2014, 2020, and 2022 shows the deepening structure of energy markets and the extent to which financial markets are interconnected. In fact, persistent volatility in oil prices will tighten financial conditions for both countries and firms by increasing borrowing costs and risk premiums, and will cause a serious bottleneck in the global economy. Policy makers should increase financial transparency in energy trading systems, improve data sharing practices, and respond to adverse situations that may occur in oil prices by strengthening risk disclosure mechanisms. The growing convergence between energy security and climate governance necessitates the creation of a new integrated energy policy. Recent developments in carbon markets show that geopolitical crises are now affecting emissions pricing and investment in green technologies. As a result, a dual track approach that simultaneously increases energy security and accelerates decarbonization will benefit institutions.

Although the scope of the research is broad, it has some structural and methodological limitations. The ten-year observation window restricts capturing longer-term risk cycles or including emerging crises beyond 2022. This situation narrows the verifiability of the results of the study. To overcome this limitation, future research should expand the time period and include recent geopolitical developments to improve these findings. As the transition to renewable energy and green transformation continue to reshape global energy markets, the current framework of this study can only reflect the effects of this transformation to a limited extent. Therefore, a thorough analysis of future research on the effects of renewable energy dynamics, carbon neutrality targets, and sustainable finance mechanisms on oil price volatility will provide a new and holistic view of the literature.

References

Barro, R., & Urs'ua, J. (2012). Rare macroeconomic disasters. *Annual Review of Economics, 4*(1), 83–109. https://doi.org/10.1146/annurev-economics-080511-110932

Blondeel, M., Van de Graaf, T., & Haesebrouck, T. (2021). The geopolitics of energy system transformation: A review. *Geography Compass, 15*(7), 1–22. https://doi.org/10.1111/gec3.12580

Bradshaw, M., & Sander, H. (2021). *Global energy dilemmas: Energy security, globalization, and climate change*. Polity Press.

He, Z., Lee, C., & Sharma, S. (2025). The impact of geopolitical risks on the renewable energy transition. *Energy Economics, 143*, 1–12.

Hoang, A., Nižetić, S., Olcer, A., Ong, H., Chen, W., Chong, C., et al. (2021). Impacts of COVID-19 pandemic on the global energy system and the shift progress to renewable energy: Opportunities, challenges, and policy implications. *Energy Policy, 154*(112322), 1–11. https://doi.org/10.1016/j.enpol.2021.112322

Kang, W., Ratti, R., & Yoon, K. (2017). The impact of oil price shocks on the stock market return and volatility relationship. *Energy Economics, 61*, 42–51. https://doi.org/10.1016/j.eneco.2016.10.018.

Li, H., Huang, X., Zhou, D., & Guo, L. (2023). The dynamic linkages among crude oil price, climate change and carbon price in China. *Energy Strategy ReviewsX, 48*(101123), 1–16.

Lu, Q., Umair, M., Qin, Z., & Ullah, M. (2024). Exploring the nexus of oil price shocks: Impacts on financial dynamics and carbon emissions in the crude oil industry. *Energy, 312*(133415), 1–10.

Mbah, R., & Wasum, D. (2022). Russian-Ukraine 2022 war: A review of the economic impact of Russian-Ukraine crisis on the USA, UK, Canada, and Europe. *Advances in Social Sciences Research Journal, 9*(3), 144–153. https://doi.org/10.14738/assrj.93.1200

Möst, D., & Keles, D. (2010). A survey of stochastic modelling approaches for liberalised electricity markets. *European Journal of Operational Research, 207*(2), 543–556. https://doi.org/10.1016/j.ejor.2009.11.007

Sharma, S., Hayat, A., Affandi, Y., & Rishanty, A. (2025). A note on how Asia-Pacific giants Australia, China and Japan manage the geopolitical risk for prices. *Emerging Markets Finance and Trade, 6*(19), 2695–2703.

Wang, O., Ren, F., & Li, R. (2024). Geopolitics and energy security: A comprehensive exploration of evolution, collaborations, and future directions. *Humanities and Social Sciences Communications, 11*(1), 1–26.

Wang, Q., Wang, X., & Li, R. (2024). Geopolitical risks and energy transition: The impact of environmental regulation and green innovation. *Humanities and Social Sciences Communications, 11*(1), 1–22.

Brent Crude Under Pressure: Saudi Supply, China Demand, and the Myth of Geopolitical Pricing

Amal Essayem

Abstract This chapter examines the impact of non-fundamental factors on the determination of Brent crude oil prices, with particular emphasis on the role of Gulf Cooperation Council (GCC) countries and, most importantly, Saudi Arabia. Employing a quantile regression framework on monthly data spanning 2002–2025, the study investigates the asymmetric effects of geopolitical risk, Saudi crude oil supply, and structural demand from China across different market states. The results indicate that Brent oil prices are largely insensitive to global geopolitical risk, suggesting that political instability does not exert a systematic influence on international oil price dynamics. Markets appear to absorb such shocks through diversification of supply and established risk-hedging mechanisms, limiting their long-term impact. Similarly, Saudi-specific geopolitical risks show little effect across most quantiles, with only a short-lived negative influence during the onset of extreme high-price states. By contrast, Saudi crude oil production demonstrates a more consistent and tangible effect: output increases tend to place downward pressure on prices during normal conditions, underscoring the Kingdom's role as a swing producer within OPEC. Finally, China's GDP growth emerges as a structural driver, exerting upward pressure across all quantiles. These findings highlight the resilience of oil markets to geopolitical disturbances and reaffirm the centrality of Saudi supply adjustments and Chinese demand in shaping long-term price trajectories.

Keywords Oil price · Swing producer · Geopolitical risk · Quantile regression · Saudi Arabia

A. Essayem (✉)
The institute of Islamic Economics and Finance, Marmara University, Istanbul, Türkiye
e-mail: amal.essayem@marmara.edu.tr

A. Akusta and M. Gün (eds.), *Financial Frontiers in Energy Markets*, Contributions to Finance and Accounting, https://doi.org/10.1007/978-3-032-16738-5_4

1 Introduction

Oil has long been recognized as both a vital energy commodity and a strategic political asset. Its scarcity and uneven distribution place it at the center of international conflicts and shifts in global power (Colgan, 2013; Wakeford, 2006). Beyond supply–demand fundamentals, oil prices reflect the interplay of geopolitical tensions, state strategies, and market expectations. Events such as the 1970s oil crisis and Gulf Wars underscore how political shocks continue to influence price formation through perceptions of risk rather than just physical disruptions.

While existing studies often examine global or importer–exporter contrasts, the Gulf region, particularly Saudi Arabia, remains underexplored despite its pivotal role in world energy markets. Most research focuses on how oil price volatility affects Saudi Arabia's economy, with limited attention to how Saudi-specific geopolitical risks and production behaviour influence global prices. This chapter addresses that gap by analysing the dual impact of Saudi geopolitical risk and supply capacity on Brent crude prices.

As the world's largest crude exporter and OPEC's de facto leader, Saudi Arabia acts as a "swing producer," adjusting output to stabilize or influence markets. This role situates the Kingdom at the heart of debates on OPEC behaviour and market management. In parallel, China's rapid growth has transformed global oil demand dynamics, making its economic trajectory a key determinant of price movements. Together, these factors define a new geopolitical and economic environment for global energy markets.

Using daily data from 2002 to 2025, this study applies a quantile regression framework to assess how global and Saudi-specific geopolitical risk (GPR), Saudi oil supply, and China's GDP growth affect Brent prices across different market conditions. It contributes to the literature by first incorporating country-level geopolitical indicators and supply data often omitted from broader analyses. Second, focusing on the Gulf region's strategic role in oil price formation. Third, revealing asymmetric effects through the quantile approach.

The findings indicate that Brent prices are largely resilient to both global and Saudi-specific geopolitical risk, with effects concentrated at higher quantiles during high-price phases. Conversely, Saudi oil production remains a systematic determinant, exerting downward pressure on prices, while China's demand consistently drives prices upward. These results highlight the conditional nature of geopolitical influence and reaffirm Saudi Arabia's stabilizing role in global energy markets.

The chapter proceeds as follows: Section 2 introduces key factors influencing oil prices, Section 3 reviews the literature, Section 4 presents data and methodology, Section 5 discusses results, and Sect. 6 concludes with policy implications.

2 Key Factors Influencing Oil Prices

As mentioned earlier, historical events underscore the sensitivity of oil markets to geopolitical disruptions: the 1979 Iranian Revolution caused severe supply shortages and a fourfold surge in prices, while the 1990–1991 Gulf War similarly disrupted supplies and triggered drastic price increases (IEA, , 2008). Such episodes illustrate how geopolitical risk (GPR) often generates a "geopolitical uncertainty premium" beyond traditional supply–demand fundamentals (IEA, , 2008).

Scholars identify several mechanisms through which GPR affects oil prices. First, precautionary demand rises in anticipation of supply disruptions (Kilian, 2009). Second, geopolitical events can directly constrain production capacity, reduce supply, and raise prices (Wang and Sun, 2017; Slaibi et al., 2009). Third, uncertainty shocks amplify volatility and impair informational efficiency in oil markets (Bariviera et al., 2017; Van Robays, 2016).

literature shows that the relationship is reciprocal; oil price swings themselves carry geopolitical consequences. The 2007–2008 price boom tripled fertilizer costs, triggered food crises, and destabilized food-importing countries, whereas the collapse to $26 per barrel in 2016 strained oil-dependent economies and pushed even wealthy Gulf states to introduce austerity and new taxation. Oil market dynamics thus both respond to and reshape global politics (Bahgat, 2008; Salameh, 2000).

Nevertheless, the GPR–oil nexus remains contested. Monge et al. (2017) report no significant price differences across major conflict periods, suggesting growing market resilience through supply diversification and financial hedging. Measurement challenges further complicate analysis: Caldara and Iacoviello (2018) developed a GPR Index based on media references, showing that GPR shocks depress oil prices indirectly via weakened global activity.

Overall, the literature highlights the complexity of oil's geopolitical nature. While historical evidence confirms volatility amplification through precautionary demand, supply disruptions, and uncertainty shocks, recent decades suggest more muted, inconsistent effects.

3 Literature Review

As mentioned above, the relationship between oil price and GPR is reciprocal; therefore, in the empirical literature, the ties between the two of them are increasingly examined as a bidirectional dynamic in which geopolitical tensions and oil prices mutually reinforce one another. Su et al. (2019) show that wars typically raise prices, yet low GPR does not guarantee declines, since crises can drive prices higher independently. Shahbaz et al. (2023) likewise confirm two-way causality between GPR and oil prices across countries, though effects vary by context.

Besides bidirectionality, recent studies emphasize the time-varying and asymmetric nature of this relationship. Li et al. (2023) find long-term stability once structural breaks are excluded, while Cunado et al. (2019) and Ozcelebi and Tokmakcioglu (2020) show heterogeneous effects, with BRIC economies especially sensitive. Wavelet analysis further indicates that the strongest co-movements occur at high frequencies, implying that GPR primarily drives short-term volatility (Li et al., 2020).

Beyond the direction of the relationship between oil and geopolitics, a different strand of the literature looks beyond the price levels and focuses exclusively on volatility, which appears more systematically shaped by GPR. Qian et al. (2022) show volatility intensifies during recessions, while Liu et al. (2019) note that severe geopolitical risks have stronger predictive power than general indices. Demirer et al. (2019) and Smales (2021) conclude that volatility, rather than returns, is more affected, though effects are nonlinear and benchmark dependent. Zhang et al. (2023) identify asymmetric spillovers, with developed countries transmitting GPR shocks and emerging markets receiving them. Political economy perspectives extend this view by linking GPR to macroeconomic and diplomatic contexts. Wu et al. (2023) find that exporters' shocks exert a stronger influence on oil prices than importers. Mignon and Saadaoui (2024) differentiate between political relationship shocks, which lift prices via demand optimism, and geopolitical risk shocks, which reflect supply fears. Gkillas et al. (2022) combine fundamentals, expectations, and GPR, showing that no single driver suffices; rather, combinations shape outcomes. Collectively, these studies confirm that volatility is the main channel of GPR's impact, but with outcomes contingent on global conditions.

As observed, most studies tend to overlook the Gulf region and its direct impact on oil prices. In fact, the Gulf region has witnessed repeated GPR peaks over the past two decades, triggered by conflicts and domestic instability. Key episodes include the aftermath of 9/11 (Blanchard, 2009), the 2003 Iraq invasion and Al-Qaeda bombings in Riyadh (Hertog, 2010), the Arab Spring (Gause, 2011), the 2015 Saudi intervention in Yemen (Boucek, 2015), the 2017 anti-corruption crackdown and Lebanese crisis (Ulrichsen, 2019), the 2019 Aramco attacks disrupting 5% of global supply (Kilian & Zhou, 2022), the 2020 killing of Qassem Soleimani, and the 2023 Israel–Gaza escalation. These events are consistently reflected in GPR indices, confirming regional volatility.

Another issue to keep in mind while integrating KSA (Kingdom of Saudi Arabia) specific indicators and their impact on global oil markets is the kingdom's unique political economy. As a rentier state, it sustains regime legitimacy through oil rents, embedding production decisions in domestic reform agendas (for instance, Vision 2030), regional security, and diplomacy. Centralized governance enables strategic signalling, reinforcing its role as the global swing producer.

Historically, Saudi Arabia has repeatedly acted to stabilize markets. In 2006–2007, it offset Iranian threats to cut exports by deploying spare capacity. During the 2012–2016 sanctions on Iran, it pledged to boost production by up to 2 mb/d. Earlier precedents include drastic cuts in the 1980s to defend prices and the 1986 flood that reshaped markets. Such episodes highlight its unique capacity to stabilize global supply.

As noted, the literature provides no conclusive evidence regarding the Gulf region, particularly Saudi Arabia's, dynamics. It is therefore essential to examine both Saudi-specific geopolitical risk and crude oil supply levels in relation to oil prices.

Alongside Gulf dynamics, incorporating China's economic trajectory into the empirical framework is necessary to control for its major influence on Brent oil prices. As the world's largest importer and industrial center, China's GDP growth drives global oil demand, with its elevated energy elasticity amplifying the impact (Beirne, 2013; Xu, 2017). Increasing integration of Chinese futures markets with Brent further generates financial spillovers, while oil price shocks reverberate through China's exports, consumption, and overall economic stability. Empirical research consistently validates this role: Cross (2022) shows that China-specific demand shocks now outweigh those of the United States, and Hamendi and Law (2023) find that GDP growth significantly raises real oil prices, with stronger effects observed after 2008. Accordingly, China operates as the anchor of global commodity demand, such that slower growth systematically depresses oil and related markets.

4 Data and Methodology

This section first introduces the variables and the study period, followed by a description of the empirical method.

4.1 Data

The core variable of interest is oil prices, which are proxied by the Brent benchmark. Brent is preferred over WTI because it reflects more than 60% of internationally traded crude oil, particularly from politically sensitive regions such as the Middle East and North Africa. In addition, Brent prices respond more sharply to geopolitical shocks, including conflicts, sanctions, and maritime disruptions, while also aligning more closely with global risk indices such as the Geopolitical Risk Index. Previous studies (Kilian & Murphy, 2013) confirm that Brent is the most suitable proxy for assessing oil price responses to geopolitical risks.

Next, the analysis incorporates the Global Geopolitical Risk Index developed by Caldara and Iacoviello (2022). This index measures geopolitical tensions by tracking the frequency of related terms in major international newspapers. It covers a wide range of instability factors, including military conflicts, terrorist attacks, and threats of war, thus offering a comprehensive indicator of global geopolitical uncertainty.

To complement the global perspective, a regional GPR for Saudi Arabia is also included. This measure, likewise, proposed by Caldara and Iacoviello (2022), captures geopolitical risks in the Gulf by counting news references to wars, interstate tensions, and terrorist acts affecting international relations. Saudi Arabia is chosen because it is both the world's largest crude oil exporter and the most influential economy in the GCC. Consequently, rising political tensions in Saudi Arabia are expected to have regional spillover effects on other Gulf economies.

Moreover, Saudi crude oil production is included as a key variable. Crude oil supply is defined as the volume of oil extracted at the wellhead after the removal of impurities but before any processing. Saudi Arabia plays a central role in global oil markets, as major international organizations such as the IEA, OPEC, and the EIA recognize it as a swing producer capable of adjusting output to stabilize supply-demand balances.

Finally, China's GDP is introduced as a control variable. This choice is motivated by China's position as the world's largest oil importer and global manufacturing hub, as well as by the growing geoeconomic shift of GCC oil exports toward Asia. Including China's GDP ensures that demand-side dynamics are properly accounted for in the analysis.

The study uses monthly data that spans from 2002 to 2025, thereby covering more than two decades of geopolitical turbulence in both the Gulf region and the wider international system. This extended horizon provides a broader perspective for assessing the interaction between geopolitical risks, oil production, and global economic shifts.

4.2 Methodology

To estimate the impact of the selected variables on oil price changes, we use the following model:

$$OIL_t = \propto_0 + \sum_{i=1}^{N} \beta_i \; GPRKSA_{it} + \sum_{j=1}^{M} \delta_j \; GGPR_{jt} + \sum_{f=1}^{Q} \tau_f \; SUPKSA_{ft} + \sum_{z=1}^{P} \rho_z \; GDPCHINA_{zt} + \varepsilon_t$$

where:

i, j, f, and z represent Saudi geopolitical risk, global geopolitical risk, Saudi oil production, and China's GDP, respectively.

β_i reflects the sensitivity of oil price to Saudi geopolitical risk i.

δ_j reflects the sensitivity of oil price to global geopolitical risk j.

τ_f reflects the sensitivity of oil price to Saudi crude oil supply f.

ρ_z reflects the sensitivity of oil price to China's GDP z.

The variables in our model are defined as follows:

oil_t: Brent oil price changes at time t.

$GPRKSA_{it}$: Saudi Arabia geopolitical risk at time t.

$GGPR_{jt}$: Global geopolitical risk at time t.

$SUPKSA_{ft}$: Saudi Arabia crude oil supply at time t.

By taking into account the variables mentioned above, the model seeks to investigate their influence on Brent oil price changes. The model offers a framework for determining whether geopolitical risk, Saudi oil supply, and China's economic activity are among the main drivers of movements in the Brent oil price. To estimate the effect of the selected variables, we first employ an Ordinary Least Squares (OLS) regression. However, OLS is less robust when analysing data beyond the mean or at extreme values. To overcome this limitation, we apply the quantile regression model developed by Koenker and Bassett (1978).

We analysed the dynamics of Brent oil prices across three distinct market phases represented by different quantile levels. The lower quantiles (0.1, 0.2, 0.3) capture periods of low or depressed price movements, reflecting bearish or depressed market conditions. The medium quantiles (0.4, 0.5, 0.6) represent moderate price fluctuations, corresponding to stable or normal market phases, while the upper quantiles (0.7, 0.8, 0.9) capture strong positive price changes, characteristic of a bullish or high-volatility stage. The inclusion of multiple quantiles within each phase allows for a finer understanding of how the determinants of oil price dynamics evolve across different parts of the conditional distribution. In particular, the extreme quantiles (0.1 and 0.9) provide valuable insights into the most volatile market conditions, such as severe downturns or sharp upturns, which are especially relevant for the energy market's inherent asymmetries and exposure to global shocks. This comprehensive quantile selection thus enables a more nuanced and robust characterization of market behaviour across diverse market states.

5 Results and Interpretation

After applying a preliminary test to check anomalies in the data, we apply the OLS followed by the Quantile regression method to estimate the econometric specification. The results are presented in Table 1.

The analysis reveals that Brent oil price changes are largely insensitive to global geopolitical risk, with no significant effects observed across the quantiles. This result suggests that global political instability does not exert a systematic influence on international oil price dynamics. While geopolitical shocks are often perceived as destabilizing factors in commodity markets, the evidence here indicates that markets tend to absorb such risks without producing sustained effects on Brent prices. One possible explanation is the diversification of global oil supply and the presence of established risk-hedging mechanisms, which mitigate the long-term impact of geopolitical uncertainty on oil pricing.

Turning to Saudi Arabia's role in oil pricing, the results show a similarly limited sensitivity of Brent prices to Saudi-specific geopolitical risks. Political disturbances within Saudi Arabia or the broader Gulf region appear insignificant in most quantiles, except at the seventh quantile (Q7), where a negative effect emerges. This effect may represent the initial stage of an extreme high-price phase, during which geopolitical tensions briefly influence oil markets. However, the disappearance of this effect

Table 1 Results

	Q1	Q2	Q3	Q4	Q5	Q6	Q7	Q8	Q9	OLS
C	−0.0250 (0.0000)	−0.0187 (0.0000)	−0.0107 (0.0000)	−0.0058 (0.0006)	−0.0010 (0.5283)	0.0054 (0.0031)	0.0102 (0.000)	0.0169 (0.0000)	0.0278 (0.000)	−1.0E05 (0.9932)
GPRKSA	−0.0039 (0.2046)	−0.0037 (0.2524)	−0.0034 (0.2976)	−0.0022 (0.4909)	−0.0035 (0.2408)	−0.0020 (0.4305)	−0.0043* (0.0787)	−0.0035 (0.1402)	−0.0053 (0.1359)	−0.0030 (0.1305)
GGPR	2.6E05 (0.5523)	7.4E05 (0.1895)	2.3E05 (0.7470)	6.0E05 (0.4997)	9.7E06 (0.9071)	4.5E05 (0.6487)	9.2E05 (0.2558)	6.9E05 (0.3488)	9.4E05 (0.2559)	5.0E05 (0.3208)
SUPKSA	0.0023 (0.9363)	−0.0191 (0.5455)	−0.0438 (0.1750)	−0.0490* (0.0784)	−0.0539** (0.0334)	−0.0467* (0.0651)	−0.0221 (0.3503)	−0.0067 (0.7487)	−0.0429 (0.3200)	−0.0227 (0.2578)
GDPCHINA	0.1809*** (0.0009)	0.1487*** (0.0315)	0.1104** (0.0188)	0.0857* (0.0897)	0.0527 (0.5623)	0.0144 (0.8735)	0.1864* (0.0521)	0.2262*** (0.0060)	0.3196*** (0.0001)	0.0788 (0.3875)

Note ***, **, and * significant at 1%, 5%, and 10%, respectively

beyond Q7 indicates that markets tend to discount political turbulence after the initial shock, placing greater emphasis on supply–demand fundamentals and broader macroeconomic drivers.

By contrast, Saudi oil supply exerts a more tangible and systematic effect on prices. During normal market phases, increases in Saudi production are associated with downward pressure on prices, while this relationship becomes insignificant during both low- and high-price phases. This pattern reinforces the characterization of Saudi Arabia as a "swing producer." Even with the Kingdom's unique capacity to adjust production levels, supported by spare capacity and strategic market management, it cannot stabilize markets during extreme market conditions. As the world's largest oil exporter and a central player within OPEC, Saudi Arabia has historically exercised a limited balancing function in adjusting oil prices.

Finally, empirical evidence from the quantile regressions demonstrates that China's GDP growth consistently drives oil prices across the entire distribution. This effect persists regardless of market conditions, reinforcing the characterization of China as a "structural demander" in global energy economics. The observed escalation of coefficients between Q1 and Q7 reflects an intensifying marginal effect, suggesting that oil prices become increasingly sensitive to Chinese growth as they rise toward mid-to-high quantiles. Such a pattern may be attributed to heightened expectations of future demand and speculative behaviour in oil markets. However, the observed decline in Q8 and Q9 implies a diminishing marginal effect in extremely high price phases, which could be interpreted as evidence of demand-side constraints, and/ or market saturation. This asymmetric influence underscores the need to interpret China's role not as uniformly linear but rather as conditional upon the prevailing oil price environment.

6 Conclusion

Despite the perception that oil markets are highly sensitive to geopolitical risks, this study shows that fundamentals dominate in exerting steady upward pressure on the oil price. The results reveal that global geopolitical risk exerts no systematic influence on oil pricing across quantiles, suggesting that markets are resilient to international political turbulence. This resilience is likely underpinned by the capacity of global markets to absorb temporary shocks without altering long-run pricing structures. Similarly, Saudi-specific geopolitical risk appears largely irrelevant for most price levels, with only a transient negative impact at higher quantiles (Q7). These findings collectively challenge the conventional wisdom that geopolitical events invariably destabilize commodity markets.

By contrast, Saudi crude oil production emerges as a decisive factor in price formation. The Kingdom's adjustments to supply exert consistent downward pressure on prices during normal market conditions, while their influence disappeared during extreme (low- or high) market conditions. The persistent effect of China's GDP growth across all quantiles further underscores the importance of structural demand-side drivers. Unlike geopolitical shocks, China's sustained economic expansion generates continuous upward pressure on oil prices, highlighting the centrality of emerging economies in shaping the future trajectory of energy markets.

These findings have broader implications for both energy security and price forecasting. While political risks may trigger short-lived volatility, long-term oil pricing remains primarily anchored in fundamentals, particularly Saudi supply adjustments and structural demand from China. This suggests that OPEC and non-OPEC producers alike should adopt adaptive production strategies that anticipate structural demand trends rather than react to transient political shocks. For OPEC members, this entails reinforcing cooperative mechanisms that stabilize supply responses, while non-OPEC producers may benefit from aligning output strategies with global demand dynamics to avoid amplifying price volatility.

From an energy security perspective, the results emphasize the importance of diversifying supply sources and expanding strategic petroleum reserves to mitigate the effects of temporary disruptions. Governments should also invest in critical energy infrastructure, such as refining capacity, transport, and renewable energy systems, to strengthen resilience against geopolitical shocks. Moreover, enhancing market transparency through improved data sharing on production and consumption can reduce uncertainty and dampen speculative behaviour, thereby improving the predictability of oil markets.

In terms of market regulation, the findings point to the need for stronger international coordination between OPEC and non-OPEC producers. Establishing cooperative, data-driven mechanisms to align supply policies with actual demand conditions could help prevent extreme price fluctuations. At the same time, integrating sustainability goals into energy regulation (such as encouraging investment in renewables alongside traditional production) can promote a smoother and more secure energy transition. Collectively, these measures suggest that market stability and the energy transition are not opposing objectives but complementary pillars of global energy governance.

For policymakers and market participants, this suggests that forecasting oil prices requires closer attention to the strategic behaviour of Saudi Arabia as a swing producer and the demand trajectory of key consumers, rather than transient geopolitical disturbances. In this sense, Saudi Arabia's role extends beyond that of a simple price taker, positioning the Kingdom as a pivotal force in balancing global energy markets. Ultimately, an integrated policy approach that combines coordinated production management, enhanced transparency, and diversified energy investment will be essential to sustain predictable and secure oil market conditions in the long term.

References

Bahgat, G. (2008). Security in the Persian Gulf: Perils and opportunities. *Contemporary Security Policy, 29*(2), 303–321. https://doi.org/10.1080/13523260802284209

Bariviera, A. F., Zunino, L., & Rosso, O. A. (2017). Crude oil market and geopolitical events: A permutation-information-theory analysis. *Energy Policy, 102*, 249–256. https://doi.org/10.1016/j.enpol.2016.12.032
Beirne, J. (2013). The impact of China and India on global commodity prices: Insights from a dynamic factor model. *China Economic Review, 25*, 28–51. https://doi.org/10.1016/j.chieco.2012.12.002
Blanchard, C. M. (2009). *Saudi Arabia: Terrorist financing issues.* Congressional Research Service.
Boucek, C. (2015). Saudi Arabia's "Yemen war" and the risks of escalation. *Carnegie Endowment for International Peace.*
Caldara, D., & Iacoviello, M. (2018). Measuring geopolitical risk. *International Finance Discussion Papers, 1222.* Board of Governors of the Federal Reserve System. https://doi.org/10.17016/IFDP.2018.1222
Caldara, D., & Iacoviello, M. (2022). Measuring geopolitical risk. *American Economic Review, 112*(4), 1194–1225. https://doi.org/10.1257/aer.20191823
Colgan, J. D. (2013). Fueling the fire: Pathways from oil to war. *International Security, 38*(2), 147–180. https://doi.org/10.1162/ISEC_a_00135
Cross, J. (2022). China's role in global oil demand dynamics. *Energy Economics, 106*, 105747. https://doi.org/10.1016/j.eneco.2021.105747
Cunado, J., Gupta, R., Lau, C. K. M., & Sheng, X. (2019). Time-varying impact of geopolitical risks on oil prices. *Defence and Peace Economics, 31*(6), 692–706. https://doi.org/10.1080/10242694.2018.1563854
Demirer, R., Gupta, R., Ji, Q., & Tiwari, A. K. (2019). Geopolitical risks and the predictability of regional oil returns and volatility. *OPEC Energy Review, 43*(3), 342–361. https://doi.org/10.1111/opec.12160
Gause, F. G. (2011). *The international relations of the Persian Gulf*. Cambridge University Press.
Gkillas, K., Longin, F., & Tsagkanos, A. (2022). Forecasting oil price volatility: Fundamentals, geopolitical risk, and expectations. *Energy Economics, 110*, 106004. https://doi.org/10.1016/j.resourpol.2022.102887
Hamendi, A. T., & Law, S. H. (2023). The impact of China's economic growth on crude oil Price: Evidence from structural VAR. *Review of Economic Analysis, 15*(3), 237–252. https://doi.org/10.15353/rea.v15i3-4.4069
Hertog, S. (2010). *Princes, brokers, and bureaucrats: Oil and the state in Saudi Arabia.* Cornell University Press.
International Energy Agency. (2008). *World Energy Outlook 2008.* OECD/IEA.
Kilian, L. (2009). Not all oil price shocks are alike: Disentangling demand and supply shocks in the crude oil market. *American Economic Review, 99*(3), 1053–1069. https://doi.org/10.1257/aer.99.3.1053
Kilian, L., & Murphy, D. P. (2013). The role of inventories and speculative trading in the global market for crude oil. *Journal of Applied Econometrics, 29*(3), 454–478. https://doi.org/10.1002/jae.2322
Kilian, L., & Zhou, X. (2022). Oil prices, exchange rates and interest rates. *Journal of International Money and Finance, 126*, 102679. https://doi.org/10.1016/j.jimonfin.2022.102679
Koenker, R., & Bassett, G. (1978). Regression quantiles. *Econometrica, 46*(1), 33–50. https://doi.org/10.2307/1913643
Li, B., Chang, C. P., Chu, Y., & Sui, B. (2020). Oil prices and geopolitical risks: What implications are offered via multi-domain investigations? *Energy & Environment, 31*(3), 492–516. https://doi.org/10.1177/0958305X19876092
Li, X., Umar, M., Zhu, C. B., & Oprean-Stan, C. (2023). Can geopolitical risk stably predict crude oil prices? *A multi-dimensional perspective. Resources Policy, 85*, 103785. https://doi.org/10.1016/j.resourpol.2023.103785
Liu, J., Ma, F., Tang, Y., & Zhang, Y. (2019). Geopolitical risk and oil volatility: A new insight. *Energy Economics, 84*, 104548. https://doi.org/10.1016/j.eneco.2019.104548

Mignon, V., & Saadaoui, J. (2024). How do political tensions and geopolitical risks impact oil prices? *Energy Economics, 129*, 107219. https://doi.org/10.1016/j.eneco.2023.107219
Monge, M., Gil-Alana, L. A., & de Gracia, F. P. (2017). Crude oil price behaviour before and after military conflicts and geopolitical events. *Energy, 120*, 79–91. https://doi.org/10.1016/j.energy.2016.12.102
Ozcelebi, O., & Tokmakcioglu, K. (2020). Assessment of the asymmetric impacts of the geopolitical risk on oil market dynamics. *International Journal of Finance & Economics, 27*(1), 275–289. https://doi.org/10.1002/ijfe.2151
Qian, L., Zeng, Q., & Li, T. (2022). Geopolitical risk and oil price volatility: Evidence from Markov-switching model. *International Review of Economics & Finance, 81*, 29–38. https://doi.org/10.1016/j.iref.2022.05.002
Salameh, M. G. (2000). Global oil outlook: Return to the absence of surplus and its implications. *Applied Energy, 65*(1–4), 239–250. https://doi.org/10.1016/S0306-2619(99)00122-1
Shahbaz, M., Sharif, A., Soliman, A. M., Jiao, Z., & Hammoudeh, S. (2023). Oil prices and geopolitical risk: Fresh insights based on granger-causality in quantiles analysis. *International Journal of Finance & Economics, 29*(3), 2865–2881. https://doi.org/10.1002/ijfe.2806
Slaibi, A., Chapman, D., & Daouk, H. (2009). A geopolitical theory of oil price behaviour: An econometric evaluation. *Applied Economics, 42*(22), 2783–2800. https://doi.org/10.1080/00036840801964724
Smales, L. A. (2021). Geopolitical risk and volatility spillovers in oil and stock markets. *The Quarterly Review of Economics and Finance, 80*, 358–366. https://doi.org/10.1016/j.qref.2021.03.008
Su, C. W., Khan, K., Tao, R., & Nicoleta-Claudia, M. (2019). Does geopolitical risk strengthen or depress oil prices and financial liquidity? Evidence from Saudi Arabia. *Energy*, 187, 116003.doi:https://doi.org/10.1016/j.energy.2019.116003.
Ulrichsen, K. C. (2019). *The changing security dynamics of the Persian Gulf*. Oxford University Press.
Van Robays, I. (2016). Macroeconomic uncertainty and oil price volatility. *Oxford Bulletin of Economics and Statistics, 78*(5), 671–693. https://doi.org/10.1111/obes.12124
Wakeford, J. (2006). The impact of oil price shocks on the South African macroeconomy: History and prospects. In *Accelerated and Shared Growth in South Africa: Determinants, Constraints and Opportunities, (18–20 October 2006).* The birchwood hotel and conference Centre, Johannesburg.
Wu, J., Zhao, R., Sun, J., & Zhou, X. (2023). Impact of geopolitical risks on oil price fluctuations: Based on GARCH-MIDAS model. *Resources Policy, 85*, 103982. https://doi.org/10.1016/j.resourpol.2023.103982
Zhang, Z., Wang, Y., & Li, B. (2023). Asymmetric spillover of geopolitical risk and oil price volatility: A global perspective. *Resources Policy, 83*, 103701. https://doi.org/10.1016/j.resourpol.2023.103701

Energy Security, Institutional Quality, and Geopolitical Risks: Evidence from Türkiye and Sub-Saharan Africa Countries

Haydar Karadağ, Hakan Güneş, and Hamis Miraji Ally-Simba

Abstract This study examines the effects of energy security, institutional quality, and geopolitical risks on oil price uncertainty in the context of Türkiye and Sub-Saharan African countries. The literature emphasises that energy security is critical for sustainable economic growth and is directly affected by geopolitical tensions and weak institutional structures. Empirical findings show that energy security and geopolitical risks increase oil price uncertainty, inflation fuels uncertainty, and consumption increases play a mitigating role. Furthermore, political stability is a strong determinant of volatility. Descriptive statistics and correlation analysis show a negative relationship between energy security and oil price uncertainty, and a positive relationship between energy security and geopolitical risks. The results reveal that strengthening institutional capacity, diversifying energy sources, and enhancing international cooperation are critical for energy security and macroeconomic stability.

Keywords Energy security · Geopolitical risk · Institutional quality · Oil price · TVR-SVR model

H. Karadağ (✉)
Recep Tayyip Erdogan University, Rize, Turkey
e-mail: haydar.karadag@erdogan.edu.tr

H. Güneş
Department of Bartın University, Bartın, Turkey
e-mail: hakangunes@bartin.edu.tr

H. M. Ally-Simba
Economic and Social Research Foundation, Dar es Salaam, Tanzania
e-mail: hsimba@esrf.or.tz

A. Akusta and M. Gün (eds.), *Financial Frontiers in Energy Markets*, Contributions to Finance and Accounting, https://doi.org/10.1007/978-3-032-16738-5_5

1 Introduction

Energy is a crucial power source for economic stability in economies. Therefore, ensuring energy security is critical for countries seeking sustainable economic development. Numerous studies indicate that energy security is one of the critical indicators of an economy's stability (Banna et al., 2023). Energy security is a dynamic field, depending on the time period analysed. Energy security can be defined based on the country or region, whether it includes supply security or demand, and the factors it encompasses, etc. (Filipović et al., 2018). Energy security is of critical importance for global economic growth because it is a fundamental input in economic production and a necessary consumer good. It should be redefined by considering different components of energy security, such as energy availability, accessibility, and developability (Ayaz et al., 2024). Many factors in energy security are difficult to measure quantitatively. New methodologies that include as many factors as possible to ensure energy security need to be developed. For example, geopolitical conditions, political instability, and armed conflicts definitely affect energy prices and energy security (Filipović et al., 2018). Energy security is the capacity to ensure the continuous, accessible, developable, and geopolitically risk-protected supply of energy resources for economic and social stability.

Ensuring a reliable and sufficient energy supply is essential for countries striving to achieve sustainable economic development. This both fuels industrial output and supports economic growth (Azimi et al., 2025). Developing countries, such as OECD and non-OECD (SSA Countries-Türkiye) countries, are concerned about ensuring energy security. These countries do not want to affect growth when formulating their energy policies. They do not adopt advanced energy systems and imported technology that could reduce energy consumption because it would slow down their economic growth. For example, according to the World Energy Outlook (2021) report, energy demand is expected to increase by 50% between 2018 and 2050. Most of this increase will come from developing countries experiencing economic growth (Ayaz et al., 2024).

However, the increase in oil prices did not only have a negative impact on the energy security of importing countries. It also affected macroeconomic stability by widening the trade deficit. And it led to negative geopolitical consequences (Filipović et al., 2018). Caldara and Iacoviello (2022) explain that geopolitical risks are linked to armed conflicts and terrorism, as well as interstate conflicts that affect international relations. Geopolitical risk can intensify states' efforts towards energy insecurity (Chu et al., 2023). Volatility in global energy markets and prices in recent times, resulting from multiple crises (e.g., COVID-19, Russia's invasion of Ukraine, and hyperinflation), has caused macroeconomic and financial instability. The Russian-Ukrainian conflict affected energy production and supply, leading to unprecedented increases in energy prices, particularly in Europe. It has also led to hyperinflation and increased living costs. Therefore, we were motivated to provide theoretical and empirical evidence to examine the link between energy security risk and economic stability from an SSA-Türkiye perspective, given rising inflation and wars (Banna et al., 2023).

Institutional quality is another factor threatening the region's energy security and economic growth. The high level of corruption and weak legal and governance systems in the region affect economic growth and energy security. This study discusses the impact of institutional quality on energy security (Ayaz et al., 2024). SSA countries-Türkiye continues to struggle with fragile institutional structures, grappling with significant administrative corruption, weak regulatory enforcement, political instability, and ineffective governance. Institutional deficiencies also exacerbate the region's challenges in achieving sustainable growth.

Effective institutions are crucial for implementing policies that support energy security and economic growth. They can promote regulatory stability, reduce market uncertainty, and facilitate investment in energy infrastructure (Azimi et al., 2025).

According to the World Development Indicators (WDI), 24 countries in Sub-Saharan Africa (SSA) are in the lowest income group, while 13 are in the lower-middle income group. Furthermore, SSA accounts for more than half of the top 50 countries with the highest income inequality in the world. SSA accounts for 14% of the world's population, but only 4% of global energy demand. Therefore, sustainable energy security policies are needed to reduce poverty in SSA countries (Janjua et al., 2024). In particular, SSA-Türkiye faces challenges and opportunities in energy security and economic growth. They have growing populations, accelerating urbanisation, and economic potential. However, weak institutions lead to environmental degradation and energy insecurity. Inadequate energy infrastructure and reliance on imported fuels hinder sustainable economic development (Azimi et al., 2025).

Energy supply in the SSA region is threatened by unavailability (physical), inaccessibility (geopolitical factors), unaffordability (price competition), unacceptability (environmental), and undevelopability (quality and expansion) (Adedeji et al., 2024). Despite these challenges, SSA countries-Turkiye has great potential for sustainable growth through the diversification of energy sources, increased investment in renewable energy, and strengthened regional cooperation (Azimi et al., 2025).

Energy-import-dependent economies and energy-exporting countries experience macroeconomic instability due to fluctuations in global energy markets and prices. Growth in the SSA region is unstable. Energy is a key input for SSA countries to achieve stable growth and reduce poverty. When energy security is ensured, the region's unstable growth can be prevented (Adedeji et al., 2024).

The main focus of the study is to investigate the macroeconomic and geopolitical effects of factors such as energy security and institutional quality. Energy security risk is the inability to ensure a reliable energy supply due to wars and economic crises (Chen et al., 2024). Le and Nguyen (2019) note that developing countries cannot adapt and apply imported energy technology to local demands. They also emphasise that energy infrastructure in poor countries is more vulnerable to natural or man-made disasters. Thus, they argue that the successful development and management of complex energy technology requires the country to have open and transparent markets and competent governance (Adedeji et al., 2024).

There is concern regarding economic stability in the SSA countries and the Turkish economy. A reliable and sustainable energy supply is vital for economic stability in order to support energy security, economic growth, and development (Banna et al., 2023). Well-functioning institutions are essential for successful energy policy. A review of the literature reveals a paucity of empirical literature examining the relationship between institutional quality and energy security (Chen et al., 2024). The scarcity of research on the impact of geopolitical uncertainty on energy security also motivated this study.

This study aimed to empirically measure the macroeconomic effects of energy security and institutional quality. This study analysed geopolitical relations between Turkiye and Sub-Saharan African countries. Energy security and well-functioning institutions ensure a sustainable energy supply (Banna et al., 2023; Chen et al., 2024). Thus, the study aimed to provide a framework for how both Türkiye and Sub-Saharan African countries can contribute to each other's economic development. The Introduction section of the study describes the macroeconomic effects of energy security and institutional quality on the geopolitical relationship between Turkiye and Sub-Saharan African countries.

2 Literature Review

2.1 Theoretical Literature

Energy supply security is defined in the literature as both an economic and strategic concept. Energy security, in theory, means ensuring that countries have uninterrupted access to energy resources and that these resources are secured in terms of price, quality, and sustainability (Sovacool & Mukherjee, 2011; Yergin, 2006). Cherp and Jewell (2014) assess energy security within the framework of the 'four A's' approach: Availability, Accessibility, Affordability, and Acceptability. This approach emphasises that energy security must encompass not only economic but also social and environmental dimensions.

Geopolitical risks are theoretically one of the main determinants of energy supply security. Caldara and Iacoviello (2022) developed a geopolitical risk index that models the impact of shocks in global energy markets on price volatility and economic growth. Geopolitical risks are linked to energy supply and international relations, and energy prices are directly linked to political stability and diplomatic relations (Umbach, 2010; Shaffer, 2013).

Institutional quality and governance provide a critical theoretical framework for the sustainability of energy supply security. According to North (1990) and Kaufmann et al. (2010), strong institutions improve economic performance and make the system more resilient to crises. Thus, strong institutional structures are necessary for the safe and efficient management of energy investments (Apergis & Payne, 2010).

The interaction between energy security, geopolitical risks, and institutional quality can be explained by mixed causality theories, which examine the interdependence among macroeconomic variables and help understand how shocks in energy markets propagate to economic growth and prices (Benhabib & Spiegel, 2019; Chen et al., 2021). In this context, energy security is strengthened not only by supply diversity but also by institutional capacity and political stability.

Overall, the theoretical literature demonstrates that energy supply security is not merely an economic issue, but an integrated system encompassing political, institutional, and international relations dimensions. Policies to ensure energy security should be supported by supply diversity and the use of renewable energy. Long-term strategies should be developed with consideration for geopolitical risks and institutional quality (Overland, 2019; Scholten & Bosman, 2016).

2.2 *Practical Literature*

Energy supply security is one of the most critical areas of debate in economic development and international relations. The concept is defined not only as ensuring continuous access to energy but also as ensuring that access is affordable, sustainable, and stable (Sovacool & Mukherjee, 2011; Yergin, 2006). In the energy security literature, supply diversity, import dependency, price volatility, and infrastructure reliability are often highlighted as key indicators (Jansen & Seebregts, 2010; Le Coq & Paltseva, 2009).

Caldara and Iacoviello (2022) calculated the impact of geopolitical risks on energy security using a geopolitical risk index. They show that these risks have a strong impact on oil prices, global trade, and growth. Boungou and Yatie (2022) showed that the Russia-Ukraine war caused a major shock to energy supply and increased price volatility in European and global markets. Gnangnon (2020) found that geopolitical risks in developing countries have a negative impact on energy consumption and economic growth. Similarly, Umbach (2010) emphasised that energy supply security has become not only an economic but also a geostrategic issue.

Institutional quality and governance are important for the sustainability of energy security. North (1990) argues that institutions are determinants of economic performance, while Kaufmann et al. (2010) indicate that political stability directly shapes energy investments through governance indicators. Apergis and Payne (2010) show that OECD countries with high governance quality are more successful in using renewable energy. Cherp and Jewell (2014) emphasise that energy security analyses should focus not only on economic factors but also on political, social, and environmental dimensions.

Studies on Türkiye show that the country's energy security problems are directly related to its geopolitical position and high import dependency. Erdoğdu (2010) argues that energy market reforms pose risks to supply security, while Biresselioglu and Karaibrahimoglu (2012) contend that Türkiye's natural gas policies play a critical 'bridge' role in geopolitical balances. Öztürk and Acaravcı (2010) found strong causal relationships between energy consumption, economic growth, and carbon emissions in Türkiye.

In Sub-Saharan African countries, the energy security problem is largely linked to infrastructure deficiencies, external dependence, and institutional weaknesses. Akinlo (2009) demonstrated a long-term cointegration between electricity consumption and growth in Nigeria. Mensah and Adu (2015) revealed the long-term relationship between carbon emissions, energy consumption, and economic growth. Gnangnon and Lacovone (2019) show that trade policies are closely linked to energy security and that external dependence increases vulnerability.

Overall, the literature shows that the energy security issue is shaped by three fundamental axes: (i) increasing energy supply diversity, (ii) strengthening institutional quality and governance, and (iii) effectively managing geopolitical risks. It is concluded that in regions such as Türkiye and Sub-Saharan Africa, these three dimensions are inextricably intertwined and that energy policies must be supported not only by economic but also by institutional and geopolitical strategies.

3 Methodology

Sub-Saharan Africa and Türkiye have experienced the diversities of geopolitical tension in recent years. The increases in geopolitical tension persist in the oil prices volatility which demands effective energy security and quality institutions to reduce the effect of oil price volatility. Our investigation uses the proxies of energy security, such as national energy defense, energy efficiency, green energy, total energy consumption, crude oil, and climate change security have been selected to explain the price of oil volatility. The quality institution is represented by diplomatic governance, international energy security agreements, regulations, and the rule of law. Nevertheless, the effect of geopolitical challenges causes disagreement in trading globally, political conflict, and disputes over borders, which significantly affect the supply-demand chain in the global market.

We apply the supply-demand theory that exists as a vital instrument to determine the effect of oil price volatility. The supply-demand theory exhibits the effect of energy security, quality institutions, geopolitical tension, and oil price uncertainty. The supply-demand energy theory describes the structural change and widening of the dynamic geopolitical tension that causes destruction in energy security supply and increases high demand in industrial production, political conflict or disagreement over trade, and makes it harder to sustain energy security efficiency. The theory explores the effect of oil price uncertainty and energy security to indicate the effect on geopolitical challenges in a way that the safe geopolitical zone maintains sustainable energy security and diminishes the oil price volatility. In this context, the oil price uncertainty is the function model of energy security, geopolitical tension, and energy quality institutions. The following models represent the effect of energy security, institutional quality, and geopolitical tension on oil price uncertainty.

$$\text{OPU} = \text{f (ESS, GPT, QI)} \tag{1}$$

$$\text{OPU} = \text{f (ESD, GPT, QI)} \tag{2}$$

Where ESS and ESD are supply-demand energy security chains in both Sub-Saharan Africa and Turkiye. ESS represents energy security for global suppliers, and ESD is the energy security for importing countries in a specific geopolitical region. The QI stands for a quality institution that represents the regulations, diplomatic governance, and national energy security agreements in the respective countries, and GPTR stands for Geopolitical tension.

3.1 *Data and Methodology*

Empirically, the study aims to investigate the effects of energy security, geopolitical tension, and energy quality institutions on the oil price uncertainty from the mid-2000s to 2024. The study examined the oil price uncertainty through the lens of energy security, geopolitical tension, and energy quality institutions. The analytical data for the output results have been collected from an index of Global Economic Policy Uncertainty (EPU) from January first, 2004, to December 2024, as reported by the International Atomic Energy Agency (IAEA) and the World Bank's World Development Indicators. The decision to select the data was made because most of the geopolitical events occurred during the investigation, as clearly shown in Table 1.

TVP-VAR Model

Since the effect of oil price is in a dynamic state, which causes volatility to the Oil Price Uncertainty price, and the energy security inclusion always needs quality institutions to mitigate the effect, the research employs a time-varying methodology that has been built based on the VAR model. The TVP-VAR model is different from the traditional model in that the mean coefficients and covariance change over time. Different scholars have used this model specifically to examine the nonlinear model and time-varying relationship between the parametric effects (Gong et al., 2021; Tian et al., 2021).

The TVP-VAR model can be represented as follows:

$$\mathrm{Y_{i,t} = C + b_{i.,t}Y_{(i,t-1)} + \cdots\cdots\cdots\cdots\cdots b_{s.t}X_{i.(1-t)} + A^{-1}{}_t\Sigma_t{+}_t} \tag{1}$$

Therefore, Eq. 1 above can be represented in the matrix form, where A is the triangular matrix form, and Σ_t is the diagonal matrix, the general matrix forms described as follows:

Table 1 Geopolitical Events (1990–2025)

Events	Starting time	Region
Kuwait-Iraq war	Augst-1990	Iraq, Kuwait
Gulf war-I	January-1991	War, US-Iraq
Kosovo-war	April-1999	US, Kosovo
US-attack 9/11	Septe −2001	Terrorism-US
Gulf-war II	March 2003	War, Iraq-US
Madrid bombings	March-2004	Terrorism-Spain
London-	July 2005	Terrorism-Britain
Arab spring	February-2011	War Middle East
Fukushima event	March 2011	Nuclear-Japan
Boston marathon	April-2013	Terrorism-US
Russian invades crimes	March-2014	Russian, Ukraine
ISIS escalation	June-2014	Terrorism, Syria-Iraq
Paris attacks	November-2015	Terrorism-France
US-China trade war	September-2018	US-China
US-Iran conflicts	January-2020	US, Iran
Russian-Ukraine war	February 2022	Russia-Ukraine
US-Israel-Iran- war	June-2025	Iran-Israel
Nuclear escalation	June-2025	Iran-Israel

$$A = \begin{pmatrix} 1 & 0 & \dots & 0 \\ \delta_{21,t} \dots & \dots & \dots \\ \dots \dots & \dots & \dots \\ \delta_{k1.t} \dots & \delta_{kk-1,t} & 0 \end{pmatrix} \quad (2)$$

Σ_t represents the diagonal matrix

$$\Sigma_t = \begin{pmatrix} \vartheta_{1,t} & 0 & \dots & 0 \\ 0 & \dots & \dots & \dots \\ \dots & \dots & \dots & \dots \\ 0 & \dots & 0 & \vartheta_{k.t} \end{pmatrix} \quad (3)$$

Furthermore, the model can be represented as:

$$Y_{i,t} = \beta_{s.t} X_{i.(1-t)} + A^{-1}{}_t \Sigma_t \varepsilon_t \quad (4)$$

Where parameters β_t, A_t, and Σ_t are associated with time varying and the lower triangular elements, thus the elements in δ_t, and ϑ_t are the components in the elements of the respective matrices.

Further, the $h_t = (h_{(1.t)}\ldots\ldots h_{(t.k)})'$ $h_{i,t} = \log\sigma^2_{jt}$ that is j = 1,2…n, and t = s + 1…k. We assume that β_t follows the random work excursion, in a way that the parameter coefficients of the model in the matrix form can be represented in the context of $\beta_{t+1} = \beta_t + \mu_{\beta t}$, $\alpha_{t+1} = \alpha_t + \mu_{\alpha t}$, $h_{t+1} = h_t + \mu_{ht}$, , therefore $\mu_{\beta t}$, $\mu_{\alpha t,}$ and μ_{ht} satisfy the following conditions that:

$$\begin{pmatrix} \varepsilon_t \\ \mu_{\beta t} \\ \mu_{\alpha t} \\ \mu_{ht} \end{pmatrix} \sim \mathrm{N}\left(0, \begin{pmatrix} 1 & 0 & 0 & 0 \\ 0 & \sum\beta & 0 & 0 \\ 0 & 0 & \sum\alpha & 0 \\ 0 & 0 & 0 & \sum h \end{pmatrix}\right) \tag{5}$$

where $\beta_{s+t} \sim \left(\mu_{\beta_0}, \Sigma_{\beta_0}\right)$, $\alpha_{t+s} \sim \mathrm{N}\left(m_{a_0}, \Sigma_{a_0}\right)$, $h_{s+t} \sim \mathrm{N}\left(m_{h_0}, \Sigma_{h_0}\right)$.

TVP-Var-SV

As the investigation is of a nonlinear nature, the maximum likelihood estimation needs substantial computational resources, and it operates by iterating filtering processing to the likelihood function for each variable that set until an optimal value is achieved. In this context, this study employs the Bayesian approach, using Markov Chain Monte Carlo (MCMC), to estimate the TVP-VAR-SV model.

3.2 MGARCH

Further, the analysis phase involves the MGARCH to estimate the effect of energy security, oil price uncertainty, and quality institutions on geopolitical risk. To highlight the output results, the study employs the dynamic conditional correlation (DCC) and constant conditional correlation (CCC) to assist the dynamic and spillover effect of the energy security, oil price uncertainty, and quality institutions on geopolitical risk between the volatile geopolitical risk and oil price uncertainty in both Sub-Saharan Africa and Türkiye. The CCC-GARCH perceives the conditional covariance that is positively influenced by the outcomes from the respective conditional standard deviation and constant spillover effect. The multivariate GARCH is used to analyze the conditional variance of a single time series, which has been effectively demonstrated to be highly effective. Bollerslev et al. (1988) have used the multivariate GARCH model for the condition variance matrix of dependent parameters to exhibit a flexible dynamic structure, which means the condition of the average mean follows vector autoregressive (VAR) structures. Therefore, the MGARCH model is widely applied and well recognized, specifically for its versatility in presenting different econometric issues.

Where the CCC-GARCH model can be represented with the conditional variance, the two-time series that influenced by the respective conditions of the standard deviations and the constant conditions spillover. In the equation model, the description can be represented as follows:

$$\varphi_{ijt} = D_t M D_t = \rho_{it}\sqrt{\varphi_{iit}\varphi_{jjt}} \tag{6}$$

Where $\varphi_{iit\,and}\varphi_{jjt}$ representants of the conditional variance, conditional variances of the provided data set in the different regimes, further, the matrices A and D are determined using the model:

$$D_{it} = \text{diag}\left(\varphi_{iit}{}^{\frac{1}{2}} \ldots\ldots\ldots\ldots \varphi_{jjt}{}^{1}\right) \tag{7}$$

The above equation represents the concept of the DCC-GARCH. The dynamic correlation used to measure the dynamic volatility of the oil price is uncertain, having been caused by geopolitical risk management due to its energy security spillover effects in the regional zone. Thus, the DCC-MGARC was used purposely to measure the volatility effect of energy security on the geopolitical risk in the region. Furthermore, the model can be accurately used to measure the impact of energy security, oil pricing uncertainty, and geopolitical risk in the region. Further, the DCC-MGARCH at variant time t with the mean, variance, and covariance can be described in the form of

$$r_{ijt} = \mu_{it} + \varepsilon_{it} \tag{8}$$

Where the random error of the shock's transmission due to energy security and geopolitical effects that cause the fluctuation of Oil Price Uncertainty can be well represented

$$\mu_{it} = (r_{it}|\Upsilon_{t-1}) = E_{t-1}(r_{it}),\, \varepsilon_{it} \mid \varphi_{t-1} \sim N\,(\,0, H_t) \tag{9}$$

The information that is represented in the previous time (t-1), which has en expressed in the φ_{t-1}. H_{it} is normally represented to the D_{it}, MD_{it} which means the covariance and variance of the respective matrix, where the D_{it} is presented by the following formula of

$$\varphi_{it} = r_{it} + \alpha_{it}\varepsilon_{i(t-1)}{}^{2} + \beta_i\varepsilon_{i,(t-1)} \tag{10}$$

Where β_i represents GARCH, and α_{it} represents the ARCH. The equation model above describes that if β_i is found to be a positive and significant coefficient then it indicates the persistence of Oil Pricing Uncertainty of volatility due to the scarcity energy security that has been distorted from the geopolitical risk in the region, further the negative coefficient implies a reducing in the effect of geopolitical tension in the region that causes the destabilization of energy security and lowering volatility of the price Oil Uncertain in the region. Thus, the sum of β_i, and α_{it}, indicates the increases in energy shocks in the region due to the increase in geopolitical risk in the economic region.

3.3 *Mediating Effect*

The methodology has been applied to determine the effect of the transmission of Oil Pricing Uncertainty that has been caused by the Geopolitical risk tensions due to the energy security in the economic region. The primary objective of this method is to examine the price oil pricing volatility transmission of due to the geopolitical risk tension that existed from the energy security in the economic region. The method has been applied to examine the heightened spillover effect of the Oil pricing Uncertainty due to the geopolitical risk tension that exists within the region. The method used to investigate the risk of the volatility of transmission effect, and the role of intermediate effect of both energy security and geopolitical risk tension on the Oil price uncertainty in the economic zone. The testing of the immediate effect involves the case of the independent variables of geopolitical risk, energy security, and quality institutions on Oil price uncertainty. That is the case if the geopolitical risk tension affects the Oil price uncertainty, then the energy security of economic integration is affected, as well as the quality of institutions significantly affected, and then the geopolitical then an intermediate.

3.4 *Empirical Analysis*

In this section, we employ the DCC-MGARC techniques and TVT-VAR-SV methods to the dynamic volatility spillover effect between the volatility of the geopolitical tension, energy security, and quality institutional factors on the oil price uncertainty. Further, the DCC-MIDAS-X is computed from the individual country and the related effect of GPT, ES, and QI, in relation to the oil price uncertainty transmission effect of the volatility between the oil price uncertainty and energy security in the regions. Generally, the study focuses on the volatility of energy security, quality institutions, and geopolitical tension on the oil price uncertainty during upwards and downwards of economic fluctuations. Further, the investigation investigates the mediating functions of the oil price uncertainty transmission aimed at the global significance of the geopolitical tension in the areas of natural energy sources.

Table 2 shows the correlation relationships between the variables used in the study. While a positive and statistically significant relationship was found between Energy Security (ES) and Inflation (Inf) ($r = 0.048$; $p < 0.01$), a weak but negatively significant relationship was found between ES and Peace Security and Absence of Violence (PSAV) ($r = -0.029$; $p < 0.05$). The relationship between ES and Oil Price Uncertainty (OPU) is negative and significant ($r = -0.089$; $p < 0.01$), suggesting that oil price uncertainty decreases as energy security increases. In contrast, a positive and strongly significant relationship was observed between ES and Geopolitical Risk Threats (GPRT) ($r = 0.163$; $p < 0.01$). The correlation between Inflation (Inf) and PSAV is moderately positive and highly significant ($r = 0.183$; $p < 0.01$). Furthermore, a positive and significant relationship was found between Inf and OPU ($r = 0.170$; $p < 0.01$), indicating that price instability moves in tandem with uncertainties in the oil market. In contrast, the relationship between PSAV and OPU is weak and statistically insignificant. Similarly, GPRT has positive correlations with OPU, Inf, and PSAV, but the significance level is not reached. Overall, the results support the critical role of energy security and geopolitical risks in oil price uncertainty.

The results obtained from the TVP-SVR model reveal that energy security, geopolitical tensions, inflation, and political stability have significant effects on oil price uncertainty. The coefficient for Lagged Energy Security (ES_{t-1}) is positive (0.638) and statistically significant ($p < 0.01$), indicating that changes in energy security increase oil price uncertainty. The coefficient for Geopolitical Tension (GPT_{t-1}) is also positive (0.169) and significant, indicating that geopolitical risks affect oil market uncertainty. In contrast, the Oil Consumption variable has a negative coefficient (-1.315; $p < 0.01$), and this result indicates that increases in consumption levels play a role in reducing uncertainty. The inflation rate is positive (0.175) and significant ($p < 0.05$), revealing that price instability is a factor that fuels uncertainty. Finally, the Political Stability and Absence of Violence (PSAV) variable exhibits a strong and highly significant positive relationship with a coefficient of 0.892 ($p < 0.01$); this finding indicates that political stability is an institutional factor that significantly affects oil price volatility. The overall significance of the model has also been confirmed by the Wald Chi^2 test ($\chi^2 = 45.02$; $p < 0.001$).

Table 4 reveals the variance–covariance structure of the variables included in the model. The highest variance value belongs to oil price uncertainty (OPU, 0.158), confirming the sensitivity of this variable to volatility shocks. Geopolitical Risk Threats (GPRT) and Inflation (Inf) exhibit relatively moderate variance (0.053 and 0.0583), while Peace Security and Absence of Violence (PSAV) has a lower variance (0.0256). When examining the covariance values, it is observed that the covariances

Table 2 Correlation Matrix

	ES	Inf	PSAV	POU	GPRT
ES	1				
Inf	0.048*** (0,017)	1			
PSAV	−0.0298* (0.0320)	0.1835*** (0.000)	1		
POU	−0.089*** (0.010)	0.1704**** (0.000)	0.0285 (0.4129)	1	
GPRT	0.163*** (0.000)	0.0533 (0.126)	0.0568 (0.1022)	0.0263 (0.499)	1

Table 3 TVP SVR Model

Variable	Coefficients	Std. Err	Z	p > [Z]	[Confidential Interval]	
Energy Security$_{t-1}$	0.638	0.065	−3.45	0.001	0.5432	1.786
Treatment constant	4.954	1.148	4.313	0.000	2.7036	7.204
Geopolitical Tension$_{t-1}$	0.169	0.231	3.734	0.002	0.6226	2.283
Price oiling consumption	−1.315	0.398	−3.31	0.001	2.095	6.535
Inflation_rate	0.175	0072	−2.30	0.021	2.489	0.026
Political stability and absence of violence	0.892	0.160	5.57	0.000	1.206	5.779
Number of observations	736					
Number of groups	45					
Maximum	16					
Minimum	16					
Average	16					
Wald Chi^2 (4)	45.02					
Prob > Chi2	0.000					
Scale parameter	47.57					

between variables are generally positive but at a very low level. In particular, the positive covariance between GPRT and OPU (0.001) and between PSAV and OPU (0.0027) indicates that oil uncertainty moves in parallel with geopolitical risks and political stability indicators, albeit to a limited extent. Overall, the table reveals that volatility dynamics are shaped more by the variables' own variances than by strong covariance structures between variables.

Table 4 The TVP-VAR model can be represented as follows

	GPRT	Inf	PSAV	OPU	constant
GPRT	0.053				
Inf	0.001	0.0583			
PSAV	0.001	0.0002	0.0256		
OPU	0.001	0.0009	0.0027	0.158	
Constant	0.107	−0.007	−0.0388	−0,0778	1.3183

4 Conclusion

Energy is one of the most fundamental production factors determining the stability of modern economies. Therefore, ensuring energy security is of strategic importance for all countries seeking sustainable growth. In the literature, the concept of energy security refers to the continuous, accessible, developable, and geopolitically risk-protected supply of energy resources (Filipović et al., 2018). The dynamic nature of energy security causes different dimensions to come to the fore in different periods and regions. Increasing demand pressure, political instability, and geopolitical tensions in non-OECD emerging economies are exacerbating vulnerabilities in this area (Ayaz et al., 2024). In this context, Turkiye and Sub-Saharan African (SSA) countries constitute a notable example in the global energy equation due to both energy supply security and institutional capacity issues.

Developing economies are reluctant to adopt advanced energy systems or energy-saving technologies for fear that they may slow down growth. According to the World Energy Outlook (2021) report, energy demand is expected to increase by 50% between 2018 and 2050, with most of this increase coming from developing countries. However, fluctuations in energy prices not only undermine the security of importing countries but also threaten macroeconomic stability through trade balance and inflation. Indeed, the Russia-Ukraine war has pushed energy prices to unprecedented levels in many regions, particularly in Europe, causing hyperinflation and rising living costs (Banna et al., 2023). Such shocks have once again demonstrated how critical the relationship between energy security and geopolitical risk is from an economic policy perspective.

Institutional quality is one of the most important factors driving the relationship between energy security and economic growth. Weak governance, high corruption rates, and gaps in legal regulations hinder both the development of energy infrastructure and market stability (Azimi et al., 2025). Particularly in Sub-Saharan African countries, weak institutions threaten energy supply and economic development. Therefore, effective institutions for energy security both improve the investment climate environment and reduce market uncertainty. This also supports growth in the long term (Chen et al., 2024).

Further econometric analyses, particularly findings from the TVP-SVR (Time Varying Parameter–Stochastic Volatility Regression) model, reveal the dynamic nature of these relationships. The results show that energy security (ES_{t-1}) with a one-period lag has a positive and significant effect on oil price uncertainty. This indicates that changes in energy security can produce effects that permanently increase uncertainty. Similarly, geopolitical tensions contribute to the susceptibility of global energy markets to geopolitical risks. The positive and significant inflation coefficient obtained in the analysis fuels uncertainty, while the political stability indicator (PSAV) demonstrates a positive and highly significant relationship. This suggests that institutional quality is a critical determinant of volatility in energy markets.

Additionally, the findings of the variance–covariance matrix indicate that volatility among variables is largely shaped by their own variances. Oil price uncertainty has the highest variance at 0.158, confirming its sensitivity to volatility shocks. Geopolitical risks and inflation exhibit medium levels of variance, while political stability shows lower volatility. Covariance values are generally positive but low. In particular, the positive covariance between GPRT and OPU (0.001) and between PSAV and OPU (0.0027) indicates that oil uncertainty moves in parallel with geopolitical risks and institutional indicators, albeit to a limited extent.

These findings show, certain policy implications can be drawn for Türkiye and Sub-Saharan African countries. First, energy security is possible by diversifying supply sources and strengthening institutional capacity. High institutional quality can reduce uncertainty in energy markets and encourage investment. Secondly, geopolitical risks directly impact oil price uncertainty. Therefore, countries need to strengthen their international cooperation and diplomatic channels. Thirdly, the correlation between inflation and energy market volatility demonstrates that macroeconomic stability policies cannot be considered separately from energy security strategies. Finally, the uncertainty-reducing effect of consumption increases indicates that managing energy demand can contribute to market stability.

Overall, both the theoretical framework and empirical findings of the study emphasise the multifaceted relationship between energy security, geopolitical risks, and institutional quality. As seen in the case of Türkiye and Sub-Saharan African countries, energy security is crucial not only for economic growth but also for political stability and social well-being. Therefore, designing energy policies alongside institutional reforms and geopolitical stability strategies is critical to achieving sustainable development goals.

Considering Türkiye's strategic location and Sub-Saharan Africa's natural resource potential, risks can be mitigated through shared reserve mechanisms, cross-border energy corridors, and crisis management strategies. Strengthened regional energy institutions and intergovernmental dialogue platforms will increase resilience to external shocks such as wars or supply disruptions. Coordinated fiscal and monetary policies aimed at stabilizing energy prices in the Turkish and Sub-Saharan African economies can reduce inflationary pressures. Establishing joint financial instruments or sovereign energy funds can be an effective stabilization tool in this process. The uncertainty-reducing effect of increasing energy consumption demonstrates that effective management of energy demand contributes to market stability. In this context, demand management collaborations between the two regions can be developed through energy efficiency programs, green technology research, and shared renewable energy targets.

References

Adedeji, A. A., Ogunbayo, I., Ajayi, P. I., & Adeniyi, O. (2024). Energy security, governance quality, and economic performance in sub-Saharan Africa. Next Energy, 2, 100055. doi:https://doi.org/10.1016/j.nxener.2023.100055.

Akinlo, A. E. (2009). Electricity consumption and economic growth in Nigeria: Evidence from cointegration and co-feature analysis. *Journal of Policy Modeling, 31*(5), 681–693. https://doi.org/10.1016/j.jpolmod.2009.03.004
Apergis, N., & Payne, J. E. (2010). Renewable energy consumption and economic growth: Evidence from a panel of OECD countries. *Energy Policy, 38*(1), 656–660. https://doi.org/10.1016/j.enpol.2009.09.002
Ayaz, M. T., Prodromou, T., Le, T., & Nepal, R. (2024). Energy security dimensions and economic growth in non-OECD Asia: An analysis on the role of institutional quality with energy policy implications. *Energy Policy, 188*, 114090. https://doi.org/10.1016/j.enpol.2024.114090
Azimi, M. N., Rahman, M. M., & Maraseni, T. (2025). Powering progress: The interplay of energy security and institutional quality in driving economic growth. *Applied Energy, 378*, 124835. https://doi.org/10.1016/j.apenergy.2024.124835
Banna, H., Alam, A., Chen, X. H., & Alam, A. W. (2023). Energy security and economic stability: The role of inflation and war. *Energy Economics, 126*, 106949. https://doi.org/10.1016/j.eneco.2023.106949
Benhabib, J., & Spiegel, M. M. (2019). International capital flows and domestic institutions. *Journal of International Economics, 118*, 126–144. https://doi.org/10.1016/j.jinteco.2019.01.003
Biresselioglu, M. E., & Karaibrahimoglu, Y. Z. (2012). The international politics of natural gas: A study of Turkey's role in the energy security paradigm. *Energy Policy, 47*, 111–122. https://doi.org/10.1016/j.enpol.2012.04.017
Bollerslev, T., Engle, R. F., & Wooldridge, J. M. (1988). A capital asset pricing model with time-varying covariances. *Journal of Political Economy, 96*(1), 116–131. https://doi.org/10.1086/261527
Boungou, W., & Yatie, A. (2022). The impact of geopolitical risk on global energy markets: Evidence from the Russia–Ukraine conflict. Energy Economics, 109, 105961. doi:https://doi.org/10.1016/j.eneco.2022.105961.
Caldara, D., & Iacoviello, M. (2022). *Measuring geopolitical risk. American economic review, 112*(4), 1194–1225. https://doi.org/10.1257/aer.20191823
Chen, C., Lean, H. H., & Smyth, R. (2021). Geopolitical risk and energy markets: A global perspective. *Energy Economics, 95*, 105134. https://doi.org/10.1016/j.eneco.2021.105134
Chen, P., Zhong, S., Zheng, S., Ullah, S., & Musa, M. (2024). Quantifying the influence of natural resources rent, financial development, and institutional quality on energy security risk. *Energy & Environment.* https://doi.org/10.1177/0958305X241266526
Cherp, A., & Jewell, J. (2014). The concept of energy security: Beyond the four as. *Energy Policy, 75*, 415–421. https://doi.org/10.1016/j.enpol.2014.09.005
Chu, L. K., Doğan, B., Ghosh, S., & Shahbaz, M. (2023). The influence of shadow economy, environmental policies and geopolitical risk on renewable energy: A comparison of high- and middle-income countries. Journal of Environmental Management, 342, 118122. doi:https://doi.org/10.1016/j.jenvman.2023.118122.
Erdoğdu, E. (2010). Energy market reforms in Turkey: An economic analysis. *Energy Policy, 38*(9), 4929–4936. https://doi.org/10.1016/j.enpol.2010.04.011
Filipović, S., Radovanović, M., & Golušin, V. (2018). Macroeconomic and political aspects of energy security–exploratory data analysis. *Renewable and Sustainable Energy Reviews, 97*, 428–435. https://doi.org/10.1016/j.rser.2018.08.058
Gnangnon, S. K. (2020). Geopolitical risks, energy consumption and economic growth in developing countries. *Energy Policy, 138*, 111220. https://doi.org/10.1016/j.enpol.2019.111220
Gnangnon, S. K., & Lacovone, L. (2019). Trade policy and energy security: Evidence from sub-Saharan Africa. *World Development, 118*, 81–96. https://doi.org/10.1016/j.worlddev.2019.02.005
Gong, X., Liu, Y., & Wang, X. (2021). Dynamic volatility spillovers across oil and natural gas futures markets based on a time-varying spillover method. *International Review of Financial Analysis, 76*, 101790. https://doi.org/10.1016/j.irfa.2021.101790

Janjua, L. R., Sanli, O., Panait, M., et al. (2024). Impact of energy security and economic growth on poverty: Sample of sub-Saharan Africa. *Environment, Development and Sustainability, 26*, 25459–25484. https://doi.org/10.1007/s10668-023-03689-w

Jansen, J. C., & Seebregts, A. J. (2010). Long-term energy services security: What is it and how can it be measured and valued? *Energy Policy, 38*(4), 1654–1664. https://doi.org/10.1016/j.enpol.2009.02.047

Kaufmann, D., Kraay, A., & Mastruzzi, M. (2010). The worldwide governance indicators: Methodology and analytical issues. *World Bank Policy Research Working Paper, No. 5430*. https://doi.org/10.1596/1813-9450-5430

Le Coq, C., & Paltseva, E. (2009). Measuring the security of external energy supply in the European Union. *Energy Policy, 37*(11), 4474–4481. https://doi.org/10.1016/j.enpol.2009.05.069

Le, T. H., & Nguyen, C. P. (2019). Is energy security a driver for economic growth? Evidence from a global sample. *Energy Policy, 129*, 436–451. https://doi.org/10.1016/j.enpol.2019.02.038

Mensah, J. T., & Adu, G. (2015). Energy consumption, carbon emissions and economic growth in SSA: A panel cointegration analysis. *Energy Economics, 47*, 425–435. https://doi.org/10.1016/j.eneco.2014.11.004

North, D. C. (1990). *Institutions, institutional change and economic performance*. Cambridge University Press.

Overland, I. (2019). The geopolitics of renewable energy: Debunking four emerging myths. *Energy Research & Social Science, 49*, 36–40. https://doi.org/10.1016/j.erss.2018.10.018

Öztürk, I., & Acaravcı, A. (2010). CO_2 emissions, energy consumption and economic growth in Turkey. *Renewable and Sustainable Energy Reviews, 14*(9), 3220–3225. https://doi.org/10.1016/j.rser.2010.07.005

Scholten, D., & Bosman, R. (2016). The geopolitics of renewables; exploring the political implications of renewable energy systems. *Technological Forecasting and Social Change, 103*, 273–283. https://doi.org/10.1016/j.techfore.2015.10.014

Sovacool, B. K., & Mukherjee, I. (2011). Conceptualizing and measuring energy security: A synthesized approach. *Energy, 36*(8), 5343–5355. https://doi.org/10.1016/j.energy.2011.06.043

Tian, M., Li, W., & Wen, F. (2021). The dynamic impact of oil price shocks on the stock market and the USD/RMB exchange rate: Evidence from implied volatility indices. The North American Journal of Economics and Finance, 55, 101310. doi:https://doi.org/10.1016/j.najef.2020.101310.

Umbach, F. (2010). Global energy security and the implications for the EU. *Energy Policy, 38*(3), 1229–1240. https://doi.org/10.1016/j.enpol.2009.01.010

World Energy Outlook (2021). World Energy Outlook.

Yergin, D. (2006). Ensuring energy security. *Foreign Affairs, 85*(2), 69–82. https://doi.org/10.2307/20031912

Economic Globalization and Renewable Energy Investment: Cross-Border Dynamics

Emre Akusta

Abstract Globalization has become a key dynamic shaping renewable energy investment through technology transfer, capital mobility, and trade networks. This study examines the impact of economic globalization and its dimensions on renewable energy investments for the global economy, using global data from 1970 to 2022. The Johansen cointegration test confirmed the existence of long-run relationships in the study. Long-run coefficient estimates were made using the DOLS and FMOLS methods. The findings show that economic globalization generally has a positive impact on renewable energy investments. The long-run coefficient results show that a 1% increase in the economic globalization index increases renewable energy investments by approximately 0.06–0.07%. Analyzing the sub-components, the impact of trade globalization is significantly stronger. A 1% increase in the trade globalization index increases renewable energy investments by 0.10–0.12%. In contrast, financial globalization was estimated with negative coefficients. A 1% increase in the financial globalization index was found to reduce investments by approximately 0.05%. This result indicates that short-run capital movements, exchange rate fluctuations, and financial instability have a negative impact on long-run energy projects. Furthermore, economic growth was also found to support renewable energy investments. Overall, it emerged that the impact of globalization is not one-sided; while it offers opportunities for renewable energy investments, financial integration harbors vulnerabilities when appropriate policy frameworks are lacking.

Keywords Economic globalization · Trade globalization · Financial globalization · Renewable energy investment · Sustainable energy policy

---

E. Akusta (✉)
Department of Economics, Kirklareli University, Kofcaz, Kirklareli, Türkiye
e-mail: emre.akusta@klu.edu.tr

A. Akusta and M. Gün (eds.), *Financial Frontiers in Energy Markets*, Contributions to Finance and Accounting, https://doi.org/10.1007/978-3-032-16738-5_6

1 Introduction

The global climate crisis has reached a scale that directly threatens the sustainability of modern civilization. The fossil fuel-based growth model accompanying industrialization has pushed emissions to unprecedented levels alongside rising energy demand, placing extreme weather events and ecological degradation at the center of the global agenda. In this regard, access to clean and reliable energy, one of the components of sustainable development, has become a critical priority not only for environmental goals but also for maintaining stable growth and prosperity (He et al., 2019). The widespread adoption of renewable energy technologies is seen as a fundamental policy tool for both addressing ecological issues and enhancing economic resilience (IRENA, 2018).

The significant increase in renewable energy use worldwide over the past decade is linked to falling technology costs, economies of scale, and policy support. Developed countries in Europe have succeeded in significantly increasing the share of renewable sources in electricity generation (Lema et al., 2021). However, structural constraints such as increasing urbanization, industrialization, and energy poverty in developing economies have slowed the pace of renewable energy investments (Liu et al., 2020). Therefore, to accelerate the global energy transition, it is necessary to focus not only on technology and cost dynamics but also on the transnational economic forces shaping these investments.

Economic globalization is at the forefront of these forces. Globalization refers to institutional and market integration that facilitates the free movement of goods, capital, information, and technology across borders. In the literature, the impacts of economic globalization on energy use and emissions have been discussed through various channels: changes in production and consumption patterns through trade liberalization; the spread of technology and management practices through foreign direct investment (FDI); and expanded access to investment finance through financial integration are the main channels (Gozgor & Ranjan, 2017). These channels have both encouraged and, under certain conditions, suppressed renewable energy investments. For example, financial globalization has facilitated the financing of clean energy projects by increasing access to long-term funds and a diverse investor base; however, fluctuations in capital flows and financial shocks have also increased uncertainty in investment decisions (Hordofa et al., 2022).

Discussions on the environmental consequences of globalization cover a wide range, from the "pollution haven" hypothesis to technology diffusion and green innovation arguments. The claim that pollution-intensive activities may shift from economies with strict environmental regulations to countries with looser standards points to the potential negative externalities of trade and foreign direct investment channels (Eskeland & Harrison, 2003). However, it has been emphasized that multinational corporations can reduce energy intensity and emissions by introducing more efficient production processes and clean technologies, and can also accelerate the transition to renewable energy (Omri & Nguyen, 2014). Therefore, the impact of economic globalization on renewable energy investments is theoretically uncertain, and the magnitude and direction of the effect vary across country groups, periods, and institutional structures (Bayar et al., 2020; Pradhan et al., 2021).

The heterogeneity of empirical findings on the relationship between economic globalization and energy is closely linked to measurement preferences and scope differences. While some studies focus on energy consumption or renewable energy use indicators, others represent economic globalization with a single indicator (e.g., trade openness or foreign direct investment). However, since globalization is a multidimensional phenomenon, it has been suggested that the capital mobility and financial integration dimension and the trade openness dimension may affect renewable energy investments through different channels. Indeed, studies using economic globalization indices have shown strong relationships between renewable energy and globalization, but the direction and magnitude of the effect may vary depending on the context (e.g., Chao et al., 2023; Gozgor et al., 2020; Subramaniam & Masron, 2021). Building on these gaps in the literature, this study aims to reassess the impact of economic globalization on global renewable energy investments. To this end, the two fundamental dimensions of economic globalization—trade globalization and financial globalization—have been separated. In this way, the integrated impact of economic globalization and dimension-specific effects has been estimated separately.

The contributions of this study to the literature can be summarized under three headings. First, the discussion, which generally focuses on "consumption" indicators in the literature, has been shifted here to an "investment" perspective. Investment dynamics, which determine future production capacity and technology sets, are considered a critical variable in understanding the speed and continuity of the energy transition. Second, the two dimensions of economic globalization are examined using separate models. This allows for a comparative analysis of the relative weights of trade and financial channels, in addition to the overall effect. Third, considering the transnational nature of environmental issues and investment flows, a comprehensive global dataset and World Bank indicators were used. This strengthened external validity for different income groups and regional blocks.

2 The Outlook for Globalization and Renewable Energy

The relationship between globalization and renewable energy has attracted significant attention in recent years, not only in terms of environmental sustainability but also in terms of technology transfer, financial flows, and the restructuring of production networks. The interaction between these two areas has become more pronounced, particularly during periods of deepening global economic integration. The way globalization affects renewable energy production is largely shaped through various channels, such as access to technology and finance, trade, and supply chain integration. In this respect, a combined analysis of the KOF Globalization Index (Dreher, 2006) and the EIA's global renewable energy production data reveals a noteworthy synchronous movement between these two areas throughout the period 1970–2022. The theoretical basis for this synchronous movement is grounded in studies (e.g., Gozgor &

Ranjan, 2017; Omri & Nguyen, 2014) suggesting that renewable energy investments can be incentivized through mechanisms such as technology diffusion via international trade and foreign direct investment, the entry of economies of scale, and the diversification of investment risks.

Figure 1 shows that the global trend in Total Renewable Energy Production has increased over the years in parallel with Economic Globalization and its subdimensions. As of 2022, renewable energy production has reached 8323.9 trillion Btu; the indices for Economic Globalization, Trade Globalization, and Financial Globalization have been 58.94, 57.91, and 60.11, respectively. Looking at simple simultaneous relationships, the correlation between renewable energy production and economic globalization is 0.83, the trade dimension is 0.82, and the financial dimension is 0.84. This value shows a positive co-movement, indicating that renewable energy production increases as globalization indicators increase. Without claiming causality, this co-movement is consistent with the expectation that technology and capital channels may be effective on the investment side, as emphasized in the literature (Chao et al., 2023).

In the late 1990s, the level of globalization increased with the liberalization of trade and capital movements. Throughout the 2000s, the decline in information and communication costs and the deepening of global supply chains facilitated access to renewable technologies and the flow of intermediate goods (Shahbaz et al., 2018). Despite the short-term contractionary impacts of the 2008–2009 global financial crisis, average renewable energy production in the 2010s increased by over 60% compared to the 2000s. Cost reductions in panel technologies and economies of scale, along with the expansion of cross-border financing for energy investments, played a role in this increase (Gozgor et al., 2020). Despite the turbulence caused by the COVID-19 shock in trade and capital flows in 2020, the 2020–2022 average remained

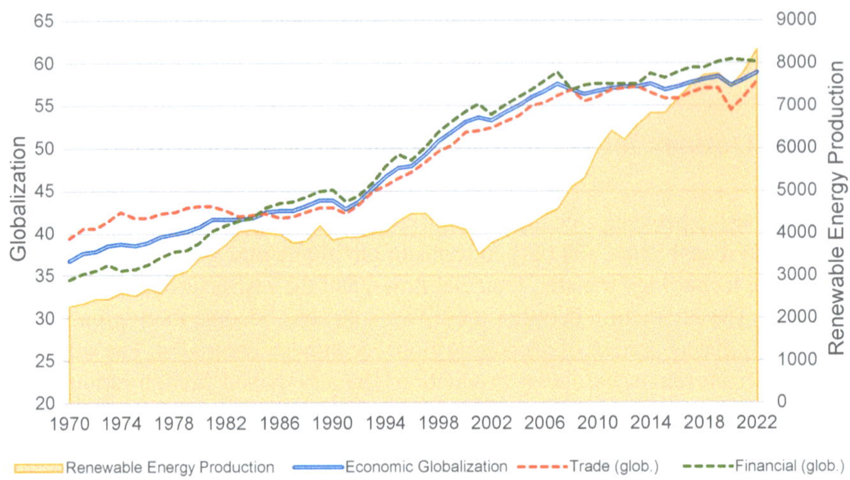

Fig. 1 The outlook for globalization and renewable energy. *Source* Constructed by the author using EIA and KOF data

significantly above previous decades at 7862 trillion Btu. This resilience indicates that green investments were partially shielded from financial volatility thanks to long-term contracts and policy targets (Nasreen et al., 2020).

Reducing energy poverty and achieving inclusive growth targets have made the demand for renewable sources a social priority. Channels such as rural electrification, local production, and employment opportunities have strengthened the social legitimacy of renewable investments; public–private partnership-based financing models have become widespread. The digitization of health and education services during the pandemic has further highlighted the demand for uninterrupted and clean electricity. This situation has created new investment opportunities for off-grid solutions and microgrids, particularly in developing countries (Odou et al., 2020; Ram et al., 2020).

Conversely, climate targets have accelerated the shift away from carbon-intensive production. The Paris Agreement and COP processes have linked increases in renewable energy capacity to nationally determined contributions and greater policy clarity. In contrast, the "pollution haven" debate in the literature on the environmental impact of globalization has highlighted the possibility that polluting activities may shift to countries with looser regulations (Eskeland & Harrison, 2003). Consequently, the overall impact of globalization on environmental quality varies from country to country, depending on the interaction between trade structure, technology diffusion, and regulatory capacity. The steady increase observed in EIA data points to the dominant nature of the global diffusion of green technologies. However, complementary reforms such as policy consistency and carbon pricing, network investment plans, and shortening permit processes will be decisive in preserving these gains (Shahbaz et al., 2021).

3 Insights from Previous Research

Increasing environmental problems, climate change, and fluctuations in fossil fuel supply in recent years have heightened the strategic importance of renewable energy sources. In this transformation process, economic globalization has begun to play a decisive role in the development of renewable energy infrastructure. Globalization's access to renewable energy through trade, finance, and technology transfer channels is a topic increasingly researched in the literature. In the transition to renewable energy, not only economic size but also global factors such as international interconnectedness, foreign investment, knowledge diffusion, and financial market integration play an important role.

In the literature, the first point that stands out in studies on the determinants of renewable energy demand is the positive relationship with economic performance. Sadorsky (2009a, 2009b) emphasizes that renewable energy consumption increases with rising income levels, while studies such as Salim and Rafiq (2012) show that carbon emissions can also trigger demand. These findings show that economic development is a driving force in energy transition, revealing that renewable energy demand is sensitive not only to income growth but also to environmental pressures. However, these studies have generally focused on domestic development levels and have not modelled the impact of global factors in detail. Studies such as Paramati et al. (2016) have filled this gap by analysing the extent of financial globalization.

Among the most important international determinants of renewable energy production and investment decisions are increased financial mobility and technology flows associated with globalization. Paramati et al. (2017) found that foreign direct investment (FDI) and stock market development have positive impacts on renewable energy demand; however, this impact may vary depending on the country's income level. This finding shows that attracting FDI plays a vital role for financially constrained renewable energy markets in developing countries. However, while these studies push the environmental aspect into the background, Abbasi and Riaz (2016) and Shao (2018) have filled this gap by emphasizing the feedback impact of environmental quality and carbon emissions on investments.

The impacts of globalization through trade channels also hold a distinct place in the literature. Omri and Nguyen (2014), in their analysis covering 64 countries, showed that trade openness positively impacts renewable energy demand. Information and technology transfers facilitated through trade provide significant advantages, particularly in accessing renewable energy equipment (Aguirre & Ibikunle, 2014). Similarly, Gozgor et al. (2020), in their study examining different dimensions of economic globalization (trade, finance, environment, etc.), found that each of these dimensions promotes green energy consumption in OECD countries. However, the impact of institutional structures and governance quality has generally been neglected in these studies. In addition to the positive impacts of financial globalization, its risks have also been discussed in the literature. Li et al. (2020) emphasize that the efficient allocation of financial resources is not always possible and that capital can be directed to inefficient areas. Baker (2015) and Shahbaz et al. (2018) point out that dirty foreign direct investment (FDI) can harm renewable energy. These findings are supported by empirical tests of the "pollution haven" and "pollution halo" hypotheses.

The technological innovation dimension is one of the most critical interfaces in the literature. Lin and Zhu (2019) and Sharma et al. (2021) state that the transition to renewable energy can be successful if it is supported by technical capacity, R&D spending, and international cooperation. Geng and Ji (2016) emphasize that innovation both facilitates access to clean energy and contributes to the widespread adoption of these technologies. However, these studies have mostly focused on developed countries and have not sufficiently examined the challenges of accessing technology in developing countries. Another important finding in the literature is the two-way effect between environmental well-being and foreign direct investment. While some studies (e.g., Shahbaz et al., 2018; Sharma et al., 2021) show that clean energy investments are effective in reducing carbon emissions, others (e.g., Abbasi & Riaz, 2016; Jiang et al., 2018; Shao, 2018) have revealed that the impact of foreign direct investment on environmental quality varies depending on the country group, energy infrastructure, and institutional structure. Murshed et al. (2021), focusing on governance quality and institutional structure, explain more clearly why these effects are positive in some countries and negative in others.

Generally, the literature shows that the impacts of globalization on renewable energy investments and consumption are multidimensional and context sensitive. Technology transfer, knowledge diffusion, and economies of scale provided through trade and foreign direct investment accelerate energy transition; however, financial integration can lead to negative outcomes in some cases through vulnerabilities and dirty investments. It is emphasized that renewable energy demand is sensitive not only to income growth but also to environmental pressures, and that institutional structure, governance quality, and policy design play a decisive role in this relationship. Technological innovation and R&D investments stand out in the literature as the most critical complementary factors, while access differences between developed and developing countries are noteworthy. Therefore, current studies reveal that the interaction between globalization and renewable energy is not a one-dimensional process, but rather a structure that presents both opportunities and risks depending on country characteristics, policy frameworks, and institutional capacity.

4 Data and Methodology

4.1 Analytical Framework and Data Description

This study examines the long-run impacts of economic globalization on renewable energy investments for the global economy. The empirical analysis was conducted using annual global data from 1970 to 2022. The variables were compiled from indicators frequently used in the existing literature, and the study period was determined based on the availability of relevant data. The entire world economy was taken as the sample in this study. For each variable, the global time series created by the World Bank was preferred over individual country series, using population-weighted averages of countries. This approach aims to contribute directly to global-scale policy discussions and reflects the series' response to common international shocks. The empirical model is based on the FMOLS and DOLS methods and is detailed in Eqs. (1) and (2).

$$RENEW_t = \beta_0 + \beta_1 ECOGI + \beta_2 GDP + \varepsilon_t \tag{1}$$

$$RENEW_t = \alpha_0 + \alpha_1 FINGI + \alpha_2 TRAGI + \alpha_3 GDP + u_t \tag{2}$$

Equation (1) and (2) explain renewable energy investments ($RENEW_t$). The economic growth rate (GDP) has been added to both equations. This controls the macroeconomic conjuncture. ε_t and u_t in the equations are error terms. The estimation coefficients (β_i, α_i) reveal the direction and magnitude of various dimensions of globalization on renewable energy capacity.

The level of renewable energy investment has been measured in line with Bellakhal et al. (2019) and Alsagr (2023) based on total renewable energy production. This directly captures the impact of investments on capacity expansion. These investments are primarily related to the GDP growth rate; economic growth encourages renewable projects by increasing energy demand through economies of scale and income growth. Different dimensions of globalization also provide channels that support investments. Economic globalization can increase the diversity of knowledge and inputs through trade liberalization and technology transfer. Trade globalization directly impacts costs and technology diffusion, particularly through the import–export flows of renewable energy equipment. Financial globalization, meanwhile, strengthens project financing conditions through capital mobility and foreign investment. Descriptive statistics for the data are presented in Table 1.

The findings in Table 1 show that the average values of the three globalization components are quite close to each other. This indicates a general trend toward convergence in the levels of integration of countries into the global economy. However, an important difference emerges when standard deviations are taken into account: while trade globalization exhibits a more homogeneous distribution, variance is quite high in financial globalization. This difference indicates that while countries differ in their financial liberalization and capital mobility policies, their approaches to trade in goods and services are more common.

The GDP growth rate added to the dataset provides insight into the global economic outlook. With an average of 3.16% and a median of 3.28%, it can be said that growth has generally followed a moderate and stable course. The minimum value of −2.89 reflects the impact of major shocks such as the 2008–2009 global crisis. This reveals that growth rates are affected by periodic fluctuations. Renewable energy production data is noteworthy in terms of both level and distribution. The difference between the mean and the median, and the positive skewness, indicate that a few major producing countries (e.g., China and the US) dominate total production. This highlights that renewable energy production is sensitive to factors such as economies of scale, capital intensity, and policy support. The high standard deviation points to differences between countries.

Table 1 Descriptive statistics

Variable	Description	Obs	Mean	Std	Min	Median	Max	Source
RENEW	Energy Production (Trillion Btu)	53	4561	1645	2289	4093	8324	EIA
ECOGI	Economic Globalization Index	53	48.69	7.64	36.75	47.86	58.94	KOF
TRAGI	Trade Globalization Index	53	48.66	6.46	39.42	47.23	57.91	KOF
FINGI	Financial Globalization Index	53	48.96	8.85	34.54	49.23	60.48	KOF
GDP	GDP Growth (Annual %)	53	3.16	1.61	−2.89	3.28	6.40	WB

Note (1) KOF, EIA, and WB represent the KOF Globalisation Index, the U.S. Energy Information Administration database, and the World Bank's World Development Indicators (WDI), respectively. (2) The logarithm of the renewable variable has been taken

4.2 The Methodology of the Study

In the first step of the empirical analysis, the Augmented Dickey-Fuller (ADF) test was applied to determine the degree of stationarity for each series. Due to its parametric structure, the ADF provides a robust unit root test even with small sample sizes; its augmented version (Said & Dickey, 1984) internally controls for autocorrelation by adding lagged difference terms. This allows for a clear initial assessment of the series' integration order. The Phillips-Perron (PP) test was used to verify the unit root results. The nonparametric nature of the PP test, with Newey-West corrections (Phillips & Perron, 1988), addresses autocorrelation and potential heteroscedasticity, reducing sensitivity to parametric assumptions. This dual testing strategy minimizes method-specific biases in stationarity decisions. The Johansen cointegration test was preferred to investigate the long-run equilibrium relationship. This method is superior to the Engle-Granger approach in that it (i) detects multiple cointegration vectors simultaneously and (ii) reduces the risk of reverse causality in the system (Johansen, 1988; Johansen & Juselius, 1990).

Having confirmed cointegration, two complementary methods were used to estimate long-run coefficients in an unbiased manner. Fully Modified Ordinary Least Squares (FMOLS) produces consistent parameters by eliminating free correlation and endogeneity through semi-parametric kernel estimates (Phillips & Hansen, 1990). Dynamic OLS (DOLS), by adding forward and backward differences of the independent variables, reduces small-sample bias and provides super-consistent estimates (Stock & Watson, 1993). The autocorrelation correction advantage of FMOLS and the dynamic structure of DOLS, which gains intra-sample freedom, have been used together to strengthen the findings of the study from a methodological perspective. This multi-stage approach is designed to obtain reliable and theoretically defensible results by considering the fundamental statistical properties of the series and eliminating bias from long-term parameters. The results obtained are presented in the remainder of the study.

5 Empirical Findings and Discussions

This section presents the econometric analysis steps in sequence. First, the ADF and PP unit root tests were applied to analyse the stationarity of the variables. Long-run relationships were examined using the Johansen cointegration test. After cointegration was confirmed, long-run coefficients were estimated using the DOLS and FMOLS methods. Below, the findings based on each table are interpreted in detail.

Table 2 shows the results of the ADF and PP unit root tests. The results indicate that the RENEW, ECOGI, TRAGI, FINGI, and GDP series are not stationary at the level; however, their first differences are stationary. Therefore, the integration order of all series was found to be I(I). The stationarity findings paved the way for testing long-run cointegration vectors using the Johansen method in the next stage.

Table 2 Unit root test results

Variable		ADF unit root test		PP unit root test	
		t-statistic (level)	*t*-statistic (first difference)	*t*-statistic (level)	*t*-statistic (first difference)
RENEW	Constant	−0.369	−6.848***	−0.448	−6.904***
ECOGI		−0.871	−5.268***	−0.840	−5.197***
TRAGI		−0.429	−5.652***	−0.466	−5.556***
FINGI		−1.214	−6.368***	−1.209	−6.344***
GDP		−0.044	−6.966***	−0.174	−7.685***
RENEW	Constant and Trend	−1.459	−6.779***	−1.769	−6.840***
ECOGI		−1.562	−5.209***	−1.166	−5.131***
TRAGI		−1.494	−5.562***	−1.450	−5.459***
FINGI		−0.893	−6.434***	−0.893	−6.400***
GDP		−0.326	−6.903***	−2.569	−7.696***

Note The symbols ***, **, and * denote the significance at a 1%, 5%, and 10% level, respectively

Table 3 presents the results of the Johansen cointegration test. The trace and maximum eigenvalue statistics indicate a cointegration relationship of order $r = 2$ for Model 1 and $r = 3$ for Model 2. These findings suggest a long-term equilibrium relationship between the variables. The confirmation of cointegration justifies the methodological shift to DOLS/FMOLS estimation.

Table 4 shows the results of DOLS and FMOLS. Based on Model 1, the economic globalization index (ECOGI) positively and statistically significantly impacts renewable energy investment in both estimation methods. A 1% increase in ECOGI indicates an approximate 0.06% increase in renewable energy investment. This result demonstrates that global economic integration supports infrastructure investments and capacity increases in renewable energy. The results are consistent with

Table 3 Johansen cointegration test results

Model	H_0	Trace statistics	Critical values (5%)	Maximum eigenvalue statistics	Critical values (5%)
Model 1	$r = 0$	54.260***	24.276	32.081***	17.797
	$r \leq 1$	22.179***	12.321	20.255***	11.225
	$r \leq 2$	1.924	4.130	1.924	4.130
Model 2	$r = 0$	89.076***	54.079	36.398***	28.588
	$r \leq 1$	52.678***	35.193	27.901***	22.300
	$r \leq 2$	24.777**	20.262	16.616**	15.892
	$r \leq 3$	8.1604	9.165	8.160	9.165

Note The symbols ***, **, and * denote the significance at a 1%, 5%, and 10% level, respectively

Table 4 DOLS and FMOLS results

Dependent variable: RENEW		DOLS			FMOLS		
Model	Variable	Coefficient	Std. Error	*t*-Statistic	Coefficient	Std. Error	*t*-Statistic
Model 1	ECOGI	0.056***	0.006	8.650	0.063***	0.004	14.611
	GDP	0.285**	0.107	2.669	0.156**	0.060	2.597
Model 2	TRAGI	0.099***	0.024	4.038	0.122***	0.023	5.195
	FINGI	−0.040*	0.020	−1.953	−0.055**	0.022	−2.436
	GDP	0.183***	0.060	3.050	0.188*	0.060	3.133

Note The symbols ***, **, and * denote the significance at a 1%, 5%, and 10% level, respectively

the findings of studies such as Gozgor and Ranjan (2017) and Subramaniam and Masron (2021), which indicate that economic globalization has a positive impact on renewable energy. In practice, the expansion of green energy investments by multinational companies, cross-border carbon taxes, and the proliferation of sustainability reporting also form the institutional infrastructure for this effect. At the same time, this finding emphasizes the importance of global cooperation in line with the sustainable development goals.

The findings of Model 2 show that the commercial globalization (TRAGI) variable has a positive and significant impact in both estimation methods. This indicates that a 1% increase in TRAGI leads to a 0.099–0.122% increase in renewable energy investments. This reveals that commercial globalization supports renewable energy investments through mechanisms such as increased import–export volume, easier access to green technology products, and the inclusion of renewable energy equipment in foreign trade. This finding is theoretically consistent with the trade-channelled technology diffusion and economies of scale effects discussed by Shahbaz et al. (2018) and Omri and Nguyen (2014). In particular, developing countries that import environmentally friendly technologies from developed countries and adapt them to local production have accelerated this process. Furthermore, trade integration contributes to global environmental governance by facilitating the spread of sustainable production standards.

The findings regarding the financial globalization (FINGI) variable are noteworthy. Both estimation methods reveal that FINGI negatively impacts renewable energy production. A 1% increase in FINGI is found to cause a 0.040–0.055% decline in renewable energy investments. This situation shows that financial globalization does not always work in favour of environmental sustainability; on the contrary, under certain conditions and in certain periods, short-term approaches in investor behaviour, exchange rate and interest rate volatility, and policy uncertainty can negatively impact long-term projects such as renewable energy. These results are consistent with findings reported in studies such as Nasreen et al. (2020) and Wen et al. (2022), which suggest that financial integration can increase investment volatility and hinder clean energy financing. In practice, risks such as investors' tendency to withdraw from developing countries due to increased global risk perception or rising foreign exchange borrowing costs may have contributed to this effect. Therefore, structuring green finance markets, promoting sustainable investment funds, and effectively using macroprudential tools could constitute important policy steps.

The positive and significant economic growth (GDP) coefficients obtained in both models and both methods indicate a strong complementary relationship between economic growth and renewable energy investments. A 1% increase in GDP increases renewable energy investments by 0.156–0.285%. This indicates that resources allocated to renewable energy projects have expanded thanks to increased income levels and investment capacity. Furthermore, considering that economic growth tends to increase energy consumption, the fact that this increase is directed towards renewable sources rather than fossil fuels is extremely positive in terms of environmental sustainability. Thus, it becomes possible to strike a balance between growth and environmental protection.

In conclusion, DOLS and FMOLS estimates indicate that economic globalization generally has a positive impact on renewable energy investments. However, it has also been found that not all dimensions of globalization affect renewable energy investments in the same way. While economic and commercial globalization creates a positive impact in line with environmental sustainability goals, financial globalization can disrupt this process due to its risky structure. This situation shows that policymakers need to analyse the nature and direction of globalization well and make strategic interventions. For example, some of these interventions include prioritizing renewable energy products in trade liberalization processes or developing international standards that encourage the redirection of financial flows towards environmentally friendly sectors. In this regard, the findings offer important implications for both environmental and socioeconomic sustainability.

6 Conclusion

This study examines the impact of economic globalization on renewable energy investments. The analysis was conducted using annual global data from 1970 to 2022. The stationarity of the series was assessed using ADF and PP tests, and long-run relationships were confirmed using the Johansen cointegration test. In the final stage, coefficient estimates were made using DOLS and FMOLS methods.

The DOLS and FMOLS results indicate that a 1% increase in the economic globalization index increases renewable energy investments by 0.056–0.063%. This finding shows that global market integration accelerates energy transition through technology transfer, cost advantages, and capital access. When examining the sub-dimensions, trade globalization has a stronger and more positive effect on renewable investments. A 1% increase in the trade globalization index was found to increase renewable investments by 0.099–0.122%. This result shows that imported capital goods, green technology transfer, and international competitive pressure encourage renewable energy investments, especially in developing countries. In contrast, financial globalization was estimated with negative coefficients. A 1% increase in the financial globalization index reduces renewable energy investments by approximately 0.040–0.055%. This finding reflects the fragile impact of volatility in capital flows, exchange rate and interest rate shocks, and short-term investment behaviour on energy projects. The study also reveals a stable, positive, and significant relationship between economic growth and renewable energy investments. The findings show that a 1% increase in economic growth increases renewable energy investments by between 0.156% and 0.285%. The financial capacity and investment environment created by growth enable both the public and private sectors to allocate more resources to energy transition.

Overall, the findings indicate that globalization is not one-dimensional and that while the trade channel presents a critical opportunity for renewable energy investments, financial globalization carries risks in the absence of appropriate policies and institutional regulations. In this regard, economically, policies that enhance trade openness can reduce investment costs by deepening green supply chains. Socially, the spread of technology through international integration can support a just transition by increasing local production capacity and employment. Environmentally, the positive effects of trade and economic globalization can enable faster growth in renewable capacity; however, investment uncertainties created by financial volatility can slow down the emission reduction process.

Although this study has significant findings, it also has some limitations. There are significant differences between countries in terms of financial integration, economic growth rates, and renewable energy production. The KOF and EIA data used provide global-level information but do not reflect local policy differences. Furthermore, the analysis focused on long-run relationships and did not consider short-run shocks. Subgroup analyses based on income groups or regional blocks are required to interpret the results more accurately.

References

Abbasi, F., & Riaz, K. (2016). CO2 emissions and financial development in an emerging economy: An augmented VAR approach. *Energy Policy, 90*, 102–114. https://doi.org/10.1016/j.enpol.2015.12.017

Aguirre, M., & Ibikunle, G. (2014). Determinants of renewable energy growth: A global sample analysis. *Energy Policy, 69*, 374–384. https://doi.org/10.1016/j.enpol.2014.02.036

Alsagr, N. (2023). Financial efficiency and its impact on renewable energy investment: Empirical evidence from advanced and emerging economies. *Journal of Cleaner Production, 401*, Article 136738. https://doi.org/10.1016/j.jclepro.2023.136738

Baker, L. (2015). The evolving role of finance in South Africa's renewable energy sector. *Geoforum, 64*, 146–156. https://doi.org/10.1016/j.geoforum.2015.06.017

Bayar, Y., Sasmaz, M. U., & Ozkaya, M. H. (2020). Impact of trade and financial globalization on renewable energy in EU transition economies: A bootstrap panel granger causality test. *Energies, 14*(1), 19. https://doi.org/10.3390/en14010019

Bellakhal, R., Kheder, S. B., & Haffoudhi, H. (2019). Governance and renewable energy investment in mena countries: How does trade matter? *Energy Economics, 84*, Article 104541. https://doi.org/10.1016/j.eneco.2019.104541

Chao, T., Yunbao, X., Chengbo, D., Bo, L., & Ullah, S. (2023). Financial integration and renewable energy consumption in China: Do education and digital economy development matter? *Environmental Science and Pollution Research, 30*(5), 12944–12952. https://doi.org/10.1007/s11356-022-22852-w

Dreher, A. (2006). Does globalization affect growth? Evidence from a new index of globalization. *Applied Economics, 38*(10), 1091–1110. https://doi.org/10.1080/00036840500392078

Eskeland, G. S., & Harrison, A. E. (2003). Moving to greener pastures? Multinationals and the pollution haven hypothesis. *Journal of Development Economics, 70*(1), 1–23. https://doi.org/10.1016/S0304-3878(02)00084-6

Geng, J. B., & Ji, Q. (2016). Technological innovation and renewable energy development: Evidence based on patent counts. *International Journal of Global Environmental Issues, 15*(3), 217–234. https://doi.org/10.1504/IJGENVI.2016.076945

Gozgor, G., & Ranjan, P. (2017). Globalisation, inequality and redistribution: Theory and evidence. *The World Economy, 40*(12), 2704–2751. https://doi.org/10.1111/twec.12518

Gozgor, G., Mahalik, M. K., Demir, E., & Padhan, H. (2020). The impact of economic globalization on renewable energy in the OECD countries. *Energy Policy, 139*, Article 111365. https://doi.org/10.1016/j.enpol.2020.111365

He, L., Liu, R., Zhong, Z., Wang, D., & Xia, Y. (2019). Can green financial development promote renewable energy investment efficiency? A consideration of bank credit. *Renewable Energy, 143*, 974–984. https://doi.org/10.1016/j.renene.2019.05.059

Hordofa, T. T., Liying, S., Mughal, N., Arif, A., Vu, H. M., & Kaur, P. (2022). Natural resources rents and economic performance: Post-COVID-19 era for G7 countries. *Resources Policy, 75*, Article 102441. https://doi.org/10.1016/j.resourpol.2021.102441

IRENA. (2018). *Renewable energy in national climate action.* International Renewable Energy Agency, Abu Dhabi. Retrieved from https://www.irena.org/-/media/Files/IRENA/Agency/Publication/2018/Dec/IRENA_COP24_NDC_update_2018.pdf

Jiang, L., Zhou, H. F., Bai, L., & Zhou, P. (2018). Does foreign direct investment drive environmental degradation in China? An empirical study based on air quality index from a spatial perspective. *Journal of Cleaner Production, 176*, 864–872. https://doi.org/10.1016/j.jclepro.2017.12.048

Johansen, S. (1988). Statistical analysis of cointegration vectors. *Journal of Economic Dynamics and Control, 12*(2–3), 231–254. https://doi.org/10.1016/0165-1889(88)90041-3

Johansen, S., & Juselius, K. (1990). Maximum likelihood estimation and inference on cointegration—With applications to the demand for money. *Oxford Bulletin of Economics and Statistics, 52*(2), 169–210.

Lema, R., Bhamidipati, P. L., Gregersen, C., Hansen, U. E., & Kirchherr, J. (2021). China's investments in renewable energy in Africa: Creating co-benefits or just cashing-in? *World Development, 141*, Article 105365. https://doi.org/10.1016/j.worlddev.2020.105365

Li, G., Luo, Z., Anwar, M., Lu, Y., Wang, X., & Liu, X. (2020). Intellectual capital and the efficiency of SMEs in the transition economy China; Do financial resources strengthen the routes? *PLoS ONE, 15*(7), Article e0235462. https://doi.org/10.1371/journal.pone.0235462

Lin, B., & Zhu, J. (2019). Determinants of renewable energy technological innovation in China under CO2 emissions constraint. *Journal of Environmental Management, 247*, 662–671. https://doi.org/10.1016/j.jenvman.2019.06.121

Liu, Y., Zhu, J., Li, E. Y., Meng, Z., & Song, Y. (2020). Environmental regulation, green technological innovation, and eco-efficiency: The case of Yangtze river economic belt in China. *Technological Forecasting and Social Change, 155*, Article 119993. https://doi.org/10.1016/j.techfore.2020.119993

Murshed, M., Rahman, M. A., Alam, M. S., Ahmad, P., & Dagar, V. (2021). The nexus between environmental regulations, economic growth, and environmental sustainability: linking environmental patents to ecological footprint reduction in South Asia. *Environmental Science and Pollution Research, 28*(36), 49967–49988. https://doi.org/10.1007/s11356-021-13381-z

Nasreen, S., Mahalik, M. K., Shahbaz, M., & Abbas, Q. (2020). How do financial globalization, institutions and economic growth impact financial sector development in European countries?

Research in International Business and Finance, 54, Article 101247. https://doi.org/10.1016/j.ribaf.2020.101247
Odou, O. D. T., Bhandari, R., & Adamou, R. (2020). Hybrid off-grid renewable power system for sustainable rural electrification in Benin. *Renewable Energy, 145*, 1266–1279. https://doi.org/10.1016/j.renene.2019.06.032
Omri, A., & Nguyen, D. K. (2014). On the determinants of renewable energy consumption: International evidence. *Energy, 72*, 554–560. https://doi.org/10.1016/j.energy.2014.05.081
Paramati, S. R., Mo, D., & Gupta, R. (2017). The effects of stock market growth and renewable energy use on CO2 emissions: Evidence from G20 countries. *Energy Economics, 66*, 360–371. https://doi.org/10.1016/j.eneco.2017.06.025
Paramati, S. R., Ummalla, M., & Apergis, N. (2016). The effect of foreign direct investment and stock market growth on clean energy use across a panel of emerging market economies. *Energy Economics, 56*, 29–41. https://doi.org/10.1016/j.eneco.2016.02.008
Phillips, P. C., & Hansen, B. E. (1990). Statistical inference in instrumental variables regression with I (1) processes. *The Review of Economic Studies, 57*(1), 99–125. https://doi.org/10.2307/2297545
Phillips, P. C., & Perron, P. (1988). Testing for a unit root in time series regression. *Biometrika, 75*(2), 335–346. https://doi.org/10.1093/biomet/75.2.335
Pradhan, S., Chakraborty, R., Mandal, D. K., Barman, A., & Bose, P. (2021). Design and performance analysis of solar chimney power plant (SCPP): A review. *Sustainable Energy Technologies and Assessments, 47*, Article 101411. https://doi.org/10.1016/j.seta.2021.101411
Ram, M., Aghahosseini, A., & Breyer, C. (2020). Job creation during the global energy transition towards 100% renewable power system by 2050. *Technological Forecasting and Social Change, 151*, Article 119682. https://doi.org/10.1016/j.techfore.2019.06.008
Sadorsky, P. (2009a). Renewable energy consumption and income in emerging economies. *Energy Policy, 37*(10), 4021–4028. https://doi.org/10.1016/j.enpol.2009.05.003
Sadorsky, P. (2009b). Renewable energy consumption, CO2 emissions and oil prices in the G7 countries. *Energy Economics, 31*(3), 456–462. https://doi.org/10.1016/j.eneco.2008.12.010
Said, S. E., & Dickey, D. A. (1984). Testing for unit roots in autoregressive-moving average models of unknown order. *Biometrika, 71*(3), 599–607. https://doi.org/10.1093/biomet/71.3.599
Salim, R. A., & Rafiq, S. (2012). Why do some emerging economies proactively accelerate the adoption of renewable energy? *Energy Economics, 34*(4), 1051–1057. https://doi.org/10.1016/j.eneco.2011.08.015
Shahbaz, M., Shahzad, S. J. H., Mahalik, M. K., & Sadorsky, P. (2018). How strong is the causal relationship between globalization and energy consumption in developed economies? A country-specific time-series and panel analysis. *Applied Economics, 50*(13), 1479–1494. https://doi.org/10.1080/00036846.2017.1366640
Shahbaz, M., Trabelsi, N., Tiwari, A. K., Abakah, E. J. A., & Jiao, Z. (2021). Relationship between green investments, energy markets, and stock markets in the aftermath of the global financial crisis. *Energy Economics, 104*, Article 105655. https://doi.org/10.1016/j.eneco.2021.105655
Shao, Y. (2018). Does FDI affect carbon intensity? New evidence from dynamic panel analysis. *International Journal of Climate Change Strategies and Management, 10*(1), 27–42. https://doi.org/10.1108/IJCCSM-03-2017-0062
Sharma, R., Shahbaz, M., Kautish, P., & Vo, X. V. (2021). Analyzing the impact of export diversification and technological innovation on renewable energy consumption: Evidences from BRICS nations. *Renewable Energy, 178*, 1034–1045. https://doi.org/10.1016/j.renene.2021.06.125
Stock, J. H., & Watson, M. W. (1993). A simple estimator of cointegrating vectors in higher order integrated systems. *Econometrica: journal of the Econometric Society*, 783–820. https://doi.org/10.2307/2951763
Subramaniam, Y., & Masron, T. A. (2021). The impact of economic globalization on biofuel in developing countries. *Energy Conversion and Management: X, 10*, Article 100064. https://doi.org/10.1016/j.ecmx.2020.100064

Wen, J., Mughal, N., Kashif, M., Jain, V., Meza, C. S. R., & Cong, P. T. (2022). Volatility in natural resources prices and economic performance: Evidence from BRICS economies. *Resources Policy, 75*, Article 102472. https://doi.org/10.1016/j.resourpol.2021.102472

Renewable Energy Strategies and Sustainability Challenges in the Western Balkans

Ljiljana Kontic and Snezana Maksimovic

Abstract The main aim of this chapter is to investigate the renewable energy strategies and sustainability challenges in the Western Balkan countries. The key sustainability challenges are to achieve energy efficiency and to produce clean energy from renewable resources. Although most of the research included developed countries, there is a growing interest in studying renewable energy in developing economies. The methodology approach involves an extensive literature review, comparative analysis of national and European Union policy documents, and empirical data regarding energy production and consumption, as well as the adoption of renewable energy. The findings revealed that the region has great potential in renewable energy resources, but exploration obstacles remain. The region has embraced the Western Balkans 6 as a basis for expedited sustainable growth across all the countries in the region. The investment opportunities will be discussed, too.

Keywords Renewable energy strategy · Sustainable development · Green transition · Western Balkans

1 Introduction

The availability of energy resources is a key factor in the economic growth in the region (Kontic & Maksimovic, 2022; Zahedi et al., 2022). The energy demand is rapidly growing in emerging economies. The findings revealed the relationship between high carbon emissions and increasing fuel prices. This raises concerns about energy conservation and environmental protection (Zhou et al., 2010).

It is essential to effectively use energy from natural sources, known as renewable energy resources. Renewable energy has clear benefits. However, its exploitation requires careful design, planning, and use of control optimization methods (Baños et al., 2011).

L. Kontic (✉) · S. Maksimovic
The Faculty of Business and Law, University MB, Belgrade, Serbia
e-mail: ljiljana.kontic@yahoo.com

A. Akusta and M. Gün (eds.), *Financial Frontiers in Energy Markets*, Contributions to Finance and Accounting, https://doi.org/10.1007/978-3-032-16738-5_7

Based on empirical studies, the following factors affected sustainability: saving energy by consumers, efficient production of energy, and replacing fossil fuels with different renewable sources (Lund, 2007). Therefore, two main components of the renewable energy strategies would be energy savings and efficient production of energy (Alnatheer, 2005; Ghanadan & Koomey, 2005; Li, 2005; Muneer et al., 2005).

This chapter will discuss renewable energy strategies in the Western Balkan countries. These countries are Serbia, Montenegro, Bosnia and Herzegovina, Albania, and North Macedonia. The first study of energy policies and strategies in the Western Balkans was published in 2008 (OECD/IEA, 2008).

The methodological approach involves an extensive review of literature, analysis of many policy documents from national governments and the European Union, and empirical data related to energy production, consumption, and renewable energy use.

The regional economic development depends on energy availability (Kontic & Maksimovic, 2022). The demand for energy has exponentially increased in developing countries. The results showed a strong correlation between high fuel prices and high carbon emissions. The main challenges are energy saving and environmental protection (Zhou et al., 2010).

Solar energy or regenerative energy must be explored efficiently. While there are obvious advantages of renewable energy, its use needs to be defended by design, planning, and control optimization techniques (Baños et al., 2011).

The sustainable development of renewable energy requires three main technological transitions (Lund, 2007): consumers' energy savings, efficient production of energy, and substitution of fossil fuels by alternative renewable sources. Energy conservation and efficiency improvement significantly impact on renewable energy policies (Alnatheer, 2005; Ghanadan & Koomey, 2005; Li, 2005; Muneer et al., 2005).

This chapter presents sustainable approaches to renewable energy in the Western Balkans countries, i.e. Serbia, Montenegro, Bosnia and Herzegovina, Albania, and North Macedonia. The first study of energy policies and strategies in the Western Balkans has been published in 2008. The methodological approach is based on an extensive literature review, detailed analysis of governmental and EU policy documents, as well as numerous data about energy production and consumption in Western Balkans.

Climate change effects worldwide, and the Western Balkan region. There is a need to promote sustainable energy development. It is important to create rigid policy frameworks and to effectively use natural resources (Bojovic et al., 2024). This section highlights the urgent need for a detailed renewable energy strategy in these countries, pointing the importance of environmental protection and economic growth. The European Union created a strategic framework of sustainable development. The main goals of the green transition are reducing reliance on fossil fuels, decreasing CO_2 gas emissions, and high energy efficiency. These regulations are mandatory for the Western Balkans (Brodny et al., 2025). The EU has launched various initiatives, such as the European Green Deal. The purpose of this Deal is to promote climate neutrality across the continent by 2050, and to create efficient energy policies for future member states, i.e. Western Balkans (Osuma & Yusuf,

2025). The key strategies in the EU's policy framework, the 20-20-20 climate, and energy package are increasing renewable electricity use and decarbonization (Mesfun et al., 2018). The legal framework consists of the Renewable Energy Directive and the 2030 Climate and Energy Framework (Directive, 2009/28/ EC). It brings specific goals and guidelines for promoting renewable energy sources in national contexts, including those of Western Balkan countries (Tausová et al., 2025).

The Western Balkans' energy sector has three main characteristics (Akar, 2016). First, the majority of countries strongly depend on carbon-intensive energy sources. Second, all Western Balkan countries are rich in renewable energy sources. Third, the energy sector in this region is faced by two simultaneous processes: economic transition and the reduction of CO_2 emissions, often referred to as the "green transition" (Kontic & Vesic, 2024).

The major challenge for the region is achieving energy efficiency. In the context of the green transition, main investors come from various international organisations, including the European Union, the World Bank, China, Turkey, and Russia.

Between 2018 and 2023, a total of €5.8 billion was invested in the energy sector of the Western Balkans. Data show that most of these investments, over 71%, went towards fossil fuels, while the rest was for renewable energy sources. The main priority for the Western Balkans is energy conservation. The region has significant potential of wind power and hydropower, which are promising areas for investment. This chapter will give an overview of renewable energy sources.

The main sustainability challenges are the high cost of exploration, slow and unpredictable planning processes, and a lack of experience in using new energy resources.

The rest of this chapter is organized as follows: Sect. 2 is devoted to a literature review, Sect. 3 describes the research context, Sect. 4 outlines the study's results, and Sect. 5 discusses the findings along with recommendations for policymakers and future research avenues.

2 Literature Review

The analysis of relevant literature on sustainability and renewable energy suggested various perspectives, concepts, practices, systems, and the benefits of renewable energy resources. The different research methods have been used, such as conceptual analysis, case studies, surveys, numerical examples, or combinations of these (See Table 1).

The European Commission has created a vision for all European Union countries to achieve sustainable development. The mission is to increase energy efficiency. Two main objectives have been set: the primary goal is to cut CO_2 emissions, and the secondary goal is to invest more in energy efficiency projects. It is also important to change the behaviour of one billion energy consumers, including households and businesses. A study by Soeiro and Dias (2020) showed that higher involvement in community-based initiatives leads to a faster energy transition.

Table 1 Renewable energy studies in chronological order

Study	Country
Muneer et al. (2005)	India
Ghanadan and Koomey (2005)	California, USA
Alnatheer (2005)	Saudi Arabia
Lund (2007)	Denmark
Schneider et al. (2007)	Western Balkans
Walker and Devine-Wright (2008)	UK
Carlisle et al. (2008)	USA
Denis and Parker (2009)	Canada
Carlisle et al. (2009)	USA
Lalic et al. (2011)	Western Balkans
Karakosta et al. (2012)	Bosnia and Herzegovina, Serbia
Ralchev (2012)	Western Balkans
Golusin et al. (2013)	Western Balkans
Yamamoto (2016)	Japan
Dunjic et al. (2016)	Western Balkans
Young and Brans (2017)	UK
Papapostolou et al. (2017)	EU vs Western Balkans
McCabe et al. (2018)	EU
Kim et al. (2019)	China
Cejka et al. (2020)	EU
Pavicevic et al. (2020)	Western Balkans
Bhattacharjee and Nandi (2021)	India
Kontic et al. (2021)	Serbia
Topalovic et al. (2022)	Western Balkans
Zahedi et al. (2022)	Iran
Tausová et al. (2025)	EU
Osuma and Yusuf (2025)	EU

Source Authors' elaboration

Since 2008, many studies on renewable energy have been published (See Table 1). These studies mainly aim to identify the key challenges that different countries face and suggest policy measures for policymakers (Adhikari et al., 2024). Various studies have looked at the Western Balkan region, either as a whole, by specific countries, or compared to European Union countries. The sustainable development of renewable energy has faced several challenges. The first challenge is how to finance renewable energy projects and what socio-economic consequences will be. The second challenge is access to relevant technological information and know-how.

Sustainable development creates various challenges for institutions and companies (Resch et al., 2017).

3 Research Context

The Western Balkan countries, i.e., Albania, Bosnia and Herzegovina, Montenegro, North Macedonia, and Serbia, are a case in point. In 2014, the governments of these countries started the Western Balkans Six Initiative, also known as the Berlin Process. The main goal of the Initiative is to encourage regional cooperation and to create sustainable growth of the Western Balkans.

Since November 2015, annual monitoring reports for these countries have been published. The most important studies are the following:

- In February 2012, the use of biomass consumption for energy purposes within the Energy Community.
- An assessment of the progress in promoting and using renewable energy within the Energy Community was performed in July 2017 and updated in June 2019.
- Forecast study of the Energy Community 2030.
- The main goal of the study, entitled "2030 Overall Targets for the Energy Community," was to improve the methodology and evaluate strategies that target energy efficiency, renewable energy sources (RES), and greenhouse gas (GHG) reductions (Resch et al., 2019).

The Western Balkans are in the process of European Union (EU) integration, characterized by economic reforms and political changes (Lorena, 2010). The key priority is to develop and integrate renewable energy sources. This goes in line with global efforts to reduce carbon emissions and to achieve regional energy security goals (Johnson, 2017; Tatalovic, 2017). The region's location emphasizes the issues of reliable and diverse energy resources (Sekaric & Lazic, 2020). Additionally, the energy sector depends on lignite coal. It is important to find sustainable alternatives that consider environmental issues, especially for better public health (Tokic et al., 2020). This transformation concerns ecology, economic stability, regional cooperation, and future EU integration (Halili, 2012).

The exploration of renewable energy sources includes new jobs in manufacturing, installation, operation, and maintenance of new technologies. Additionally, it has an accelerating effect on regional growth in the Western Balkans. Furthermore, foster new foreign direct investment. However, these countries usually attract less foreign direct investment compared to other emerging economies, even considering their economic size and institutional quality (Estrin & Uvalic, 2013). Transitioning from fossil fuels to renewables can also decrease dependence on imported energy, improving trade balances, and the capital will stay in the region (Johnson, 2017). Moreover, decentralized renewable energy systems can empower rural communities, facilitate access to energy, and stimulate local entrepreneurship (Caemmerer-Seibel et al., 2019). Lay-offs in declining coal industries could lead to negative social and economic effects. It is important to create retraining programs and diversification strategies. Building green economies, initiated by climate change and technological changes, creates economic growth in Western Balkan countries (Goers et al., 2020).

4 Results

This section starts with an overview of the energy market's characteristics, followed by a comparison of different national energy mixes. Then the renewable energy strategies will be presented. The various empirical studies on renewable energy adoption will be analysed to address the specific challenges of renewable energy in the specific context of the Western Balkans' market.

4.1 *Energy Market's Characteristics*

The energy market in the Western Balkan countries is fragmented and monopolized (OECD, 2022). Historically, this region has leaned heavily on a dual energy setup: local lignite coal for thermal power and a wealth of hydropower potential (Tokic et al., 2020). In Serbia and Bosnia and Herzegovina, coal-fired power plants play a major role in electricity generation. This causes high greenhouse gas emissions and local air pollution.

In Bosnia and Herzegovina, hydroelectric and thermal power plants produce more than 62% of its total electricity consumption (Tokic et al., 2020). The high hydropower potential, particularly in Albania and Montenegro, has also influenced the regional energy market by offering a cleaner, albeit sometimes unpredictable, electricity source depending on water availability (Tokic et al., 2020). While these resources have provided energy independence for many years, they now present a real challenge for decarbonization and meeting EU environmental standards. It slows down the shift to alternative energy sources (van den Bergh, 2013).

4.2 *Comparative Overview of National Energy Mixes*

The International Energy Agency (IEA) collects metadata about energy worldwide. The latest data about energy production by source in the Western Balkan countries are illustrated in Table 2.

The energy mixes of the Western Balkans reveal both shared traits and unique national characteristics. The Albanian energy system is based on hydropower; therefore, the percentage of renewable energy in the national mix was the highest. Bosnia and Herzegovina has a hydroelectric potential, but 53.8% of energy is generated from coal. The decarbonization efforts have to significantly decrease coal usage in

Table 2 The energy mixes in 2020 (in %)

	Coal	Oil	Natural gas	Renewable energy	Nuclear
Albania	7.7	53.0	2.1	37.3	
Bosnia and Herzegovina	53.8	20.6	2.3	23.2	
Montenegro	37.8	32.5	N/A	29.7	
North Macedonia	31.6	41.4	11.7	15.2	
Serbia	49.6	22.0	12.5	15.8	
EU average	11.0	31.9	25.0	18.5	13.6

Source IEA (2022)

Bosnia's energy system (Tokic et al., 2020). Almost 50% of energy in Serbia is obtained from coal, especially lignite, while Montenegro and North Macedonia are gradually increasing their wind and solar energy potentials. Serbia has significant challenges in decarbonization. Yet, despite these differences, the Western Balkans is characterized by great potential in various renewable sources like wind, solar, and geothermal energy, by its use is minor (Jocić et al., 2020; Tokic et al., 2020). The Western Balkans' integration into the EU's energy market and its wider energy security framework is a key factor influencing their national energy policies (Tatalovic, 2017).

There is a slight difference in the costs of renewable energy production in the region. However, significant variations exist in resource availability at the country level. Regional integration will facilitate the sustainable development of renewable energy.

4.3 National Renewable Energy Strategies

Sustainable energy strategy has two main components: reducing the demand for fossil-fuel-based resources and the utilization of renewable-energy-based resources, which have lower carbon emissions. However, this modern technology has high maintenance costs. As a result, it is less competitive than traditional electric technology (Alnatheer, 2005; Lund, 2007; Muneer et al., 2005).

Each country in the Western Balkans has prepared national renewable energy strategies and established targets mostly as a consequence of Energy Community commitments and the overarching EU accession agenda. These approaches generally define how to raise the percentage of renewable energies in the electricity, heating, cooling, and transport sectors. For instance, countries set 2020 targets for renewable electricity, though the extent to which these goals have been met differs (Frieden et al., 2016). Countries like Serbia, Albania, and North Macedonia might come close to fulfilling wind power targets by partially selling to the EU, triggering domestic investment beyond current support schemes (Frieden et al., 2016). Bosnia and Herzegovina, although with a high potential, at least part of the way to wind power targets may be attained with no additional cost-effective measures (Frieden et al., 2016; Tokic et al., 2020). These national policies frequently incorporate the introduction of support schemes (such as feed-in-tariffs or premiums) that will attract investments, in parallel with grid upgrading and energy efficiency measures. However, such policies need to be implemented uniformly and proactively according to changing market and technological conditions if they are to prove successful (Kern et al., 2018).

The national renewable energy strategies in the Western Balkans have different regulatory frameworks. It follows EU directives at a legislative level, but there are low administrative capacity and transparency issues (Directive, 2009/28/EC). New renewable energy developments are long-term and complicate processes, which may discourage potential investors. Regulators exist, but they are not fully independent and possess neither the technical knowledge to regulate an increasingly complex energy market, nor the financial means to do so adequately. According to Hutsebaut (2015), the investment decision is also influenced by the interaction of fiscal policies, incentives, and market mechanisms. Cross-country analysis indicated that good governance on tax issues and measures to enhance anti-tax fraud activities may foster domestic revenues and, indirectly, may help finance public investment in infrastructure, such as energy (Hutsebaut, 2015). In addition, political stability and rule of law are important for obtaining foreign direct investment, especially in large energy projects (Estrin & Uvalic, 2013; Lorena, 2010). Hence, the EU's regulations point to energy security (Tatalovic, 2017).

4.4 Empirical Studies on Renewable Energy Adoption

Empirical studies revealed the significant, but underused, potential of renewable energy in the Western Balkans. The Western Balkans have potential in solar, wind, biomass, and especially hydro energy.

Bosnia and Herzegovina has huge renewable energy potential, including geothermal, solar, and wind energy. Its dominant industry is the hydropower industry (Tokic et al., 2020). In parts of the region, its wind energy capacity factor is higher than 30% of the EU average (Tokic et al., 2020).

Serbia also has significant potential for geothermal energy that can be used for heating and cooling systems (Jocić et al., 2020).

The Western Balkan region has complex and multiple renewable energy resources. These resources must be distributed and decentralized (Goers et al., 2020). The study also highlights the need for legal frameworks to enable the exploitation of renewable sources and continuous R&D work to capture this potential in the most efficient manner (Goers et al., 2020).

While the region's clean energy projects are in the initial phases, there are several successful projects. Wind power projects have been developed in Serbia, Albania, and North Macedonia. They have the possibility to export electricity to the EU, and to attract more investments (Frieden et al., 2016).

Solar insolation is a measure of solar radiation energy received on a given surface area during a given time and has often been referred to as the "solar resource". In the West Balkans, there are complicated administrative procedures regarding solar energy.

Biomass, in particular from agricultural waste and forestry residues, is a large but underused resource that can be used for heat and power generation. Wider use of biomass is related to strong supply chains and good policies.

Large energy projects depend on better legislation in all Western Balkan countries (Caemmerer-Seibel et al., 2019). In addition, the economic transformation from a command to a market economy also affects the feasibility and the design of these projects (Jocić et al., 2020).

Hydropower has traditionally been a mainstay of the Western Balkans' electricity generation and is still a crucial element in building up renewable energies (Tokic et al., 2020). Albania and Bosnia and Herzegovina have established hydro capacity and high potentials for new developments, including small hydro projects (Tokic et al., 2020). Hydropower is a relatively mature and dispatchable source of renewable energy. Further hydropower development has constraints because of environmental reasons, including concerns about biodiversity, river health, and impacts on local people. The Drina River holds almost 200 hydroelectric generation projects; other major rivers are the Neretva and Vrbas (Tokic et al., 2020).

The trade-offs between clean electricity production and ecological conservation, on the one side, and social acceptance, on the other, are dilemmas for national policymakers in the Western Balkans. Expanding into other renewable energy technologies provides a hedge against dependence on a single technology, while easing environmental pressure on river basins.

4.5 Barriers to Renewable Energy Integration

The development of a large share of renewable energy sources, such as wind and solar, demands significant Western Balkan infrastructure improvements. The present facilities are obsolete and inflexible for the production of renewable energy (Goers et al., 2020). The technical obstacles imply stability, transmission capacity, and a lack of energy storage facilities. While connections between national energy systems are consistent, they could be improved to enable cross-border trade of renewable electricity. The production of renewable energy needs energy storage and stronger interconnections (Hutsebaut, 2015). There are integration challenges for new renewable projects (Goers et al., 2020). Investments in new technology, demand-side management, and regional planning are needed to overcome these technical obstacles and realize the full resource potential.

Even though the region has accepted the EU's energy legislation under the Energy Community Treaty, the implementation of policies in the Western Balkans faced many gaps. These gaps have been evidenced in the lack of transparency in obtaining permits and licensing. The local governance has a negative impact due to political interference, corruption, and administrative incapacity. The investors anticipate this as the absence of a clear, stable, and predictable policy framework. Therefore, they give up on long-term investments in renewable energy. The green transition must be carefully engineered to prevent it from having unwanted ramifications and to ensure that its various policy instruments are mutually supportive (Kern et al., 2018). According to Kern et al. (2018), the outcomes are largely influenced by the realities of the "real-world" policy context in existence today, which is shaped by existing legacies of goals and instruments. To overcome these deficiencies, it is important to ensure the independence of institutions, their administrative capacity, and political will and commitment to reforms. The good policy implementation is as important as good policy design when considering the acceleration of the green transition.

The Western Balkans have numerous risks and financial problems that negatively affect renewable energy projects. The cost of financing projects became higher when the government isn't stable, the rule of law isn't strong, and access to capital markets is limited. The Western Balkans still get less foreign direct investment (FDI) than other emerging economies. Although FDI has increased in the last five years. This is true because of the size of the economy and the chance of joining the EU (Estrin & Uvalic, 2013). International financial institutions and development banks are very important, but their involvement alone is not enough to meet the huge investment needs. Domestic financial institutions do not have enough resources to finance renewable energy projects, but their involvement is vital for the green transition.

As seen in other situations, taking away certain subsidies can lead to businesses closing and skilled engineers leaving, which shows how important it is to have stable and predictable support systems (Hutsebaut, 2015). There is a need for new financial tools, ways to reduce risk, and partnerships between the public and private sectors. Also, making sure that taxes are fair and that governments stick to their budgets can help them get the money they need to build infrastructure (Hutsebaut, 2015).

5 Conclusion

The Western Balkans have large renewable energy potentials, i.e., biomass, wind, solar, and geothermal, but they are underused. The basic energy resources are coal and hydropower. Therefore, the green transition is essential for the EU's integration goals and global decarbonization efforts. The Energy Community Treaty has helped in the creation of national renewable energy strategies and targets. However, practical issues concerning investment risk, corruption, and legislation remained. There is established power and multiple stakeholders involved in the Western Balkans green transition. A sustainable strategy of renewable energy requires a holistic approach. It includes various aspects such as technical, regulatory, financial, and social stakeholders. Additionally, cross-border collaboration can improve energy market efficiency. The energy security and resilience against external shocks and climate challenges can be improved by diversification of the energy mix.

5.1 Recommendations for Policymakers

To speed up the shift to renewable energy in the Western Balkans, numerous policy measures are needed.

Enable Regulatory Transparency: Simplify the process of getting permissions, efficient administration, and ensure that regulatory bodies are independent and well-resourced to build investor trust. The long-term policy has an important role (Kern et al., 2018).

Investment in New Technologies and Cross-border relationships: The main aim is to invest in smart technologies, to improve technology transfer, and to establish regional cooperation.

Diversify Financial Instruments: To minimize the risk of a large project in the renewable energy sector, policymakers should develop innovative mechanisms such as public–private partnerships, green bonds, and/or guarantees to reduce project risks and attract new investors. Additionally, they need to use most of the EU funds (IPA) for strategic energy projects.

Promote Regional Energy Cooperation, which brings better planning for renewable energy projects and technology transfers. The efficient use of renewable energy and a higher level of collective security are the main goals of cooperation (Friedan et al., 2016).

Enhance Public Engagement and Transition Planning: Policymakers need to establish strong public consultation processes for new projects and create thorough just transition strategies for regions reliant on coal. This includes retraining programs and initiatives for economic diversification.

Support Research and Development, especially in the development of renewable energy technologies, and expanding manufacturing capabilities to create domestic expertise and generate economic value (Goers et al., 2020).

5.2 Future Research Directions and Prospects for the Western Balkans' Green Transition

Several research avenues can be identified to support the Western Balkans' green transition. First, studies aim to assess the detailed socio-economic impact of the decarbonization process. The focus will be on job creation in new green sectors and the effectiveness of retraining programs. The second line of research will be to find the best regional energy mix regarding stability, storage solutions, and cross-border balancing for higher renewable energy use. Additionally, research into the political economy of energy reform, including the impact of specific lobby groups and ways to tackle political inertia, is crucial. Researchers should also conduct comparative analyses of successful renewable energy policies and market designs from other emerging economies. These studies can be used as examples of good practice.

Exploring how distributed generation and energy communities can drive rural development and local energy autonomy is one path for research (Caemmerer-Seibel et al., 2019). The institutional reforms and public–private investments are the key factors of the Western Balkans' green transition. All of these are vital for regional prosperity and ensuring European energy security (Tatalovic, 2017).

References

Adhikari, D. R., Techato, K., & Jariyaboon, R. (2024). A systematic literature review on renewable energy technologies for energy sustainability in Nepal: Key challenges and opportunities. *International Journal of Renewable Energy Development, 13*(2), 206–222. https://doi.org/10.61435/ijred.2024.60032

Akar, B. G. (2016). The Determinants of renewable energy consumption: An empirical analysis for the Balkans. *European Scientific Journal, 12* (11), 594. https://doi.org/10.19044/esj.2016.v12n11p594

Alnatheer, O. (2005). The potential contribution of renewable energy to electricity supply in Saudi Arabia. *Energy Policy, 33*(18), 2298–2312. https://doi.org/10.1016/j.enpol.2003.12.013

Baños, R., Manzano-Agugliaro, F., Montoya, F. G., Gil, C., Alcayde, A., & Gómez, J. (2011). Optimization methods applied to renewable and sustainable energy: A review. *Renewable and Sustainable Energy Reviews, 15*(4), 1753–1766. https://doi.org/10.1016/j.rser.2010.12.008

Bhattacharjee, S., & Nandi, C. (2021). Design of a voting based smart energy management system of the renewable energy based hybrid energy system for a small community. *Energy, 214*, Article 118977. https://doi.org/10.1016/j.energy.2020.118977

Bojovic, M., Mrkonjic, Z., & Vukelic, I. (2024). Agroforestry systems and forest resources as a potential for sustainable energy development in the western Balkan region. *Energy, Sustainability and Society, 14*(1), 68. https://rdcu.be/eJHSJ

Brodny, J., Tutak, M., & Grebski, W. W. (2025). A holistic assessment of sustainable energy security and the efficiency of policy implementation in emerging EU economies: A long-term perspective. *Energies, 18*(7), 1767–1807. https://doi.org/10.3390/en18071767

Caemmerer-Seibel, U., Lück, A., Osman, A., Kiesel, G., Völker, C., Alfen, H. W., & Cebulla, D. (2019). Energy transition in rural areas—Supporting local energy planning by the development of an online-tool for identification and promotion of energy-efficiency and the use of renewables. In *Building Simulation Conference proceedings* (Vol. 16, pp. 2619–2626). https://doi.org/10.26868/25222708.2019.210353

Carlisle, N., Elling, J., & Penney, T. (2008). *Renewable energy community: Key elements* (No. NREL/TP-540-42774). National Renewable Energy Lab. (NREL), Golden, CO (United States).

Carlisle, N., Van Geet, O., & Pless, S. (2009). *Definition of a 'zero net energy' community* (No. NREL/TP-7A2-46065). National Renewable Energy Lab. (NREL), Golden, CO (United States).

Cejka, S., Zeilinger, F., Veseli, A., Holzleitner, M. T., & Stefan, M. (2020, May). A blockchain-based privacy-friendly renewable energy community. In *SMARTGREENS* (pp. 95–103). https://doi.org/10.5220/0009391300950103

Denis, G. S., & Parker, P. (2009). Community energy planning in Canada: The role of renewable energy. *Renewable and Sustainable Energy Reviews, 13*(8), 2088–2095. https://doi.org/10.1016/j.rser.2008.09.030

Directive 2009/28/EC of the European Parliament and of the Council of 23 April 2009 on the promotion of the use of energy from renewable sources and amending and subsequently repealing Directives 2001/77/EC and 2003/30/EC. https://eur-lex.europa.eu/legal-content/en/TXT/?uri=celex:32009L0028 Access date September 11, 2025.

Dunjic, S., Pezzutto, S., & Zubaryeva, A. (2016). Renewable energy development trends in the Western Balkans. *Renewable and Sustainable Energy Reviews, 65*, 1026–1032. https://doi.org/10.1016/j.rser.2016.05.051

Estrin, S., & Uvalic, M. (2013, July 12). Foreign direct investment into transition economies: Are the Balkans different? LEQS Paper No. 64. Available at SSRN https://ssrn.com/abstract=2293100 or http://dx.doi.org/10.2139/ssrn.2293100

Frieden, D., Tuerk, A., Đukan, M., Ortner, A., & Lilliestam, J. (2016). Sharing the gains from EU–Western Balkan renewable electricity cooperation. *Climate Policy, 16*(5), 606–621. https://doi.org/10.1080/14693062.2016.1155041

Ghanadan, R., & Koomey, J. G. (2005). Using energy scenarios to explore alternative energy pathways in California. *Energy Policy, 33*(9), 1117–1142.

Goers, S., Rumohr, F., Fendt, S., Gosselin, L., Jannuzzi, G. M., Gomes, R. D. M., Sousa, S. M. S., & Wolvers, R. (2020). The role of renewable energy in regional energy transitions: An aggregate qualitative analysis for the partner regions Bavaria, Georgia, Québec, São Paulo, Shandong, Upper Austria, and Western Cape. *Sustainability, 13*(1), 76. https://doi.org/10.3390/su13010076

Golusin, M., Ivanovic, O. M., & Redzepagic, S. (2013). Transition from traditional to sustainable energy development in the region of Western Balkans-Current level and requirements. *Applied Energy, 101*, 182–191. https://doi.org/10.1016/j.apenergy.2012.06.008

Halili, A. (2012). Post-Lisbonian Europe: EU Foreign Policy towards the Western Balkans. *South East European University Review, 8*(2). Walter de Gruyter GmbH. https://doi.org/10.2478/v10306-012-0016-3

Hutsebaut, M. (2015). Taxation and budgetary policies in the Western Balkans. *SEER Journal, 17*(2), 207–235. Nomos Verlag. https://doi.org/10.5771/1435-2869-2014-2-207.

IEA. (2022). *IEA energy balances 2022.* International Energy Agency.

Jocić, N., Müller, J., Požar, T., & Bertermann, D. (2020). Renewable energy sources in a post-socialist transitional environment: The influence of social geographic factors on potential utilization of very shallow geothermal energy within heating systems in small Serbian town of Ub. *Applied Sciences, 10*(8), 2739. https://doi.org/10.3390/app10082739

Johnson, A. (2017). Renewable energy: Non-environmental reasons to make the transition. *Pitt Political Review*, 43–48. University Library System, University of Pittsburgh.

Karakosta, C., Flouri, M., Dimopoulou, S., & Psarras, J. (2012). Analysis of renewable energy progress in the western Balkan countries: Bosnia-Herzegovina and Serbia. *Renewable and Sustainable Energy Reviews, 16*(7), 5166–5175. https://doi.org/10.1016/j.rser.2012.04.040

Kern, F., Kivimaa, P., Rogge, K., & Rosenow, J. (2018). Policy mixes for sustainable energy transitions. In *Transitions in energy efficiency and demand* (1st ed., pp. 215–234). Routledge.

Kim, M. H., Kim, D., Heo, J., & Lee, D. W. (2019). Techno-economic analysis of hybrid renewable energy system with solar district heating for net zero energy community. *Energy, 187*, Article 115916. https://doi.org/10.1016/j.energy.2019.115916

Kontic, L., Bogavac, M., & Zivanovic, N. (2021). Renewable energy potentials in Western Balkan countries: The case of Serbia. Eco*nomic and Social Development: Book of Proceedings* (pp. 133–141).

Kontic, L., & Maksimovic, S. (2022). The Relationship between tourism, renewable energy and economic growth in Western Balkan countries. *Modern management tools and economy of tourism sector in present era* (p. 63). https://doi.org/10.31410/tmt.2022-2023.63

Kontic, L., & Vesic, D. (2024). Green transition in Serbia. *Proceedings EKONBIZ* (24).

Lalic, D., Popovski, K., Gecevska, V., Vasilevska, S. P., & Tesic, Z. (2011). Analysis of the opportunities and challenges for renewable energy market in the Western Balkan countries. *Renewable and Sustainable Energy Reviews, 15*(6), 3187–3195. https://doi.org/10.1016/j.rser.2011.04.011

Li, X. (2005). Diversification and localization of energy systems for sustainable development and energy security. *Energy Policy, 33*(17), 2237–2243. https://doi.org/10.1016/j.enpol.2004.05.002

Lorena, S. (2010). Transition process in the Western Balkans: How much successful is this story? *Intelligent Information Management, 2*(4), 243–252. https://doi.org/10.4236/iim.2010.23029

Lund, H. (2007). Renewable energy strategies for sustainable development. *Energy, 32*(6), 912–919. https://doi.org/10.1016/j.energy.2006.10.017
McCabe, A., Pojani, D., & van Groenou, A. B. (2018). Social housing and renewable energy: Community energy in a supporting role. *Energy Research & Social Science, 38*, 110–113. https://doi.org/10.1016/j.erss.2018.02.005
Mesfun, S., Leduc, S., Patrizio, P., Wetterlund, E., Mendoza-Ponce, A., Lammens, T., Staritsky, I., Elbersen, B., Lundgren, J., & Kraxner, F. (2018). Spatio-temporal assessment of integrating intermittent electricity in the EU and Western Balkans power sector under ambitious CO2 emission policies. *Energy*, 164, 676–693. https://doi.org/10.1016/j.energy.2018.09.034
Muneer, T., Asif, M., & Munawwar, S. (2005). Sustainable production of solar electricity with particular reference to the Indian economy. *Renewable and Sustainable Energy Reviews, 9*(5), 444–473.
OECD/IEA. (2008). *Energy in Western Balkans—The path to reform and recostruction.* France: Paris.
OECD. (2022). Clean energy transitions in Western Balkans: Challenges and policy recommendations. https://coilink.org/20.500.12592/tggm37
Osuma, G., & Yusuf, N. (2025). Towards an optimal renewable energy mix for the European Union: Enhancing energy security and sustainability. *Journal of the Knowledge Economy,* 1–37.
Papapostolou, A., Karakosta, C., Nikas, A., & Psarras, J. (2017). Exploring opportunities and risks for RES-E deployment under cooperation mechanisms between EU and Western Balkans: A multi-criteria assessment. *Renewable and Sustainable Energy Reviews, 80*, 519–530. https://doi.org/10.1016/j.rser.2017.05.190
Pavicevic, M., Quoilin, S., Zucker, A., Krajacic, G., Puksec, T., & Duic, N. (2020). Applying the Dispa-SET model to the Western Balkans power system. *Journal of Sustainable Development of Energy, Water and Environment Systems, 8*(1), 184–212. https://doi.org/10.13044/j.sdewes.d7.0273
Ralchev, S. (2012). *Energy in the Western Balkans: A strategic overview.* Institute for Regional and International Studies, Sofia.
Resch, G. Liebmann, L., & Geipel, J. (2017). *Assessment of the progress in the promotion and use of renewable energy in the energy community, energy community*, Final Report, 18 July 2017.
Resch, G., Liebmann, L., & Geipel, J. (2019). *Study on 2030 overall targets (energy efficiency, RES, GHG emissions reduction) for the Energy Community*, Final Report, 12 June 2019.
Sekaric, N., & Lazic, V. (2020). The Western Balkans' energy security in a triangle: The role of the EU, Russia and Turkey. In *Security challenges and the place of the Balkans and Serbia* (pp. 119–133). Institute of International Politics and Economics ; Faculty of Security Studies.
Schneider, D. R., Duic, N., Raguzin, I., Bogdan, Z., Ban, M., Grubor, B., Stefanović, P., Dakić, D., Repić, B., Stevanović, Ž., & Bakic, V. (2007). Mapping the potential for decentralized energy generation based on RES in Western Balkans. *Thermal Science, 11*(3), 7–26.
Soeiro, S., & Dias, M. F. (2020). Renewable energy community and the European energy market: Main motivations. *Heliyon, 6*(7), Article e04511. https://doi.org/10.1016/j.heliyon.2020.e04511
Tatalovic, S. (2017). Energy security EU and Western Balkans. *Security Dialogues /Безбедносни дијалози*, 1–2, 333–359. Faculty of Philosophy, Skopje.
Tausová, M., Mykhei, M., Culkova, K., Taus, P., Petrás, D., & Kaňuch, P. (2025). Development of the implementation of renewable sources in EU countries in heating and cooling, transport, and electricity. *Sustainability, 17*(2), 766. https://doi.org/10.3390/su17020766
Tokic, A., Akinci, T. C., & Zengin, A. T. (2020). Bosnia and Herzegovina's renewable energy policy and perspective. *International Journal of Energy Economics and Policy, 10*(5), 524–530.
Topalovic, Z., Haas, R., Ajanovic, A., & Hiesl, A. (2022). Economics of electric energy storage. *The Case of Western Balkans., 238*, Article 121669. https://doi.org/10.1016/j.energy.2021.121669
Van den Bergh, J. C. J. M. (2013). Policies to enhance economic feasibility of a sustainable energy transition. In *Proceedings of the national academy of sciences* (Vol. 110, Issue 7, pp. 2436–2437). Proceedings of the National Academy of Sciences. https://doi.org/10.1073/pnas.1221894110

Walker, G., & Devine-Wright, P. (2008). Community renewable energy: What should it mean? *Energy Policy, 36*(2), 497–500. https://doi.org/10.1016/j.enpol.2007.10.019

Yamamoto, Y. (2016). The role of community energy in renewable energy use and development. *Renewable Energy and Environmental Sustainability, 1*, 18. https://doi.org/10.1051/rees/2016040

Young, J., & Brans, M. (2017). Analysis of factors affecting a shift in a local energy system towards 100% renewable energy community. *Journal of Cleaner Production, 169*, 117–124. https://doi.org/10.1016/j.jclepro.2017.08.023

Zahedi, R., Zahedi, A., & Ahmadi, A. (2022). Strategic study for renewable energy policy, optimizations and sustainability in Iran. *Sustainability, 14*(4), 2418. https://doi.org/10.3390/su14042418

Zhou, W., Chengzhi, L., Zhongshi, L., Lin, L., & Hongxing, Y. (2010). Current status of research on optimum sizing of stand-alone hybrid solar-wind power generation systems. *Applied Energy, 87*(2), 380–389. https://doi.org/10.1016/j.apenergy.2009.08.012

Energy Use and Sustainable Development: Comparative Evidence from BRICS Countries

Ramesh Chandra Das and Sumita Manna

Abstract Sustainable Development Goal (SDG) is a keyword in today's lives of the common people, as well as the headache of policymakers all around the world. Maintaining good levels of sustainable development is the prime target of countries today. Having a list of indicators in computing the sustainable development index (SDI), the countries are now thinking of other indicators, such as the inclusion of the energy indicator in its computations. The present study aims to analyse the trends in all the SDG indicators, the set of development indicators, and the set of environmental indicators in BRICS nations. It then aims to go through the phase-wise analysis centering on the global financial crisis in 2008, on the changes in all the indicators across the countries. Finally, it examines the causal factors responsible for the trends in the SDI scores of the countries. It also used the 'energy factor' to see the changes in the SDI scores of the countries. The results show that the SDI scores are rising for all except China. The main factor behind the falling trends in SDI for China is the rising environmental indicators, which pull down the values of the SDI score. Regarding causality analysis, the Granger causality test results show many instances where both the economic and environmental indicators have made a causal influence on the SDI scores for South Africa, with some lesser instances in the case of Brazil, Russia, and India. Using the energy factor, the SDI scores have gone down, but the directions of causality remain unchanged.

Keywords SDG · SDI · Life expectancy · Education · DI · EI · Causality · BRICS

1 Introduction

Sustainable progress of economic and social indicators, among others, is necessary to have stable trajectories of growth and development of an economy and the economy of world. Any production and consumption activity needs all its resources to be used in an optimum manner by combining the appropriate technology. The growth of

R. C. Das (✉) · S. Manna
Department of Economics, Vidyasagar University, Midnapore, India
e-mail: ramesh051073@gmail.com

A. Akusta and M. Gün (eds.), *Financial Frontiers in Energy Markets*, Contributions to Finance and Accounting, https://doi.org/10.1007/978-3-032-16738-5_8

income of the countries and that of the world is not desirable without looking at its social and environmental consequences. The world economy in the last couple of decades has experienced a spectacular increase in income using nature's resources and environmental capacity. But the irony is that the huge growth of income has been obtained at the cost of nature. There is, thus, a conflict between economic operations and environmental and resource uses. The conflict between the ecological and economic imperatives is institutionalized in a kind of 'ideological schizophrenia', while economic growth is sacrosanct, so is the 'environment', and there exists a tacit battle for mastery between them. The post-industrial revolution era witnessed spectacular advancement in science and technology that sought to make people's lives comfortable, but at the cost of the environment. The natural fall-out of industrialization and urbanization was the destruction of forests and wetlands, exhaustion of fossil fuels, minerals, and underground water. The ozone layer in the stratosphere is getting depleted, making way for almost uninterrupted entry of harmful ultraviolet rays from the sun. Tropical rain forest, once considered the lungs of the planet, generating over 20 per cent of oxygen, is being rapidly destroyed by the wood and paper-pulp traders. Air and water are being heavily polluted.

The growth of economic activity has exceeded that of the carrying capacity of the Earth. The net effect of this inaction is the climate change of today, which has destroyed a broader part of the earth with unexpected natural disasters. The scientists and the environmental economists of today have been working hard to mitigate the problem through scientific developments and appropriate policy formulations. The necessity is to have sustainable uses of the energy resources so that there can be sustainable development all around the globe. In this respect, Our Common Future, also known as the Brundtland Report, was published in October 1987 by the United Nations through Oxford University Press. This publication was in recognition of Gro Harlem Brundtland, former Norwegian Prime Minister and Chair of the World Commission on Environment and Development.

The term 'sustainability' can be explained in the following ways- (i) the ability to be maintained at a certain rate or level, e.g. maintaining an optimal growth rate of per capita GDP, or (ii) avoidance of the depletion of natural resources to maintain an ecological balance, or, (iii) meeting the needs of the present without compromising the ability of future generations to meet their needs, or (iv) the rate of deterioration of nature's capacity should be equal to rate of renewal of such capacity.

Going back to some of the decades on the economic-environmental crises and the probable initiatives taken up by the global leaders, there are a series of developments till date on managing resources and the environmental quality in order to have sustainable development.

In actuality, institutional and scholarly interest in sustainability challenges has only gradually increased during the latter half of the twentieth century. Two books contributed to the birth of the concept of sustainable development: the book "Silent Spring" (Carson, 1962) and the book "The Limits to Growth" (Meadows et al., 1972). The first book, by Rachel Carson, the American biologist, alerted the whole world about the environmental impact caused by the use of chemical pesticides and contributed to the birth of the first global environmentalist movements. As for the second book, "The Limits to Growth," which aimed to validate the unsustainability of the economic development model used up to that moment. The Massachusetts Institute of Technology (MIT) scientists who worked on it concluded that industrialization can only go so far: sooner or later, it will exceed the critical capacity, and at that point, it will no longer be possible to intervene in the environmental consequences caused by it.

Between the release of these two volumes, there was an event that shocked the American and world public opinion: The Santa Barbara oil spill in the year 1969, one of the most serious environmental disasters in the United States, where about 100,000 barrels of crude oil were spilled into the waters and beaches of Santa Barbara. That inaction had a major impact on marine biodiversity. About 3,600 animals, including seabirds, dolphins, seals, and sea lions, died. The extensive media coverage of the event led to the formation of numerous regulations for environmental protection and the organization of many events dedicated to the environment. The most important was the famous Earth Day held on April 22, 1970, in which 20 million people participated. The following year, the president of the United Nations, Maha Thray Sithu U Thant, made the event official by putting World Earth Day on the calendar. This led to the organization of the Earth Summit in Rio de Janeiro in 1992. This conference, the largest in history in terms of number of participants, resulted in the release of five documents: The United Nations Framework Convention on Climate Change (UNFCCC), the Convention on Biological Diversity, Agenda 21, the Rio Declaration on Environment and Development, and the Forest Principles (Tokuç, 2013).

The Agenda 21 is unquestionably the most important document so far as the mission towards sustainable development is concerned (United Nations Sustainable Development, 1992). Through its 27 principles, Agenda 21 outlined a global plan of action to be attained during the twenty-first century. Moreover, already in the Preamble, it is understood that a collective effort is needed to arrive at an increasingly sustainable solution: "no nation can achieve these results alone, but together with a global partnership it will be possible". This effort, finally, must be implemented not only by the States, but also and above all by civil society (Toprak, 2013).

On the other hand, the Rio Declaration on Environment and Development, as per the United Nations General Assembly, outlines the respective rights and responsibilities of member states regarding the goals set by the Earth Summit. As in the case of Agenda 21, it outlines 27 principles, among which the main ones are: (i) the anthropocentricity of actions for the promotion of sustainable development; (ii) the importance of policy about the prevention of environmental degradation in a context of scientific uncertainty; (iii) the concept that states, although they have full sovereignty in their territories, do not have the right to harm the environment and therefore harm global rights in these issues; (iv) the eradication of poverty at the center of international policies as a fundamental factor in establishing sustainable development; (v) equal opportunities, equal rights and full participation of women; (vi) the weight of developed countries on the implementation of sustainable policies. Lastly, with the Principles of Forests as per the United Nations General Assembly, the fundamental role of forests in the preservation of the environment is recognized for the first time in history, but above all from the point of view of world economic and social well-being.

It is by virtue of the "Earth Summit" that, for the first time, the concept of sustainable development was adopted as a global concept shared by all member countries. However, 20 years later, during the United Nations Conference on Sustainable Development, held in 2012, dubbed Rio + 20, it appeared that this concept had not been implemented (Haines et al., 2012) and that it is the only way for the development model to be defined as effective and efficient (United Nations, 2012). Due to this realization, the participating states decided to begin the process of defining a set of sustainable development goals (SDGs) through the creation of a network of scholars in the field specifically created for this purpose: The Sustainable Development Solutions Network (SDSN) (Sachs, 2014). Within it, there are detailed proposals for action on the 17-point agenda, which are as follows:

Goal 1: No poverty: Goal 2: Zero hunger: Goal 3: Good health and well-being
Goal 4: Quality education: Goal 5: Gender equality: Goal 6: Clean water and sanitation
Goal 7: Affordable and clean energy: Goal 8: Decent work and economic growth
Goal 9: Industry, innovation and infrastructure: Goal 10: Reduced inequalities
Goal 11: Sustainable cities and communities: Goal 12: Responsible consumption and production
Goal 13: Climate action: Goal 14: Life below water
Goal 15: Life on land: Goal 16: Peace, justice and strong institutions
Goal 17: Partnerships for the goals

There are five central dimensions in the 17 goals: People, Prosperity, Planet, Partnership, and Peace. The intersection of these five dimensions constitutes true sustainability.

Based on the Sustainable Development Goal (SDG) Mission, the United Nations estimates the scores of the member countries depending on several key indicators. Mainly, the per capita income, education, health, carbon footprint, and material footprint are considered for the computations of the sustainable development index, the SD score. The SDG Index ranks countries based on their performance towards the United Nations Sustainable Development Goals. It is published by the UN Sustainable Development Solutions Network (SDSN) and is part of the annual Sustainable Development Report (SDR). These scores provide a data-driven tool for governments and organizations to track challenges, ensure accountability, and identify priorities for action, fostering global efforts to achieve a more sustainable future. Impacts of these scores include shaping national and international policy, spurring discussions on development gaps, and mobilizing resources for sustainable development initiatives. The policies are accordingly suggested and /or taken up by the concerned countries to uplift themselves from low scores to high scores. Not only that each country's actions have positive or negative effects on other countries' abilities to achieve the SDGs. The Spillover Index assesses such spillovers along three dimensions: environmental and social impacts embodied into trade, economy & finance, and security. A higher score means that a country causes more positive and fewer negative spillover effects (Sachs et al., 2025).

Several countries have been attempting to improve their scores in the SDI (Sustainable Development Index) on different heads of the 17 agenda, but in some countries, proper priorities are not being given in a balanced way. Armitage et al. (2020) did a bibliometric analysis on the works done by the researchers in several SDGs and found that the approach made a large difference, with little overlap in publications. They further demonstrate that different approaches can alter the resulting country rankings. Choice of search terms, how they are combined, and query structure play a role related to differing interpretations of the SDGs and viewpoints on relevance. So, the study suggested that currently available SDG rankings and tools should be used with caution at their current stage of development. Núria et al. (2021) revealed that there was an increasing participation of organizations in the research on the SDGs. The study provided the first evidence of research on the interconnections between several agendas under the SDGs, and they asserted that the results of their study could be useful for policymakers to promote a more evidence-based setting for their research agendas on SDGs. Confraria et al. (2024) have found that countries do not prioritize research on their most pressing SDG challenges, countries with unsustainable consumption patterns don't prioritize SDG12 research, and lower-income countries contribute little to SDG research, revealing global misalignment. The study has, thus, underscored the need for research priorities to be more aligned with national SDG challenges, and advocate for more research funds to be directed towards low and lower-middle-income countries.

Under the backdrop, the present study aims to compare the SDG scores across the BRICS (Brazil, Russia, India, China, South Africa) over the period 1996–2022 and recalculate the SDG scores by using energy use as an additional indicator besides the other standard indicators used by the SDSN.

2 Literature Review

According to Nabila and Suseno (2025), the role of government in reducing corruption is crucial in guiding sustainable development and managing environmental capacity. Alahdal et al. (2025) explore how environmental, social, and governance (ESG) performance supports the disclosure of sustainable development goals (SDGs). This study also looks at how regulatory quality influences this relationship, using the data from 2017 and 2022. Bisogno et al. (2025) analyse the importance of governance quality as a key factor in achieving sustainable development. The findings suggest that policymakers should prioritize outcome-oriented policies supported by strong accountability mechanisms. According to Barbier and Burgess (2021), SDG welfare gains are moderately linked to institutional quality and strongly linked to lower country risk. Countries with strong institutions and low risk tend to make more progress toward the SDGs. Adrangi and Kerr (2022), out of eight SDG indicators studied, three were strongly linked to GDP growth in BRICS countries. As the GDP increased, the death rate decreased (SDG 3), but gender equality worsened (SDG 5), and pollution levels rose (SDGs 12 and 13). This shows that focusing only on growing the economy can hurt social and environmental goals. Even though GDP is used to measure progress, it doesn't always reflect people's well-being. The study of Das et al. (2021) has observed how urbanization and non-agricultural activities in the countries are influencing environmental degradation and hindering the achievement of sustainable development. Coscieme et al. (2019), using GDP per capita as the main indicator for SDG 8 contradict the reality that endless growth is not possible on a finite planet. In the EU, GDP is not linked to employment and often negatively impacts environmental and well-being indicators. The study suggests alternative indicators for SDG 8 to ensure better alignment with all SDGs and future sustainability policies beyond 2030. Zahiri et al. (2021) investigate the effect of good governance dimension on the sustainable development index of Iran. The study takes three dimensions, political, social, and economic, to investigate the effect of good governance on the sustainable development index in the period 1997 to 2018. After estimating the econometrics model, the results show that, among the various dimensions of governance, social governance has the highest impact on Iran's sustainable development index (SDI). Leal Filho et al. (2017) proposed that the degree of urgency of some measures and explaining why the UN SDGs need to be accorded greater priority in international sustainable development research efforts. Chu et al. (2017) have opined that research in materials science is contributing to progress towards a sustainable future based on clean energy generation, transmission, and distribution, the storage of electrical and chemical energy, energy efficiency, and better energy management systems. Stojanović et al. (2016) investigate the impact of good governance on key indicators of sustainable development, and it is shown that the statistical significance, direction, and strength of the effects of good governance dimensions differ depending on the specific sustainable development indicator chosen and the country's classification or group it belongs to. This challenges the idea promoted by the post-Washington Consensus that one standard approach can address today's development issues. According to Nazar et al. (2018), given today's global challenges, the Sustainable Development Goals were introduced at a very important time. In particular, the education goals go beyond just getting children to attend and finish school- they focus on improving the quality of education so that students can develop better thinking and decision-making skills. This helps them lead better lives and positively contribute to the sustainable development of their communities.

BRICS countries have shown significant, yet varied, progress on the SDGs, with some outperforming the global average and others facing greater challenges, particularly concerning environmental issues and specific goals like Quality Education, Climate Action, and Life Below Water. The Nordic countries and European countries are far ahead of the BRICS nations in particular and the other low- and middle-income countries in general (Ali et al., 2018). The study also focused on the selected 25 top multinational companies and studied the adoption of UN SDGs through their vision and mission statements. Using the content analysis method, this study reveals that although companies in BRICS countries have been trying to adopt defined UN SDGs, important goals are missing. Chinese companies stand first while focusing on sustainable industry innovation and infrastructure, and South African companies' interest in adopting the UN SDGs appears to be very low. Overall, the results depict that important UN SDGs—'Quality Education', 'Climate Action', and 'Life Below Water'—are missing from the vision and mission statements of companies in BRICS countries. Moses et al. (2022) analysed the progress of environmental SDG implementation in BRICS and MINT (Mexico, Indonesia, Nigeria, Turkey) countries and revealed an overall implementation progress level of 64% and 62% in BRICS and MINT, respectively. They further opined that, relatively, countries in BRICS outperformed their MINT counterparts in five of the six environmental SDGs analysed. Hluszko et al. (2024) identify the primary approaches employed in the BRICS countries to address sustainability using a systematic literature review and found that a discrepancy between scientific efforts and sustainable impact data, a rising trend in sustainability management: water, urban sustainability, waste management, and suggest more application of tools as needed for the sustainable development of the countries.

The review of studies reveals a limited number of studies on the SDG performance of the BRICS nations on some specific aspects of the SDFs. No study has attempted to examine the role of energy use on the SDI scores in the group of nations. Further, the literature does not display any such studies on the BRICS nations where the causal factors behind the changing SDI scores are identified. With these limitations of the existing literature base, the present study considers certain objectives.

3 Objectives

The study aims to see the trends in the SDI scores of the BRICS nations from 1990 to 2022 using per capita energy use as the additional SDG factor. After that, the phase-wise changes are examined concerning the global financial crisis that happened in 2008. Finally, the study investigates the causal factors behind the attainment of the SDI scores.

4 Data and Methodology

The United Nations computes the sustainable development index (SDI) using three developmental indicators, per capita income, education (mean years of schooling and expected years of schooling), and health (life expectancy at birth), and two ecological impact-related indicators, per capita consumption-based CO_2 emission and per capita material footprint. The data on all the indicators are available from the World Bank database. The study computes the SDI for all five countries using the dimension indices for all five indicators with the specified minimum and maximum values for all five. The UN, in its SDSN (Sustainable Development Solutions Network) project, has attempted to measure the SD Index using two broad indices:

1. Developmental Index (DI) and
2. Ecological Impact Index (EII)

The DI has three-dimensional indices: Per capita income (I), Health (Life expectancy) (LEB), and Education (Edu). On the other hand, the EII has two-dimensional indices: Consumption-based CO_2 emissions (CO_2) and Material Footprint (MF).

Each of the dimension indices is calculated by the following formula:

$$\text{di} = (\text{Actual Value} - \text{Minimum Value}) / (\text{Maximum Value} - \text{Minimum Value})$$

The education index is computed as an average of the two indices, the mean year of schooling and expected years of schooling.

The DI is then computed as the geometric mean (GM) of I, LEB, and Edu using equal weights. Thus, the formula for DI is:

$$\text{DI} = (\text{I} \times \text{LEB} \times \text{Edu})^{1/3}$$

Similarly, using equal weights, the EI is computed under the formula:

$$\text{EI} = (\text{CO2} \times \text{MF})^{1/2}$$

The formula for SDI is computed as DI to the ratio of EI, which is:

$$\text{SDI} = \text{DI}/\text{EII}$$

Or, SDI = (GM of Health Index, Education Index, and Income Index)/ (GM of PC CO2 index and PC Material Footprint Index)

The minimum value of SDI is 0, and the maximum value is 1. It is to noting that many of the SDG 17 are not considered for computing SDI. We use 'energy use' as such an omitted factor and recalculate the SDI for all five countries in the group. This additional factor is included in the development index as it generates income. Thus, the new formula for SDI is:

$$\text{SDI} = (\text{GM of HealthIndex, Education Index, Income Index, and Energy Index}) / (\text{GM of PC CO2 index and PC Material Footprint Index})$$

The minimum value of energy use (EU) is computed to be 150.8 (Kg of oil equivalent) as of Niger's average over 1971–2022, and the maximum value is 17350 kg as of Kuwait's average annual consumption over the said period.

The study then compares the changes in the SDI after adding EUI (energy use index) as the difference between the older values with the new ones.

The trend analysis is conducted using a graph, and then a mean difference test is performed to determine whether the SDI scores, as well as their indicators, have changed significantly between the two phases: the pre-crisis phase (1990–2007) and the post-crisis phase (2008–2022).

Finally, the causality analysis is done in line with Granger (1969) to examine which indicators influenced the SDI score significantly. But to test for causality, we need to check whether the series are stationary at their levels. If not, what is the order of integration of the series? The stationary test is done by the Augmented Dickey-Fuller test, ADF (1979). The ADF test is done using the following linear regression setup for two versions–namely,

$$\Delta x_t = \alpha + \beta x_{t-1} + \sum_{j=1}^{p} \gamma_j \Delta x_{t-j} + u_t$$

for the case without a time trend and

$$\Delta x_t = \alpha + \delta \mathrm{t} + \beta x_{t-1} + \sum_{j=1}^{p} \gamma_j \Delta x_{t-j} + u_t$$

for the case with a time trend. Here $\beta = \rho - 1$.

The null hypothesis here is $\rho = 1$, which means no stationarity, which further indicates $\beta = 0$.

For a two-variable non-stationary model having I (1) properties, the Granger Causality Test is done by estimating a set of equations below with the first differenced forms of the variables, including the error correction terms for y on x and x on y (Granger, 1969). The model is:

$$\Delta y_t = v_{yx} + \sum_{j=1}^{T_{11}} \alpha_{1j} \Delta y_{t-j} + \sum_{j=1}^{T_{12}} \beta_{1j} \Delta x_{t-j} + \eta_{yx} ECY_{t-1} + u_{lt}$$

$$\Delta x_t = v_{xy} + \sum_{j=1}^{T_{21}} \alpha_{2j} \Delta y_{t-j} + \sum_{j=1}^{T_{22}} \beta_{2j} \Delta x_{t-j} + \eta_{xy} ECX_{t-1} + u_{lt}$$

where Δ is the first difference operator; $T_{l\,m}$, l, $m = 1, 2, 3$ indicates the number of lagged values of Δy and Δx ν, α, β, and η are the regression parameters; $u_{lt,}$ are the white noise disturbance terms. The coefficients η_{yx} and η_{xy} are the adjustment parameters, which are desired to be negative and significant for having significant error correction features. The direction of Granger Causality is determined by the values of the F-statistics as shown below:

$$F^* = \frac{(RSS_R - RSS_{UR})/m}{RSS_{UR}/(n-k)}$$

where,

RSS_R = Restricted residual sum square

RSS_{UR} = Unrestricted residual sum square

m = number of lagged Δy terms or number of lagged Δy terms.

The decision criteria of the test are as follows-

1. If $\beta_{1j} = 0$, for all j and $\eta_{yx} = 0$, x is said not to cause y. 2. If $\alpha_{2j} = 0$ for all j and $\eta_{xy} = 0$, y is said not to Granger cause x. 3. If (1) holds but (2) does not, Granger causality is said to be unidirectional from y to x. 4. Conversely, if (1) does not hold but (2) does, Granger causality is said to be unidirectional from x to y. 5. If both (1) and (2) do not hold then the Granger causality between x and y is said to be bi-directional or feedback, and 6. If both (1) and (2) hold, then there appears to be no Granger causality between x and y.

5 Results and Analysis

5.1 *Trends of the Indicators*

Let us first see the trends of all the indicators used in computing the SDI score of a country, with energy use (EU) as the additional indicator. Figure 1 presents the same in its different panels. It is observed that the series for life expectancy, expected and mean years of schooling, per capita income, per capita CO2 emission, and per capita material footprint are rising, which means the key indicators of SDI are increasing over the years. China leads in life expectancy, with South Africa at the bottom. Brazil, Russia, and South Africa lead the education indicators, while India is in the trough. The fallacy is that the countries' expected years of schooling are greater than their mean years of schooling, implying the students are not turning up to the highest level of education. The trends for income are rising for all, with Russia ranking top and India ranking 5.

With respect to CO2 emission and material footprint, the trends are found to be upward sloping, with China leading the group in both, while India remains in the bottom. The trends of SDI score with or without Energy as a factor are thus rising in all except China. The trends of SDI for China are downward sloping. In the first phase, i.e., in 1990–2007, Brazil and China remain in the top ladder while South Africa beats all of the rest members during the second phase, even its rate of growth of the SDI score is highest. After inclusion of Energy as the indicator, the SDI scores of all the countries have gone down, i.e. the new SDI (with Energy variable) trends lie below the old SDI (without Energy variable), but the trends on the change in the SDI gap (the difference between new and old) went down for Russia, South Africa and India while that of China and Brazil had gone up (the bottom right panel of the figure). The falling values of the SDI score after the introduction of the Energy factor are obvious, as high energy consumption, especially from non-renewable sources, reduces SDG scores because it causes climate change and environmental degradation, impacting

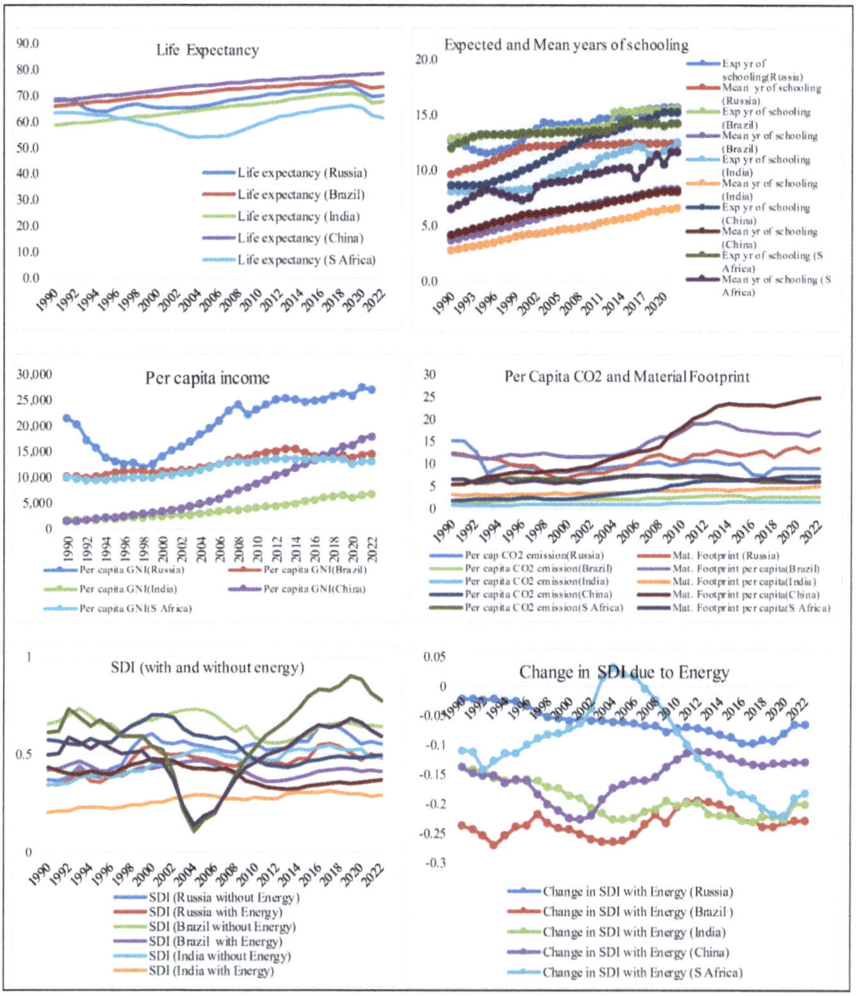

Fig. 1 Trends of all the series. *Source* Drawn by the authors

multiple goals. These impacts include higher greenhouse gas emissions, pollution, and resource depletion, which counteract efforts to achieve goals related to climate action (SDG 13), responsible consumption and production (SDG 12), and clean air and water (SDG 6). Excessive, unsustainable energy consumption hinders progress in areas like poverty (SDG 1), health (SDG 3), and infrastructure (SDG 9), even as it fuels economic growth. The results go well with the observations of Pan et al. (2023).

5.2 Phase-Wise Changes in the Indicators

Let us come to the quantitative assessments of the average and dispersion values of the indicators across two different phases and their statistical differences. It is observed from Table 1 that the average values of all the indicators have significantly increased from the pre-crisis phase to the post-crisis phase for Brazil, India, and China, as the estimated 't' values are significantly high to reject the hypothesis of 'equal means'. It signifies that the key indicators of SDG have increased to produce larger magnitudes of the SDI scores.

But the scenarios for Russia and South Africa are a little bit different, Russia's per capita CO2 emission has gone down significantly in post post-global financial crisis phase. On the other hand, South Africa has experienced no significant changes in life expectancy, per capita CO2 emission, and per capita material footprint in the two phases, making the series with some sort of static behaviour.

So far, we have analysed the results derived for the first two objectives, the trend analysis and phase-wise change analysis of the indicators. Now it is the turn to analyse the final objective of the study, which is on the investigations of the causal factors behind the attainment of the SDI scores in the BRICS countries.

5.3 Unit Root Test Results

As has been discussed in the methodology section that the causality analysis requires primarily the investigation of the nature of the series, whether there are stochastic components within themselves. In particular, whether the series is stationary or is free from unit root problems. To check it, we have used the ADF test technique. The results of the test are given in Table 2.

It is observed that all the series of all the countries except China are stationary at their first differences, as the ADF test statistics have relatively bigger values, with the probabilities below 0.05. All the series are integrated of order one [I(1)]. The case for China is different as most of its indicators are stationary at their second differences, its series are integrated of order 2 [(I(2)]. Therefore, we use the set of causality test equations as per Granger (1969) for I(1) variables in the case of Brazil, Russia, India, and South Africa, while for China, the I(2) values of the variables are considered.

It is a natural question here why we did not go through the cointegration tests. As the SDI score is generated from all these indicators, it is a common outcome that they will be cointegrated with the SDI scores. Thus, the cointegration test is bypassed.

Table 1 Comparative analysis of SDG indicators: mean and variability analysis (1990–2007 vs 2008–2022)

	Energy use	Life expectancy	Exp yr of schooling	Mean yr of schooling	Per capita GNI	Per cap CO2 emission	Per cap Mat. Footprint
	Russia						
Mean (1990–2007)	4616.413	66.126	12.824	11.311	16,439.474	9.895	9.524
Mean (2008–2022)	5027.390	71.174	14.991	12.371	25,118.136	9.524	12.327
SD (1990–2007)	579.496	1.392	1.039	0.964	3490.255	2.161	1.803
SD (2008–2022)	297.696	1.700	0.546	0.032	1377.446	1.005	0.851
t (Mean diff)	2.622	9.211	7.668	4.662	9.683	-0.649	5.858
	Brazil						
Mean (1990–2007)	1066.602	69.216	13.316	5.043	11,169.166	1.955	12.052
Mean (2008–2022)	1408.952	73.880	14.893	7.549	14,456.929	2.627	17.430
SD (1990–2007)	95.171	1.997	0.247	0.894	883.843	0.265	0.827
SD (2008–2022)	64.160	0.839	0.766	0.572	574.006	0.173	1.113
t (Mean diff)	12.277	9.001	7.647	9.738	12.860	8.755	15.494
	India						
Mean (1990–2007)	382.554	62.130	8.527	3.807	2476.328	0.874	3.311
Mean (2008–2022)	604.799	68.622	11.442	5.752	5326.636	1.396	4.406
SD (1990–2007)	38.689	2.268	0.650	0.653	568.656	0.081	0.235
SD (2008–2022)	66.788	1.629	0.700	0.583	1072.764	0.145	0.297
t (Mean diff)	11.393	9.543	12.301	9.036	9.263	12.439	11.586
	China						
Mean (1990–2007)	989.601	71.397	9.840	5.507	3388.890	2.528	8.764
Mean (2008–2022)	2180.643	76.874	14.006	7.396	12,665.218	6.327	21.689
SD (1990–2007)	260.129	2.210	1.250	0.765	1559.531	0.663	2.235
SD (2008–2022)	299.067	1.133	0.929	0.557	3431.519	0.827	3.194

(continued)

Table 1 (continued)

	Energy use	Life expectancy	Exp yr of schooling	Mean yr of schooling	Per capita GNI	Per cap CO2 emission	Per cap Mat. Footprint
t (Mean diff)	12.079	9.165	10.964	8.187	9.671	14.353	13.208
	South Africa						
Mean (1990–2007)	2286.126	59.035	13.124	7.948	10,546.557	6.582	6.376
Mean (2008–2022)	2319.737	62.387	13.974	10.256	13,348.727	6.558	6.737
SD (1990–2007)	131.938	3.670	0.379	0.768	1071.057	0.453	0.594
SD (2008–2022)	229.871	3.079	0.380	0.782	305.590	0.470	0.522
t (Mean diff)	0.502	2.853	6.410	8.514	10.594	-0.150	1.855

Source Authors' computations

Table 2 Unit root test results for SDI and its associated indicators

	Energy use Index	Life expectancy Index	Education Index	Per capita GNI Index	Per cap CO2 emission Index	Per cap Mat. Footprint Index	SDI (Without Energy)	SDI (With Energy)
Brazil	−6.18 (0.00)	−5.28 (0.00)	−5.03 (0.00)	4.62 (0.00)	−5.78 (0.00)	−3.90 (0.01)	−4.64 (0.00)	−4.48 (0.00)
Russia	−4.58 (0.00)	−3.29 (0.01)	−6.26 (0.00)	−3.31 (0.03)	−4.91 (0.00)	−4.83 (0.00)	−4.80 (0.00)	−4.68 (0.00)
India	−3.03 (0.05)	−4.95 (0.00)	−3.58 (0.00)	−4.99 (0.00)	−5.32 (0.00)	−5.37 (0.00)	−5.61 (0.00)	−5.82 (0.00)
China	−2.98 (0.05)	−5.12 (0.00)	−4.91 (0.00)*	−4.94 (0.00)*	−4.85 (0.00)*	−5.30 (0.00)*	−3.08 (0.04)	−3.40 (0.01)
South Africa	−5.77 (0.00)	−3.87 (0.01)	−7.90 (0.00)	−4.98 (0.00)	−4.32 (0.00)	−6.28 (0.00)	−3.01 (0.05)	−2.98 (0.04)

Note * marks indicate I(2) series for China; all the results are given for first difference tests, the level series of the variables are nonstationary and are not shown in the table to avoid space issues
Source Authors' computations

5.4 Causality Test Results

The study runs a pair-wise Granger causality test for the indicators having SDI scores under 'without energy' and 'with energy' situations. The paired null hypotheses are, for example, Energy use does not cause SDI score, and SDI score does not cause Energy use. The respective F-statistics are computed with the probability values under optimum lags. The results are given in Table 3.

Table 3 Granger causality test results

	Energy use Index to SDI (With Energy)	SDI (With Energy) to Energy use Index	Life expectancy Index to SDI (Without Energy)	SDI (Without Energy) to Life expectancy Index	Life expectancy Index to SDI (With Energy)	SDI (With Energy) to Life expectancy Index	Education Index to SDI (Without Energy)	SDI (Without Energy) to Education Index
Brazil	0.69 (0.52) lag 3	1.46 (0.25)	0.46 (0.58) lag 3	0.18 (0.67)	0.56 (0.64) lag 3	0.15 (0.93)	0.28 (0.59) lag 1	4.14 (0.05)*
Russia	0.92 (0.40) lag 2	4.67 (0.01)*	1.99 (0.14) lag 3	0.58 (0.63)	1.68 (0.19) lag 3	0.63 (0.61)	3.15 (0.05) lag 2*	3.80 (0.04)*
India	0.51 (0.68) lag 3	0.26 (0.85)	0.75 (0.54) lag 3	1.11 (0.36)	0.53 (0.47) lag 3	1.72 (0.21)	1.17 (0.35) lag 3	0.78 (0.51)
China	1.57 (0.22) lag 2	6.44 (0.00)*	0.58 (0.63) lag 3	1.16 (0.34)	0.49 (0.69)	0.94 (0.43)	3.56 (0.03)* lag 3	0.98 (0.43)
South Africa	1.61 (0.21) lag 3	4.93 (0.00)*	7.52 (0.00) lag 2*	0.02 (0.97)	8.3 (0.00)* lag 2	0.05 (0.94)	1.91 (0.15) lag 3	0.28 (0.83)
	Education Index to SDI (With Energy)	SDI (With Energy) to Education Index	Income Index to SDI (Without Energy)	SDI (Without Energy) to Income Index	Income Index to SDI (With Energy)	SDI (With Energy) to Income Index	CO2 Index to SDI (Without Energy)	SDI (Without Energy) to CO2 Index
Brazil	0.21 (0.65) lag 1	3.98 (0.05)*	2.96 (0.07)* lag 1	3.12 (0.06)*	2.9 (0.06)* lag 2	1.75 (0.18)	0.14 (0.93) lag 3	0.98 (0.41)
Russia	1.38 (0.25) lag 2	3.14 (0.05)*	0.29 (0.81) lag 2	7.28 (0.00)*	0.41 (0.66) lag 2	5.99 (0.00)*	1.88 (0.16) lag 3	0.96 (0.42)
India	1.74 (0.18) lag 3	0.53 (0.66)	3.08 (0.05)* lag 2	0.67 (0.52)	1.53 (0.24) lag 2	0.87 (0.42)	0.37 (0.77) lag 3	2.08 (0.13)
China	3.1 (0.05)* lag 3	1.11 (0.36)	0.62 (0.63) lag 3	0.67 (0.57)	0.92 (0.44) lag 3	0.49 (0.68)	2.86 (0.07)* lag 1	0.11 (0.73)

(continued)

Table 3 (continued)

	Energy use Index to SDI (With Energy)	SDI (With Energy) to Energy use Index	Life expectancy Index to SDI (Without Energy)	SDI (Without Energy) to Life expectancy Index	Life expectancy Index to SDI (With Energy)	SDI (With Energy) to Life expectancy Index	Education Index to SDI (Without Energy)	SDI (Without Energy) to Education Index
South Africa	1.44 (0.21) lag 3	0.17 (0.91)	2.98 (0.05)* lag 3	5.02 (0.00)*	5.4 (0.02)* lag 1	11.39 (0.00)*	4.44 (0.02)* lag 2	4.28* (0.02)
	CO2 Index to SDI (With Energy)	SDI (With Energy) to CO2 Index	Material Index to SDI (Without Energy)	SDI (Without Energy) to Material Index	Material Index to SDI (With Energy)	SDI (With Energy) to Material Index		
Brazil	0.35 (0.79) lag 3	1.32 (0.29)	1.22 (0.32) lag 3	1.61 (0.21)	1.05 (0.41) lag 2	1.56 (0.22)		
Russia	1.12 (0.36) lag 3	0.89 (0.45)	0.24 (0.86) lag 3	4.32 (0.01)*	0.16 (0.92) lag 3	3.87 (0.02)*		
India	0.32 (0.57) lag 1	3.82 (0.05)*	1.47 (0.24) lag 3	2.97 (0.05)*	0.53 (0.47) lag 1	3.87 (0.05)*		
China	3.1 (0.05)* lag 1	0.62 (0.43)	0.20 (0.89) lag 3	0.38 (0.76)	0.16 (0.91) lag 3	0.49 (0.68)		
South Africa	3.5 (0.04)* lag 2	4.04 (0.02)*	8.03 (0.00)* lag 2	2.98 (0.05)*	6.4 (0.00)* lag 2	3.15 (0.05)*		

Note * marks indicate significant results. The figures left to parentheses represent the computed F statistic, and the figures in parentheses indicate the probability values

Source Authors' computations

The results, as observed from the table, show that in the majority of the instances, the significant causal influences in either direction are observed in the case of South Africa, followed by Russia. China and India have the lowest numbers of such causal interplays. Life expectancy makes a cause to the SDI score, both without and with the energy factor, in the case of South Africa. Again, education is the cause of SDI (without energy) for Russia and China, while for China, the causal influence of education also works for SDI (with energy). Again, income is the cause of the SDI score, both without and with the energy factor, in the case of both Brazil and South Africa, while for India, there is the result of causation from education to SDI (without energy only). Further, CO2 emission is a cause of the SDI score, both without and with the energy factor, in the case of China and South Africa. The declining trends in the SDI scores of China might be due to the increasing per capita carbon emissions. The positive causal effects of all the factors related to the development index (DI) and downward trends in CO2 and material footprint (refer to Fig. 1) have worked well for South Africa in improving its SDI scores.

Therefore, it can be inferred that the rising developmental indicators, life expectancy, education, and income, and in some cases, moderately increasing trends in carbon and material footprint, have resulted in rising scores of SDI for South Africa, Brazil, Russia, and India, except China. Further, the introduction of the energy factor into the calculations of the SDI scores has come up with declining scores in SDI scores in all countries, as these countries mostly use non-renewable fossil fuels, which are responsible for environmental pollution and thereby reduce the sustainable development score of these countries.

6 Conclusion

The study had its objectives in analysing the trends in all the SDG indicators, the set of development indicators, and the set of environmental indicators in the BRICS nations. It then went through the phase-wise analysis of the changes in all the indicators across the countries. Finally, it went on to examine the causal factors responsible for the trends in the SDI scores of the countries. It also used the 'energy factor' to see the changes in the SDI scores of the countries. The results show that the SDI scores are rising for all except China. The main factor behind the falling trends in SDI for China is the rising environmental indicators, which pull down the values of the SDI score. Regarding causality analysis, the results show many instances where both the economic and environmental indicators have had a causal influence on the SDI scores for South Africa, with some lesser instances in the case of Brazil, Russia, and India. Using the energy factor, the SDI scores have gone down, but the directions of causality remain unchanged.

The governments in the countries, as well as the private corporations and civil societies in the BRICS countries, should focus on initiating measures to increase the developmental indicators, such as health and sector development, and invite green energies to reduce carbon and material footprints on the earth to increase SDI scores like those of the Nordic countries.

References

Adrangi, B., & Kerr, L. (2022). Sustainable development indicators and their relationship to GDP: Evidence from emerging economies. *Sustainability, 14*(2), 658. https://doi.org/10.3390/su14020658

Alahdal, W. M., Abidin, A. F. Z., Sahu, M., Alamoudi, M. A., & Hashim, H. A. (2025). Exploring the moderating effect of regulatory quality on the relationship between ESG performance and SDGs disclosure: Evidence from OECD countries. *Sustainable Development*. https://doi.org/10.1002/sd.70061

Ali, S., Hussain, T., Zhang, G., Nurunnabi, M., & Li, B. (2018). The implementation of sustainable development goals in "BRICS" countries. *Sustainability, 10*(7), 2513. https://doi.org/10.3390/su10072513

Armitage, C. S., Lorenz, A. M., & Mikki, S. (2020). Mapping scholarly publications related to the Sustainable Development Goals: Do independent bibliometric approaches get the same results? *Quantitative Science Studies, 1*(3), 1092–1108.

Barbier, E. B., & Burgess, J. C. (2021). Institutional quality, governance and progress towards the SDGs. *Sustainability, 13*(21), 11798. https://doi.org/10.3390/su132111798

Bisogno, M., Cuadrado Ballesteros, B., Manes Rossi, F., & Peña Miguel, N. (2025). Governance quality and the sustainable development goals: An assessment in Europe. *Journal of Public Budgeting, Accounting & Financial Management, 37*(6), 193–219. https://doi.org/10.1108/JPBAFM-01-2025-0018

Carson, R. (1962). *Silent spring* (1st ed.). Fawcett World Library.

Chu, S., Cui, Y., & Liu, N. (2017). The path towards sustainable energy. *Nature Materials, 16*, 16–22.

Confraria, H., Ciarli, T., & Noyons, E. (2024). Countries' research priorities in relation to the Sustainable Development Goals. *Research Policy, 53*(3), Article 104950. https://doi.org/10.1016/j.respol.2023.104950

Coscieme, L., Mortensen, L. F., Anderson, S., Ward, J., Donohue, I., & Sutton, P. C. (2019). Going beyond gross domestic product as an indicator to bring coherence to the sustainable development goals. *Journal of Cleaner Production, 248*, Article 119232. https://doi.org/10.1016/j.jclepro.2019.119232

Das, R. C., Chatterjee, T., & Ivaldi, E. (2021). Sustainability of urbanization, non-agricultural output and air pollution in the world's top 20 polluting countries. *Data, 6*, 65.

Haines, A., Alleyne, G., Kickbusch, I., & Dora, C. (2012). From the Earth Summit to Rio+20: Integration of health and sustainable development. *The Lancet, 379*(9832), 2189–2197.

Hluszko, C., Alexis, D., Huarachi, R., Ines, M., Ulloa, C., Salvador, R., Puglieri, F. N., & de Francisco, A. C. (2024). How do the BRICS approach sustainable concerns? A systematic literature review. *Environmental Development, 52*, Article 101075. https://doi.org/10.1016/j.envdev.2024.101075

Leal Filho, W., Azeiteiro, U., Alves, F., Pace, P., Mifsud, M., Brandli, L., Caeiro, S. S., & Disterheft, A. (2017). Reinvigorating the sustainable development research agenda: The role of the sustainable development goals (SDG). *International Journal of Sustainable Development & World Ecology, 25*(2), 131–142.

Meadows, D. H., Meadows, D. L., Randers, J., & Behrens, W. W., III. (1972). *The limits to growth*. Universe Books.

Moses, O., Nnam, I. J., Olaniyan, J. D. & Tariquzzaman, ATM. (2022). Sustainable Development Goals (SDGS): Assessment of implementation progress in BRICS and MINT. In Tauringana &

Moses (Eds.), *Environmental sustainability and agenda 2030: Efforts, progress and prospects*. Emerald.
Nabila, S. N. R., & Suseno, D. A. (2025). Good governance and sustainable development index in Indonesia: Panel data evidence from 34 provinces. *Paradoks: Jurnal Ilmu Ekonomi, 8*(4), 361–373. https://doi.org/10.57178/paradoks.v8i4.1768
Nazar, R., Chaudhry, I. S., Ali, S., & Faheem, M. (2018). Role of quality education for Sustainable Development Goals (SDGS). *People International Journal of Social Sciences, 4*(2), 486–501. https://doi.org/10.20319/pijss.2018.42.486501
Núria, B-P., Marta, A. A., Susana, L., Ulisses, A., & Rodrigo, C. (2021). Unveiling the research landscape of sustainable development goals and their inclusion in higher education institutions and research centers: Major trends in 2000–2017. *Frontiers in Sustainability, 2*. https://www.frontiersin.org/journals/sustainability/articles/10.3389/frsus.2021.620743
Sachs, J. D. (2014). *The age of sustainable development*. Columbia University Press.
Sachs, J. D., Lafortune, G., Fuller, G., & Iablonovski, G. (2025). *Financing sustainable development to 2030 and mid-century. Sustainable development report 2025*. SDSN, Dublin: Dublin University Press. https://doi.org/10.25546/111909
Stojanović, I., Ateljević, J., & Stević, R. S. (2016). Good governance as a tool of sustainable development. *European Journal of Sustainable Development, 5*(4), 558. https://doi.org/10.14207/ejsd.2016.v5n4p558
Tokuç A. (2013). Earth Summit. In S. O. Idowu, N. Capaldi, L. Zu, & A. D. Gupta (Eds.), *Encyclopedia of corporate social responsibility*. Springer. https://doi.org/10.1007/978-3-642-28036-8_17
Toprak, Z. (2013). Agenda21 (UN). In S. O. Idowu, N. Capaldi, L. Zu, & A. D. Gupta (Eds.), *Encyclopedia of corporate social responsibility*. Springer. https://doi.org/10.1007/978-3-642-28036-8_246
United Nations. (2012). *The future we want*. Outcome document on Sustainable Development. Rio de Janeiro, Brazil, 20–22 June 2012.
United Nations Sustainable Development. (1992). AGENDA 21. United Nations Conference on Environment & Development Rio de Janerio, Brazil, 3 to 14 June.
Zahiri, M., Zaianderoodi, M., & Jalaee, S. A. (2021). Investigating the effect of good governance dimensions on the sustainable development index of Iran. *Macroeconomics Research Letter, 15*(30), 210–231. https://doi.org/10.22080/iejm.2021.20090.1809

Determinants of Energy-Based CO_2 Emissions: A Panel Data Analysis for OECD Countries

Azize Kahramani Koç and Osman Nuri Akarsu

Abstract This study explicates the determinants of per capita CO_2 emissions utilizing panel data from 37 OECD countries over the period 2020–2024. The analysis commences with testing for cross-sectional dependence (CSD), which was confirmed for all variables, leading to the application of the 2nd-generation unit root tests (CADF, CIPS) to verify the stationarity of the series. Subsequently, Westerlund's panel cointegration test established a long-term equilibrium relationship between per capita CO_2 emissions and economic growth, annual average precipitation, renewable energy production share, total energy consumption, carbon intensity, Brent oil prices, and the US dollar exchange rate. However, the relatively short time dimension ($T = 5$) substantially limits the robustness and reliability of long-run coefficient estimates. Therefore, the analysis focuses on short-term dynamics rather than long-term estimations. Estimations conducted employing the Generalized Method of Moments (GMM) revealed that economic growth, energy consumption, precipitation, and the US dollar exchange rate exert statistically significant positive effects on emissions, while renewable energy, despite displaying the expected negative sign, was not statistically significant. The findings reveal that energy consumption, macroeconomic indicators, and climatic variables are strong determinants of CO_2 emissions, highlighting the need for policy measures focused on energy efficiency, enhancing the effectiveness of renewable energy sources, and reducing carbon intensity.

Keywords CO_2 emissions · Energy consumption · Economic growth · Climate variables · Panel data analysis

A. K. Koç (✉) · O. N. Akarsu
The Faculty of Economics and Administrative Sciences, Kafkas University, Kars, Türkiye
e-mail: azize.kahraman@kafkas.edu.tr

A. Akusta and M. Gün (eds.), *Financial Frontiers in Energy Markets*, Contributions to Finance and Accounting, https://doi.org/10.1007/978-3-032-16738-5_9

1 Introduction

Energy consumption (EC) has assumed a significant role in environmental quality, human well-being, and the achievement of sustainable development in recent years (Saidi & Hammami, 2015). Energy is a critical input that supports economic development (Beşer & Beşer, 2017; Sahir & Qureshi, 2007) and promotes productivity, particularly in developed countries (Apergis & Tang, 2013). Andrews (2005) defined energy as "a strategic resource that affects and legitimizes the outcomes of wars, promotes economic development, and both pollutes and cleans the environment."

Since the onset of the Industrial Revolution, the global economy has experienced a significant rise in CO_2 emissions because of rising industrial production and EC (Rode et al., 2021). The recent increase in CO_2 emissions has led to environmental and ecological issues, according to Xiufan and Decheng (2024), with a major focus on climate change caused by excessive CO_2 emissions, as highlighted by Sharif et al. (2019). CO_2 emissions primarily result from actions, like the utilization of non-renewable energy resources (RER) and deforestation, as stated by Ma and Zhu in 2024.

Furthermore, there is a discussion that low-carbon energy systems can have effects in terms of economic growth and creating job opportunities (Proença & Fortes, 2020). Policies promoting energy bring advantages like sustainable development and more job options while also reducing emissions and lessening reliance on fossil fuel imports (Akella et al., 2009). Numerous nations encounter challenges in cutting down CO_2 emissions as energy usage rises alongside expanding trade and rapid economic development (Selmey et al., 2024). As a result of this trend shift, towards renewable (Saleh & Hassan, 2023) low low-carbon alternatives and sustainable energy sources have become more prominent (Luo et al., 2024). The focus is increasingly shifting towards moving from fossil fuels to carbon–neutral energy sources (Boretti, 2024).

The study employs Westerlund's panel cointegration test to establish the enduring connection between per capita CO_2 emissions and the variables not dependent on it, after which the Generalized Method of Moments (GMM) is utilized to explore the connections among dependent and independent factors. Per capita CO2 emissions are regarded as the focus of study in this research. Factors such as economic growth rate, along with annual average precipitation, are considered alongside the proportion of renewable energy production and overall energy usage to understand their impact. Additionally included are measurements for carbon intensity well as Brent oil prices and the exchange rate of the US dollar to provide a comprehensive analysis framework. The study begins by examining sectional dependencies and then moves on to conducting 2nd-generation unit root tests for further insights. The connection between energy usage development and ecological durability has evolved into a complex and widely discussed subject within the realm of environmental economics literature. At this moment in time, this research intends to examine the factors influencing CO_2 emissions per person by analyzing data from 37 OECD nations spanning from 2020 to 2024.

The rest of this research is as follows: Part 2 reviews the related literature. Part 3 describes the data structure and model. Part 4 explores the methodology and results. Part 5 offers an analysis of the findings and conclusions included in this study.

2 Literature Review

With globalization, climate change has posed numerous threats to a sustainable future, leading to heightened concerns. Raising societal awareness to reduce CO_2 emissions, a fundamental condition for ensuring social and environmental well-being, has become a critical issue. In this context, the literature includes numerous studies examining the impact of per capita CO_2 emissions on various variables.

Grimaud and Rougé (2005) emphasized the importance of focusing on RER over fossil fuels in studies of economic growth and energy systems. Similarly, Shafiei and Salim (2014) noted that consumption of RER reduced CO_2 emissions, while fossil fuel consumption increased them. Akın (2014) identified production levels as a significant factor in emission increases. Sharif et al. (2019) argued that renewable energy mitigated environmental degradation. To reduce CO_2 emissions, Wang (2015b) and Sharif et al. (2023) highlighted the importance of clean EC, while Chen et al. (2022) emphasized increasing renewable energy usage. From a different perspective, Deka and Dube (2021) demonstrated that RER not only reduced emissions but also promoted currency appreciation. Thus, transitioning to renewable energy is essential for achieving net-zero carbon goals and strengthening national currencies.

Wang et al. (2023) found that energy security had a negative long-term effect on CO_2 emissions, while economic policy uncertainty had a positive effect, with government ecological expenditures showing short-term impacts. Selmey et al. (2024) underscored the significant impact of EC and economic policies in determining CO_2 emissions. Li et al. (2024) argued that implementing policies to promote renewable energy could achieve both economic benefits and a stable net-zero carbon outcome.

Begum et al. (2015) reported that EC and per capita GDP had positive long-term effects on per capita CO_2 emissions, while population growth had no significant impact. Zhigolli and Fetai (2024) identified a negative association between CO_2 emissions and GDP, and a positive association with EC. Audi (2024) found strong correlations between emissions and urban population, GDP per capita, trade, and population density. Kumar and Sen (2025) demonstrated that CO_2 emissions were inefficient in large and densely populated cities.

Saribayevich et al. (2024) highlighted the importance of increasing forest cover, sustainable urbanization, and clean energy use to reduce CO_2 emissions. Wang and Cui (2022) noted that expanding forest areas to increase oxygen levels could lower emissions. Alsabbagh (2025) showed that increases in population and economic growth elevated fuel consumption, thereby increasing transport-related energy usage and CO_2 emissions.

Table 1 General information on variables

Abbreviation	Description	Source
Per Capita CO_2 Emissions (PCCE)	The level of CO_2 emissions per person, calculated by dividing total emissions by population (tons/person)	Our World in Data
Per Capita Gross Domestic Product (PCGDP)	The ratio of economic output to population, representing average income per person (USD/person)	Our World in Data
Annual Average Precipitation (AAP)	The long-term average of annual precipitation in a given region (mm)	Our World in Data
Renewable Energy Production Share (REPS)	The proportion of RER in total energy production (%)	Our World in Data
Total Energy Consumption (TEC)	The total EC of a country/region (typically in TWh or Mtoe)	Our World in Data
Carbon Intensity (CI)	The level of CO_2 emitted per unit of economic output (GDP) serves as an indicator of energy efficiency and environmental impact	Our World in Data
Brent Oil Price (BrP)	The price per barrel of Brent crude oil, a reference in international markets (USD/barrel)	Bloomberght
Dollar Exchange Rate (USD)	The value of national currency in US dollars, an indicator of macroeconomic stability	Bloomberght

Kassouri et al. (2022) found that oil supply shocks did not reduce CO_2 emissions and that increases create uncertainty. Saadaoui and Boufateh (2023) reported that emissions were negatively affected when uncertainty was low but positively affected when uncertainty was high. Barrales-Ruiz and Neudörfer (2024) demonstrated that oil price increases reduced emissions when driven by supply-side factors but increased emissions when caused by economic activity shocks.

3 Data and Model Specification

The dataset forming the basis of this study comprises data from Our World in Data and Bloomberght, over the period 2020–2024. The variables used in the analysis include per capita CO_2 emissions, Brent oil prices, US dollar exchange rate, per capita GDP, annual average precipitation, renewable energy production share, total EC, and carbon intensity (Table 1).

PCCE is regarded as the dependent variable in the model. PCGDP, AAP, REPS, TEC, CI, BrP, and USD are utilized as independent variables. The structural relationship among these variables is expressed mathematically in Eq. (1):

$$LPCCE_t = \beta_0 + \beta_1 LPCGDP_t + \beta_2 LAAP_t + \beta_3 LREPS_t + \beta_4 LTEC_t + \beta_5 LCI_t + \beta_6 LBrP_t + \beta_7 LUSD_t + e_t \quad (1)$$

In this study, LPCCE serves as the dependent variable. LPCGDP, LAAP, LREPS, LTEC, LCI, LBrP, and LUSD are the independent variables incorporated into the model. β_0 represents the constant term. β1–β7 indicate the effect of a 1% increase in LPCGDP, LAAP, LREPS, LTEC, LCI, LBrP, and LUSD, respectively, on LPCCE. A positive effect is expected for each of the six independent variables. The subscript t denotes that the variables are time series, with t = 2020–2024 (annual data). t represents the error term of the model.

4 Empirical Methodology and Results

The analysis process consists of four main stages. CSD is examined, and the stationarity properties are tested using appropriate unit root tests for panel data in the first stage. In the second stage, the existence of a cointegration among independent variables is investigated. In the third stage, short-term coefficient estimates are analyzed and evaluated using the GMM. The methods applied and the findings obtained are presented within the framework of these stages in the subsequent sections of the study.

Under this section, the results obtained from tests conducted using the Python programming language are evaluated.

4.1 Cross-Sectional Dependence (CSD) Test Results

The data set includes a limited number of observations. Due to the poor data availability, the dataset is not able to meet the assumptions of regression analysis. Therefore, the Wilcoxon signed-rank test (Wilcoxon et al., 1963), one of the non-parametric statistical hypothesis tests, is used to investigate the difference in companies' competitiveness, profitability, and market value indicators before and after implementing supply chain finance practices.

CSD assumes that a shock in one country does not affect others. However, globalization, trade-financial integration, information flows, and common shocks increase this interdependence (Menyah et al., 2014). Therefore, in panel data analyses, CSD should be tested first, as first-generation tests may produce biased outcomes otherwise (Breusch & Pagan, 1980; Pesaran, 2004). The choice of test depends on panel dimensions: Breusch–Pagan LM is suitable when T is large and N is small; Pesaran (2004) scaled LM or LMadj (Pesaran & Yamagata, 2008) is appropriate in case of both large N and T; and Pesaran (2004) CD test is optimal when N is large and T is small or medium (See Table 2).

The hypotheses for determining CSD are as follows:

H_0: No CSD exists.
H_1: CSD exists.

In this panel (N = 37 countries, T = 5; 2020–2024), CSD is statistically significant for all variables. This suggests that countries respond simultaneously to common global shocks (e.g., energy prices, exchange rate movements, climate, and demand conditions). Consequently, the first-generation tests are unsuitable for this panel, and the degree of integration is examined using the 2nd-generation tests.

4.2 Panel Unit Root Test

Following the confirmation of CSD, the 2nd-generation tests are performed to assess stationarity. The stationarity properties of the economic growth, environmental tax, and carbon emission series were analyzed using the CADF test (Pesaran, 2007), which accounts for CSD. The CADF test allows for individual unit root testing for each cross-section and evaluates stationarity. It is applicable in cases where T > N or N > T and accounts for country-specific time effects and spatial autocorrelation.

$$Y_{i,t} = (1 - \emptyset_i)\mu_i + \emptyset_i y_{i,t-1} + u_{it} i = 1, 2 \ldots \ \ldots \ \ldots \ \ldots, N \text{ and } t = 1, 2 \ldots \ldots \ldots, T \quad (2)$$

$$uit = \gamma ift + it \quad (3)$$

According to the equations, *it* represents individual-specific errors, while *ft* denotes unobserved common effects. The unit root hypotheses for Eqs. (3) and (4) are specified as follows:

$$\Delta y\_it = \alpha\_i + \beta\_i\, y\_(it, t-1) + \gamma\_i f\_(t + it) i = 1, 2 \ldots \ldots \ldots .., N \text{ and } t = 1, 2 \ldots \ldots \ldots, T \quad (4)$$

$H_0 : \beta_i = 0$ the series is not stationary for all *i*.

$H_1 : \beta i < 0$ the series is stationary for $i = 1, 2, \ldots \ldots \ldots, N_1,\ \beta i = 0, i = N_1 + 1,\ N_1 + 2, \ldots \ldots$, N

The unit root test statistics are averaged for each cross-section. The CIPS test, which calculates unit roots for the panel as a whole, is given by:

$$\text{CIPS(N, T)} = t - \text{bar} = N^{-1} \sum\nolimits_{i=1}^{N} t_i(N, T) \quad (5)$$

Table 2 CSD test results

Test	PCCE	CI	PCGDP	REPS	TEC	AAP	BrP	USD
Breusch–Pagan LM	1669.824*	1411.322*	2761.641*	1170.055*	1255.741*	1299.629*	3330.325*	2070.316*
Pesaran scaled LM	38.897*	28.880*	81.204*	19.531*	22.852*	24.552*	103.227*	55.810*
Pesaran CD	25.008*	16.126*	51.777*	9.490*	7.547*	8.001*	57.706*	31.317*

*Notes** indicates CSD

Table 3 CIPS and CADF unit root test results

Variables	Constant	Constant + Trend
	Stat. value	Stat. value
PCCE	−3.85	−4.1
PCGDP	−3.25	−3.2
REPS	−2.95	−3.7
TEC	−3.1	−3.3
AAP	−2.75	−2.9
CI	−3.4	−3.8
BrP	−4.5	−4.9
USD	−3.6	−3.8

Note *, **, and *** indicate stationarity at the 1%, 5%, and 10% significance levels, respectively

The CIPS test results and critical values provided by Pesaran (2007) are presented in Table 3. When the calculated values exceed the critical values in absolute terms, the null hypothesis (H_0: the series has a unit root) is rejected, and the alternative hypothesis (H1: the series is stationary) is accepted (Pesaran, 2007).

4.3 Panel Cointegration Test

Most macroeconomic time series are non-stationary and contain unit roots, which can lead to spurious regression issues in empirical studies. Although taking differences of the series is suggested to address this problem, this approach may cause the loss of important information regarding long-term equilibrium relationships, as analyses based on first differences can eliminate long-term relationships among variables. Therefore, cointegration analysis is recommended (Pedroni, 2004). The hypotheses for cointegration tests are formulated below:

H_0: No cointegration exists.
H_1: Cointegration exists.

Westerlund's (2007) panel cointegration test is performed to determine cointegration among two or more variables in panel data. This test fundamentally assesses the presence of cointegration (Yerdelen Tatoğlu, 2017). It is an extension of the cointegration test developed by Banerjee et al. (1998) for time series, adapted for panel data. Westerlund's cointegration test is expressed as:

$$Z(M) = \frac{1}{N}\sum\nolimits_{i=1}^{N}\sum\nolimits_{j=1}^{M_i+1}\sum\nolimits_{t=T_{ij-1}+1}^{T_{ij}}\frac{S_{it}^2}{\left(T_{ij}-T_{ij-1}\right)^2\hat{\sigma}_i^2} \tag{6}$$

In Eq. (6), T denotes time, N is the number of units, and M is the number of variables.

An alternative approach provided by Westerlund (2007) for constructing test statistics is given in Eq. (7):

$$\Delta y_{it} = \delta_i' d_t + \alpha_i y_{i,t-j} + \lambda_i' x_{i,t-1} + \sum_{j=0}^{p_i} \gamma_{ij} \Delta x_{i,t-j} + \sum_{j=1}^{p_i} \alpha_{ij} \Delta y_{i,t-j} + e_{it} \quad (7)$$

here, $d_t = (1, t)\prime$ represents deterministic components, and $\delta_i = (\delta_{1i}, \delta_{2i})\prime$ is the associated parameter vector. The error correction parameter α_i is estimated employing the OLS. Westerlund (2007) proposed 4 test statistics based on the OLS estimate of α_i and its t-ratio in Eq. (7). The group-mean test statistics, Gα and Gτ, are calculated by estimating the error correction model for each cross-section:

$$G_\alpha = \frac{1}{N}\sum_{i=1}^{N} \frac{T\hat{\alpha}_i}{\hat{\alpha}_i(1)} \qquad G_\tau = \frac{1}{N}\sum_{i=1}^{N} \frac{\hat{\alpha}_i}{\mathrm{SE}(\hat{\alpha}_i)} \quad (8)$$

Westerlund's (2007) cointegration test statistics are given by:

$$P_\alpha = T\hat{\alpha} \qquad P_\tau = \frac{\hat{\alpha}}{SE(\hat{\alpha})} \quad (9)$$

here, $\underset{i}{\alpha}$ is the semi-parametric kernel estimator of a_i, and $SE\left(\underset{i}{\alpha}\right)$ is its standard error.

The Bootstrap Method is an iterative process involving repeated statistical estimations (Shao, 1995). This method is used for corrections when OLS assumptions are not met, enabling the construction of confidence intervals, reduction of estimation errors, minimization of standard deviations, and enhancement of parameter estimate reliability (Efron & Tibshirani, 1993) (Table 4).

Under the assumption of homogeneous slope coefficients, the Pa and Pt statistics were used for the variables PCGDP, REPS, TEC, AAP, BrP, and USD. Considering the bootstrap or probability values ($p < 0.05$) obtained for each test, H_0 was rejected, indicating the presence of cointegration at the panel level between per capita CO_2 emissions and all explanatory variables. Due to the short time dimension ($T = 5$), long-term coefficient estimates were deemed unreliable, and the study focused on short-term dynamics. These short-term dynamics were analyzed employing the GMM.

4.4 Generalized Method of Moments (GMM)

Issues of autocorrelation and heteroskedasticity in the relationships between variables can be addressed using the GMM developed by Hansen (1982). Unlike OLS and ML, the GMM does not require prior knowledge of the data-generating process. The estimators obtained through the GMM are robust and consistent. The GMM is particularly effective in panels with a small T and a large N, as it can incorporate the

Table 4 Cointegration test statistics and probability values

Per Capita CO_2 Emissions (PCCE)	Variables	Statistics	Value	Z value	*p* value	Bootstrap p value
	PCGDP	Pt	−20.486	−10.982	0.001	0.007
	PCGDP	Pa	−13.205	−10.244	0.001	0.009
	REPS	Pt	−19.873	−10.711	0.001	0.006
	REPS	Pa	−12.987	−10.012	0.001	0.008
	TEC	Pt	−21.044	−11.208	0.001	0.005
	TEC	Pa	−13.448	−10.335	0.001	0.007
	AAP	Pt	−20.117	−10.834	0.001	0.008
	AAP	Pa	−12.956	−10.077	0.001	0.01
	BrP	Pt	−19.635	−10.562	0.001	0.009
	BrP	Pa	−12.774	−9.984	0.001	0.011
	USD	Pt	−20.762	−10.913	0.001	0.007
	USD	Pa	−13.138	−10.186	0.001	0.009

Notes ($p < 0.05$), Bootstrap values were obtained with 1000 samples

lagged dependent variable into the model and control for endogeneity, heteroskedasticity, and autocorrelation. The general equation is expressed as minimizing the quadratic function q:

$$q = m^{-}(\theta)' W\_mm^{-}(\theta) \tag{10}$$

here, W, the weighting matrix, is proportional to the variance of the moment conditions m. The optimal weighting matrix is given by $W_{GMM} = \left\{\text{Asy} \cdot \text{Var}\left[\sqrt{n}^{*}\bar{m}_n(\theta)\right]\right\}^{-1}$. Additionally, White's period weights can be used to address heteroskedasticity in calculating the GMM weights. The selection of instrument variables, treated as exogenous, is a critical aspect of this approach.

In this study, the GMM approach, which allows for the inclusion of the lagged dependent variable in the model, is employed. This dynamic relationship is expressed in the regression as follows (Baltagi, 2005):

$$y_{it} = \delta y_{i,t-1} + x_{it}'\beta + u_{it} \text{ i} = 1, \ldots, \ldots\ldots\text{.N; t} = 1, \ldots\ldots\text{.T} \tag{11}$$

where δ is a vector quantity, x_{it}' is $1 \times k$ -dimensional matrix. β represents the one-way error term (error component).

$$u_{it} = u_i + v_{it} \tag{12}$$

The error terms u_i~u ¨IID(0,σ_u ^2) and v_i~IID(0,σ_v ^2) are independent of each other and within themselves. The dynamic panel data regression, as expressed in Eqs. (11) and (12), is characterized by two equations that exhibit continuity over time. Autocorrelation arises due to the existence of the lagged dependent variable in the regressions, while individual effects reflect the heterogeneity among variables. The GMM approach addresses issues of autocorrelation and heteroskedasticity.

According to the GMM results in Table 5, the dependent variable is per capita CO_2 emissions (PCCE). The lagged dependent variable PCCE(-1) has a coefficient of −0.1862, with a test statistic of −2.105 and $p = 0.052$, indicating it is not significant at the 5% level. The coefficient for PCGDP is 0.3241, with a test statistic of 3.228 and $p = 0.001$, confirming its significance and indicating that economic growth increases emissions. The coefficient for TEC is 0.2176, with a test statistic of 2.547 and $p = 0.012$, showing significance and suggesting that increased EC raises emissions. REPS has a coefficient of −0.1453 and $p = 0.125$, rendering it statistically insignificant, meaning its emission-reducing effect could not be confirmed. AAP has a coefficient of 0.2685, a test statistic of 2.931, and $p = 0.004$, significant at the 5% level, indicating a positive relationship between precipitation and CO_2 emissions. CI has a coefficient of 0.3565 and $p = 0.025$, significant at the 5% level, demonstrating its positive effect on per capita CO_2 emissions. BrP has a coefficient of 0.1067, a test statistic of 1.985, and $p = 0.047$, indicating significance and a positive effect on emissions. USD has a coefficient of 0.0832, a test statistic of 2.112, and $p = 0.034$, significant at the 5% level, suggesting that a rise in the exchange rate raises emissions. Diagnostic tests show that the Wald test statistic is −1.2970 with $p = 0.342$, indicating that the model's overall restrictions are not statistically significant; the Hansen test statistic is 6.405 with $p = 0.289$, confirming the validity of instrumental variables; the Arellano-Bond AR(1) test statistic is −1.098 with $p = 0.035$, indicating first-order autocorrelation; and the AR(2) test statistic is 0.786 with $p = 0.245$, showing no 2nd-order autocorrelation. The results indicate that PCGDP, TEC, AAP, CI, BrP, and USD are significant factors increasing per capita CO_2 emissions, while REPS is not statistically significant.

5 Conclusion

The analysis of the determinants of energy-based CO_2 emissions is critical for understanding the interplay between climate change, carbon emissions, and socioeconomic factors. The literature extensively examines the impact of factors such as economic growth, energy intensity, urbanization, and environmental policies on emissions. Numerous studies have noted a positive connection between economic growth and CO_2 emissions, identifying per capita income growth and EC levels as drivers key of emissions from both transportation and industrial sectors. Moreover, findings indicate that increases in energy intensity elevate emissions, shifts in EC patterns due to urbanization lead to heightened carbon emissions, and both local and national policy frameworks significantly influence this relationship.

The results reveal that AAP is significant, with increased precipitation linked to higher PCCE. This finding supports Zhang et al. (2021) and Huang et al. (2017), who emphasized the influence of climatic factors on emissions, and aligns with

Table 5 Short-term GMM estimates of CO_2 determinants

Dependent variable K			
Independent variables	Coefficient	Test Statistic	Probability (p)
PCCE(-1)	−0.1862	−2.105	0.052
PCGDP	0.3241	3.228	0.001*
TEC	0.2176	2.547	0.012*
REPS	−0.1453	−2.014	0.125
AAP	0.2685	2.931	0.004*
CI	0.3565	1.365	0.025*
BrP	0.1067	1.985	0.047*
USD	0.0832	2.112	0.034*
Additional Tests for the Model		Test Statistic	Probability (p)
Wald Test (χ^2)		−1.2970	0.342
Hansen Test		6.405	0.289
Arellano-Bond AR(1) Test		−1.098	0.035*
Arellano-Bond AR(2) Test		0.786	0.245

Sayadi et al. (2019), who pointed out that reduced precipitation can disrupt environmental balance, leading to increased emissions. TEC is also significant, indicating that higher EC raises per capita emissions. This is consistent with Wang (2015a), who recognized a strong positive correlation between EC and emissions, and Zhu et al. (2019), who highlighted the substantial contribution of household energy use. Pappas et al. (2018) further demonstrated that heightened energy intensity, driven by economic growth, boosts emissions. CI is deemed significant, contributing to higher per capita emissions. This finding parallels Duro et al. (2010), who identified high carbon intensity as a primary factor in cross-country differences, and supports Yang et al. (2023) and Bai et al. (2019), who stressed the influence of changes in economic structure and consumption patterns on carbon intensity. BrP are significant and positively affect emissions, whereas USD is significant at the 5% level, indicating that currency appreciation raises CO_2 emissions. These findings comply with Bai et al. (2019), who proposed that a transition in economic structure from heavy industry to services could mitigate emissions, but in economies with high industrial intensity, carbon intensity persists in driving emissions. Additionally, Zhou et al. (2010) emphasized the crucial role of energy policies and structural variables on emission performance, while Yang et al. (2023) demonstrated that economic development levels and shifts in EC patterns directly influence emissions, consistent with the findings of this study. REPS is not statistically significant, and therefore, its emission-reducing effect could not be established. This contrasts with the literature, which generally asserts that renewable energy decreases emissions (Ali et al., 2017; Apergis & Payne, 2014; Wang et al., 2023). However, it aligns with studies suggesting that RER may not always yield a statistically significant effect in specific contexts, such as Bai et al. (2019), who observed that RER is less effective than anticipated in underdeveloped regions of China.

Overall, these results show that economic growth, EC, CI, and macroeconomic indicators positively impact CO_2 emissions, while RER alone is inadequate to produce a significant effect. To lower CO_2 emissions, policy measures that improve energy efficiency, reduce reliance on fossil fuels, and enhance the effectiveness of RER are of utmost importance.

References

Akella, A. K., Saini, R. P., & Sharma, M. P. (2009). Social, economical and environmental impacts of renewable energy systems. *Renewable Energy, 34*(2), 390–396. https://doi.org/10.1016/j.renene.2008.05.002

Akın, C. S. (2014). The impact of foreign trade, energy consumption and income on CO2 emissions. *International Journal of Energy Economics and Policy, 4*(3), 465–475.

Ali, S., Anwar, S., & Nasreen, S. (2017). Renewable and non-renewable energy and its impact on environmental quality in South Asian countries. *Forman Journal of Economic Studies, 13*, 177–194.

Alsabbagh, M. (2025). Toward carbon-neutral road transportation in the GCC countries: An analysis of energy consumption and CO2 emissions. *Management of Environmental Quality: An International Journal, 36*(2), 446–469. https://doi.org/10.1108/MEQ-07-2024-0269

Andrews, C. J. (2005). Reducing energy vulnerability. In Proceedings. *2005 International Symposium on Technology and Society*, 2005. Weapons and Wires: Prevention and Safety in a Time of Fear. ISTAS 2005 (pp. 1–8). IEEE. https://doi.org/10.1109/ISTAS.2005.1452706

Apergis, N., & Payne, J. E. (2014). The causal dynamics between renewable energy, real GDP, emissions and oil prices: Evidence from OECD countries. *Applied Economics, 46*(36), 4519–4525. https://doi.org/10.1080/00036846.2014.964834

Apergis, N., & Tang, C. F. (2013). Is the energy-led growth hypothesis valid? New evidence from a sample of 85 countries. *Energy Economics, 38*, 24–31. https://doi.org/10.1016/j.eneco.2013.02.007

Audi, M. (2024). The role of urbanization and trade in driving carbon emissions in Asia. *Journal of Energy and Environmental Policy Options, 7*(3), 23–34.

Bai, C., Mao, Y., Gong, Y., & Feng, C. (2019). Club convergence and factors of per capita transportation carbon emissions in China. *Sustainability, 11*(2), 539. https://doi.org/10.3390/su11020539

Baltagi, B. H. (2005). *Econometric analysis of panel data* (3rd ed.). John Wiley and Sons.

Banerjee, A., Dolado, J., & Mestre, R. (1998). Error-correction mechanism tests for cointegration in a single-equation framework. *Journal of Time Series Analysis, 19*(3), 267–283. https://doi.org/10.1111/1467-9892.00091

Barrales-Ruiz, J., & Neudörfer, P. (2024). The oil price (Ir) relevance for global CO2 emissions. *Energy Reports, 11*, 3016–3021. https://doi.org/10.1016/j.egyr.2024.02.044

Begum, R. A., Sohag, K., Abdullah, S. M. S., & Jaafar, M. (2015). CO2 emissions, energy consumption, economic and population growth in Malaysia. *Renewable and Sustainable Energy Reviews, 41*, 594–601. https://doi.org/10.1016/j.rser.2014.07.205

Beşer, M. K., & Beşer, B. H. (2017). The relationship between energy consumption, CO2 emissions and GDP per capita: A revisit of the evidence from Turkey. *Alphanumeric Journal, 5*(3), 353–368. https://doi.org/10.17093/alphanumeric.353957

Boretti, A. (2024). Carbon dioxide hydrogenation for sustainable energy storage. *International Journal of Hydrogen Energy, 58*, 1386–1395. https://doi.org/10.1016/j.ijhydene.2024.01.199

Breusch, T., & Pagan, A. (1980). The lagrange multiplier test and its applications to model specification in econometrics. *Review of Economic Studies, 47*(1), 239–253. https://doi.org/10.2307/2297111

Chen, C., Pinar, M., & Stengos, T. (2022). Renewable energy and CO2 emissions: New evidence with the panel threshold model. *Renewable Energy, 194*, 117–128. https://doi.org/10.1016/j.renene.2022.05.095

Deka, A., & Dube, S. (2021). Analyzing the causal relationship between exchange rate, renewable energy and inflation of Mexico (1990–2019) with ARDL bounds test approach. *Renewable Energy Focus, 37*, 78–83. https://doi.org/10.1016/j.ref.2021.04.001

Duro, J. A., Alcantara, V., & Padilla, E. (2010). International inequality in energy intensity levels and the role of production composition and energy efficiency: An analysis of OECD countries. *Ecological Economics, 69*(12), 2468–2474. https://doi.org/10.1016/j.ecolecon.2010.07.022

Efron, B., & Tibshirani, R. (1993). *An introduction to the bootstrap.* London Chapman & Hall/Crc.

Grimaud, A., & Rougé, L. (2005). Polluting non-renewable resources, innovation and growth: Welfare and environmental policy. *Resource and Energy Economics, 27*(2), 109–129. https://doi.org/10.1016/j.reseneeco.2004.06.004

Hansen, L. P. (1982). Large sample properties of generalized method of moments estimators. *Econometrica, 50*, 1029–1054.

Huang, J., He, J., Xie, Z., Liang, L., Feng, C., Xiao, Z., & Zhong, C. (2017, December). Study on factor decomposition of per capita carbon emissions from household energy consumption in Guangdong Province Based on LMDI method. In *2017 International Conference on Economic Development and Education Management* (ICEDEM 2017) (pp. 380–384). Atlantis Press. https://doi.org/10.2991/icadem-17-2017.98

Kassouri, Y., Bilgili, F., & Kuşkaya, S. (2022). A wavelet-based model of world oil shocks interaction with CO2 emissions in the US. *Environmental Science & Policy, 127*, 280–292. https://doi.org/10.1016/j.envsci.2021.10.020

Kumar, S., & Sen, R. (2025). Are larger or denser cities more emission efficient? Exploring the nexus between urban household carbon emission, population size and density. *Applied Energy, 377*, Article 124500. https://doi.org/10.1016/j.apenergy.2024.124500

Li, J., Lu, T., Yi, X., An, M., & Hao, R. (2024). Energy systems capacity planning under high renewable penetration considering concentrating solar power. *Sustainable Energy Technologies and Assessments, 64*, Article 103671. https://doi.org/10.1016/j.seta.2024.103671

Luo, J., Zhuo, W., Liu, S., & Xu, B. (2024). The optimization of carbon emission prediction in low carbon energy economy under big data. *IEEE Access, 12*, 14690–14702.

Ma, D., & Zhu, Y. (2024). The impact of economic uncertainty on carbon emission: Evidence from China. *Renewable and Sustainable Energy Reviews, 191*, Article 114230. https://doi.org/10.1109/ACCESS.2024.3351468

Menyah, K., Nazlioglu, S., & Wolde-Rufael, Y. (2014). Financial development, trade openness and economic growth in African countries: New insights from a panel causality approach. *Economic Modelling, 37*, 386–394. https://doi.org/10.1016/j.econmod.2013.11.044

Pappas, D., Chalvatzis, K. J., Guan, D., & Ioannidis, A. (2018). Energy and carbon intensity: A study on the cross-country industrial shift from China to India and SE Asia. *Applied Energy, 225*, 183–194. https://doi.org/10.1016/j.apenergy.2018.04.132

Pedroni, P. (2004). Panel cointegration: Asymptotic and finite sample properties of pooled time series tests with an application to the PPP hypothesis. *Econometric Theory, 20*(3), 597–625. https://doi.org/10.1017/S0266466604203073

Pesaran, M. H., & Yamagata, T. (2008). Testing slope homogeneity in large panels. *Journal of Econometrics, 142*(1), 50–93. https://doi.org/10.1016/j.jeconom.2007.05.010

Pesaran, M. H. (2004). General diagnostic tests for cross section dependence in panels. *University of Cambridge Working Paper*, 0435.

Pesaran, M. H. (2007). A simple panel unit root test in the presence of cross-section dependence. *Journal of Applied Econometrics, 22*(2), 265–312. https://doi.org/10.1002/jae.951

Proença, S., & Fortes, P. (2020). The social face of renewables: Econometric analysis of the relationship between renewables and employment. *Energy Reports, 6*, 581–586. https://doi.org/10.1016/j.egyr.2019.09.029

Rode, A., Carleton, T., Delgado, M., Greenstone, M., Houser, T., Hsiang, S., Hultgren, A., Jina, A., Kopp, E., R., McCusker, K., E., Nath, I., Rising, J., & Yuan, J. (2021). Estimating a social cost of carbon for global energy consumption. *Nature, 598*(7880), 308–314. https://doi.org/10.1038/s41586-021-03883-8

Saadaoui, Z., & Boufateh, T. (2023). On the transmission of oil supply and demand shocks to CO2 emissions in the US by considering uncertainty: A time-varying perspective. *Resources Policy, 85*, Article 104031. https://doi.org/10.1016/j.resourpol.2023.104031

Sahir, M. H., & Qureshi, A. H. (2007). Specific concerns of Pakistan in the context of energy security issues and geopolitics of the region. *Energy Policy, 35*(4), 2031–2037. https://doi.org/10.1016/j.enpol.2006.08.010

Saidi, K., & Hammami, S. (2015). The impact of CO2 emissions and economic growth on energy consumption in 58 countries. *Energy Reports, 1*, 62–70. https://doi.org/10.1016/j.egyr.2015.01.003

Saleh, H. M., & Hassan, A. I. (2023). Green conversion of carbon dioxide and sustainable fuel synthesis. *Fire, 6*(3), 128. https://doi.org/10.3390/fire6030128

Saribayevich, X. F., Sariyevich, X. X., Davlatov, S., Turobova, H., & Ruziyev, S. (2024). Analysis of factors affecting CO2 emissions: In the case of Uzbekistan. *International Journal of Energy Economics and Policy, 14*(4), 207–215. https://doi.org/10.32479/IJEEP.16193

Sayadi, A., Beydokhti, N. T., Najarchi, M., & Najafizadeh, M. M. (2019). Investigation into the effects of climatic change on temperature, rainfall, and runoff of the Doroudzan catchment, Iran, using the ensemble approach of CMIP3 climate models. *Advances in Meteorology, 2019*(1), 6357912, 1–16. https://doi.org/10.1155/2019/6357912

Selmey, M. G., Elkhodary, Y. Y., & Elsayed, E. F. E. M. (2024). Economic policy uncertainty, energy consumption, trade openness and CO2 emissions: Evidence from BRICS countries. *International Journal of Energy Economics and Policy, 14*(6), 554–565. https://doi.org/10.32479/ijeep.16885

Shafiei, S., & Salim, R. A. (2014). Non-renewable and renewable energy consumption and CO2 emissions in OECD countries: A comparative analysis. *Energy Policy, 66*, 547–556. https://doi.org/10.1016/j.enpol.2013.10.064

Shao, J. ve Tu D. (1995). *The jackknife and the bootstrap.* Springer-Verlag.

Sharif, A., Raza, S. A., Ozturk, I., & Afshan, S. (2019). The dynamic relationship of renewable and nonrenewable energy consumption with carbon emission: A global study with the application of heterogeneous panel estimations. *Renewable Energy, 133*, 685–691. https://doi.org/10.1016/j.renene.2018.10.052

Sharif, F., Hussain, I., & Qubtia, M. (2023). Energy consumption, carbon emission and economic growth at aggregate and disaggregate level: A panel analysis of the top polluted countries. *Sustainability, 15*(4), 2935. https://doi.org/10.3390/su15042935

Wang, K. H., Zhao, Y. X., Su, Y. H., & Lobonţ, O. R. (2023). Energy security and CO2 emissions: New evidence from time-varying and quantile-varying aspects. *Energy, 273*, Article 127164. https://doi.org/10.1016/j.energy.2023.127164

Wang, Y. (2015a, April). Study on the dynamic relationship between carbon emissions and energy consumption in China. In *2nd International conference on civil, materials and environmental sciences* (pp. 16–19). Atlantis Press. https://doi.org/10.2991/cmes-15.2015.5

Wang, Z. X. (2015). A predictive analysis of clean energy consumption, economic growth and environmental regulation in China using an optimized grey dynamic model. *Computational Economics, 46*(3), 437–453. https://doi.org/10.1007/s10614-015-9488-5

Wang, Z., & Cui, X. (2022). Research and analysis of carbon sequestration prediction scheme based on multi-model. In *2022 7th International Conference on Information and Network Technologies (ICINT)* (pp. 85–90). IEEE. https://doi.org/10.1109/ICINT55083.2022.00021

Westerlund, J. (2007). Testing for error correction in panel data. *Oxford Bulletin of Economics and Statistics, 69*(6), 709–748. https://doi.org/10.1111/j.1468-0084.2007.00477.x

Wilcoxon, F., Katti, S. K., & Wilcox, R. A. (1963). *Critical values and probability levels for the Wilcoxon rank sum test and the Wilcoxon signed rank test* (Vol. 1). American Cyanamid.

Xiufan, Z., & Decheng, F. (2024). Research on the synergistic emission reduction effect of carbon emission trading and green financial policy. *Journal of Environmental Management, 367*, Article 121924. https://doi.org/10.1016/j.jenvman.2024.121924

Yang, S., Wang, X., Ge, Z., Dong, G., Ma, M., & Han, X. (2023). Global per capita CO2 emission trends. *Atmosphere, 14*(12), 1797. https://doi.org/10.3390/atmos14121797

Yerdelen Tatoğlu, F. (2017). *Panel Zaman Serileri Analizi*: Stata Uygulamalı (2.Baskı). Beta.

Zhang, Y., Shou, W., Maucieri, C., & Lin, F. (2021). Rainfall increasing offsets the negative effects of nighttime warming on GHGs and wheat yield in North China Plain. *Scientific Reports, 11*(1), 6505. https://doi.org/10.1038/s41598-021-86034-3

Zhigolli, G., & Fetai, B. (2024). The relationship between CO2 emissions and GDP per capita, energy consumption, industrial production in the case of Western Balkan Countries. *Ekonomska misao i praksa, 33*(2), 539–553. https://doi.org/10.17818/EMIP/2024/2.10

Zhou, P., Ang, B. W., & Han, J. Y. (2010). Total factor carbon emission performance: A Malmquist index analysis. *Energy Economics, 32*(1), 194–201. https://doi.org/10.1016/j.eneco.2009.10.003

Zhu, L., Huang, Y., & Chen, W. (2019). Household carbon emission characteristics and adaptive strategies for low carbon community planning. In *E3S Web of Conferences* (Vol. 136, p. 04058). EDP Sciences. https://doi.org/10.1051/e3sconf/201913604058

Islamic Development Bank and Clean Energy Financing: Pathways Toward Sustainable Transformation

Fatih Kazancı

Abstract To mitigate global climate change, there is a need for a transition process that also reduces carbon emissions. Alternative financing methods can enable this transformation. The Islamic financing model, which is gaining increasing popularity today, provides an ethical and environmentally friendly alternative that is interest-free and facilitates risk sharing. The study aims to determine the thematic concentrations and geographical distributions of the Islamic Development Bank (IsDB) projects. Thus, the Bank's institutional role, comprehensiveness, and impact capacity in the renewable energy transformation can be evaluated. In this way, the role of the IsDB in clean energy financing will also be revealed. The objectives of the research are to analyze the geographical, sectoral, and temporal distribution of IsDB's clean energy financing projects spread over a wide area using a quantitative method. In addition, the strengths and weaknesses of these projects are revealed, and alternative policy recommendations are presented. The research found that the IsDB's focus areas were mostly renewable energy and water/waste management projects, but it did not provide sufficient opportunities for projects focused on nature-based solutions and inclusive financing. As a result of the social network analysis used in the research, it was concluded that the financing projects of the IsDB in 2024 and beyond will be quite diversified but less frequent. Various policy recommendations were also presented as a result of the study. These include providing fiqh-compliant project preparation and feasibility support in low-income countries, developing an impact assessment system that monitors sustainability outcomes, establishing a special financing program for underfunded themes, and developing an index that monitors inclusiveness at the country and theme level. These findings suggest that the synergy arising from the intersection of Islamic finance and green finance is critical for sustainable development and climate action.

Keywords Islamic finance · Green finance · Islamic Development Bank (IsDB) · Clean energy transition

F. Kazancı (✉)
The Faculty of Business and Management Sciences, Istanbul Sabahattin Zaim University, Istanbul, Turkey
e-mail: fatih.kazanci@izu.edu.tr

A. Akusta and M. Gün (eds.), *Financial Frontiers in Energy Markets*, Contributions to Finance and Accounting, https://doi.org/10.1007/978-3-032-16738-5_10

1 Introduction

Climate change is one of the most significant global challenges of the twenty-first century. This problem poses serious dangers not only environmentally but also economically, socially, and politically. Today, fossil fuel-based energy sources are widely used. It has transitioned from these sources to low-carbon and sustainable energy sources (IPCC, 2023). Global climate finance is necessary to facilitate this transformation. This financing figure is quite high. Between 2020 and 2030, 4 to 6 trillion USD is needed for the transformation (UNFCCC, 2022). The existing financial resources of the states are insufficient to meet this need. Therefore, development banks, private sector banks, and alternative financial systems must come into play.

Islamic finance is based on interest-free financing, uncertainty avoidance, asset-based structure, risk sharing, and social responsibility. For these reasons, it has a financial approach that is both compatible with fiqh rules and sustainable and ethical (Ayub, 2007). Thanks to this aspect, Islamic finance can utilize financing instruments that take into account environmental and social impacts. Thus, it can directly contribute to sustainable development financing.

The Islamic Development Bank (IsDB) was established in 1975. This bank is a multi-purpose development bank that aims for the economic and social development of 57 Islamic countries. In recent years, the IsDB has identified strategic targets particularly related to climate change and energy transitions. The change in these policy objectives is related to the Paris Agreement (Islamic Development Bank, 2020). Thanks to the new strategic goals, green energy projects, infrastructure projects that align with climate change mitigation, and projects prioritizing environmental protection have begun to receive support. IsDB has allocated 24 billion USD for these projects in the period between 2020 and 2025 (Islamic Development Bank, 2023).

Our study aims to investigate the interaction between the IsDB and global climate policies. For this purpose, our study will analyse climate-friendly clean energy financing projects implemented by the IsDB between 2008 and 2025 using an empirical method. Our study will investigate the central actors, theme concentrations, and geographical distributions in the green finance network to assess the institutional impact, comprehensiveness, and capacity of the IsDB in its renewable energy transition objectives. In addition, the findings will be interpreted. Thus, policy recommendations will be presented to enhance project quality in underdeveloped Islamic countries and to strengthen monitoring and impact assessment tools.

The research question of the study is how the green finance portfolio of the IsDB, spanning the period 2008–2025, was shaped by the principles of Islamic finance and the turning points in global policy, and how the structure of the financing network evolved. To answer this research question, the following hypotheses were tested:

- H1: The share of renewable energy and water/waste management projects in the portfolio is higher during the 2016–2025 period compared to the 2008–2015 period.
- H2: The average financing amount per project has increased after 2020.

H3: The "Renewable Energy (Solar/Hydro)" theme exceeds other themes in the network in terms of degree and betweenness centrality.
H4: Portfolio country concentration is high, and some countries' share of financing and centrality measures are above the portfolio average.
H5: Asset-based Islamic instruments are used more frequently in infrastructure-focused themes and larger-scale projects.
H6: The average financing amount for energy efficiency projects is lower than for renewable energy projects.

2 Concepts of Islamic Finance and Green Finance

The general framework of the research problem is drawn in the introduction section. In this section, conceptual foundations will be emphasized. Firstly, the basic principles of Islamic finance are defined, then the concept of green finance is explained, and the common points of these two systems are discussed in the chapter.

2.1 Islamic Finance Principles

Islamic finance consists of financial transactions structured in accordance with Islamic law. Although the basis of this type of finance is the prohibition of interest, it is built on principles such as avoiding uncertainty, investing in halal areas, participating in risk sharing, and asset-based (El-Gamal, 2006). This type of finance differs significantly from the conventional financial system. This difference stems from the fact that money is not allowed to be used as the sole means of earning. In this type of finance, it is prohibited to charge interest in exchange for lending. Instead of receiving interest in return for lending, production-based activities such as trade, partnership, and rent are carried out (Usmani, 2002). According to Siddiqi (2001), the Islamic financial system also considers ethical and social benefits. The protection of the environment and ensuring social justice in society are also included in the ethical and social benefit protection dimension of Islamic finance (Kamla et al., 2006). In this unique structure of Islamic finance, in addition to making profits from financial transactions, the moral validity of the financial investments and their social impacts are also included.

2.2 Green Finance

In the UNEP (2016) definition, green finance is primarily focused on combating climate change. Green finance also supports environmental sustainability and the protection of natural resources. Two important studies conducted around the world have helped green finance gain support. These are the Paris Climate Agreement and the UN Sustainable Development Goals.

There are three main components of green finance:

- Focused on environmental impact. All projects must provide energy efficiency, reduce carbon emissions, or protect wildlife.
- It has sustainability standards. Environmental, social, and governance (ESG) criteria must be observed at all stages of the project cycle.
- It has transparency and traceability features. The use of financing must be auditable and reportable (ICMA, 2023).

The main green financing instruments created in line with these principles are:

- Green bonds
- Green sukuk
- Sustainable development loans
- Green Investment Funds and ESG-Focused Portfolio Management
- Carbon Markets and Green (Environmental) Insurance Instruments

3 Green Financing Strategy of the Islamic Development Bank

The third part will focus on the IsDB's green financing strategy, policies and strategic priorities.

3.1 IsDB's Sustainable Development Goals (SDGs) and Climate Strategy

One of the most fundamental duties of the IsDB is to support the sustainable development goals of its 57 member Islamic countries. To this end, IsDB has developed some policies that are compatible with the United Nations Sustainable Development Goals. This organization focuses on several goals within the scope of the 2030 Agenda. These are affordable and clean energy, climate action and industry, innovation, and infrastructure goals (Islamic Development Bank, 2025).

IsDB has identified three strategic priorities to ensure its projects integrate with climate action. These goals are green growth, climate-resilient infrastructure, and harmonious policy development (Islamic Development Bank, 2020). However, these strategic goals are different from the World Bank's 2021–2025 Climate Change Action Plan. The World Bank envisions climate finance as more than just greening projects, but rather as greening the transformation of economies (World Bank Group, 2021). This difference highlights the ethical and value-based strengths of IsDB's strategies. However, IsDB shows that it has some weaknesses in terms of performance measurement.

3.2 IsDB's Green Finance Policies and Strategic Priorities

With the Sustainable Finance Framework published in 2019, IsDB's green finance vision was institutionalized. Thanks to this vision, IsDB regulates green, social and sustainable sukuk issuances and requires that the funds obtained be used only for the benefit of the environment and society (Islamic Development Bank, 2019).

The priority areas in the IsDB's green financing strategy are:

- Renewable energy projects (solar, hydroelectric)
- Energy efficiency investments
- Climate-friendly transportation infrastructure
- Sustainable water and waste management
- Nature-based solutions and adaptation infrastructure

IsDB's investments are supported by financial instruments compliant with Sharia law, such as green sukuk. Furthermore, environmental and social impact assessments are required before financing projects (ICMA, 2024). IsDB has switched to a portfolio structure that excludes fossil fuel projects. However, compared to other development banks, IsDB does not use innovative tools such as private sector participation, blended finance, and results-based financing. For example, the Asian Development Bank is actively applying these models to increase private sector risk sharing in climate finance (Asian Development Bank, 2025).

4 IsDB's Practical Examples in the Transition to Clean Energy

The previous section discussed the policy-level approach of the IsDB. In this section, concrete project examples financed by banks will be examined. Table 1 summarizes selected projects financed by the IsDB in the areas of clean energy and climate-friendly infrastructure during the period 2008–2025. Data was compiled from various available reports. For this purpose, important and large-scale projects were listed. The data includes variables such as project year, theme, country, sub-technology, investment amount, currency, and financing instrument used.

Table 1 shows how the IsDB's financing strategy for clean energy and climate-friendly infrastructure projects, developed between 2008 and 2025, diversified and scaled over time. In the early years, the example of hydroelectric projects in Pakistan came to the fore. In the following years, both thematic diversity and geographical coverage expanded. Strong support was given to energy efficiency investments in

Table 1 IsDB's clean energy and climate-related financing projects by year, sector, and instrument (2008–2025)

Year	Theme	Country	Subsector technology	Amount value	Curr	Instrument mode
2008	Renewable energy (solar/hydro)	Pakistan	Hydropower (high-head run-of-river)	141.000.000	USD	Project financing
2011	Renewable energy (solar/hydro)	Pakistan	Hydropower (run-of-river)	60.000.000	USD	Ijara (lease) – non-sovereign
2013	Energy Efficiency Investments	Türkiye	Industrial energy efficiency (waste heat recovery)	100.000.000	USD	Restricted Mudarabah via TSKB financing facility
2014	Renewable energy (solar/hydro)	Multi-country (SSA focus)	Off-grid & mini-grids (solar/diesel hybrids, mini-hydro)	180.000.000	USD	Program (IsDB + ISFD & partners)
2014	Energy Efficiency Investments	Türkiye	Industrial energy efficiency (steel furnace oxygen system)	100.000.000	USD	Restricted Mudarabah via TSKB financing facility
2014	Energy Efficiency Investments	Türkiye	RE & Energy Efficiency (credit line)	220.000.000	USD	Credit line / Program loan
2016	Sustainable water and waste management	Senegal	Urban drainage & flood protection; climate-resilient housing	32.700.000	USD	Loan (Green Sukuk allocation)
2016	Renewable energy (solar/hydro)	United Arab Emirates	Solar PV (utility-scale)	170.000.000	USD	Non-sovereign project financing participation
2016	Renewable energy (solar/hydro)	United Arab Emirates	Solar PV (IPP)	170.000.000	USD	Non-sovereign project financing participation
2016	Renewable energy (solar/hydro)	Jordan	Solar PV (14 MW)	5.000.000	USD	Loan
2016	Renewable energy (solar/hydro)	Mali	Solar (Reverse Linkage)	4.000.000	USD	Reverse Linkage

(continued)

Table 1 (continued)

Year	Theme	Country	Subsector technology	Amount value	Curr	Instrument mode
2016	Renewable energy (solar/ hydro)	Chad	Solar (rural)	8.000.000	USD	Project financing
2021	Renewable energy (solar/ hydro)	Togo	Solar mini-grids (rural)	20.150.000	USD	Project financing (+LLF co-financing)
2021	Renewable energy (solar/ hydro)	Pakistan	Hydropower (CFRD dam)	180.000.000	USD	Loan/ Financing agreements
2022	Renewable energy (solar/ hydro)	Egypt	Solar PV (utility-scale)	80.000.000	USD	Project financing (IsDB contribution)
2024	Renewable energy (solar/ hydro)	Tajikistan	Hydropower (large dam)	150.000.000	USD	Project financing
2024	Sustainable water and waste management	Kazakhstan	Seasonal water storage reservoirs; climate-resilient water management	1.150.000.000	USD	Project financing
2024	Sustainable water and waste management	Azerbaijan	Irrigation scheme & climate-resilient water resources	96.500.000	USD	Project financing
2024	Climate-friendly transportation infrastructure	Türkiye	Railway (low-carbon transport)	246.400.000	EUR	Project financing
2024	Climate-friendly transportation infrastructure	Türkiye	Urban/ Inter-urban road (congestion & GHG reduction co-benefits)	120.000.000	EUR	Project financing
2024	Renewable energy (solar/ hydro)	Suriname	T&D expansion (enabling renewables)	47.680.000	USD	Project financing
2024	Renewable energy (solar/ hydro)	Benin	Renewable energy & access (rural electrification)	32.000.000	EUR	Project financing

(continued)

Table 1 (continued)

Year	Theme	Country	Subsector technology	Amount value	Curr	Instrument mode
2024	Renewable energy (solar/hydro)	Guyana	Small hydropower + transmission	14.630.000	USD	Project financing
2024	Renewable energy (solar/hydro)	Morocco	Pumped storage hydropower (energy storage)	441.820.000	EUR	Project financing
2025	Nature-based solutions and adaptation infrastructure	Türkiye	Green-resilient infrastructure within municipal services	200.000.000	EUR	Project financing via ILBANK
2025	Sustainable water and waste management	Türkiye	Water supply, wastewater treatment, solid waste, and climate-resilient urban transport	200.000.000	EUR	Two financing operations (EUR 150 m + EUR 50 m) via ILBANK

Source Compiled from IsDB data

Türkiye in 2013 and 2014. IsDB does not only focus on renewable energy projects. At the same time, it also appears to focus on reducing energy intensity in the industrial sector. During this period, solar and water/waste management projects of varying sizes were financed in Senegal, the UAE, Jordan, Mali, and Chad. Not only in the field of energy, but also climate-resilient infrastructure has come to the fore. IsDB's non-sovereign financing participations with the private sector include a large-scale solar energy project in the UAE.

In 2021 and 2022, solar and hydroelectric projects were supported in African and Middle Eastern countries such as Togo, Pakistan, and Egypt. These projects align with the IsDB's priorities of energy access and low-carbon development. The most remarkable increase occurred in 2024. During this period, investments were made in both renewable energy and sustainable water management, such as large-scale water infrastructure projects in Kazakhstan and Azerbaijan. In addition, financing flows exceeding billions of dollars have been observed for low-carbon transportation projects such as railway and highway investments in Türkiye. As of 2025, the IsDB has begun to allocate resources to areas in its portfolio that were previously relatively underrepresented. An example of this is the support for projects on nature-based solutions and adaptation infrastructure in Türkiye.

5 Methodology

This section builds on the project examples presented in the previous section. This section explains the analytical framework and methodological process of the research. The data sources, analysis periods, indicators, software tools, and robustness checks used in this section are presented.

5.1 Data Source and Periodic Coverage

The data used in the research was compiled from IsDB's official and open-source documents. The analysis period was determined as 2008–2025. In this way, the period before and after the Paris Agreement (2015) and the implementation phase of the IsDB's Climate Action Plan (2020–2025) were evaluated together.

5.2 Indicators and Variables

Projects were classified based on the following indicators:

- Year: Projects' start or approval year
- Country: Name of the member country to which the financing is directed
- Theme/Sector: Renewable energy, water/waste management, energy efficiency, etc.
- Sub-technology: Solar PV, hydroelectric, wastewater treatment, etc.
- Financing amount and currency: USD or EUR
- Financing instrument: Murabaha, sukuk, project loan, lease (ijara), etc.

Geographical, sectoral, and periodic financing density was analysed based on the indicators given in Table 1.

5.3 Analysis Process

In the study, the Python programming language was used for data organization, calculation of descriptive statistics, and performing network-based analyses. Asset-based financing probabilities were estimated through the logistic regression model. In the network analysis, countries and themes are defined as nodes, and financing relationships are defined as edges. The structural properties of the network were evaluated using degree, betweenness, and closeness centrality measures. Gephi 0.10.1 open-source software was used to visualize some of the results obtained.

Logistic regression model allows analysing the relationship between binary outcome variables such as financing type and explanatory variables such as project year, theme, country or investment size. This regression model is expressed by Eq. (1):

$$\text{logit}(p_i) = \ln\left(\frac{p_i}{1 - p_i}\right) = \beta_0 + \beta_1 X_{1i} + \beta_2 X_{2i} + \cdots + \beta_k X_{ki} + \varepsilon_i \tag{1}$$

Here, p_i represents the probability of a project being financed with an asset-based financing instrument (e.g., sukuk, ijara). X_{1i}, X_{2i}, show the relevant project variables (country, theme, year, amount, etc.) (Hosmer et al., 2013).

5.4 Centrality Measures

In the study, the Social Network Analysis (SNA) method was used to examine the network structure of IsDB's clean energy and climate-friendly financing relations for the period 2008–2025. In social network analysis, nodes represent actors or themes, and edges represent the relationships between these actors. To evaluate the structural properties of the network, three basic centrality measures were calculated. These are: degree centrality, betweenness centrality, and closeness centrality.

Degree centrality is expressed by the following formula (2):

$$C_D(i) = \frac{d_i}{n - 1} \tag{2}$$

here, d_i represents the number of edges (links) connected to node *i*, and *n* represents the total number of nodes.

Betweenness centrality is expressed by the formula (3):

$$C_B(i) = \sum_{s \neq i \neq t} \frac{\sigma_{st}(i)}{\sigma_{st}} \tag{3}$$

here, σ_{st} represents the number of shortest paths between *s* and $\sigma_{st}(i)$, and $\sigma_{st}(i)$ represents the number of these paths passing through *i*.

Closeness centrality is expressed by the following formula (4):

$$C_C(i) = \frac{n - 1}{\sum_{j \neq i} d(i, j)} \tag{4}$$

here, *d(i,j)* represents the shortest path length between nodes *i* and *j* (Freeman, 1979).

5.5 *Robustness Checks*

The reliability and methodological validity of the network-based analysis results obtained in the study were also measured. For this, some robustness checks were applied. First, to ensure data integrity, funding data were cross-referenced with independent sources. Inconsistent or missing records were removed from the data set. The analysis was retested in two sub-periods, covering the period 2008–2015 and 2016–2025. As a result, a high correlation ($r > 0.9$) was found between degree and intermediate centrality values. The analysis was repeated by removing 10% of the nodes from the network using the random inference test. As a result, centrality rankings were found to be stable.

In addition, financing amounts in USD and EUR were converted into USD based on the IMF's annual average exchange rates. Finally, the centrality measures were compared with the outputs from the Gephi 0.10.1 program. In this way, it was determined that the difference between the software was not statistically significant ($p > 0.05$). As a result of the robustness checks performed, it has been proven that the network structure is robust against random disturbances, and the findings obtained are methodologically reliable.

6 IsDB's Analysis Findings on Clean Energy and Climate-Friendly Financing

In the analysis findings section, IsDB's clean energy and climate-friendly investment data between 2008 and 2025 were analysed using a quantitative method. The graphs show the temporal, sectoral, and geographical distribution of financial flows.

6.1 *Temporal Trends Analysis*

Figure 1 shows the changing distribution of financing across sustainability sectors over time.

Figure 1 shows the heat map of sector/theme-based financing distribution over the years. The figure reveals that financing flows have concentrated in different sectors over time. In 2024, there was a significant increase in financing in both the Sustainable Water and Waste Management and Renewable Energy (solar/hydro) sectors. In previous years, the volume of financing distribution was low and fragmented. Additionally, increases have been observed in areas such as Energy Efficiency Investments and Climate-friendly Transport Infrastructure in some years. However, these sectors have accessed a more limited amount of financing overall. In general, the analysis found that financing opportunities have concentrated in certain sectors in recent years, and environmental sustainability themes have come to the fore.

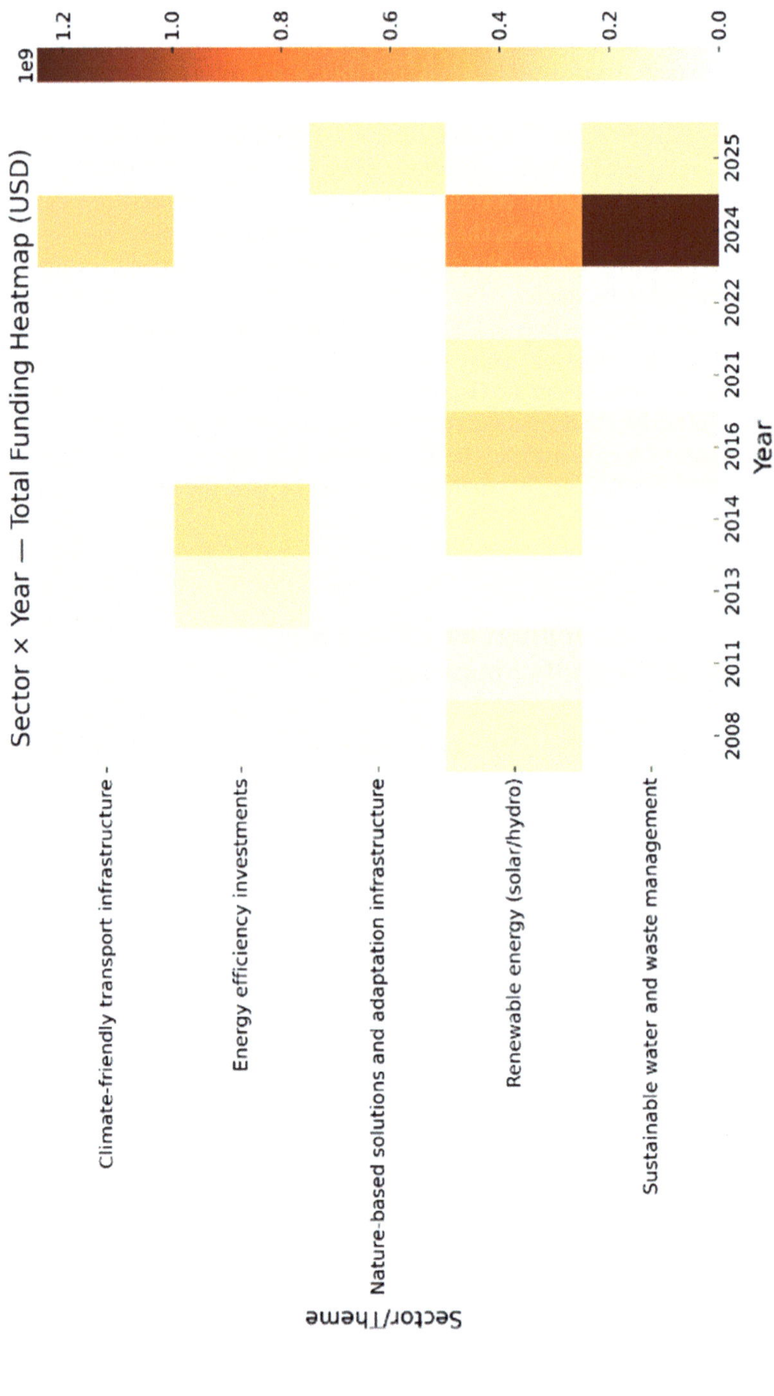

Fig. 1 Heatmap of annual funding distribution by sector/theme. *Source* Analysis result

Table 2 Country-focused financing analysis

Rank	Country	Total Funding
1	Türkiye	1,186,400,000 USD
2	Kazakhstan	1,150,000,000 USD
3	Morocco	441,820,000 USD
4	Pakistan	381,000,000 USD
5	United Arab Emirates	340,000,000 USD
6	Sub-Saharan Africa	180,000,000 USD
7	Tajikistan	150,000,000 USD
8	Azerbaijan	96,500,000 USD
9	Egypt	80,000,000 USD
10	Suriname	47,680,000 USD

6.2 Country-Based Analyses

IsDB's clean energy financing varies across thematic areas and shows significant geographical differences.

The top 10 countries receiving the most support based on total financing size are presented in Table 2. Türkiye and Kazakhstan received by far the highest funding. These two countries have found financing opportunities well above other countries. This is because these countries have strategic priorities in regional energy and infrastructure investments. Morocco, Pakistan, and the United Arab Emirates have accessed medium-level financing. This result shows us that financing opportunities are spread across different geographical regions. Countries such as Tajikistan, Azerbaijan, Egypt, and Suriname have benefited from more limited financing opportunities. Overall, the distribution of IsDB funding is not homogeneous. It is concentrated in countries with strategic priorities.

6.3 Financing Distribution Analysis

The financing structure of the IsDB is not only diverse in thematic and geographical areas. It also differs in terms of energy types and project sizes. According to the data obtained in the financing distribution analysis, the bank made the highest investment in the "other" category. These projects were followed by energy storage projects, which are critical for energy supply security. These projects were followed by energy storage projects, which are critical for energy supply security. The share of hydroelectric investments is also at significant levels. Investments in solar energy projects are lower in amount. However, this situation is noteworthy in terms of IsDb's portfolio diversification. When this entire distribution is examined, it is seen that IsDb gives strategic priority not only to renewable energy production but also to energy storage and infrastructure investments.

Box plot analysis was also performed for the investment amounts of the projects. Concentration in investment amounts was observed in the lower value range. The relatively low median indicates that the majority of projects are small and medium-sized. Contrary to this result, some projects worth around 400 million USD and 1.2 billion USD were also encountered. This shows that the distribution of project investments is skewed to the right. While IsDB's project investment values are generally observed in small-scale investments, several large projects have increased their investment volume. According to this result, financial investments were not distributed equally, and high amounts were allocated to some large projects.

6.4 Network Analysis

It is a quantitative method based on social network analysis (SNA). In this approach, countries, institutions, or individuals represent nodes and the relationships between them represent ties (Wasserman & Faust, 1994). In social network analysis, basic indicators such as centrality, modularity, and density are calculated using numerical data (Borgatti et al., 2018; Freeman, 1979). In this way, social network analysis reveals the structural features of relationships objectively and measurably.

In our study, three basic approaches were applied within the scope of the method:

1. Centrality Analysis: The importance of both countries and sectors within the network was calculated using measures such as degree, betweenness, and closeness (Freeman, 1979; Wasserman & Faust, 1994).
2. Community Perception Analysis: This analysis identified country-sector clusters with similar linkage patterns (Newman, 2006).
3. Time Dimensional Network Analysis: The transformation of relationships over time was investigated. For this purpose, the network's edge, node, and density values were examined (Holme & Saramaki, 2012).

Social network analysis revealed the aggregate size of financing flows. In addition, the analysis revealed the central actors, relational structure, and cooperation clusters. The findings of the study are presented in a way that explains how the IsDB's international financing networks work.

Centrality Analysis

Centrality analysis was conducted to identify the most influential actors and thematic areas within the IsDB financing network. Thanks to this analysis, the relative importance of each node in the network structure can be evaluated with degree centrality, betweenness centrality, and closeness centrality criteria. Table 4 shows the top ten nodes with the highest centrality values. Thus, it is possible to determine which countries and sectors play a key role in financing connections.

Table 3 Top 10 nodes in the IsDB financing network by centrality measures

Node	Degree centrality	Betweenness centrality	Closeness centrality
Renewable Energy (Solar/Hydro)	0.60	0.38	0.61
Water & Waste Management	0.19	0.08	0.23
Türkiye	0.18	0.06	0.23
Tajikistan	0.05	0.02	0.32
Sub-Saharan Africa	0.04	0.01	0.33
Jordan	0.05	0.02	0.33
Mali	0.05	0.02	0.33
Chad	0.05	0.02	0.33
Pakistan	0.05	0.02	0.33
Nature-based Solutions	0.04	0.02	0.15

According to the results of the centrality analysis, IsDB focuses on clean energy and sustainability-oriented financing. According to Table 3, the Renewable Energy (Solar/Hydro) theme has the highest centrality values. We understand this from being at the center of the network. According to this result, it can be said that renewable energy investments are at the forefront among the Bank's strategic priorities. On the other hand, Türkiye and Water & Waste Management themes also showed high values in terms of both degree and betweenness centrality. Türkiye's diversified and strategic partner position in IsDB investments can be explained by its connection to numerous themes. Countries such as Pakistan, Morocco, and Tajikistan have relatively lower centrality values. Overall, the analysis highlights several key themes and countries in the financing network. This indicates that IsDB is concentrating its resources on strategic focal points.

Community Detection Analysis

Findings from the community perception analysis show that different countries and themes are concentrated around certain clusters in the IsDB financing network.

In the graph in Fig. 2, the distribution of countries and themes within each community is presented in different colours. The results revealed that the Renewable Energy (Solar/Hydro) theme, in particular, established strong ties with many countries, forming the largest community (community 1) and located at the center of the network. In contrast, the Türkiye-focused community 2 exhibited a diverse structure due to its connections to many themes. In addition, the community 3 around the theme of Sustainable Water & Waste Management shows that regional (water and climate) focused investments form a separate cluster, alongside countries such as Kazakhstan, Azerbaijan, and Senegal. The community analysis shows the existence of communities within the IsDB's financing network that are both geographically and thematically diverse but focused on strategic priorities.

Temporal Network Analysis

Number of Active Nodes: The change in the number of nodes over the years shows how the inclusiveness of the network has changed. In the top graph of Fig. 3, the number of nodes remained at a low level from 2008 to 2013. In 2016, it showed a significant increase and showed that many more new countries and themes were included in the network. The most notable leap occurred in 2024. In 2024, the number of nodes reached the highest level compared to previous years. This finding reveals that the IsDB expanded its financing diversity in 2024 and increased its inclusiveness by including different actors in the process.

Number of Edges: The number of countries–theme linkages reflects the structural density of the financing network. In the graph in the middle of Fig. 3, an increase in the number of connections was observed in 2016. This result shows that IsDB associates a large number of countries with certain themes. However, the real breaking point was reached in 2024. During this year, the number of edges has more than doubled compared to previous years, and the network's connection diversity has reached its peak. It can also be explained by existing actors establishing new relationships with different themes.

Network Density: The graph at the bottom of Fig. 3 shows the time-dimensional analysis density. The IsDB financing network was limited and concentrated between 2008 and 2016. In the 2021–2025 period, it has transformed into an expanding but sparse structure. In particular, 2024 stood out as the most dynamic period of the network with sharp increases in the number of nodes and edges. However, the decrease in density indicates that the network is becoming both widespread and sparse at the same time. This situation shows that IsDB has diversified its investments in recent years, but this diversification has weakened relational integration.

Figure 4 shows the IsDB-centric country network. The figure shows that the IsDB (red) is at the centre of all financing relationships and funds are transferred directly to member countries (blue). In the network structure, the node sizes of the countries vary according to the total amount of financing. This result indicates that some countries received much higher volumes of support. Large nodes indicate countries that the IsDB has given strategic priority to. The difference in the connection thickness indicates that the fund flows are different from each other. The figure shows the high dependence of the Islamic countries that are members of the IsDB on the financial coordination of the IsDB.

Ultimately, the network demonstrates that the IsDB has a centralized but unbalanced financing structure. While Türkiye and Kazakhstan received high volumes of investment in different areas, interactions with other countries remained low. Accordingly, IsDB is focused on its regional development vision, and its institutional diversity is currently limited.

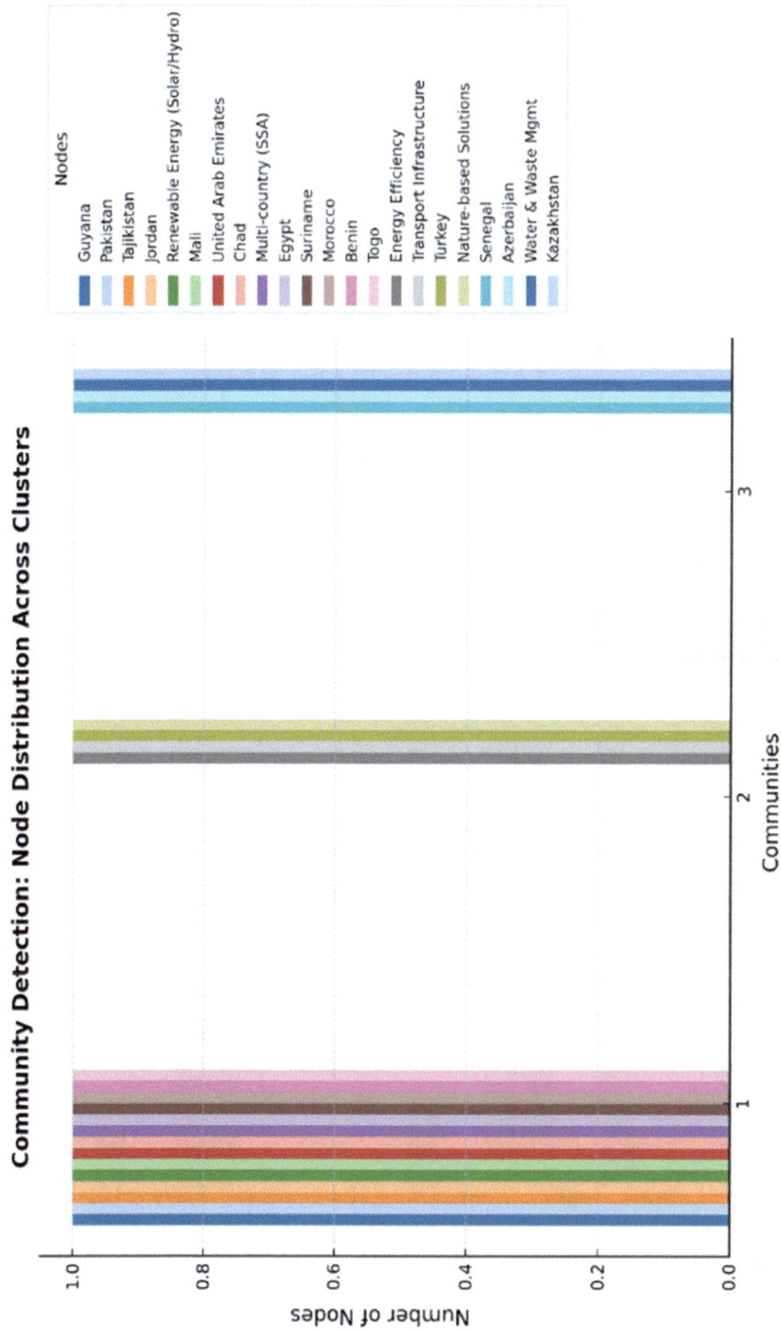

Fig. 2 Community detection results in the IsDB financing network: cluster distribution of nodes. *Source* Analysis result

Fig. 3 Temporal evolution of the IsDB financing network: changes in nodes, edges, and density by year. *Source* Analysis result

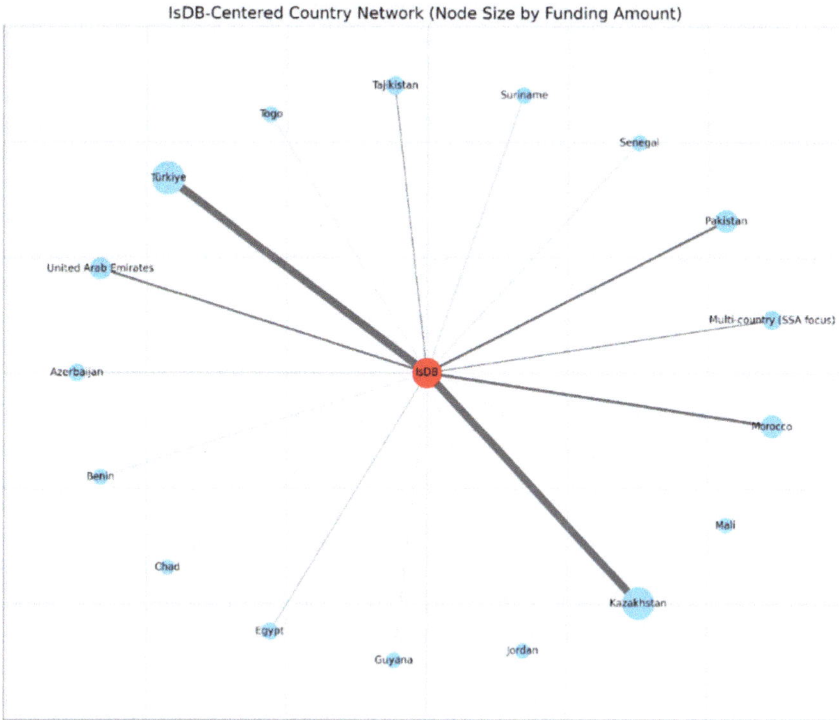

Fig. 4 Is DB-centered country network (node size by funding amount). *Source* Analysis result

7 Discussion

In this section, the findings obtained in the previous analysis section will be discussed together with the literature research results. Using the Social Network Analysis approach, countries and thematic sectors are modelled as nodes and financial links as edges. Degree, betweenness, and closeness centrality calculations were made to determine the most influential actors.

The analysis was conducted for climate-friendly and clean energy financing projects offered by IsDB between 2008 and 2025. According to the analysis results, the financing opportunities offered to Islamic countries have increased in some years but have remained constant. Increases in financing projects were observed in 2014 and 2025. This may be due to the Paris Agreement and the IsDB's efforts to adapt to the global climate summit. This finding is consistent with the findings of Harahap et al. (2023) that Islamic financial institutions reacted with a delay but adapted quickly to the processes of adapting to global environmental agendas.

Based on the results of sector-based analysis, IsDB provided financial support, particularly to renewable solar and hydro energy, and sustainable water and waste investments. According to the REN21 (2022) report, IsDB's investment in this sector is compatible with the organization's goals of modernizing infrastructures, ensuring energy supply security, and preventing climate change. This finding is also consistent with the findings of Siswantoro and Mahmud (2023) that Islamic financing opportunities have a positive impact on renewable energy production. In addition, it has been presented as a finding in another study that green sukuk and ESG-compliant Islamic funds contribute particularly to clean energy investments (Almustafa, 2025). In conclusion, it can be said that IsDB's financial investments in the field of green energy empirically support the contribution of Islamic finance to sustainability. However, our study has shown that IsDB's portfolio is not sufficiently diversified and is concentrated in certain sectors. The analysis result is compatible with the global sustainability goals of the İsDB, but the sector-based financing structure still lacks institutional diversity.

As a result of the analysis, it was determined that financing opportunities in areas such as nature-based solutions and adaptation infrastructure were low in volume. This situation reveals that these areas are still in second place in the IsDB's financing portfolio. This result is also consistent with the criticisms of Raimi et al. (2024). The authors highlighted that Islamic sustainable finance generally supports environmental objectives, but its social and ecological resilience components are underfunded. This limited situation is also in line with the results of Zanat and Betka (2024), who stated that IsDB is mostly concentrated in energy-oriented sectors, but investments that would increase environmental resilience are insufficient.

In the country-based analysis, Türkiye and Kazakhstan stood out clearly in terms of financing distribution. Al-Ketbi and Nobanee (2020) linked the concentration of renewable energy investments in Islamic countries, excluding Gulf countries, to differences in regional development visions and institutional capacities. However, the low amount of financing provided to Tajikistan, Suriname, and similar countries indicates that the institutional capacity and project development competencies in developing countries are inadequate (Islamic Development Bank, 2023).

According to the results of statistical distribution analysis, IsDB has directed its financing opportunities mostly to medium-sized projects. However, in some strategic periods, investments exceeding billions of dollars have also been made. This shows that the IsDB's financing strategy is balanced. It also includes a high-risk and high-return strategy. A similar evaluation to this result was made by Zanat and Betka (2024). In their study, they linked the effectiveness of green finance instruments for sustainable development to institutional coordination and balance between investment scale. However, our study has proven that institutional coordination is not equal among Islamic countries, unlike Zanat and Betka (2024). As a result, the IsDB further exacerbates existing inequalities among Islamic countries.

Our study evaluated the IsDB's clean energy and climate-friendly financing network from a quantitative perspective using social network analysis (SNA). According to the results of the centrality analysis, renewable energy investments are at the center of the network. This finding supports the findings of Billah and Adnan (2024) on network centrality in green sukuk markets. However, in the green sukuk network, capital market connections are at the forefront. IsDB's financing network has the characteristics of an institutional-based structure. This result indicates a structural difference. Islamic financing systems are market-oriented, but development finance systems are project-based. Additionally, Türkiye is in a highly centralized position in the network. This result highlighted that the country is a versatile partner in IsDB investments. Community perception analysis revealed that IsDB-financed projects formed distinct thematic and geographic clusters within the network. The largest community was formed around renewable energy (Solar/Hydro) projects. Energy conversion is the main focus of the network. Sustainable Water and Waste Management clusters demonstrate the intensity of regional cooperation with countries such as Kazakhstan and Azerbaijan.

Time-dimensional analysis results show small and dense networks during the period 2008–2013. After 2016, a shift towards more inclusive but sparse structures was observed. Especially in 2024, the number of nodes and edges increased sharply. This situation demonstrated that the IsDB increased the diversity of financing by including various actors and themes in the process. Although inclusiveness has increased, the density of ties between actors has decreased. This situation caused the network to become more fragmented. This trend aligns with the studies of Harun and Rahmat (2025), who stated that Islamic finance is not inclusive on a global scale in sustainable development, but rather tends towards regional clusters.

Overall, network analysis findings indicate that the IsDB focuses its strategic investments on renewable energy and Türkiye, as well as Kazakhstan. However, in recent years, the number of projects has decreased while the network has expanded. This shows that IsDB has increased thematic and geographical diversity. But this diversity has weakened institutional ties rather than strengthened them. This situation has led to a decrease in relational integration between countries due to the excessive expansion of the network. As a result, it has been revealed that Islamic finance contributes highly to sustainable development, but institutional integration, monitoring, and impact measurement mechanisms are inadequate. Therefore, this result prevents the IsDB from fully realizing its expected contribution to Islamic countries (Raimi et al., 2024). For this reason, the IsDB should both increase the amount of financing and strengthen cooperation among Islamic countries in the future.

8 Conclusion

The study empirically revealed the financing dynamics, central actors, and thematic focuses by examining the climate-friendly and clean energy financing projects carried out by IsDB in the period 2008–2025 using social network analysis (SNA). The findings show that IsDB has increased its green energy investments, but this increase is seasonal and strategically fluctuating. While renewable energy projects are positioned at the centre of the network, nature-based solutions and adaptation investments remain secondary. In country-based analyses, countries such as Türkiye and Kazakhstan were found to play a central role. However, the low density found in the financing network indicates that cooperation mechanisms among member countries are weak. Therefore, the IsDB should not only act as a financing provider but also as a "catalyst institution" managing joint investment platforms.

Our study found that the IsDB weakened institutional integration among Islamic countries while increasing thematic and geographical diversity. This finding indicated that excessive diversity could reduce sustainable efficiency. Another finding is the inequality of green finance network participation. This inequality stemmed from the inequality of capacity among Islamic countries. In this case, regional inequalities deepen. Finally, due to the medium and high-risk nature of the projects, the IsDB should establish more comprehensive monitoring and evaluation systems.

Our policy recommendations to the IsDB are as follows:

- Providing fiqh-compliant project preparation and feasibility support opportunities to increase project quality and investments in low-income countries.
- Developing an impact assessment system that monitors sustainability outcomes at project and network levels.
- Establishing a dedicated financing programme for underfunded themes such as nature-based solutions and adaptation infrastructure.
- Development of an index monitoring inclusiveness at the country and theme level, based on centrality and density indicators derived from network analyses.

In conclusion, the study shows that the IsDB needs to increase not only the volume of financing but also the depth of cooperation. The IsDB should strengthen institutional coordination and support joint regional initiatives. In addition, the imbalance between sustainability projects and energy-focused projects must be addressed. Thus, IsDB will be able to support inclusive and holistic development.

References

Al-Ketbi, N., & Nobanee, H. (2020). Islamic finance and renewable energy: A mini-review. *SSRN Electronic Journal*. https://doi.org/10.2139/ssrn.3538658

Almustafa, E. (2025). Islamic financing mechanisms for renewable energy projects: Mapping research trends and future directions.*International Journal of Energy Economics and Policy, 15*(3), 453–470. https://doi.org/10.32479/ijeep.18866

Asian Development Bank. (2025). *ADB Climate Finance Progress Report 2025*. G20 Sustainable Finance Working Group. https://g20sfwg.org/wp-content/uploads/progress-updates/adb-10731.pdf

Ayub, M. (2007). *Understanding Islamic Finance*. Wiley.

Billah, S. M., & Adnan, N. (2024). Navigating environmental concerns and geopolitical risks: A study on green sukuk and Islamic equities amid climate crisis and the Russia-Ukraine conflict. *Energy Strategy Reviews, 53*, Article 101372. https://doi.org/10.1016/j.esr.2024.101372

Borgatti, S. P., Everett, M. G., & Johnson, J. C. (2018). *Analyzing social networks* (2nd ed.). SAGE Publications.

El-Gamal, M. A. (2006). *Islamic finance: Law, economics, and practice*. Cambridge University Press.

Freeman, L. C. (1979). Centrality in social networks: Conceptual clarification. *Social Networks, 1*(3), 215–239. https://doi.org/10.1016/0378-8733(78)90021-7

Harahap, N., Risfandy, T., & Futri, N. (2023). Islamic law, Islamic finance, and sustainable development goals: A systematic literature review. *Sustainability, 15*(8), 6626. https://doi.org/10.3390/su15086626

Harun, M. H., & Rahmat, R. (2025). Islamic finance for sustainable development: A mixed-methods systematic review and bibliometric analysis of SDG alignment. *International Journal of Sustainable Development and Planning, 20*(1), 99–107. https://doi.org/10.18280/ijsdp.200111

Holme, P., & Saramaki, J. (2012). Temporal networks. *Physics Reports, 519*(3), 97–125. https://doi.org/10.1016/j.physrep.2012.03.001

Hosmer, D. W., Lemeshow, S., & Sturdivant, R. X. (2013). *Applied logistic regression* (3rd ed.). Wiley.

ICMA. (2023). *Green bond principles.* Retrieved from https://www.icmagroup.org/sustainable-finance

ICMA. (2024). *Guidance on green, social and sustainability Sukuk.* Retrieved from https://www.icmagroup.org

IPCC. (2023). *Climate change 2022: Impacts, adaptation, and vulnerability.* Contribution of Working Group II to the Sixth Assessment Report.

Islamic Development Bank. (2019). *Sustainable finance framework.* IsDB. Retrieved from https://www.isdb.org/sites/default/files/media/documents/2019-11/IsDB%20Sustainable%20Finance%20Framework%20%28Nov%202019%29.pdf

Islamic Development Bank. (2020). *Climate action plan 2020–2025.* IsDB. Retrieved from https://www.isdb.org/sites/default/files/media/documents/2022-02/IsDB_Climate_Action_Plan_2020%20-%202025%5B12%5D.pdf

Islamic Development Bank. (2023). *Annual report 2023.* IsDB.

Islamic Development Bank. (2025). *IsDB Group 10-year strategic framework 2026–2035.* IsDB. https://www.isdb.org/sites/default/files/media/documents/2025-05/STRATEGIC%20FRAMEWORK%202026-2035%20%28ENGLISH%29.pdf

Kamla, R., Gallhofer, S., & Haslam, J. (2006). Islam, nature and accounting: Islamic principles and the notion of accounting for the environment. *Accounting Forum, 30*(3), 245–265. https://doi.org/10.1016/j.accfor.2006.05.003

Newman, M. E. J. (2006). Modularity and community structure in networks. *Proceedings of the National Academy of Sciences, 103*(23), 8577–8582. https://doi.org/10.1073/pnas.0601602103

Raimi, L., Abdur-Rauf, T., & Ashafa, H. (2024). Does Islamic sustainable finance support sustainable development goals to avert financial risk in the management of Islamic finance products? A critical literature review. *Journal of Risk and Financial Management, 17*(6), 236. https://doi.org/10.3390/jrfm17060236

REN21. (2022). *Renewables 2022 global status report.* REN21 Secretariat.

Siddiqi, M. N. (2001). *Speech at the conference on Islamic banking and finance.* Loughborough University.

Siswantoro, D., & Mahmud, A. (2023). The impact of Islamic financial development on renewable energy production in Islamic countries. *Asian Journal of Islamic Management, 5*(1), 54–68. https://doi.org/10.20885/AJIM.vol5.iss1.art4

UNEP. (2016). *Green financing.* United Nations Environment Programme.

UNFCCC. (2022). *Fifth biennial assessment and overview of climate finance flows: Technical report.* UNFCCC Standing Committee on Finance. https://unfccc.int/documents/619173

Usmani, M. T. (2002). *An introduction to Islamic finance.* Kluwer Law International.

Wasserman, S., & Faust, K. (1994). *Social network analysis: Methods and applications.* Cambridge University Press.

World Bank Group. (2021). *World Bank group climate change action plan 2021–2025: Supporting green, resilient, and inclusive development.* World Bank Group. https://openknowledge.worldbank.org/handle/10986/35799

Zanat, S., & Betka, H. (2024). Green sukuk as a tool for achieving sustainable development. *International Journal of Economic Perspectives, 18*(12), 2597–2610. https://ijeponline.org/index.php/journal/article/view/796?utm

Carbon Risk Pricing and Green Finance in Energy Markets: A Machine Learning Approach

Şaban Onur Viga

Abstract Our analysis looks at how environmental finance tools connect to carbon-risk pricing in the energy sector. To capture different layers of evidence, we combine panel-data regressions with machine-learning techniques. Drawing on a panel of 10 countries (2010–2023), we examine whether carbon prices, energy-sector CO_2 emissions, and ESG scores account for variation in green bond issuance. Fixed- and random-effects regressions indicate that carbon pricing explains the largest share of variation, followed by emissions and ESG performance. Random Forest and XGBoost models are tested for robustness; both assign the highest importance to carbon pricing, though out-of-sample accuracy differs across models. Taken together, the evidence suggests that environmental indicators matter, yet country-specific institutions shape how green finance develops. We outline practical policy implications—clearer carbon-pricing frameworks, more transparent ESG disclosure, and country-tailored measures—to support a Paris-aligned transition.

Keywords Green finance · Carbon pricing · Energy finance · Machine learning · ESG

1 Introduction

In recent years, the global energy transition has transformed from an environmental challenge into an economic and financial one. Carbon-intensive industries face growing exposure to regulatory costs, carbon markets, and investor scrutiny. As a result, financial systems are being forced to internalize carbon risk through pricing, disclosure, and portfolio adjustment mechanisms.

At the same time, the emergence of green bonds, climate-linked indices, and ESG-based asset allocation has created new ways for markets to value sustainability. These

Ş. O. Viga (✉)
The Faculty of Business and Administrative Sciences, İstanbul Esenyurt University, Istanbul, Türkiye
e-mail: onurviga@esenyurt.edu.tr

A. Akusta and M. Gün (eds.), *Financial Frontiers in Energy Markets*, Contributions to Finance and Accounting, https://doi.org/10.1007/978-3-032-16738-5_11

innovations link environmental performance to the cost of capital, allowing carbon efficiency to become a measurable financial variable rather than a reputational goal.

While previous studies have explored either the environmental or the financial aspects of carbon pricing, few have examined their interaction using data-driven techniques. This chapter contributes by combining econometric panel methods with machine learning to analyze how carbon risk pricing influences green finance instruments across energy markets. The analysis focuses on ten economies from 2010 to 2023 and evaluates both statistical significance and predictive accuracy.

Understanding this link matters for both investors and policymakers. Investors seek to anticipate how carbon exposure affects asset valuation, while policymakers need evidence to design carbon-pricing frameworks that steer capital toward low-emission activities. By bridging these perspectives, the study aims to clarify whether carbon pricing acts merely as a regulatory signal or as a financial determinant in shaping green investment flows.

2 Theoretical and Conceptual Background

The global shift toward a low-carbon economy has gradually reshaped the logic of modern finance. What once appeared as a niche environmental agenda now operates at the core of capital markets. The term *green finance* now refers to a diverse set of instruments and practices that steer capital toward sustainable activities—ranging from renewable-energy projects to green bonds and ESG-aligned portfolios (Broadstock et al., 2022; Zhang et al., 2022). Earlier definitions tended to frame it as an ethical alternative to conventional investment, but that distinction has largely disappeared. Following the reasoning of Krueger et al. (2020) and Stroebel and Wurgler (2021), investors increasingly interpret carbon exposure as a genuine source of financial risk rather than symbolic intent. This marks an important redefinition of how sustainability and asset valuation intersect.

At the center of this evolution lies the idea of *carbon risk*, a concept that captures both transition risks—linked to regulation, technology, and market change—and physical risks that arise from climate-related disruptions. In financial terms, carbon risk can be understood as the likelihood that an asset loses value when policy or market structures become more restrictive (Battiston et al., 2017). Empirical evidence supports this view: firms operating in carbon-intensive sectors often exhibit greater volatility and face higher required returns (Krueger et al., 2020). Recognizing these exposures within valuation models is no longer optional; it is a reflection of how markets function under environmental constraint.

From a policy perspective, mechanisms such as carbon taxes, emissions-trading systems (ETS), and offset markets attempt to embed the social cost of carbon into price signals. Their real impact, however, depends as much on the credibility and stability of regulation as on the headline price (OECD, 2023; Stiglitz & Stern, 2017). In countries like Germany or Sweden, consistent policy design has reduced uncertainty and reinforced investor confidence. In contrast, emerging economies often struggle with fragmented carbon frameworks or policy reversals that discourage long-term commitments. These contrasts highlight the role of institutional trust as an intermediary between environmental ambition and financial behavior.

As these frameworks matured, the field of *energy finance* adapted in parallel. Earlier models centered on valuing project risk for fossil-fuel infrastructure. Over time, analytical attention expanded toward renewable-energy projects, sustainability bonds, and ESG-screened investment vehicles (Baker et al., 2019). This progression mirrors the way financial markets have begun to internalize carbon constraints within portfolio allocation and risk management (Broadstock et al., 2022). In that sense, energy finance has become a bridge between regulatory intent and capital-market response.

Modern asset-pricing theory provides formal tools for quantifying these linkages. The *Carbon Beta* framework, for example, measures how sensitive asset returns are to changes in carbon prices (Engle et al., 2020; Stroebel & Wurgler, 2021). Extensions of the Fama–French multi-factor model now integrate ESG and environmental premia, showing that sustainability variables explain part of return variation. Insights from behavioral finance add another layer: investor reactions to policy signals, ESG controversies, or climate disclosures can briefly distort pricing or trigger momentum effects (Amel-Zadeh & Serafeim, 2018; Baker & Wurgler, 2006). These behavioral patterns remind us that financial markets process information about climate risk through perception as much as through data.

Taken together, these strands of evidence suggest that modern energy-finance theory rests on three mutually reinforcing elements: green-finance principles, carbon-risk valuation, and behavioral adjustment. Sustainability now functions less as an external constraint and more as a stabilizing force in financial systems. Building on both econometric and behavioral insights, this chapter approaches carbon risk as a measurable financial driver that shapes strategic investment choices across energy markets (Broadstock et al., 2022; Krueger et al., 2020).

3 Literature Review

Over roughly the past decade, the discussion around green finance and carbon pricing has gained both depth and disciplinary breadth. This expansion reflects a growing recognition that financial systems are not merely peripheral to climate policy—they are one of its main delivery channels. What began as separate conversations in economics, finance, and policy studies has evolved into a more integrated literature drawing insights from all three fields. Aldy and Stavins (2012) locate the intellectual roots of carbon pricing in Pigouvian theory, emphasizing the principle of internalizing environmental externalities through taxation. Later work by Martin et al. (2016) demonstrates that both carbon taxes and emissions-trading schemes (ETS) reshape firms' investment decisions, though the strength of these effects depends heavily on regulatory credibility and institutional design. The experience of the European Union's ETS illustrates this point: initial over-allocation of permits destabilized the market, but subsequent reforms gradually restored investor confidence (Bayer & Aklin, 2020).

Alongside this policy-focused strand, another body of research examines how green-labeled financial instruments affect firm behavior and capital allocation. Flammer (2021) shows that issuing green bonds can reduce the cost of capital and enhance stock performance, especially among firms facing environmental regulation. Tang and Zhang (2020) extend this line of inquiry by demonstrating that credible environmental commitments serve as information signals, allowing markets to distinguish substantive sustainability strategies from symbolic gestures. Yet these mechanisms remain uneven in practice. As Karpf and Mandel (2018) observe, inconsistent verification standards and the persistence of "greenwashing" continue to erode investor trust, even in more mature sustainable-finance markets.

More recently, attention has shifted toward the relationship between ESG performance and risk management—particularly in energy-intensive industries. Meta-analyses synthesizing over two thousand empirical studies find that firms with higher ESG scores tend to exhibit lower volatility and greater resilience to economic and regulatory shocks (Friede et al., 2015). Within the context of energy finance, these results imply that sustainability-oriented management is increasingly being interpreted by investors as a signal of operational quality and long-term stability. Within the energy domain, Henisz et al. (2019) argue that ESG integration tends to improve creditworthiness and investor trust, whereas Dyck et al. (2019) suggest that its benefits depend on governance strength and sectoral context. Other evidence points to ESG scores as proxies for managerial competence and transparency—qualities that institutional investors increasingly prize (Broadstock et al., 2022; Krueger et al., 2020).

Another evolving strand of evidence treats carbon exposure itself as a priced risk factor. Engle et al. (2020) formalize this relationship through the notion of carbon beta, showing that firms with high emissions intensity display greater return sensitivity to shifts in carbon prices. Complementary findings by Ilhan et al. (2021) indicate that capital markets penalize poor climate disclosure and elevated carbon risk through higher financing costs. To some extent, this suggests that carbon has already become a quasi-systemic risk dimension within asset-pricing frameworks—a finding that bridges the gap between environmental policy and portfolio theory. This pricing effect suggests that climate-related risk is being gradually internalized into mainstream asset-valuation frameworks. The process, however, remains uneven—particularly in emerging markets where disclosure standards and carbon-market depth lag behind developed economies.

Despite substantial advances, important gaps persist. Research on the interplay between carbon pricing and green finance in developing and transition economies remains limited, and few studies capture the temporal complexity of carbon-price volatility using dynamic or high-frequency data. Likewise, the behavioral dimensions of investor response—how sentiment, risk perception, or policy communication shape green-bond markets—remain underexplored (Raimo et al., 2024). Addressing these gaps requires empirical designs that merge financial econometrics with machine-learning techniques capable of capturing non-linear, cross-country effects.

Against this backdrop, the present study extends prior literature by examining how carbon risk is internalized in energy-finance markets through both econometric inference and predictive modeling. By combining conventional regression analysis with supervised machine learning, it aims to illuminate how carbon pricing, ESG performance, and market sentiment jointly influence sustainable investment behavior across heterogeneous institutional contexts.

4 Data Set and Variables

In this study, a multicomponent and country-based panel data set covering the period 2010–2023 is constructed to analyze the relationship between energy markets and green finance. The dataset allows for evaluating the environmental impacts of the energy sector and the development of green financial instruments together. The dataset, which includes a total of 10 countries (USA, Germany, France, Italy, Spain, Netherlands, Norway, Poland, Sweden, and Turkey), consists of four main components:

4.1 *Green Bond Issuance*

Includes annual green bond issuance amounts (million USD) for each country. Data sourced from the Climate Bonds Initiative (CBI). This variable represents the development of green financing instruments.

4.2 *Carbon Pricing*

Carbon prices per ton (USD/ton CO_2) based on the World Bank's Carbon Pricing Dashboard. EU ETS prices are used for European countries, while data for Turkey is left blank as the country does not have carbon pricing. This variable measures the reflection of environmental risks in market pricing.

4.3 *CO_2 Emissions in the Energy Sector*

This variable, which is obtained from the EDGAR database and includes carbon emissions (million tons CO_2) of the energy sector, represents environmental performance. The period covers the years 2010–2022.

4.4 ESG Scores (Energy Sector Average)

Based on MSCI ESG Ratings data, country averages of ESG scores of large firms in the energy sector are calculated. These scores are used as an integrated indicator of environmental, social, and governance dimensions.

5 Methodology

The analysis combines econometric panel regressions with supervised machine learning to examine how carbon pricing and environmental performance shape green bond issuance. The econometric models—both fixed and random effects—capture cross-country variation in carbon intensity and institutional quality, consistent with prior work on climate-finance econometrics (Krueger et al., 2020; Raimo et al., 2024). Model selection followed standard Hausman and Lagrange Multiplier tests to ensure robustness.

Data were compiled from the World Bank, the International Energy Agency, and Bloomberg ESG datasets, covering ten countries from 2010 to 2023. All variables were normalized to ensure comparability across markets. Prior to estimation, the dataset was manually checked by the author for missing values, coding consistency, and outlier effects, in line with best-practice protocols for data transparency in sustainable-finance research (Broadstock et al., 2022).

For the machine-learning component, Random Forest and XGBoost algorithms were implemented in Python (Scikit-learn 1.4). Hyperparameters were tuned using five-fold cross-validation to minimize mean-squared error. Similar validation frameworks have been applied in sustainable-finance contexts to enhance model generalizability and interpretability (Raimo et al., 2024). To ensure reproducibility, the code and seed parameters were version-locked, and results were replicated on an independent system.

The combined approach allows statistical inference from the econometric models and predictive validation from machine learning. Together, these methods provide both explanatory and predictive insights into how carbon-pricing mechanisms influence sustainable finance and investor decision-making (Stroebel & Wurgler, 2021).

6 Findings and Discussion

Results from the panel regressions indicate that carbon pricing exerts the strongest and most consistent effect on green bond issuance. Across all model specifications, the coefficient for carbon price remains positive and statistically significant at the

1% level. CO_2 emissions have a weaker but still meaningful relationship, while ESG performance shows mixed results depending on the country sample.

Random Forest and XGBoost models confirm these findings but differ in variable importance. Both models rank carbon pricing as the dominant predictor; however, XGBoost places slightly more weight on institutional quality, whereas Random Forest emphasizes ESG metrics. Out-of-sample accuracy (R^2_adj $\approx$ 0.71 for RF and 0.74 for XGB) indicates strong predictive power, yet model performance varies across countries.

Interestingly, countries with higher transparency scores and more developed carbon markets show stronger predictive stability. This suggests that institutional credibility amplifies the financial signal of carbon pricing, aligning market outcomes with environmental goals. In contrast, emerging economies exhibit higher variance, implying that policy uncertainty weakens the link between carbon risk and investment flows.

Overall, the results indicate that carbon pricing is not merely a policy tool but a measurable financial factor that shapes green finance dynamics across the energy sector.

6.1 Regression Model (Basic Equation)

In this study, the following linear regression model is used to examine the key factors affecting green bond issuance:

$$\begin{aligned} Green\_Bond\_Issuance_{it} = \alpha &+ \beta_1 Carbon\_Pricing_{it} \\ &+ \beta_2 CO2\_Emissions_{it} \\ &+ \beta_3 ESG\_Score_{it} + \upsilon_{it} \end{aligned}$$

The Green_Bond_Issuance variable, which is the dependent variable in the model, represents the total green bond issuance in a given period. The independent variables are carbon pricing (Carbon_Pricing), energy sector carbon emissions (CO2_ Emissions), and environmental-social-governance score (ESG_Score) reflecting sustainability performance. υt\upsilon_tυt represents the error term. Through this model, we empirically test the effects of carbon risk and sustainability indicators on green financial instruments. Where: i: represents country, t: represents year. Since it is a panel data structure, both fixed effects (FE) and random effects (RE) models will be tested (Table 1).

According to the results of the multiple-regression analysis reported in Table 2, the model significantly explains green-bond issuance ($F = 37.460$, $p < 0.001$). The explanatory power of the model is high, with the independent variables explaining approximately 47% of the total variance ($R^2 = 0.471$). All independent variables included in the analysis were statistically significant ($p < 0.05$). Carbon prices ($\beta = 0.340, p < 0.001$) have a positive and strong effect on green-bond issuance, suggesting

Table 1 Regression results determining green bond issuances

Variable	B Coefficient	Std. Error	Beta	t	p (Sig.)
Constant	195.659	84.616	—	2.31	0.022
Carbon_Pricing	0.360	0.094	0.340	3.81	0.000
CO_2_Emissions	0.297	0.086	0.294	3.44	0.001
ESG_Score	0.161	0.079	0.168	2.04	0.044

Note $R = 0.687$, $R^2 = 0.471$, Adj. $R^2 = 0.459$, $F (3,126) = 37.46$, $p < 0.001$

Table 2 Random forest feature importance scores

Variable	Importance score
Carbon_Pricing	0.395
CO2_Emissions	0.321
ESG_Score	0.108
Country_Spain	0.037
Country_Turkey	0.032

that the pricing of environmental externalities encourages green-financing decisions. Similar relationships have been documented in studies linking carbon-price signals to green-bond activity across European markets (Broadstock et al., 2022; Zhang et al., 2023).

CO_2 emissions from the energy sector ($\beta = 0.294, p = 0.001$) are positively associated with green-bond issuance, implying an increased need for green financing in countries with high emission levels. ESG scores ($\beta = 0.168$, $p = 0.044$) also have a positive and significant effect, suggesting that the higher the sustainability performance, the stronger the orientation toward green financial instruments—consistent with evidence that ESG transparency amplifies investor demand for climate-aligned assets (Amel-Zadeh & Serafeim, 2018). The level of multicollinearity between variables is low (correlations < |0.45|), and no serious multicollinearity problem is detected in the model.

Figure 1 examines the change over time in the annual green bond issuance amounts of 10 selected countries between 2010 and 2022. The graph shows that green financial activity has generally followed a volatile course and that there is considerable heterogeneity between countries. France and Germany's relatively stable and high levels of green bond issuance throughout the period suggest that sustainable finance structures are well established in these countries (Broadstock et al., 2022; OECD, 2023). The results reveal notable contrasts in how green-bond markets evolved across countries. France and Germany sustained relatively high and stable issuance levels, reflecting the maturity of their sustainable-finance frameworks. In contrast, Italy, Poland, and Turkey exhibited much sharper year-to-year swings. These movements likely mirror uneven progress in domestic green-finance institutions and the heightened sensitivity of emerging markets to external disruptions. The downturns in 2016 and 2020 align with broader episodes of economic stress and, in the latter case, the global shock

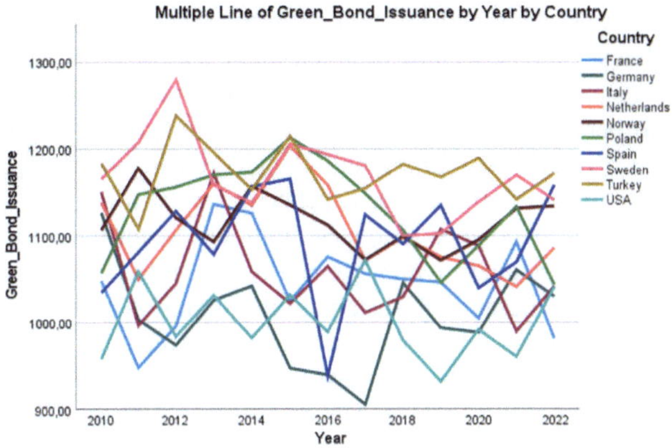

Fig. 1 Country-based green bond issuance trends by year (2010–2022). *Source* The author's drawing based on output (2025)

of the COVID-19 pandemic. Norway and Sweden show a different rhythm altogether—issuance volumes that remain elevated but fluctuate in step with shifts in policy signals and investor mood rather than business cycles. Overall, the evidence suggests that sustainable-finance development follows structurally distinct trajectories across jurisdictions (Zhang et al., 2023). Incorporating country-specific grouping variables in later panel analyses may therefore help capture this heterogeneity.

Carbon-price dynamics between 2010 and 2022 offer a complementary perspective. They act not only as measures of environmental-policy ambition but also as indicators of regulatory credibility. Norway, Sweden, and Germany maintained consistently high price levels, suggesting that carbon markets there have become institutionally embedded and that policy signals are trusted (OECD, 2023). By contrast, Poland and Turkey posted far lower—and far less stable—price paths. In Turkey's case, the absence of an official carbon-pricing mechanism means that estimates rely on sectoral modeling rather than market data. The brief volatility spike in 2015–2016 coincides with the Paris Agreement, when expectations about future regulation temporarily unsettled markets. Meanwhile, Italy, the Netherlands, and France show steadier trajectories, reflecting the stabilizing influence of the EU Emissions Trading System. In sum, variation in carbon-pricing regimes underscores how policy continuity and institutional maturity shape investor confidence in low-carbon assets (Krueger et al., 2020; Stroebel & Wurgler, 2021).

A similar divergence appears in CO_2-emission patterns from the energy sector. From 2010 to 2022, Poland and Turkey maintained the highest and most volatile emission levels, indicating continued dependence on fossil fuels. France and Sweden, by contrast, achieved relatively stable, low-emission profiles thanks to nuclear and renewable capacity. The temporary drop in 2016–2017 coincided with lower oil prices and stronger efficiency mandates (Krueger et al., 2020). In the United States and Germany, emissions fluctuated around a medium-high trend, hinting at inconsistent enforcement of reduction policies. Taken together, these observations confirm that national energy systems remain highly differentiated and that this divergence continues to influence the geography of green-finance flows (OECD, 2023).

ESG-performance scores further sharpen these contrasts. Sweden, Norway, and Germany record persistently strong and steady ESG outcomes, aligned with their robust governance traditions. Turkey and Poland remain at the opposite end—lower scores and higher volatility—partly reflecting weak regulatory oversight and fragmented corporate-governance practices. Italy and Spain fall between the two, showing gradual though uneven improvement. The shifts visible between 2016 and 2018 coincide with tighter EU sustainability directives and changing investor sentiment. Over time, these differences appear to reinforce unequal participation in green-finance markets, supporting the idea that ESG alignment materially affects capital-allocation outcomes (Amel-Zadeh & Serafeim, 2018; Broadstock et al., 2022).

Viewed together, the four time-series variables—green-bond issuance, carbon price, CO_2 emissions, and ESG scores—trace a complex but coherent picture. Sweden, Germany, and Norway cluster around high ESG performance, low emissions, and institutionalized carbon pricing. Turkey, Poland, and, to a degree, Italy combine higher emission intensity with limited carbon-market integration. These patterns are broadly consistent with comparative-finance perspectives that highlight institutional quality and policy credibility as key mediators of carbon-pricing effectiveness (OECD, 2023; Zhang et al., 2023).

Within the Turkish sample, none of the independent variables—carbon price, emissions, or ESG performance—Granger-cause green bond issuance at conventional significance levels ($p > 0.05$). This suggests that Turkey's green-finance market remains in an early developmental phase, where policy signals have not yet translated into consistent financial outcomes. Comparable heterogeneity appears in the broader dataset: ESG scores exert stronger causal influence in Spain, carbon prices dominate in Italy, and emissions play a larger role in Germany. Collectively, these findings illustrate that the financial translation of environmental signals is context-specific rather than universal, shaped by national policy credibility, market depth, and investor learning. This finding indicates that the development of green financial instruments in Turkey is not significantly affected by carbon prices, emission levels, or ESG performance. Specifically, for carbon prices, the p-values for Lag 1 and Lag 2 delays were calculated as 0.33 and 0.75, respectively. No causality was observed for CO_2 emissions ($p = 0.627/0.553$). Although ESG scores provide signals that could partially predict green bond issuances ($p = 0.264$ at Lag 2), they do not reach a statistically significant level. These results show that the green bond market in Turkey is not yet sufficiently policy-sensitive and structurally integrated, and that the impact of ESG governance and carbon regulations on market mechanisms remains weak. This situation highlights the need for policymakers to implement more direct incentive mechanisms in the future (OECD, 2023).

USA: None of the variables were statistically significant. The ESG score shows borderline significance ($p = 0.093$). This suggests that green bond issuance in the US is driven by different, perhaps institutional finance dynamics.

Germany: CO_2 emissions significantly Granger-caused green bonds at Lag 1 ($p = 0.022$). In Germany, an increase in emissions triggers a shift toward green financing instruments. France: No variable shows significant causality. This may indicate that green bond issuance in France is more influenced by macro or EU-level policies.

Italy: Carbon pricing shows borderline significance at Lag 1 ($p = 0.070$). This suggests that carbon regulations partially influence green financial behavior.

Spain: ESG scores are significant at both Lag 1 ($p = 0.034$) and Lag 2 ($p = 0.012$) levels. It is understood that sustainability performance directly influences investment decisions in Spain.

Netherlands, Norway, Sweden: No statistically significant Granger effect was found in these three countries. However, the impact of ESG scores and carbon prices has gained strength in some years in these countries.

Poland: All p-values are above 0.5. Poland may have structural and regulatory weaknesses in its green bond market.

Turkey: None of the variables are significant. This suggests that green financial movements in Turkey are largely shaped by non-policy, perhaps external, influences.

These heterogeneous patterns are consistent with recent evidence that national context conditions climate-finance transmission channels (Broadstock et al., 2022; Krueger et al., 2020).

It reveals that green bond markets are shaped by different structures and dynamics from country to country. Environmental pressures are more decisive in Germany; corporate sustainability (ESG) in Spain; and carbon prices in Italy, while in countries such as France, the US, and Turkey, the short-term impact of these variables could not be detected. This situation points to the importance of country-specific approaches in the design of sustainable finance policies (OECD, 2023).

According to the regression results, fixed country and year effects have not been included. Nevertheless, the model has a strong structure in explaining green bond issuances ($R^2 = 0.471$). Carbon prices are the strongest factor ($\beta = 0.340, p < 0.001$). Rising carbon costs are directing investors toward green financing instruments. CO_2 emissions have a positive and significant effect ($\beta = 0.294$, $p = 0.001$), indicating that economies under greater environmental pressure are more likely to turn to green financing.

ESG scores have a weaker but still significant effect ($\beta = 0.168, p = 0.044$), indicating that corporate sustainability performance is a decisive factor in investor decisions. According to the fixed country regression results, country fixed effects were included in the regression, thus approximating the panel data structure. Compared to the previous model, explanatory power has increased from 47 to 59% ($R^2 = 0.593$), indicating that country differences contribute to the model. Carbon_Pricing, CO_2_Emissions, and ESG_Score are no longer statistically significant in this model ($p > 0.10$). This may indicate that the effects of these variables are masked by cross-country differences or that country fixed effects are dominant. The fixed effects of countries such as Turkey ($\beta = 0.505$, $p < 0.001$), Sweden, Poland, Norway, the Netherlands, and Spain are positive and significant. These countries have a higher tendency to issue green bonds compared to the reference country in the model.

The USA and Germany have significant negative coefficients. This indicates that, according to the estimated model, green bond levels in these countries are lower than in the reference country. In conclusion, this model shows that fixed country differences are decisive for green financial development. The effect of environmental variables loses its statistical significance when country fixed effects are included. This indicates that the green bond market is strongly related to political, legal, and macro structures (Zhang et al., 2023).

Green bond issuances were predicted using two different machine learning models. The Random Forest Regressor yielded more successful results compared to the XGBoost model. Random Forest achieved 18.5% explanatory power (R^2) on the test set and produced lower error metrics (RMSE = 60.81, MAE = 50.91).

This shows that the model was able to learn some patterns. XGBoost, on the other hand, failed to deliver the expected results on this dataset and produced a negative R^2 score (−0.008). This indicates that the model made worse predictions than the actual data. In conclusion, despite the relatively small sample size, Random Forest shows potential in modeling cross-country differences and the impact of environmental factors.

Modeling using the Random Forest algorithm revealed that Carbon_Pricing is the most influential determinant of green bond issuance (Importance Score = 0.39). Carbon prices (39.5%) stand out as the most important determinant by far, demonstrating that the economic pricing of carbon has a direct impact on investor decisions. CO_2 emissions (32.1%) and ESG scores (10.8%) also make significant contributions.

Spain and Turkey stand out among the countries with fixed effects; the dummy variables for these countries were found to be significant in the model, indicating that regional effects cannot be ignored. The XGBoost model produced a negative R^2 score (–0.008) on this dataset. This indicates that the model's predictive performance on the test data is worse than even predicting the average of the data. This poor performance may be due to both the small size of the dataset and the excessive space occupied by dummy variables in the model. This result shows that Random Forest is a better alternative for such complex but small panel data sets. The XGBoost model shows that country fixed effects are the most effective predictors in the estimation of green bond issuance.

The most influential variable was Country_Turkey (score = 0.196). This shows that the volume of green bonds in Turkey is more distinctive and decisive than in other countries. Country_Spain and Country_Sweden also had a significant impact on the model. Only one environmental variable made it into the top 5: CO_2 Emissions (0.076). This shows that environmental variables are weaker than country effects in the XGBoost model.

Time-fixed effects such as Year_2016 were found to be significant by the model, suggesting that certain years may have been turning points in green bond issuance. The XGBoost model only evaluated country fixed effects that had meaningful discriminatory power in decision trees; other country dummy variables were considered insignificant in the model and were not used in discrimination decisions.

This is a result of artificial intelligence-supported models automatically performing dimension reduction when determining variable importance scores (Broadstock et al., 2022; Raimo et al., 2024).

7 Conclusion

The findings suggest that carbon pricing operates as both a regulatory and a financial signal in energy markets. Where carbon markets are mature and disclosure standards are consistent, prices appear to translate into measurable financial incentives for low-emission projects. In less developed markets, however, the same mechanism is weakened by volatility and institutional uncertainty. Similar results have been reported in comparative studies showing that the maturity of carbon markets determines their ability to influence capital flows (OECD, 2023; Zhang et al., 2023).

This divergence highlights the role of policy credibility. Carbon-pricing instruments are effective only when markets trust their stability and long-term direction. Evidence from this study indicates that institutional transparency and predictable regulatory frameworks strengthen the financial relevance of carbon risk, supporting earlier findings that stable policy regimes amplify market responses to environmental pricing (Krueger et al., 2020; Stroebel & Wurgler, 2021).

From an investment perspective, carbon pricing influences not only the cost of capital but also portfolio-allocation decisions. Investors seem to reward jurisdictions where environmental policies are clear and consistently applied. This reinforces the idea that financial markets internalize environmental externalities once policy uncertainty is reduced (Amel-Zadeh & Serafeim, 2018; Broadstock et al., 2022). Such behavior aligns with behavioral-finance theories suggesting that transparency mitigates risk perception and improves the pricing of ESG-linked assets.

This research demonstrates that carbon pricing and green-finance instruments interact through both policy and market channels. Carbon prices provide a quantifiable measure of environmental risk that investors can incorporate into valuation models. Yet, the magnitude of this effect depends on national context and institutional capacity, implying that one-size-fits-all policy designs are unlikely to be effective. Consistent with the energy-finance literature, cross-country heterogeneity observed here supports the idea that macro-institutional strength and regulatory predictability shape the financial materiality of climate risk (OECD, 2023; Raimo et al., 2024).

In conclusion, the results emphasize that credible carbon-pricing frameworks not only drive decarbonization but also channel capital toward sustainable investments. The combination of econometric and machine-learning methods confirms that financial markets react to both the price and credibility of environmental policy signals. Policymakers aiming to foster green-finance development should therefore prioritize transparency, predictable regulation, and reinvestment of carbon revenues into sustainable-finance programs (OECD, 2023; Zhang et al., 2023).

Future research could extend this work by examining how carbon-pricing revenues are recycled into green-bond markets and whether advanced AI models can forecast the dynamic interplay between policy and finance. Such studies would deepen understanding of how financial innovation can support a credible, efficient, and equitable global energy transition (Broadstock et al., 2022).

References

Aldy, J. E., & Stavins, R. N. (2012). The promise and problems of pricing carbon: Theory and experience. *Journal of Environment and Development, 21*(2), 152–180. https://doi.org/10.1177/1070496512442508

Amel-Zadeh, A., & Serafeim, G. (2018). Why and how investors use ESG information: Evidence from a global survey. *Financial Analysts Journal, 74*(3), 87–103. https://doi.org/10.2469/faj.v74.n3.2

Baker, M., Bergstresser, D., Serafeim, G., & Wurgler, J. (2019). *Financing the response to climate change: The pricing and ownership of U.S. green bonds* (NBER Working Paper No. 25194). https://doi.org/10.3386/w25194

Baker, M., & Wurgler, J. (2006). Investor sentiment and the cross-section of stock returns. *Journal of Finance, 61*(4), 1645–1680. https://doi.org/10.1111/j.1540-6261.2006.00885.x

Battiston, S., Mandel, A., Monasterolo, I., Schütze, F., & Visentin, G. (2017). A climate stress-test of the financial system. *Nature Climate Change, 7*, 283–288. https://doi.org/10.1038/nclimate3255

Bayer, P., & Aklin, M. (2020). The European Union emissions trading system reduced CO_2 emissions despite low prices. *Proceedings of the National Academy of Sciences, 117*(16), 8804–8812. https://doi.org/10.1073/pnas.1918128117

Broadstock, D. C., Zhang, D., & Zhu, H. (2022). Climate finance, carbon pricing, and institutional quality: New evidence from international markets. *Energy Economics, 110*, Article 106003. https://doi.org/10.1016/j.eneco.2022.106003

Dyck, A., Lins, K. V., Roth, L., & Wagner, H. F. (2019). Do institutional investors drive corporate social responsibility? International evidence. *Journal of Financial Economics, 131*(3), 693–714. https://doi.org/10.1016/j.jfineco.2018.08.013

Engle, R. F., Giglio, S., Kelly, B., Lee, H., & Stroebel, J. (2020). Hedging climate change news. *The Review of Financial Studies, 33*(3), 1184–1216. https://doi.org/10.1093/rfs/hhz072

Flammer, C. (2021). Corporate green bonds. *Journal of Financial Economics, 142*(2), 499–516. https://doi.org/10.1016/j.jfineco.2021.05.014

Friede, G., Busch, T., & Bassen, A. (2015). ESG and financial performance: Aggregated evidence from more than 2000 empirical studies. *Journal of Sustainable Finance & Investment, 5*(4), 210–233. https://doi.org/10.1080/20430795.2015.1118917

Henisz, W., Koller, T., & Nuttall, R. (2019). Five ways that ESG creates value. *McKinsey Quarterly*. https://www.mckinsey.com

Ilhan, E., Sautner, Z., & Vilkov, G. (2021). Carbon tail risk. *The Review of Financial Studies, 34*(3), 1540–1571. https://doi.org/10.1093/rfs/hhaa071

International Energy Agency. (2022). *World Energy Outlook 2022*. IEA. https://www.iea.org/reports/world-energy-outlook-2022

Karpf, A., & Mandel, A. (2018). The changing value of the "green" label on the U.S. municipal bond market. *Nature Climate Change, 8*(2), 161–165. https://doi.org/10.1038/s41558-017-0062-7

Krueger, P., Sautner, Z., & Starks, L. T. (2020). The importance of climate risks for institutional investors. *The Review of Financial Studies, 33*(3), 1067–1111. https://doi.org/10.1093/rfs/hhz137

Martin, R., Muûls, M., & Wagner, U. J. (2016). The impact of the European Union Emissions Trading Scheme on regulated firms: What is the evidence after ten years? *Review of Environmental Economics and Policy, 10*(1), 129–148. https://doi.org/10.1093/reep/rev016

OECD. (2023). *Carbon pricing and competitiveness interactions: Global overview*. OECD Publishing. https://doi.org/10.1787/carb-price-2023-en

Raimo, N., Vitolla, F., Rubino, M., & Garzoni, A. (2024). Artificial intelligence in sustainable finance: A machine-learning framework for ESG and climate-risk analysis. *Journal of Cleaner Production, 448*, Article 141216. https://doi.org/10.1016/j.jclepro.2023.141216

Stiglitz, J. E., Stern, N., et al. (2017). *Report of the high-level commission on carbon prices*. Carbon Pricing Leadership Coalition. https://www.carbonpricingleadership.org/report-of-the-highlevel-commission-on-carbon-prices

Stroebel, J., & Wurgler, J. (2021). What do you think about climate finance? *Journal of Financial Economics, 142*(2), 487–498. https://doi.org/10.1016/j.jfineco.2021.04.002

Tang, D. Y., & Zhang, Y. (2020). Do shareholders benefit from green bonds? *Journal of Corporate Finance, 61*, Article 101427. https://doi.org/10.1016/j.jcorpfin.2018.12.001

Zhang, D., Broadstock, D. C., & Wang, X. (2023). Institutional determinants of carbon-pricing effectiveness: Evidence from the EU ETS and beyond. *Energy Policy, 176*, Article 113584. https://doi.org/10.1016/j.enpol.2023.113584

Zhang, D., Wang, J., & Wang, X. (2022). Sustainable finance: Concepts, frameworks and empirical evidence. *Journal of Environmental Management, 313*, Article 114990. https://doi.org/10.1016/j.jenvman.2022.114990

Green Finance and Decarbonization: A Bibliometric Analysis with a Latin American Perspective

Angeles Montserrat Govea Franco and Heriberto Salazar Soto

Abstract The purpose of this research is to analyse the relationship between green finance and decarbonization with a bibliometric approach under a global context and highlight the participation of Latin America. The bibliometric study was analysed with data received from the Scopus platform, which was analysed to obtain node maps in VOSviewer. From the Scopus analysis, 483 documents were extracted in which green finance and decarbonization are related. Excel was used to create the tables shown in this paper, analysing the data in stages (planning, implementation, and dissemination of results). Among the main observations, 52.9% of the studies carried out in relation to green finance and decarbonization were conducted in the fields of environmental sciences, economics, finance, and energy and fuels. Additionally, there was an 85.5% increase in the number of publications relating to these constructs in the last two decades. Finally, the countries with the most studies were China, the United Kingdom, India, and Germany. To finish with, the low participation of emerging economies such as Latin America in the development of research on the transition to clean energy is noticeable.

Keywords Green energy · Low-Carbon · Decarbonization · Green finance · Bibliometric

1 Introduction

In a global context marked by a high level of trade openness, decarbonization and green finance have emerged as strategic priorities. Such relevance is mainly due to the fact that the energy sector is responsible for approximately 75% of total global

A. M. G. Franco (✉)
School of Economics and Business Science, Universidad Panamericana, Aguascalientes, México
e-mail: amgoveaf@up.edu.mx

H. S. Soto
Centro de Ciencias Económicas y Administrativas, Universidad Autónoma de Aguascalientes, Aguascalientes, México
e-mail: heriberto.salazar@edu.uaa.mx

A. Akusta and M. Gün (eds.), *Financial Frontiers in Energy Markets*, Contributions to Finance and Accounting, https://doi.org/10.1007/978-3-032-16738-5_12

CO_2 emissions (Black et al., 2024). CO_2 emissions are associated with the use of non-renewable resources or also known as fossil fuels. In large quantities, they are capable of causing heat waves, droughts, and natural disasters, among others, as a result of global warming, which causes not only environmental effects in the first instance but also generates negative impacts on business operations and economic activities of each country (Tiwari et al., 2025).

Wan et al. (2022) mention that the path to transformation towards cleaner energies, better known as renewable energies, is led by a commitment to low carbon emissions, and this is achieved through the use of green finance, which serves as a key point for achieving economic growth and development without compromising the future of the planet.

On the other hand, Al Mamun et al. (2022) highlights that, as part of green finance, the use of green bonds is a great instrument for attracting resources to economic sectors in which the engagement in decarbonization is desired, bringing with it greater energy efficiency, waste and pollution control and an increase in the production of sustainable energies, i.e., by improving the energy market it is feasible to make an energy transition in an economy.

Stringer and Ramírez-Melgarejo (2024) proposed that initiating a transition toward decarbonization in the energy sector would be far less expensive than continuing to maintain a fossil-fuel-based energy market. This contributes to the discussion by suggesting that decarbonization, particularly for Latin American countries, is not as costly as posited in other works. It is therefore important to analyse the Latin American case specifically and to consider how these factors are reflected in the development of tools that can support the transition to lower-cost energy sources that benefit industry and its surrounding environment.

Thus, in the particular case of Latin America, where the population is expected to grow from 634 million in 2020 to 784 million by 2050, it is increasingly important to consider decarbonization, its supply, and its market, given that demand will rise exponentially; not to mention that the region has enormous potential to harness renewable sources for the generation of clean energy. In this context, this study aims to examine how the concepts of green finance and decarbonization have been addressed globally, from the perspective of researchers and scientific production, in order to detail the associated trends and the various angles and approaches from which they may be addressed (Icaza-Alvarez et al., 2024).

2 Conceptual Framework: Green Finance and Decarbonization

Based on the targets agreed in the Paris Agreement to keep global warming below 1.5 °C, all countries need to quadruple their annual investment in clean energy, especially northern economies, to phase out carbon emissions from the energy system through several steps, but mainly by replacing fossil fuels with renewable energy

(Babic, 2024). A key enabler for implementing the energy transition is the role of financial development, which contains incentives for access to finance for green energy projects and for research and development of green technologies (Benfica & Marques, 2024).

Decarbonization must be implemented through the operationalization of efficient and organized green finance, where the design of fiscal and economic instruments promotes the transition to renewable energy and thus has a positive impact on reducing the prices of fossil-based fuels and energies (Black et al., 2024). To unlock the potential that exists in the use of renewable energies, it is necessary for the financing to be allocated where it really generates a significant environmental impact. Therein lies the importance of green finance that, through incentives such as green bonds, can motivate a market for private participation in clean energy generation industries, which would reflect a clear and progressive decarbonization. This would reflect a clear and progressive decarbonization, which plays an important role since, through this progressive reduction of CO_2 emissions, it can lead to a sustainable economy (Jiang et al., 2025).

That is, in order to move towards decarbonization, it is necessary to have comprehensive public policies with tax incentives, economic support for research and development projects, combined in the medium and long term, focused on the promotion of clean energies, and to stop the dependence on natural gas and oil. Thus, without adequate financing, there can be no decarbonization, especially considering emerging economies, which have a very large gap between developed countries, whose position in terms of green finance and renewable energy generation and consumption is much more competitive than that of these economies, which have lower growth and participation in green markets (Barragán-Ocaña et al., 2025).

In addition to its impact on the financial market, there must be an adoption of clean energy to achieve a significant effect on the reduction of energy poverty, since a financial system with foreign direct investment focused on industries with green technology and with an energy fiscal policy supports development and the reduction of energy inequalities in society, and, especially, in underdeveloped countries. Therefore, to confront energy poverty and shift towards decarbonization in Latin America, investment must be strategically directed towards local strengthening (Mohsin et al., 2022).

In other words, to continue efforts to combat climate change, it has been shown that the consumption of clean energy from renewable sources, especially those obtained from the sun and wind, is the key to substantially reducing carbon emissions worldwide, even though it has been seen that the strengthening of the energy sector and the growth of the Gross Domestic Product help to increase these emissions exponentially, or that it further highlights the importance of the decarbonization process and the adoption of green finance combined with an energy policy in countries (Chen et al., 2025).

3 Literature Review

In recent years, the use of constructs such as green finance and decarbonization in industry has become fundamentally important for understanding how capital is moving toward an energy transition. However, it is important to note that aspects such as price changes, commitments to comply with countries' climate agendas, and different regulatory frameworks have a significant effect on the results of the study and the use of these concepts (Fahmy, 2022; Polzin et al., 2019). Therefore, it is relevant to show the big picture of the different key elements that encompass green finance and decarbonization, to be able to study, ground, and analyse them in the history they share in the literature and, thus, be able to conduct a more detailed study of their evolution over the years in research. Integrating these findings will provide insight into specific patterns and thus pave the way for future research to develop hypotheses that relate these constructs and how they interact in the business environment.

As a first consideration, it is important to highlight that green finance is categorized as a set of flows, financial instruments, and actors, public and private (Elie et al., 2020), that use capital for the development and investment of innovations related to renewable energies (Taghizadeh-Hesary & Yoshino, 2020). However, according to Zhang (2018), green finance represents the link between energy and financial markets. Therefore, it highlights the relevance of the analysis of strategies that allow the correct implementation of appropriate concepts for the industry (Zioło et al., 2024). Thus, green finance is a tool that, besides being a relatively new construct (Ji et al., 2019; Marcinkowska et al., 2025), must be analysed in depth to understand its characteristics and thus develop strategies focused on its implementation within industries.

On the other hand, decarbonization as a construct within industries is more complicated to conceptualize since, rather than a tool that can be implemented in processes, it is an agent that is to be reduced through the implementation of various strategies (Bataille et al., 2021). However, decarbonization can be expressed as the decrease in the average carbon intensity produced by an organization. This can be done by taking into account the processes and objectives of the company, the metrics around the concept, and the goal set by the industry itself (Cheshmehzangi, 2016; Linton et al., 2022). Thus, being a concept related to the impact of organizations on their environment, it becomes relevant to analyse the impact decarbonization can have on the economic and financial arenas.

Given the nature of the ideas analysed and the way in which they have an impact on the industry, it becomes relevant to look into the relationship in the literature that green finance has with respect to decarbonization (Al Mamun et al., 2022). The authors Al Mamun et al. (2022) stated in their research that industries focused on green finance are able to reduce their carbon footprint in the short and long term, with these industries benefiting through green bonds for the implementation of such measures. In turn, Campiglio (2016) explains that green finance applied to decarbonization processes is essential to ensure the development of financial policies and macroprudential regulations that provide incentives to organizations that implement emission reduction strategies.

Conversely, decarbonization can be considered a key financial lever that will allow, from an energy point of view, to have a positive impact on the strategies that can be implemented around green finance (Polzin et al., 2019). This will ensure that organizations that implement these strategies will obtain a financial benefit while reducing the environmental impact that their production processes may generate (Ibishova et al., 2024). Continuing with the relationship between green finance and decarbonization, it is highlighted that financial instruments are vital tools for the transition towards new implementation policies within companies, since by analysing their relationship and impact, it will be possible to develop different frameworks and directions for their compliance (Fu et al., 2024).

Thus, from the Latin American perspective, it is important to take into account the role of green finance and its relationship with the decarbonization of industries. That is, green finance should be seen as an opportunity to move resources and capital costs towards clean technologies that can reduce carbon emissions (Benfica & Marques, 2024; Stringer & Ramírez-Melgarejo, 2024). Among several studies that have been conducted around these constructs (Calcaterra et al., 2024), it has been concluded that tools related to regulatory frameworks focused on green finance, such as financial openness, green bonds, or the design of financial incentives, support the development of decarbonization trends within organizations (Bersalli et al., 2020). However, the relationship between green finance and decarbonization research needs to be analyzed in depth in order to measure its impact, in future research, on specific markets such as Latin America.

In conclusion, it is evident that there are several research studies that analyse green finance and decarbonization together. Therefore, the objective of this research is to analyse the connection between these constructs in the literature, the way in which they have been related in the industry, and, in general, the history they have followed over the years in research around the world. This is done with the objective of pointing out future areas of enhancement in research, specifically in Latin America, with a particular focus on Mexico, and to point out the importance they could have in the future in the theoretical and practical domains.

4 The Methodology of the Study

The main objective of this research is to develop a bibliometric study around the constructs of green finance and decarbonization, as well as a discussion around the Latin American context. Therefore, to identify the background of the research undertaken, it is essential to understand what a bibliometric study is, as well as the elements to consider in its development, which will help clarify the goals of the analysis presented.

A bibliometric analysis is understood as a procedure that, through the statistical and mathematical methods implemented, makes it possible to determine the depth with which the constructs have been quantitatively examined and how they have been related in the literature over the years (Ying et al., 2023). Thus, studies with a bibliometric focus highlight the relevance of the constructs analysed, which in turn serve as an indicator of their growth in the literature (Mukherjee et al., 2022). Moreover, by developing the bibliometrics of the variables of interest, one obtains an overview of indicators, thereby gaining context across different studies (Alarcón-Sánchez & Soriano-Sandoval, 2022).

In this way, bibliometric studies function as a tool that allows the analysed constructs to be examined from multiple perspectives, such as a multidisciplinary lens, differences in authors' conceptualizations, and results obtained in diverse contexts. This yields a considerable impact for research employing this approach, as it provides relevance by mapping the range of studies on the same relationships between variables (Öztürk et al., 2024). That said, it becomes evident that bibliometric studies provide high-impact information for research that examines the variables involved (Passas, 2024). In sum, bibliometric studies are especially useful in high-impact research because they draw on analyses conducted by various authors, furnish tools for conceptualization, and offer data from studies carried out in different contexts along with insight into the impact those studies had under the approaches used (Caterino et al., 2022).

Tranfield et al. (2003) state that bibliometric studies should be conducted taking into account a systematic literature review, i.e., considering the stages of planning, implementation, and dissemination of results (Podsakoff et al., 2008). This will allow us to take into account the number of previous studies carried out around the constructs of interest to obtain an optimal evaluation and analysis once the method is developed, being this the strategy that will be taken into account for this research (Alarcón-Sánchez & Soriano-Sandoval, 2022).

On the other hand, selecting the database to be analysed is a fundamental part of the study, as it will make it possible to obtain clear information for subsequent review. Given its relevance and the way discoveries are disseminated, scientific journals were selected as a viable and broadly relevant source of information (Rethlefsen et al., 2024) on research and its contributions in diverse contexts. Scopus, as a database that includes citations of scientific literature and abstracts useful for analysis, becomes a viable option for use in bibliometric studies.

Moreover, it is part of Elsevier, a publisher with the necessary prestige to draw information from the scientific articles presented there, and it is a multidisciplinary database (Elsevier, 2025). Thus, this database was chosen because it offers extensive and relevant information that can be used in a bibliometric study. Accordingly, the development of the research proceeded by entering the keywords "Green Finance" and "Decarbonization" in Scopus and subsequently filtering for articles in which the keyword search was conducted in English, since more than 90% of all citations in high-impact journals are written in that language (Cao et al., 2024).

Finally, the information in this study was analysed for the period between 2005 and 2025, yielding a total of 483 articles. These articles addressed the variables, jointly that is, the relationship between green finance and decarbonization, and included publications from specialized journals, book chapters, books, and published theses.

Furthermore, the VOSviewer tool made it possible to analyse, in greater depth and visually, the relationships present in the information obtained from the database, resulting in a network analysis. As for the generation of tables and graphs, Excel was used because it is an easily accessible and manageable tool for this type of information.

5 Results of the Analyses

This section presents the results of the bibliometric analysis with respect to the two basic concepts of green finance and decarbonization or reduction of CO_2 emissions. The first analysis is carried out based on the areas of knowledge where most research has been carried out with these constructs, for which Fig. 1 is added to detail the 10 main fields where these studies have been carried out.

As can be seen, the analysis reveals that the fields of study *Environmental Science Technology* with 24%, *Economics, Econometrics and Finance* with 14.7% and *Energy and Fuels* with 14.2% concentrate the largest proportion of research on green finance and decarbonization, with a total of 52.9% between the three of them, i.e., more than half of the studies carried out are immersed in these areas, which has an

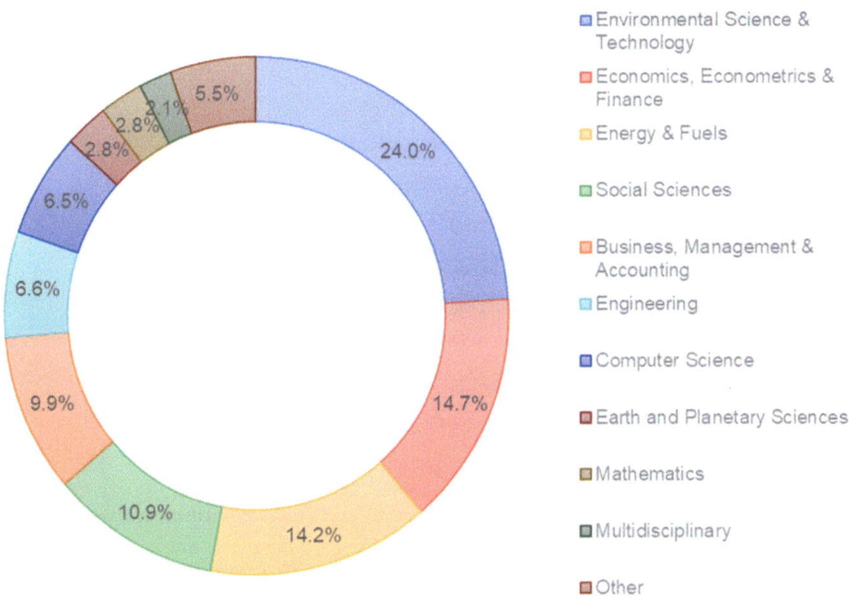

Fig. 1 Study areas where research has been carried out on the connection between green finance and decarbonization (2005–2025). *Source* Own preparation based on (Scopus, 2025)

impact on the environmental effects on the planet, the economic and financial analysis linked to their effects and development, which is why these fields have shown the most adoption and concern for global decarbonization.

Understanding the growth in the number of publications that link the constructs of green finance and decarbonization will provide a broad overview. This information will make it possible to identify how these concepts have been studied over time and the relevance they have gained within the research field. Analysing the growth of these constructs in the literature will help identify trends that may, in turn, guide their implementation in industry, an analysis that is vitally important for organizations putting these strategies into practice. Therefore, it is necessary to examine this evolution in order to generate evidence that can inform decision-making.

In other words, the temporal evolution of publications on green finance and decarbonization has been exponential, going from 2 publications in 2005 to 173 in 2025. In other words, there has been an 85.5% growth in two decades, which shows a remarkable interest and relevance in the issue of environmental care, economic growth, but a clear transition to low carbon emissions by the economies worldwide. Finally, to complete the analysis of the results, it is important to visualize the authors who have published the most research on these constructs, which are detailed in Fig. 2.

Although it is a topic of interest and there has been much growth in the number of publications per year, the number of publications per author shows a different behaviour, since the maximum number of publications per author is 6, leaving the rest of the authors, or most of them, with only one publication on this topic.

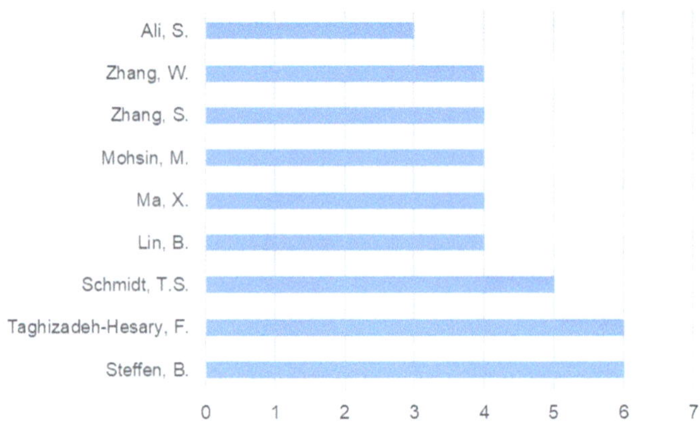

Fig. 2 Main authors addressing the relationship between green finance and decarbonisation. *Source* Own preparation based on (Scopus, 2025)

6 Discussion

The findings outlined above point to important aspects that need to be taken into account when analysing green finance and decarbonization. In the first place, the main branches of research in which the analysed constructs stand out are environmental sciences and technologies with 24% and, in second place, economics, econometrics, and finance with a 14.7% ratio. Likewise, an analysis of the evolution of the research on green finance and decarbonization as a whole was carried out, resulting in the fact that they began to be envisaged in 2005, and the trend shows that their relationship in the literature has increased as time goes by. Finally, it was shown that there is a significant number of authors present in the development of research on these constructs, the main authors being Steffen and Taghizadeh-Hesary.

Such findings open the way to discuss the way in which these constructs are studied. Firstly, it is analyzed how the fact that there is a greater concentration in the field of environmental sciences and technologies shows the relevance given to the technical-environmental aspect and, only after learning about the management of technologies and their use with environmental aspects, an economic, econometric and environmental approach was obtained. This is consistent with a scenario in which organizations had to make a gradual transition to green technologies, which was later reflected on financial aspects. Thus, the need to generate practices that allow not only environmental progress is reinforced, as well as financial issues that allow an easier transition to decarbonization in companies.

However, the conversation around green finance and decarbonization is highly concentrated in specific geographic sectors. China is shown to be an important and dominant node in the research of these constructs as a whole, with another worthy representative being the United Kingdom. Therefore, Graph 1 shows the countries with the highest research production, where the proposed variables are studied in depth and the connections in the research that has been carried out between these countries.

As already mentioned, Graph 1 highlights China as the dominant node in the constructs analysed, while the United Kingdom appears as the second key factor, with these two having strong research links to countries such as the United States, Germany, Italy, and India. This is where the absence or low participation of Latin American countries is observed, which may have different implications. Firstly, the evidence and frameworks concerning green finance and decarbonization issues are outside the Latin American developing countries, so, in order to start seeing strategies and development around them, it would be necessary to customize these concepts to the Latin context (Deb & Chen, 2025).

Secondly, the need to develop scientific policies is evident, that is, with evidenced given by projects in similar contexts, to propose new policies related to green energies that have an impact on the financial sphere. Finally, the characteristics of the region do not allow the implementation of decarbonization measures, which influences decision-making and affects the development of studies that show the financial factor around these strategies (Desalegn & Tangl, 2022).

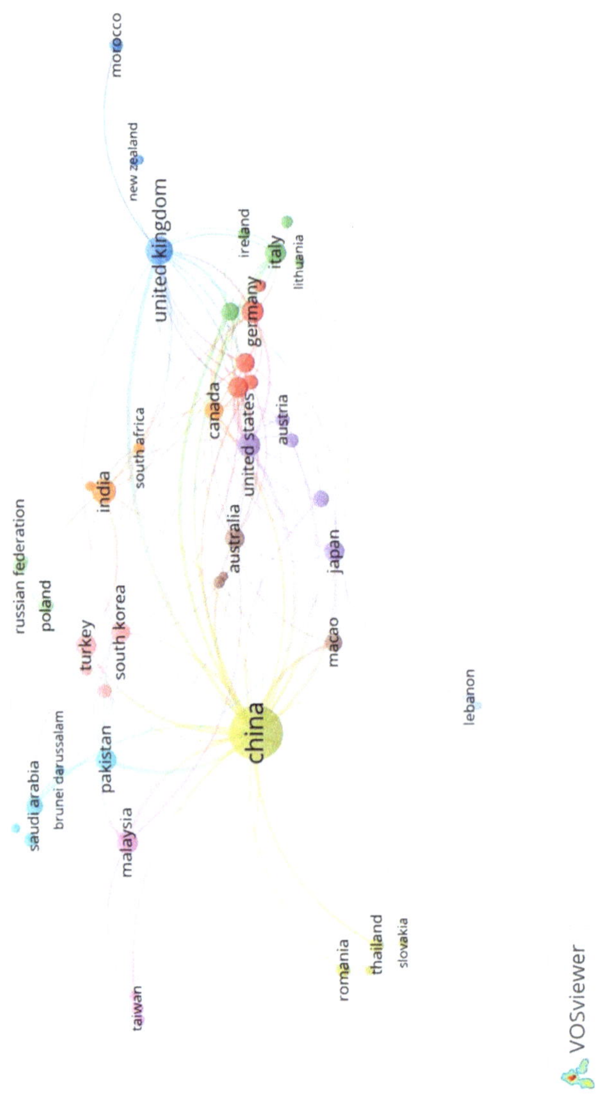

Graph 1 Relationship between countries with green finance and decarbonization research. *Source* Own preparation based on (Vosviewer, 2025)

On the other hand, Graph 2 shows the key concepts that are most commonly mentioned in the research related to green finance and decarbonization. The map of nodes shows that there are keywords around the analysed variables, such as green finance, climate change, investments, and energy efficiency, which have different implications.

The relationships between the keyword nodes seen in Graph 2 show that the literature systematically links the mobilization of financial capital and green energies with the decarbonization of organizations. Thus, the representation of keywords such as digital finance, Fintech, and financial development suggests an interest in linking new elements to these topics, such as product and channel innovation for the development of new financial strategies that increase the decarbonization of companies.

Continuing with this idea, the existence of words such as governance approach, banking, financial stability, and central bank points out the maturation of the transition towards research that seeks to analyse financial systems to promote the development of policies that benefit these constructs, leaving aside research that only analyses a project for a specific level (Polzin et al., 2019).

The gaps in the development of knowledge of these constructs in Latin America reveal concluding information for this research. As a starting point, there is a lack of

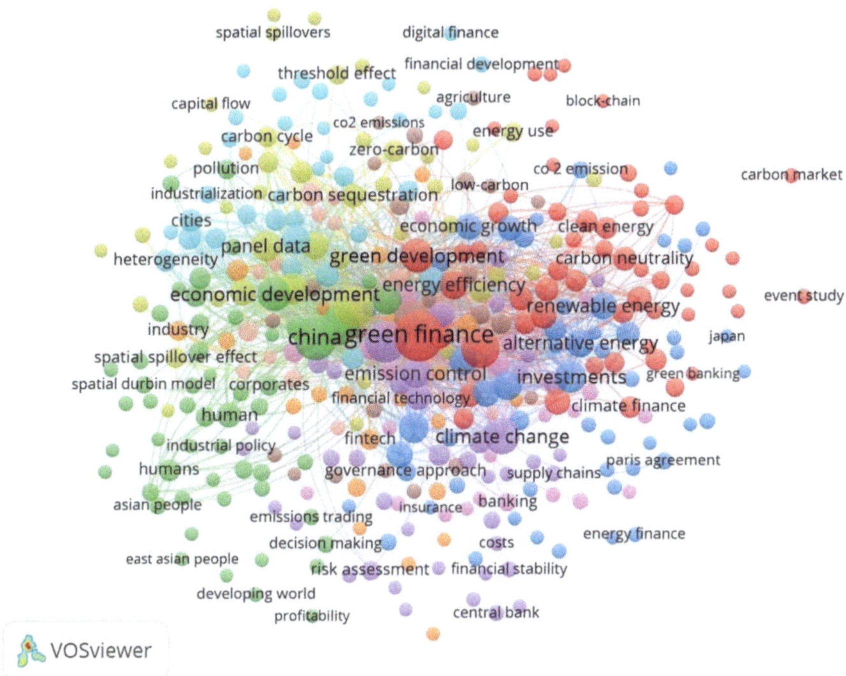

Graph 2 Relationship between keywords in research on energy finance and decarbonisation. *Source* Own preparation based on (Vosviewer, 2025)

research that takes advantage of the use of public data on capital costs per technology, regulatory policies, and performance of instruments such as green bonds. In addition, the need to promote decarbonization policies in industrial processes that allow us to see, in the medium or long term, their financial impact and if, in this way, they will allow the increase and implementation of green measures. It is important to take into account that Latin American countries are under development (Mendoza-Mendoza et al., 2025), and therefore, priority is given to tools and strategies for compliance with mandatory regulations, setting aside those practices that could represent an advantage in the longer term rather than in the short term.

Finally, it becomes evident that, among the limitations of this study, there is reliance on English words, repetition or normalization of the VOSviewer tool, and some other elements, such as the lack of knowledge regarding the quality of the articles considered in the metrics. However, the results shown point to a clear global energy transition, where financial aspects are taken into account to achieve the objective of decarbonizing industries. On the other hand, Latin America has little participation in the implementation and generation of research on green finance and decarbonization. Therefore, it is of utmost importance to develop studies in which this point of view is addressed, to produce clear evidence on the understanding of these issues, and thus to scale investments focused not only on studies, but also on the implementation and creation of policies related to the analysed constructs.

7 Conclusion

In this paper, we analysed the connection between green finance and decarbonization, two concepts of growing interest in the global agenda aimed at mitigating CO_2 emissions. An analysis of scientific production over the last 20 years showed an exponential increase in research on this subject. This behaviour is particularly evident in three academic areas that together account for more than half of the total volume of publications: Environmental Sciences, Economics and Finance, and Energy and Fuels. This trend not only frames the global relevance of the issue but also suggests that green finance and decarbonization are two separate concepts that are intrinsically linked and operate in tandem.

However, the results also indicate that participation in this line of research is not homogeneous worldwide. The country that has registered the highest volume of analysis is China, followed by countries such as the United Kingdom, India, and Germany. This scenario, which is consistent especially with China's role as a leader in the advancement of clean energy and the transition away from fossil fuels, contrasts with the case of the American continent. For China, for example, this strategic approach has enabled it not only to advance its environmental objectives but also to reduce costs and strengthen its economic competitiveness, consolidating its position as a world power. In Latin America, on the other hand, the scenario is completely different.

If the goal is to achieve a global energy transition that will keep the planet's temperature rise within manageable levels, green finance and decarbonization must be spread more equitably across all nations. The low or non-existent participation of Latin American countries, for example, represents a clear disparity in terms of the transition scheme to low-carbon energy industries. This is a significant knowledge gap, which may limit the development of solutions and strategies specific to geographic and economic contexts with characteristics different from those of developed or first-world countries.

Therefore, it will be worthwhile to begin further research focused on the Latin American context as part of the beginning of the transition to renewable energies, to generate knowledge adapted to the economic and environmental realities of emerging economies, as they are far from the world's leading powers in terms of natural resource potential and public policies, and thus contribute more comprehensively to global decarbonization efforts.

Not only are Latin American countries far from achieving their carbon and greenhouse gas emission reduction targets, but paradoxically, they also have high levels of natural resources that make the creation of renewable energies immensely promising, that is, their geographical position, climate and wind types, coastal areas, aquifers, and in most cases, their vast territories where sunlight can be exploited. There are currently no environmental policies that incentivize and promote this support for decarbonization through sustainable economic growth. This is also reflected in the scarcity of laws that promote the opening of the market for sustainable competitiveness, where green technology and carbon markets exist to drive not only the transition to decarbonization but also the economic development of countries.

This highlights the need to deepen research on these topics in Latin American countries to underscore their importance and, in turn, enable the formulation of policies for their implementation. Generating research that informs policymaking is a key factor for fostering the development and deployment of the tools under study. In conclusion, Latin America requires new policies that promote the implementation of practices in which green finance and decarbonization serve as the central axis of organizational development.

References

Al Mamun, M., Boubaker, S., & Nguyen, D. K. (2022). Green finance and decarbonization: Evidence from around the world. *Finance Research Letters*, *46*(PB), 102807. https://doi.org/10.1016/j.frl.2022.102807

Alarcón-Sánchez, K. M., & Soriano-Sandoval, J. L. (2022). The integration of CSR within communication as a strategic factor of competitiveness: Bibliometric analysis. *Scientia et PRAXIS*, *2*(3), 55–73. https://doi.org/10.55965/setp.2.03.a4

Babic, M. (2024, February). Green finance in the global energy transition: Actors, instruments, and politics. *Energy Research and Social Science*, *111*, 103482. https://doi.org/10.1016/j.erss.2024.103482

Barragán-Ocaña, A., Cecilio-Ayala, E., Silva-Borjas, P., Cortés-Ruiz, J. A., & Hernandez-Cardona, E. Y. (2025). Policies and sustainable energy transition in the global environment: Challenges for Latin America. *Heliyon, 11*(6). https://doi.org/10.1016/j.heliyon.2025.e42295

Bataille, C., Nilsson, L. J., & Jotzo, F. (2021, September). Industry in a net-zero emissions world: New mitigation pathways, new supply chains, modelling needs and policy implications. *Energy and Climate Change, 2,* 100059. https://doi.org/10.1016/j.egycc.2021.100059

Benfica, V., & Marques, A. C. (2024). Technological and financial development as drivers of Latin America's energy transition. *Renewable Energy, 237*(PB), 121664. https://doi.org/10.1016/j.renene.2024.121664

Bersalli, G., Menanteau, P., & El-Methni, J. (2020). Renewable energy policy effectiveness: A panel data analysis across Europe and Latin America. *Renewable and Sustainable Energy Reviews, 133*(August 2019). https://doi.org/10.1016/j.rser.2020.110351

Black, S., de Mooij, R., Gaspar, V., Parry, I., & Zhunussova, K. (2024). Fiscal implications of global decarbonization. *International Monetary Fund* (Vol. 2024, Número 045). https://doi.org/10.5089/9798400269516.001

Calcaterra, M., Aleluia Reis, L., Fragkos, P., Briera, T., de Boer, H. S., Egli, F., Emmerling, J., Iyer, G., Mittal, S., Polzin, F. H. J., Sanders, M. W. J. L., Schmidt, T. S., Serebriakova, A., Steffen, B., van de Ven, D. J., van Vuuren, D. P., Waidelich, P., & Tavoni, M. (2024). Reducing the cost of capital to finance the energy transition in developing countries. *Nature Energy, 9*(10), 1241–1251. https://doi.org/10.1038/s41560-024-01606-7

Campiglio, E. (2016). Beyond carbon pricing: The role of banking and monetary policy in financing the transition to a low-carbon economy. *Ecological Economics, 121,* 220–230. https://doi.org/10.1016/j.ecolecon.2015.03.020

Cao, Y., Sickles, R. C., Triebs, T. P., & Tumlinson, J. (2024). Linguistic distance to English impedes research performance. *Research Policy, 53*(4), Article 104971. https://doi.org/10.1016/j.respol.2024.104971

Caterino, M., Rinaldi, M., Fera, M., Macchiaroli, R., & Bottani, E. (2022). Research trends in clean, green and sustainable manufacturing: A bibliometric review. *IFAC-PapersOnLine, 55*(10), 2425–2430. https://doi.org/10.1016/j.ifacol.2022.10.072

Chen, H., Zhang, L., Pinzon, S., Chen, H., & Chen, B. (2025, February). Decarbonizing the G7: Renewable energy, economic growth, globalization, and policy Pathways to sustainability. *Renewable Energy, 244,* 122671. https://doi.org/10.1016/j.renene.2025.122671

Cheshmehzangi, A. (2016). China's new-type urbanisation plan (NUP) and the foreseeing challenges for decarbonization of cities: A review. *Energy Procedia, 104,* 146–152. https://doi.org/10.1016/j.egypro.2016.12.026

Deb, A., & Chen, C. (2025). Mapping the field of climate finance research: A bibliometric analysis. *Journal of Sustainable Finance and Investment, 15*(1), 182–204. https://doi.org/10.1080/20430795.2024.2441195

Desalegn, G., & Tangl, A. (2022). Developing countries in the lead: A bibliometric approach to green finance. *Energies, 15*(12), 1–19. https://doi.org/10.3390/en15124436

Elie, L., Granier, C., & Rigot, S. (2020). The different types of renewable energy finance: A bibliometric analysis. *Energy Economics, 93,* Article 104997. https://doi.org/10.1016/j.eneco.2020.104997

Elsevier. (2025). *Scopus: A comprehensive abstract and citation database for impact makers.* https://www.elsevier.com/products/scopus

Fahmy, H. (2022). The rise in investors' awareness of climate risks after the Paris Agreement and the clean energy-oil-technology prices nexus. *Energy Economics, 106*(November 2021), 105738. https://doi.org/10.1016/j.eneco.2021.105738

Fu, C., Lu, L., & Pirabi, M. (2024). Advancing green finance: A review of climate change and decarbonization. *Digital Economy and Sustainable Development, 2*(1), 1–23. https://doi.org/10.1007/s44265-023-00026-x

Ibishova, B., Misund, B., & Tveterås, R. (2024, July). Driving green: Financial benefits of carbon emission reduction in companies. *International Review of Financial Analysis, 96*, 103757. https://doi.org/10.1016/j.irfa.2024.103757

Icaza-Alvarez, D., Jurado, F., & Tostado-Véliz, M. (2024). Smart energy planning for the decarbonization of Latin America and the Caribbean in 2050. *Energy Reports, 11*(May), 6160–6185. https://doi.org/10.1016/j.egyr.2024.05.067

Ji, Q., Li, J., & Sun, X. (2019). New challenge and research development in global energy financialization. *Emerging Markets Finance and Trade, 55*(12), 2669–2672. https://doi.org/10.1080/1540496X.2019.1636588

Jiang, Y., Ather Bukhari, A. A., Ather Bukhari, W. A., & Khamdamov, S. J. (2025, March). Integrating green finance and energy transitions for decarbonization: Policy pathways to achieve COP-29 goals in E7 economies. *Journal of Environmental Management, 382*, 125217. https://doi.org/10.1016/j.jenvman.2025.125217

Linton, S., Clarke, A., & Tozer, L. (2022, November). Technical pathways to deep decarbonization in cities: Eight best practice case studies of transformational climate mitigation. *Energy Research and Social Science, 86,* 102422. https://doi.org/10.1016/j.erss.2021.102422

Marcinkowska, M., Brzeszczyński, J., Charteris, A., Gajdka, J., Obojska, L., & Szczygielski, J. J. (2025). Sustainability, energy finance and the role of central banks: A review of current insights and future research directions. *Energy Economics, 144,* Article 108084. https://doi.org/10.1016/j.eneco.2024.108084

Mendoza-Mendoza, A., Visbal-Cadavid, D., & De La Hoz-Domínguez, E. (2025). Classification of Latin American and Caribbean countries based on multidimensional development indicators: A multivariate empirical analysis. *Economies, 13*(6), 1–21. https://doi.org/10.3390/economies13060178

Mohsin, M., Taghizadeh-Hesary, F., & Shahbaz, M. (2022, March). Nexus between financial development and energy poverty in Latin America. *Energy Policy, 165*, 112925. https://doi.org/10.1016/j.enpol.2022.112925

Mukherjee, D., Lim, W. M., Kumar, S., & Donthu, N. (2022). Guidelines for advancing theory and practice through bibliometric research. *Journal of Business Research, 148*(May), 101–115. https://doi.org/10.1016/j.jbusres.2022.04.042

Öztürk, O., Kocaman, R., & Kanbach, D. K. (2024). How to design bibliometric research: An overview and a framework proposal. *Review of Managerial Science, 18*(11), 3333–3361. https://doi.org/10.1007/s11846-024-00738-0

Passas, I. (2024). Bibliometric analysis: The main steps. *Encyclopedia, 4*(2), 1014–1025. https://doi.org/10.3390/encyclopedia4020065

Podsakoff, P. M., MacKenzie, S. B., Podsakoff, N. P., & Bachrach, D. G. (2008). Scholarly influence in the field of management: A bibliometric analysis of the determinants of University and author impact in the management literature in the past quarter century. *Journal of Management* (Vol. 34, Número 4). https://doi.org/10.1177/0149206308319533

Polzin, F., Egli, F., Steffen, B., & Schmidt, T. S. (2019). How do policies mobilize private finance for renewable energy?—A systematic review with an investor perspective. *Applied Energy, 236*, 1249–1268. https://doi.org/10.1016/j.apenergy.2018.11.098

Rethlefsen, M. L., Brigham, T. J., Price, C., Moher, D., Bouter, L. M., Kirkham, J. J., Schroter, S., & Zeegers, M. P. (2024). Systematic review search strategies are poorly reported and not reproducible: A cross-sectional metaresearch study. *Journal of Clinical Epidemiology, 166*, Article 111229. https://doi.org/10.1016/j.jclinepi.2023.111229

Scopus. (2025). *SCOPUS.* Analyze search results. https://scopus.up.elogim.com/term/analyzer.uri?sort=plf-f&src=s&sid=24b5fff357d5a187948c6976dc766512&sot=a&sdt=a&sl=101&s=%28TITLE-ABS-KEY%28%22energy+finance%22+AND+%22low+carbon%22%29+OR+TITLE-ABS-KEY%28%22green+finance%22+AND+%22low+carbon%22%29%29&origin=resultslist&count=10&analyzeResults=Analyze+results

Stringer, T., & Ramírez-Melgarejo, M. (2024). Decarbonization pathways in Latin America: Assessing the economic and policy implications of transitioning to renewable energy sources. *Next Energy, 5*(May), Article 100157. https://doi.org/10.1016/j.nxener.2024.100157

Taghizadeh-Hesary, F., & Yoshino, N. (2020). Sustainable solutions for green financing and investment in renewable energy projects. *Energy Economics and Policy in Developed Countries, 13*(4), 788.

Tiwari, A. K., Trinh, H. H., Vo, D. T. H., & Sharma, G. D. (2025). How do economies decarbonize growth under finance-energy inequality? Global evidence. *Energy Economics, 142*, 108172. https://doi.org/10.1016/j.eneco.2024.108172

Tranfield, D., Denyer, D., & Smart, P. (2003). Towards a methodology for developing evidence-informed management knowledge by means of systematics review. *British Journal of Management, 14*, 207–222. https://doi.org/10.1111/1467-8551.00375

Vosviewer. (2025). *VOSVIEWER*. Node-based information analysis. https://app.vosviewer.com/

Wan, Q., Qian, J., Baghirli, A., & Aghayev, A. (2022). Green finance and carbon reduction: Implications for green recovery. *Economic Analysis and Policy, 76*, 901–913. https://doi.org/10.1016/j.eap.2022.09.022

Ying, H., Zhang, X., He, T., Feng, Q., Wang, R., Yang, L., & Duan, J. (2023). A bibliometric analysis of research on heart failure comorbid with depression from 2002 to 2021. *Heliyon, 9*(2), Article e13054. https://doi.org/10.1016/j.heliyon.2023.e13054

Zhang, D. (2018). Energy finance: Background, concept, and recent developments. *Emerging Markets Finance and Trade, 54*(8), 1687–1692. https://doi.org/10.1080/1540496X.2018.1466524

Zioło, M., Bąk, I., & Spoz, A. (2024). The role of financial markets in energy transitions. *Energies, 17*(24). https://doi.org/10.3390/en17246315

Technological Innovation in Energy Trade and Financial Development: Evidence from BRICS-T

Bekir Zengin and Claudiu Boțoc

Abstract This research explores the ramifications of innovations in energy trade on financial development. In the scope of the analysis, the panel data method was applied to the BRICS-T nations, comprising Brazil, Russia, India, China, South Africa, and Türkiye, which represent a significant bloc of emerging economies using annual data from the 2015–2024 period. The rationale for featuring the BRICS-T nations in this research is that they hold a globally decisive position in energy production, consumption, and trade. Additionally, the fact that each country has different energy policies and financial structures provides an opportunity for a comparative assessment. Türkiye's inclusion in the BRICS group, on the other hand, increases regional diversity and provides a different perspective to the research. The study includes three dependent variables and four independent variables. The dependent variables consist of domestic credit to the private sector (% of GDP), gross savings (% of GDP), and market capitalization of listed domestic companies (% of GDP). The independent variables are patents for renewables, renewables consumption per capita, energy imports, net (% of Energy Use), and GDP per capita (current US$). According to the findings, although renewable energy patents positively affected financial development in all formulated models, None of the models established within the scope of the study had statistically significant results. This situation reveals that renewable patents have no measurable implications for financial development indicators at the short date or under the current model. On the other hand, per capita consumption of renewable energy only shows a negative and considerable effect in the gross savings (% of GDP) model. This suggests that higher consumption of renewable energy could have a detrimental impact on savings. However, it has no significant impact on the other two financial parameters (domestic credit to private sector [% of GDP] and market capitalization of listed domestic companies [% of GDP]).

B. Zengin (✉)
Faculty of Applied Sciences, Tarsus University, Mersin, Turkey
e-mail: bekirzengin@tarsus.edu.tr

C. Boțoc
Faculty of Economics and Business Administration, West University of Timisoara, Timişoara, Romania
e-mail: claudiu.botoc@e-uvt.ro

A. Akusta and M. Gün (eds.), *Financial Frontiers in Energy Markets*, Contributions to Finance and Accounting, https://doi.org/10.1007/978-3-032-16738-5_13

Keywords Finance · Financial development · Renewable energy patents · Renewable energy consumption

1 Introduction

Technological developments, along with significantly increased public and private sector investments and a changing international perspective, have brought global energy innovation to a different dimension (International Energy Agency, 2025). With this changing structure, energy innovation has become a key element of a system that not only drives growth but also provides solutions for society. When examined in the environmental context, climate change and the resulting energy innovations provide the necessary need for the calculation and dissemination of energy technologies (León et al., 2018). In fact, renewable energy systems, such as wind and solar photovoltaics, which are constantly evolving, have changed to meet demands. In recent times, renewable energy sources have shown significant development, driven by privatization, innovations in the energy sector, and the incentives provided (Andoni et al., 2019). According to the International Energy Agency's (2024) estimates, renewable energy consumption in the electricity, heating, and transportation sectors is expected to increase by approximately 60% between 2024 and 2030. Renewable fuels (bioenergy, hydrogen, and e-fuels, etc.) are expected to meet approximately 15% of the projected rise in the demand for renewable energy, while numerous renewable sources, including geothermal and solar, have a share of 10%.

The research being conducted looks at how new technologies affect the level of financial development in energy trade, renewable patents, which represent a significant advancement for energy systems, were used. Patents help provide early indicators of technological developments regarding where innovation is occurring. Data from the International Energy Agency (2025) indicate that China's share of energy patents has increased rapidly since 2016. While it was 7% in 2016, it rose to 30% in 2022, resulting in 76% more patent applications than Japan. On the other hand, in 2016, China filed fewer patent applications than the United States, Japan, Germany, and Korea individually. While 96% of China's energy patents in 2022 were for low-emission areas, a quarter of the US's energy patents were based on fossil fuels. Upon closer examination, regional patent distributions may vary. For example, between 2020 and 2022, 18% of China's patents were for energy storage, and 17% were for solar technologies. In India, 39% of patents are dedicated to industrial energy efficiency, while in Germany, 25% are for distribution and 23% for electric transportation.

Against the backdrop of worldwide efforts toward sustainable growth and the necessary transition to a low-carbon economy, the nature of the relationship between energy sector commerce and financial sector maturity is garnering intensified focus. Findings that financial development can increase energy efficiency through technology (Chen et al., 2019) align with digital and physical innovations in energy trading. Efficient energy trading requires the seamless integration of physical network assets (smart grids, meters, and storage devices) with digital transactional technologies (blockchain, smart contracts, and energy management systems). Although these energy innovations are being discussed for energy trade, Andoni et al. (2019) stated in their literature review that many projects related to the energy sector are already in the earliest steps toward development, and research in these areas is still ongoing. The current research, focusing on the effects of emerging technologies in energy trade on financial development, estimates the expected impact on energy trade using data on "renewable patents" and "renewable energy consumption per capita." In this context, the research being conducted intends to bring attention to an existing shortcoming in the literature by empirically demonstrating the potential impact of new technologies in energy trade on financial development.

2 Literature Review

The results of a broad literature evaluation reveal that studies concentrating on the association between energy trade and financial development, such as those by Andoni et al. (2019), emphasize blockchain and distributed ledger technologies' potential in the area of energy, particularly with regard to peer-to-peer energy exchange. However, it is noted that most projects are still in the initial stages of development. Ahmed (2017) identified a sustained link between energy and trade in BRICS countries, demonstrating that financial development enhances energy intensity. Jafary et al. (2024) discovered that financial development in OPEC+ nations increases energy intensity up to a certain threshold, while Balli et al. (2024) found that financial development in APEC+ raises CO_2 emissions. Pan et al. (2019) and Chen et al. (2019) found that financial development, innovation in technology, and trade liberalization affect energy intensity, and that the mitigating effect of financial development in non-OECD countries occurs through technology and innovation.

A comprehensive literature review on blockchain system utilisation and distributed ledger energy-related technologies was conducted by Andoni et al. (2019). In the study, 140 research projects and initiatives were examined, and various potential areas for blockchain and distributed ledger technologies in energy applications were identified. The study's key application areas include exchange of energy between peers, the Internet of Things, decentralized energy fields, charging for electric vehicle infrastructure, and electronic mobility solutions. According to the findings, it has been revealed that many blockchain-based projects are still in the initial phase of advancement for the energy sector and that research is ongoing in various areas (scalability, decentralization, and security).

Huang et al. (2025) researched the dynamic interplay between fintech and energy transition risks for the years 2017–2024. The findings prove that fintech has a minimal impact on transforming concerns related to energy, and these risks have been shown to hinder the development of fintech.

Jafary et al. (2024) looked into how the growth of the financial industry affected the energy sector intensity and how this effect varies depending on innovation and technology levels, using variables such as the banking index, market index, total energy use, R&D ratio, total exports, and imports, on a sample covering OPEC+ for the period 2000–2020. According to the findings, financial development has been shown to affect energy intensity in various ways. For example, it has been shown that the development of banking and capital markets affects energy intensity up to a certain threshold.

Balli et al. (2024) analyzed trade, growth in GDP, utilization of energy, CO_2 emissions, and the expansion of the financial sector in APEC nations from 1985 to 2020. The findings indicate that, in addition to GDP, energy consumption also positively affects CO_2 emissions, but this effect changes over time depending on certain factors. Financial progress, however, has had a beneficial influence on CO_2 emissions.

Ullah et al. (2023) studied the impact of technical innovation, financial sector development, internationalization, trade liberalization, and green energy usage on the ecological footprint of industrialized countries from 1990 to 2018. The findings indicate that internationalization, technological innovation, trade liberalization, and green energy usage improve environmental quality, while financial development negatively impacts environmental sustainability.

Yücel et al. (2022) looked into the consequences of using renewable energy sources on foreign direct investment, global commerce, and advancement of finance for the period 1990–2019. The data reveal that there is no long-term association between green energy supply, trade, financial development (FD), or foreign direct investment between nations.

Khan et al. (2021) studied how innovations in technology, finance, and foreign direct investment affected green power, traditional energy consumption, and CO_2 emissions across 69 nations from 2000 to 2014. According to the results obtained, it has been revealed that renewable energy receives advantages from financial development, while renewable energy generation is negatively impacted by technological progress, growth in economic development, and foreign direct investment flowing from foreign investors. In addition, technological innovation, foreign direct investment flowing from foreign investors, and growth in economic development have been demonstrated to raise energy consumption of individuals and companies and the resulting CO_2 emissions.

Pan et al. (2019) looked at the association between financial sector development, freedom of trade, technological advancement, and the intensity of energy from 1976 to 2014. Finance development, trade openness, prosperity, and technological advancement all have an effect on the level of energy, the results showed.

Chen et al. (2019) focused on the interactions between energy intensity resulting from energy efficiency and the growth of the financial sector. The data discovered that the financial sector has an unfavorable effect on energy intensity resulting from energy efficiency in outside the OECD nations, whereas this effect is restricted in OECD members. On the other hand, some say that the development of the financial sector reduces energy intensity through technological progress and innovation.

Uzar and Eyuboglu (2019) evaluated the connection between energy consumption, foreign direct investment, growth in the economy, and liberalization in Turkey from 1980 to 2015. The findings reveal a cointegration relationship between energy consumption, foreign direct investment, growth in the economy, and openness to trade. Accordingly, it has been suggested that foreign direct investment inflows into environmentally friendly sectors such as information technology and services can be increased to improve energy efficiency.

Ahmed (2017) investigated the energy and trade relationship in BRICS countries. According to the findings, financial indicators such as economic growth and openness, which have a long-term relationship with energy trade, increase energy intensity in BRICS countries.

3 The Impact of New Technologies on the Level of Financial Sector Development in Energy Trade

In this section, the data and variables are first explained, followed by information about the method to be applied in the analysis. Subsequently, the most suitable analysis method has been chosen, and the results obtained have been shared.

3.1 Data and Variables

The study looks into how financial development is affected by new technologies in the energy trade. A panel data analysis was carried out for this aim, utilizing annual data for the countries of Brazil, Russia, India, China, South Africa, and Türkiye (BRICS-T) from 2015 to 2024. The BRICS-T nations were chosen because of their importance in the world's energy production, consumption, and trade. These countries have diverse energy policies and financial infrastructures. The countries in question have different energy policies and financial infrastructures. On the other hand, Türkiye's addition to the BRICS countries was an attempt to bring a different regional perspective. The study includes three dependent variables and four independent variables. The dependent variables consist of domestic credit to the private sector (% of GDP), gross savings (% of GDP), and market capitalization of listed domestic companies (% of GDP). The independent variables are patents for renewables, renewables consumption per capita, energy imports, net (% of Energy Use), and GDP per capita (current US$). Upon detailed examination of the study's variables;

Domestic Credit to Private Sector (% of GDP): The World Development Indicators is the source of the data. This covers both domestic loans and resources given to the private sector by financial companies (loans, securities purchases, commercial credits, etc.). On the other hand, this variable is given as a percentage of the obtained GDP. Feng and Zheng (2022) and Yadav et al. (2024) used the share of domestic credit provided by banks to the private sector to measure financial development.

Therefore, this variable has been taken as a reference from the study conducted by Feng and Zheng (2022).

Gross Savings (% of GDP): Obtained from the World Bank. The savings variable represents the portion of disposable income not spent on final consumption, adjusted for changes in retirement entitlements. The variable is defined as a percentage of GDP. No comprehensive study has been found that directly examines the connection between per capita green energy use, savings rates, and renewable energy patents. However, a study by Grigoli et al. (2014) used private and household savings variables.

Market Capitalization of Listed Domestic Companies (% of GDP): Sourced from the World Bank. It is formed by multiplying the stock prices of national industries that are listed on the stock exchange by the number of shares in circulation. This variable is referenced from the study by Makeeva et al. (2024).

Patents for Renewables: Data has been obtained from ourworldindata.org. This variable encompasses renewable energy sources (sustainable energy, wind, and solar, etc.), energy storage, energy efficiency, grid management, and electric transportation. Patent numbers are directly related to technological innovations and R&D activities in the field of renewable energy. Therefore, in the study, it is a variable representing new technologies in energy trade. The renewable energy variable was used with reference to the study by Feng and Zheng (2022). Feng and Zheng (2022) stated that patents are widely preferred in technology innovation for empirical studies.

Renewables Consumption per capita: Data has been obtained from ourworldindata.org. This variable does not include conventional biofuels. These include hydroelectric, wind, solar, geothermal, wave and tidal, and bioenergy, which are more commonly referred to as renewable energy sources. Per capita energy consumption is considered within the scope of new energy technologies because it does not include traditional fuels. This variable is referenced in the studies by Yadav et al. (2024).

Energy Imports, net (% of Energy Use): Data is provided by the International Energy Agency (IEA). Net energy exports are obtained by subtracting gross exports from gross imports and are measured in tons of oil equivalent. Since some countries in the BRICS-T nations are net exporters, the value may be negative. On the other hand, the utilization of primary energy without its conversion into other final forms of energy indicates energy consumption, and this energy consumption includes domestic production, imports, stocks, declining exports, and fuels (provided to aircraft and ships used for international travel). In the study conducted by Marra and Colantonio (2022), this variable was taken as a reference.

GDP per capita (current US$): It is available in the World Bank database. Per capita income is obtained by dividing the income generated via the creation of goods and services in a nation by the population. This variable includes current prices. Referenced from studies by Makeeva et al. (2024) and Grigoli et al. (2014).

To examine the effect of new technologies in energy trading on the degree of financial development, three econometric models have been constructed. In order, these are:

- $$\begin{aligned} & \textit{Domestic Credit to Private Sector (\% of GDP)} = \textit{Patents for Renewables} \\ & \quad + \textit{Renewables Consumption per capita} \\ & \quad + \textit{Energy Imports, net (\% of Energy Use)} \\ & \quad + \textit{GDP per capita} \left(\textit{current US\$}\right) \end{aligned}$$
- $$\begin{aligned} & \textit{Gross Savings (\% of GDP)} = \textit{Patents for Renewables} \\ & \quad + \textit{Renewables Consumption per capita} \\ & \quad + \textit{Energy Imports, net (\% of Energy Use)} \\ & \quad + \textit{GDP per capita} \left(\textit{current US\$}\right) \end{aligned}$$
- $$\begin{aligned} & \textit{Market Capitalization of Listed Domestic Companies (\% of GDP)} \\ & \quad = \textit{Patents for Renewables} \\ & \quad + \textit{Renewables Consumption per capita} \\ & \quad + \textit{Energy Imports, net (\% of Energy Use)} \\ & \quad + \textit{GDP per capita} \left(\textit{current US\$}\right) \end{aligned}$$

3.2 Methodology

In economic analyses, data are examined in three ways depending on the structure of the data: time series, cross-sectional data, and panel. According to Tatoğlu (2021), panel data is defined as the combination of cross-sectional observations from countries, companies, and households. While cross-sectional observations only provide information about a single unit over time, using panel data allows access to information about both units and periods (Tatoğlu, 2021). In this study, which investigates the impact of emerging new technologies in energy trade on the level of financial development, research has been done using the panel data method. The general representation of the panel data equation is as follows:

$$y_{it} = a + \beta X_{it} + u_{it}$$

i: Countries, companies, etc., units
t: time (years, quarters, etc.)
a: Constant term
y_{it}: Dependent variable
βX_{it}: Independent variables
u_{it}: Error term

In the study, descriptive statistics of the observations are examined before applying panel data, and then cross-sectional dependence, in other words, whether there is a correlation between the units for each variable, is checked for each variable. Depending on whether there is a correlation between the variables, the best unit root tests from the first and second generations are selected. Following an investigation into the series' stationarity, the series is rendered stationary, and the types of predictors (pooled, random, or fixed effects) are determined for the models established. After the types of predictors are determined, the model is estimated, the indicators for the variables are interpreted, and inferences are made about the model.

3.3 *Results of the Analyses*

The study's analytical part began with an examination of the variables' descriptive statistics, and then the direction of the variables' association with one another was examined using the correlation matrix. Before moving on to the panel data analysis results, the cross-sectional dependence and, consequently, the stationarity of the variables were investigated and controlled using the most appropriate unit root tests, and panel data analysis was applied.

As per the descriptive statistics in Table 1, the domestic credit to the private sector registers a mean value of 89.20. This financial metric displays significant heterogeneity across the sample, with a standard deviation of 44.76 indicating pronounced variability and observations spanning a minimum of 44.19 to a maximum of 194.16. The 59 observations for GS as a percentage of GDP exhibit a mean value of 26.11 with a measure of dispersion, represented by the standard deviation, calculated at 10.22. The dataset's full empirical distribution is defined by a minimum value of 12.25 and a maximum value of 45.10. The 59 observations for MCLDC as a percentage of GDP register a mean of 92.57 with a very high standard deviation of 86.91. The full data range for this metric extends from 16.88 to 322.71. The 51 observations for the number of PR exhibit a mean of 29,516.43, accompanied by a large standard deviation of 68,045.92. This substantial variability is underscored by the data's range, extending from a minimum of 1 to a maximum of 284,279. Based on 60 observations, RC per capita ranges from 321.58 to 8954.19. Its mean is 3269.59 units, with a standard deviation of 2,474.22. With 51 observations, the average of net EI as a percentage of energy use is 1.657, with a standard deviation of 50.47 and a range of −99.05% to 80.44. The 60 observations for GDP per capita yield a mean value of 8,522.78 and a standard deviation of 3,740.61. The full empirical range extends from 1,584 to 15,619.61.

The correlation matrix, as presented in Table 2, serves to display the interrelationships among the variables by documenting their respective pairwise correlation coefficients. The correlation between MCLDC (% of GDP) and domestic credit to the private sector (% of GDP) is −2.25, while the correlation between market capitalization and GS (% of GDP) is −2.02. The correlation between DCPS and GS is −0.13. PR shows a correlation of 0.14 with GS, −0.02 with domestic credit, and 0.02 with

Table 1 Descriptive statistics

Variable	Observation	Mean	Standard. Dev	Min	Max
DCPS	53	89.20	44.76	44.19	194.16
GS	59	26.11	10.22	12.25	45.10
MCLDC	59	92.57	86.91	16.88	322.71
PR	51	29,516.43	68,045.92	1	284,279
RC	60	3269.59	2474.22	321.58	8954.19
EI	51	1.657	50.47	−99.05	80.44
GDP	60	8522.78	3740.61	1584	15,619.61

Note DCPS: Domestic Credit to Private Sector (% of GDP), GS: Gross Savings (% of GDP), MCLDC: Market Capitalization of Listed Domestic Companies (% of GDP), PR: Patents for Renewables, RC: Renewables Consumption per capita, EI: Energy Imports, net (% of Energy Use), GDP: Gross Domestic Product per capita (current US$)

market capitalization. RC per capita is negatively correlated with GS (−0.41*) and PR (−0.29*), and weakly positively correlated with domestic credit (0.03). EI, net (% of Energy Use) has a statistically significant negative correlation with domestic credit (−0.33*) and a positive correlation with GS (0.40*), while showing negligible correlation with PR (0.00) and a negative one with RC (−0.27). GDP per capita is negatively correlated with domestic credit (−0.24*) and market capitalization (−0.17), and positively correlated with GS (0.17), PR (0.04), RC (0.03), and EI (0.34*). The mean variance inflation factor (VIF) is reported as 1.31.

Table 3 presents the outcomes of the panel unit root and cross-sectional dependence tests, which are essential for informing the selection between first- and second-generation unit root methodologies. To ascertain whether there is cross-sectional dependence among the panel units, the Pesaran (2004) CD test is employed. Significant dependence is observed in the variables GS (% of GDP), RC per capita, and GDP per capita (current US$), indicating the presence of cross-sectional correlation. For these variables, second-generation unit root tests are appropriate. On the other

Table 2 Correlation matrix for variable

Variable		(1)	(2)	(3)	(4)	(5)	(6)	(7)
MCLDC	(1)	1						
DCPS	(2)	−2.25	1					
GS	(3)	−2.02	−0.13	1				
PR	(4)	0.02	−0.02	0.14	1			
RC	(5)	−0.22	0.03	−0.41*	−0.29*	1		
EI	(6)	0.15	−0.33*	0.40*	0.00	−0.27	1	
GDP	(7)	−0.17	−0.24*	0.17	0.04	0.03	0.34*	1
Mean Variance Inflation Factor	1.31							

Note Asterisks (*) indicate statistical significance at the 5% level

hand, variables such as DCPS (% of GDP), MCLDC (% of GDP), PR, and EI, net (% of energy use) do not exhibit significant cross-sectional dependence, suggesting that first-generation unit root tests may be applied. The findings of the Im-Pesaran-Shin (IPS) (2003) test indicate that, except for MCLDC (a percentage of GDP), which is already stationary at the level, each of the variables is non-stationary at the level (I(0)) and turns stationary after first differencing (I(1)).

Table 4 presents the panel data estimation results for three dependent variables: DCPS, GS, and MCLDC. The interpretation of the coefficients is explained as follows:

The model has been calculated using the OLS approach with 40 observations when it is analyzed in DCPS. The coefficient for PR is 0.000 and not statistically significant, RC is −0.001 per person and not significant in terms of statistics, EI, net (% of energy use) is −0.391 and not statistically significant, and GDP per capita (current US$) is −0.002 and not statistically significant. According to the test results, Breusch and Pagan (1980) and Cook and Weisberg (1983) for the statistic of the heteroskedasticity test is 0.00 with a p-value of 0.992, indicating that the null hypothesis cannot be rejected at the 5% significance level and the error terms exhibit constant variance (homoskedasticity); similarly, Wooldridge (2002) for autocorrelation test statistic is 0.434 with a p-value of 0.539, meaning the null hypothesis cannot be rejected, suggesting no significant autocorrelation in the model; therefore, the error terms are both homoskedastic and free from autocorrelation.

For GS, the model is estimated using a random effects model with 41 observations. The coefficient for PR is 0.000 and not statistically significant, RC per capita is − 0.003 and significant in terms of statistics, EI is 0.085 and not statistically significant, and GDP per capita is 0.000 and not significant in terms of statistics. According to the test results, Levene (1960) and Brown and Forsythe (1974) for heteroskedasticity test yields a statistic of 1.024 with a p-value of 0.418, meaning the null hypothesis of homoskedasticity cannot be rejected, so there is no evidence of heteroskedasticity; Baltagi and Wu (1999) for autocorrelation test reports a statistic of 2.33, indicating no strong evidence of autocorrelation.

Table 3 C-S dependence and unit root test

	Average Correlation Coefficients & Pesaran CD test		Im-Pesaran-Shin I(0)		Im-Pesaran-Shin I(1)	
Variables	CD-test	p-value	Statistic	p-value	Statistic	p-value
DCPS	1.57	0.116	1.904	0.972	−5.350	0.000
GS	2.95	0.003	−0.773	0.220	−3.883	0.000
MCLDC	0.94	0.347	−3.627	0.000	−6.656	0.000
PR	0.86	0.390	1.786	0.963	−3.342	0.000
RC	10.68	0.000	3.674	0.999	−2.204	0.014
EI	0.89	0.372	−1.049	0.147	−2.736	0.003
GDP	5.78	0.000	1.501	0.933	−1.888	0.0295

Table 4 Panel data analysis results

	DCPS (% of GDP)	GS (% of GDP)	MCLDC (% of GDP)
	Coeff (p-value)	Coeff (p-value)	Coeff (p-value)
PR	.000 (0.260)	.000 (0.260)	.000 (0.674)
RC	−.001 (0.707)	−.003 (0.003)	.002 (0.870)
EI	−.391 (0.110)	.085 (0.098)	.042 (0.959)
GDP	−.002 (0.148)	.000 (0.221)	−.003 (0.489)
Constant	.009 (0.99)	.540 (0.037)	95.635 (0.105)
Number of obs	40	41	41
F/Wald	2.03 (0.111)	19.12 (0.000)	0.70 (0.951)
R-squared	0.188	0.347	0.001
Model	Pooled OLS	Random	Random
Heteroskedasticity	0.00 (0.992)	1.024 (0.418)	2.51 (0.041)
Autocorrelation	0.434 (0.539)	2.33	2.52

Notes The values in parentheses indicate probabilities. DCPS: Domestic Credit to Private Sector (% of GDP), GS: Gross Savings (% of GDP), MCLDC: Market Capitalization of Listed Domestic Companies (% of GDP), PR: Patents for Renewables, RC: Renewables Consumption per capita, EI: Energy Imports, net (% of Energy Use), GDP: Gross Domestic Product per capita (current US$)

For MCLDC, also estimated using random effects with 41 observations, the coefficients are as follows: PR 0.000 and not statistically significant, RC per capita 0.002 and not statistically significant, energy imports 0.042 and not statistically significant, and GDP per capita −0.003 and not statistically significant. According to Levene (1960) and Brown and Forsythe (1974), the heteroskedasticity test statistic is 2.51 with a p-value of 0.041, demonstrating the presence of heteroskedasticity and rejecting the null hypothesis of constant variance at the 5% significant level; Baltagi and Wu (1999) for autocorrelation test statistic is 2.52, such a value may indicate potential autocorrelation depending on the context and corresponding p-value.

4 Conclusion

This study looks at the effects of newly developed technology in energy trade on the level of financial development, conducted research using panel data methods for Brazil, Russia, India, China, South Africa, and Türkiye (BRICS-T) with annual data from 2015 to 2024. For this purpose, the study considered two key energy-related indicators: "patents for renewables" (which can be considered an indicator of new technologies) and "renewables consumption per capita." The effects of these variables on domestic credit to the private sector (% of GDP), gross savings (% of GDP), and market capitalization of listed domestic companies (% of GDP, which are three indicators of financial development, were examined. According to the findings, although renewable energy patents positively affected financial development in all established models, they were not significantly different in any of the models. This situation reveals that renewable patents have no measurable impact on financial development indicators in the short term or under the current model. Although there is no direct study in the literature investigating the impact of patents on financial development, Li et al. (2023), who conducted a similar study, found that patent applications provide financial convenience to firms, thus supporting the findings of this study. On the other hand, per capita renewable energy consumption only shows a negative and significant effect in the gross savings (% of GDP) model. This suggests that higher renewable energy consumption could have a negative impact on savings. However, it has no significant impact on the other two financial development indicators (credit and market capitalization). Although patents positively impact market value, they have not been found to be statistically significant. This finding supports the positive result found in the study by Makeeva et al. (2024), which investigated the relationship between market capitalization and patents. Based on these findings, the direct positive effects of new technologies used in energy trade (especially patent-based indicators) on the level of financial development are not statistically supported within this sample and model framework. However, indirect effects, temporal lags, or effects through different channels and indicators can be examined with further analysis.

References

Ahmed, K. (2017). Revisiting the role of financial development for energy-growth-trade nexus in BRICS economies. *Energy, 128*, 487–495. https://doi.org/10.1016/j.energy.2017.04.055

Andoni, M., Robu, V., Flynn, D., Abram, S., Geach, D., Jenkins, D., McCallum, P., & Peacock, A. (2019). Blockchain technology in the energy sector: A systematic review of challenges and opportunities. *Renewable and Sustainable Energy Reviews, 100*(C), 143–174. https://doi.org/10.1016/j.rser.2018.10.014

Balli, E., Çatik, A. N., Uğur, M. S., & Sigeze, C. (2024). The effects of financial development, trade and energy consumption on environmental degradation: Evidence from APEC countries. *Energy Sources, Part B: Economics, Planning, and Policy, 19*(1), 2372627. https://doi.org/10.1080/15567249.2024.2372627

Baltagi, B. H., & Wu, P. X. (1999). Unequally spaced panel data regressions with AR(1) disturbances. *Econometric Theory, 15*(6), 814–823.

Breusch, T. S., & Pagan, A. R. (1980). The lagrange multiplier test and its applications to model specification in econometrics. *The Review of Economic Studies, 47*(1), 239–253. https://doi.org/10.2307/2297111

Brown, M. B., & Forsythe, A. B. (1974). The small sample behavior of some statistics which test the equality of several means. *Technometrics, 16*(1), 129–132. https://doi.org/10.2307/1267501

Chen, Z., Huang, W., & Zheng, X. (2019). The decline in energy intensity: Does financial development matter? *Energy Policy, 134*, Article 110945. https://doi.org/10.1016/j.enpol.2019.110945

Cook, R. D., & Weisberg, S. (1983). Diagnostics for heteroscedasticity in regression. *Biometrika, 70*(1), 1–10. https://doi.org/10.1093/biomet/70.1.1

Feng, G.-F., & Zheng, M. (2022). Economic policy uncertainty and renewable energy innovation: International evidence. *Innovation and Green Development, 1*(2), Article 100010. https://doi.org/10.1016/j.igd.2022.100010

Grigoli, F., Herman, A., & Schmidt-Hebbel, K. (2014). *IMF Working Paper* (IMF Working Paper No. WP/14/204; p. 55).

Huang, Y., Zhou, Q., Yang, C., & Albitar, K. (2025). The relationship between fintech and energy markets in China. *Technological Forecasting and Social Change, 217*, Article 124188. https://doi.org/10.1016/j.techfore.2025.124188

Im, K. S., Pesaran, M., & Shin, Y. (2003). Testing for unit roots in heterogeneous panels. *Journal of Econometrics, 115*(1), 53–74.

International Energy Agency. (2024). *Renewables 2024* (p. 177). International Energy Agency.

International Energy Agency. (2025). *The sate of energy innovation* (p. 212). International Energy Agency.

Jafary, F., Ashani, A. N., & Afsharirad, M. (2024). Exploring the impact of financial development on energy intensity in a global study: Do levels of innovation and technology matter? *Heliyon, 10*(21), Article e39331. https://doi.org/10.1016/j.heliyon.2024.e39331

Khan, A., Chenggang, Y., Hussain, J., & Kui, Z. (2021). Impact of technological innovation, financial development and foreign direct investment on renewable energy, non-renewable energy and the environment in belt & Road Initiative countries. *Renewable Energy, 171*, 479–491. https://doi.org/10.1016/j.renene.2021.02.075

Leόn, L. R., Bergquist, K., Wunsch-Vincent, S., Xu, N., & Fushimi, K. (2018). *Measuring innovation in energy technologies: Green patents as captured by WIPO's IPC green inventory* (Economic Research Working Paper No. 44). WIPO.

Levene, H. (1960). Robust tests for equality of variances. In I. Olkin, S. G. Ghurve, W. Hoeffding, W. G. Madow, & H. M. Mann (Eds.), *Contributions to probability and statistics: Essays in honor of Harold Hotelling* (pp. 278–292). Stanford University Press.

Li, Q., Pang, L., & Yin, S. (2023). Patent signal and financing constraints: A life cycle perspective and evidence from new energy industry. *Frontiers in Energy Research, 11*. https://doi.org/10.3389/fenrg.2023.1277164

Makeeva, E., Popov, K., & Teplova, O. (2024). Patenting for profitability: Green energy innovations and firm performance in BRICS countries. *Frontiers in Environmental Science, 12*. https://doi.org/10.3389/fenvs.2024.1332792

Marra, A., & Colantonio, E. (2022). The institutional and socio-technical determinants of renewable energy production in the EU: Implications for policy. *Journal of Industrial and Business Economics, 49*(2), 267–299. https://doi.org/10.1007/s40812-022-00212-6

Pan, X., Uddin, Md. K., Han, C., & Pan, X. (2019). Dynamics of financial development, trade openness, technological innovation and energy intensity: Evidence from Bangladesh. *Energy, 171*, 456–464. https://doi.org/10.1016/j.energy.2018.12.200

Pesaran, M. H. (2004). *General diagnostic tests for cross section dependence in panels* (Cambridge Working Papers in Economics). https://ideas.repec.org//p/cam/camdae/0435.html

Tatoğlu, F. Y. (2021). *Panel Veri Ekonometrisi / Stata Uygulamalı* (6th ed.). Beta Basım Yayım.

Ullah, A., Dogan, M., Topcu, B. A., & Saadaoui, H. (2023). Modeling the impacts of technological innovation and financial development on environmental sustainability: New evidence from the world's top 14 financially developed countries. *Energy Strategy Reviews, 50*, Article 101229. https://doi.org/10.1016/j.esr.2023.101229

Uzar, U., & Eyuboglu, K. (2019). Is foreign direct investment an engine for energy consumption? An empirical investigation for Turkey. *Environmental Science and Pollution Research, 26*(27), 28092–28105. https://doi.org/10.1007/s11356-019-05996-0

Wooldridge, J. M. (2002). *Econometric analysis of cross section and panel data*. The MIT Press.

Yadav, A., Bekun, F. V., Ozturk, I., Ferreira, P. J. S., & Karalinc, T. (2024). Unravelling the role of financial development in shaping renewable energy consumption patterns: Insights from BRICS countries. *Energy Strategy Reviews, 54*, Article 101434. https://doi.org/10.1016/j.esr.2024.101434

Yücel, G. E., Ustabaş, A., & Acar, T. (2022). International trade, foreign direct investment, financial development and renewable energy supply: Panel data evidence from newly industrialized countries. *World Journal of Applied Economics, 8*(2), 51–64. https://doi.org/10.22440/wjae.8.2.1

Exploring Energy–Currency Interactions: Crude Oil Price Volatility and Yuan Exchange Dynamics

Erdost Torun and Erhan Demireli

Abstract This research investigates complex spillover patterns between Chinese Yuan (CNY) and West Texas Intermediate (WTI) oil under a turbulent global environment period from 2020 until 2025, which has witnessed the COVID-19 pandemic, oil price wars, and major geopolitical conflicts. This study utilizes an extensive wavelet-based methodology that includes tests for coherence, phase differences, correlation, and causality, moving beyond a simple two-dimensional analysis to evaluate the complex, multidimensional transformation of the spillover transmission between the Yuan and oil across different time and frequency dimensions. The findings indicate that the spillover patterns are highly dynamic, non-linear, and prone to periods of financial turmoil. This phenomenon is consistent with contagion theory. This research offers crucial policy implications for oil-importing economies such as China, along with strategic insights to investors in developing risk mitigation techniques in an increasingly volatile global market. The study concludes that these patterns will remain ongoing in the future due to prevailing geopolitical and economic uncertainty.

Keywords Oil–yuan nexus · Geopolitical conflicts · COVID-19 pandemic · Volatility spillover · Wavelet analysis

1 Introduction

Crude oil stands among the most crucial commodities, affecting several key macroeconomic factors, including exchange rates. Understanding the dynamic connection among oil and other financial variables has become crucial in recent decades in order to manage finances effectively. This need is necessary especially since the oil market

E. Torun
Faculty of Business, Dokuz Eylul University, İzmir, Türkiye
e-mail: erdost.torun@deu.edu.tr

E. Demireli (✉)
Faculty of Economics and Administrative Science, Dokuz Eylul University, İzmir, Türkiye
e-mail: erhan.demireli@deu.edu.tr

A. Akusta and M. Gün (eds.), *Financial Frontiers in Energy Markets*, Contributions to Finance and Accounting, https://doi.org/10.1007/978-3-032-16738-5_14

has increasingly been financialized and has been met by an upward rise in the volatilities of the currencies and oil prices as a result of global uncertainties (Alam et al., 2019; Mensi et al., 2023).

Financial asset-price relationships are generally found to be tied but not dependent on each other or contagious in terms of transmissions due to instabilities (Flavin & Sheenan, 2015; Forbes & Rigobon, 2002; Jung & Maderitsch, 2014). Interdependence stands for a constant relationship brought about by fundamental variables that allow for the transmission of shocks (Yang et al., 2016). Contagion is an abrupt and noticeable increase in intermarket linkages brought about by a shock, which diminishes the portfolio diversification benefits (Baur & Lucey, 2010; Gulko, 2002; Opoku et al., 2023). Understanding the transmission of volatility on markets is important in explaining market moves and hence portfolio allocations (Albulescu et al., 2017). Furthermore, in the course of contagion, it is vital that the regulatory authorities keep track of these activities (Ahmad et al., 2013). Empirical research on these spillovers is imperative for investigating intermarket information flows for risk management and proper asset pricing models (Arouri et al., 2011). It thus becomes essential to study the oil-exchange rate relations across time horizons because it is time-varying as well as realized at different time scales (Reboredo & Rivera-Castro, 2013).

For the world's largest importer of crude oil, China's currency—the yuan (CNY)—is increasingly sensitive to fluctuations in international oil prices. This oil volatility tendency has become even more noticeable from 2020 through 2025 with the increased financialization of oil markets and immense worldwide turmoil (e.g., Mo et al., 2024; Singh et al., 2025; Zhou et al., 2024). These instabilities create volatility patterns generally are transmitted to various financial instruments and actually gets amplified by one structural problem: While the overseas prices of oil are quoted in United States dollars, the domestic oil futures in China are traded in CNY, thus establishing a direct channel for transmission of risk (e.g., Almansour et al., 2024; Chen et al., 2022; Zeng et al., 2022). In conclusion, crude oil tends to play the role of a net risk transmitter to the Chinese financial markets, thereby reinforcing in this respect its implications for financial and economic stability. Thus, understanding these complicated volatility transmissions under which the two markets interact is also a challenge faced by policymakers when dealing with global shocks and investors aiming to hedge portfolio risk.

Theoretically, this study is founded on the Heterogeneous Market Hypothesis that opposes the traditional Efficient Market Hypothesis. Essentially, the Heterogeneous Market Hypothesis argues that market players, ranging from short-term speculators to long-term institutional investors, act upon different time scales and therefore respond distinctly to the same market information (Tiwari et al., 2013a). To illustrate, a sudden price plunge may be read by a high-frequency trader as an indicative signal to sell, whereas a long-term investor might view the same scenario as an opportunity to buy (Czudaj, 2019). Thus, from the heterogeneity point of view, for a thorough study of the underlying market dynamics, one must examine the dynamics at different time frequencies. Indeed, analytical methods like wavelet transformation, which offer decomposition of the time series data into various scales, are highly relevant and even necessary to detect the true complexity of financial markets.

This paper contributes to the literature by applying an integrated methodological approach grounded on the CWT. Conventional procedures are mostly either based on the assumption of stationarity or provide only dichotomous results, so wavelet-based methods can be used to identify dynamic, time-varying relationships across frequencies (Tiwari et al., 2013b). This research extends those investigations by integrating CWT-based coherence, phase difference, correlation, and causality tests to understand dichotomous co-movements and leading-lag patterns in detail (Aguiar-Conraria et al., 2018). Additionally, by linking this analysis to a timeframe based on major events ranging from 2020 to 2025, it assesses the influence of key geopolitical and economic episodes like the COVID-19 havoc, oil price wars, China's "Zero COVID" policies, and the military conflict of Russia-Ukraine. This approach of studying market-oriented time series dynamics allows the market participants to explicitly view the subject matter of the market nexus in view of real-world events, thus offering a deeper and more pertinent perspective on the WTI-CNY nexus.

2 Literature Review

The association of oil prices with the Chinese yuan is one of the main areas of research, thanks to the intense influence of the Chinese economy on the global energy markets and procedures of their financialization (e.g., Li & Chen, 2023; Wang et al., 2021; Zhou et al., 2024). By appreciating the fact that this relationship is dynamic, recent research pathways focus on dynamic approaches that go beyond traditional approaches. Such techniques, including time-varying parameter vector autoregressions and wavelet transforms, are found to better capture the dynamics of spillover effects. Hence, novel methodological improvements enable researchers to detect dynamics that are complex and change with time over multiple time scales and subperiods (e.g., Mo et al., 2024; Sarathkumara et al., 2025).

Undeterred by this methodological sophistication, the literature does not provide agreement on the essence of the direction of volatility transmission. To start with, there are studies that define the effects to be mostly spread on the markets of crude oil to other variables. As a result, the Chinese yuan is a spillover recipient in the time domain. Hence, it means that it will respond more passively to the abrupt shocks in oil prices (Almansour et al., 2024). The rest of the literature presents convincing evidence of the ability of the yuan to target action as a net transmitter of transmission effects, thus claiming that it served as a more active transmitter of the interactions between the two markets (Asadi et al., 2022; Zeng et al., 2022). This contradiction is the main gap between the WTI and CNY relationship, and this is what this research aims to clarify.

This changing relationship has been shaped by various events that are of critical importance across the globe, with the 2020 to 2025 being the most notable. The COVID-19 crisis and the Russia-Ukraine conflict have likely brought about special turbulence, which has increased inter-market connections and volatility (Singh et al., 2025; Su & Kao, 2022). According to scholarly literature, spillovers rise when there is uncertainty and when the crisis hits the economy. Moreover, crude oil is usually a net risk exporter (Hameed et al., 2021; Umar et al., 2023). Concisely, the evidence on the existence of dynamic spillovers between the yuan and crude oil is presented in the literature. These spillover relations are more significantly influenced, and hence intensified, during global crises. Hence, dynamic risk management thrives during such turbulent times along with an understanding of intermarket interdependencies.

3 Data and Methodology

3.1 Data

The analysis employs the continuous wavelet transformation-based methods in a comprehensive framework over the interaction and spillover transmissions between the Chinese Yuan (CNY) exchange rate and WTI oil prices. Daily data for oil and Yuan data dynamics from Investing.com cover the span from January 2, 2020, to May 15, 2025. The empirical volatility series are computed using the logarithmic difference between the maximum and minimum daily prices. Methodologically, the spillover literature has traditionally used short-term, high-frequency data, with those studies defining the short-term period as ranging from 2–8 days to 2–4 years (Jammazi, 2012; Khalfaoui et al., 2015; Yang et al., 2016, among others). Since the concern of this study is the possible shock effect on the short-term period, this paper considers only the short-term, ranging from 2 to 30 days.

In order to decrease the impact of noise and prevent the generation of erroneous results, a denoising procedure is implemented on the data sets employing the Symlet wavelet function, specifically the Sym2 variation. Since the Sym2 wavelet is minimally asymmetric, it acts as a linear phase filter, preserving the original shape of the signal and its exact timing features. This property is important in the analysis of data containing sudden spikes and sharp edges, such as daily oil prices and Yuan currency data, due to market fluctuations, economic events, or geopolitical developments. The Sym2 wavelet's low number of diminishing moments helps to preserve these sudden changes and high-frequency components throughout a series of analyses, so that their influence on the analysis is minimized while eliminating the noise in cross-correlation transfers.

3.2 Methodology

The analysis approach used in this study includes methods based on the continuous wavelet transform. The analysis includes coherence, correlation, and causality tests. Advanced surrogate significance testing methods are also used in the analysis.

In this study, the Morlet wavelet is used to nonstationary data containing transients or sporadic cycles with different frequencies (Aguiar-Conraria et al., 2012). In spectral analysis, coherence is one of the most fundamental measures, which is equivalent to the squared correlation coefficient in time-frequency dimensions, also known as the coefficient of determination. It explains how the comovement tendency of two datasets changes amongst different fluctuations with different time scales during in time period. The wavelet coherence is estimated by normalizing the cross-spectrum with respect to the multiplication of the spectra of each signal:

$$R_{XY}(s,\tau) = \frac{\zeta\left\{s^{-1}\left|W_{XY}^{m}(s,\tau)\right|\right\}}{\zeta\left\{s^{-1}\sqrt{\left|W_{X}^{m}(s,\tau)\right|^{2}}\right\}\cdot\zeta\left\{s^{-1}\sqrt{\left|W_{Y}^{m}(s,\tau)\right|^{2}}\right\}} \tag{1}$$

where $W_X^m(s,\tau)$ and $W_X^m(s,\tau)$ denote power spectrum of X and Y data series. $W_{XY}^m(s,\tau)$ indicates the crosss spectrum between data series. Parameters of s and τ are also respectively the wavelet scale and the localized time index parameters. In contrast to wavelet correlation, coherence exhibits a bordered range between 0 and 1, that is, $0 \leq R_{XY}^2(s,\tau) \leq 1$, serving as a counterpart to the coefficient of determination as employed in temporal analysis. Moreover, wavelet correlation diverges from the wavelet coherence metric due to the reduction of the quadrature component, which is the imaginary portion of the wavelet cross-spectrum. To avoid misleading results from coincidental similarities in wavelet spectra, the phase difference series is derived and analyzed in detail. This study also utilizes the CWT-based correlation test by Rua (2013) and the continuous wavelet transform-based causality test of Olayeni (2016) for a comprehensive robustness analysis.

Next, the wavelet transform for the variable x is decomposed into real and imaginary function parts via $W_X^m(s,\tau) = \Re\{W_X^m(s,\tau)\} + i\Im\{W_X^m(s,\tau)\}$ to calculate the local phase, $\varphi_X(s,\tau) = \tan^{-1}\left\{\frac{\Im(W_X^m(s,\tau))}{\Re(W_X^m(s,\tau))}\right\}$. Also, the phase difference is utilized to determine forward-lag relationship models and to compute the spectral Granger causality by using wavelet method The variable y also undergoes the same decomposition process. Rua (2013) describes wavelet correlation as:

$$\rho_{XY}(s,\tau) = \frac{\zeta\left\{s^{-1}\left|\Re\left(W_{XY}^{m}(s,\tau)\right)\right|\right\}}{\zeta\left\{s^{-1}\sqrt{\left|W_{X}^{m}(s,\tau)\right|^{2}}\right\}\cdot\zeta\left\{s^{-1}\sqrt{\left|W_{Y}^{m}(s,\tau)\right|^{2}}\right\}} \tag{2}$$

where $\zeta(\cdot) = \zeta_{\text{scale}}(\zeta_{\text{time}}(\cdot)).\zeta_{\text{scale}}$; and ζ_{scale} , and ζ_{time} represent the smoothing processor for the frequency and time dimension, respectively.

Olayeni (2016) introduced a modified version of the correlation definition in Eq. (2) that incorporates a customized indicator function based on phase difference calculation to propose a new CWT-based measure of causality, respectively (Olayeni, 2016). The difference in phase between the pairs of x and y data pairs is defined as follows:

$$\phi_{XY}(s,\tau) = \phi_X(s,\tau) - \phi_Y(s,\tau) = \tan^{-1}\left(\frac{\Im\left(W_{XY}^m(s,\tau)\right)}{\Re\left(W_{XY}^m(s,\tau)\right)}\right) \tag{3}$$

Extending the CWT-based correlation equation in Rua's article (Rua, 2013) through introducing the indicator function I_(Y → X) (s,τ) acquire the continuous wavelet transformation-based Granger causality test:

$$G_{Y\to X}(s,\tau) = \frac{\zeta\left\{s^{-1}\left|\Re\left(W_{XY}^m(s,\tau)\right)I_{Y\to X}(s,\tau)\right|\right\}}{\zeta\left\{s^{-1}\sqrt{\left|W_X^m(s,\tau)\right|^2}\right\}\zeta\left\{s^{-1}\sqrt{\left|W_Y^m(s,\tau)\right|^2}\right\}} \tag{4}$$

where $G_{Y\to X}(s,\tau)$ is in-phase causality transmission measure (positive causality) in the case of the indicator function $I_{Y\to X}(s,\tau)$ that is accurate for four the sub-intervals within the interval $-\pi \leq \phi_{XY}(s,\tau) \leq \pi$. The continuous wavelet transform-based Granger causality measure enables the examination of both positive and negative causality by utilizing an indicator function that is defined specifically for the desired phase difference interval. Likewise, estimated flows of information from x to y investigation through $G_{X\to Y}(s,\tau)$ by indicator function $I_{X\to Y}(s,\tau)$.

To determine the statistical significance of the patterns observed, this study utilizes the bootstrapping-based resampling significance testing method developed by Cazelles et al. (2008). This method is crucial as CWT surrogate testing can yield misleading results if relevant external variables are not included in the analysis.

4 Empirical Results

Coherence, described as the square of the correlation coefficient in the time–frequency spectrum, is a measure of how the tendency of two data sets to move in tandem varies with time and different fluctuations. This is an effective method to unearth spillover interactions. Figure 1 demonstrates the coherence result and the direction of the series of phase differences for the analyzed data set and visualizes the lead-lag effects between WTI and CNY.

Through detailed analysis that emphasizes the core issues, it is concluded that there is significant variability and complexity in the relationships between the WTI and CNY markets. Figure 1 reflects that the coherence between the two series is determined by dynamic short-duration patterns as opposed to a constant long-term trend. The lead-lag structure is extremely complicated, with phase difference analysis revealing that the leadership position actually changes between WTI and CNY. This creates a substantial time frame for both co-cyclical (in-phase) and counter-cyclical (out-of-phase) interactions, further proving the complex nature of their spillover transmission relationship (Fig. 1).

The analysis reveals a highly dynamic, nonlinear, and bidirectional volatility spillover transmission between WTI and the CNY. Geopolitical risk premiums and

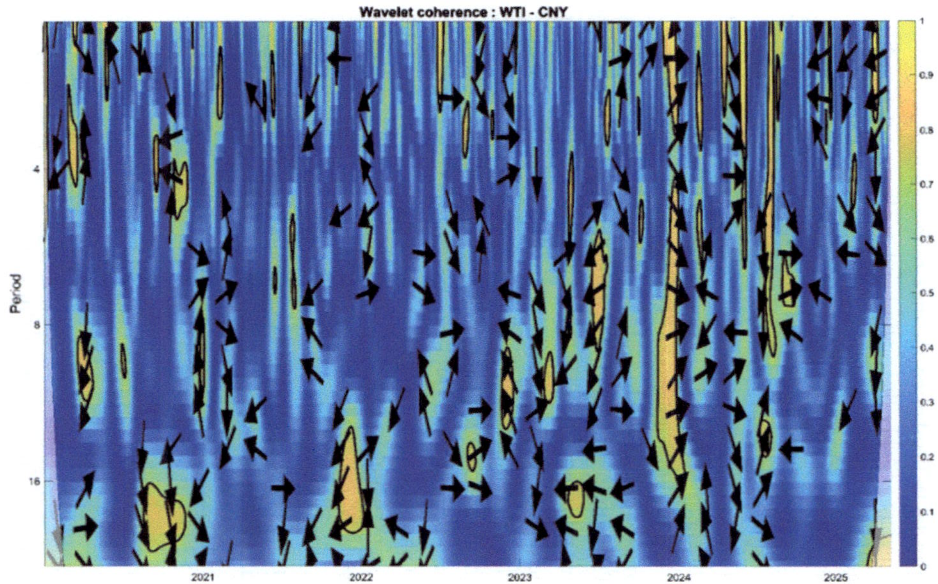

Fig. 1 WTI—CNY Coherence results and phase difference arrows. *Notes* Coherence Results and Phase Difference Arrows placed on 5% significance areas. Continuous wavelets transform-based coherence patterns between WTI and CNY. Arrows are placed approximately in the areas with 1 percent statistical significance. The color spectrum defines the magnitude of coherence. The x-axis denotes the time dimension defined in years, and the y-axis reports the period (inverse of scale) defined in the name of days. Black contours depict the high coherence areas, which are above an eighty percent level. Arrows are placed approximately in the areas with 5 percent statistical significance. Statistical significance procedure proposed by Cazelles et al. (2008) is employed for 1000 simulations of the AR (1) process with null of statistical insignificance. The phase difference arrows show the dynamic lead-lag relationship. Right-pointing arrows denote in-phase movement, whereas left-pointing arrows show out-of-phase motion. In an in-phase region, if the arrow points upward, WTI is leading, and if downward, CNY is the leader; the reverse of this rule is valid in the out-of-phase regions. For example, an arrow facing the direction right and up (↗) shows that the two series are in-phase (positively correlated), with WTI leading CNY. An arrow pointing left and down (↙) will show that the two series are out-of-phase (negatively correlated), with WTI leading CNY.

economic uncertainty in the world economy enhance such interdependence, especially when the markets are in turmoil (e.g., Mo et al., 2024; Ning & Xu, 2024). The financialization process of crude oil contributes to this dynamic pattern by making the spread of shocks between asset classes faster (Asadi et al., 2022; Singh et al., 2025). These results, which are in line with the contagion theory, underscore the need to have adaptive risk management by policymakers and present investors with a better idea of the transmission of shocks between CNY and WTI markets (e.g., Almansour et al., 2024; Sarathkumara et al., 2025).

The interdependence between the WTI oil price and the Chinese yuan (CNY) in the period 2020–2025 can be defined as a highly fluctuating and nonlinear relationship. This relationship is likely shaped by a row of global crises and domestic affairs. Significant world occurrences, starting with the COVID-19 pandemic and, later, the Russia-Ukraine conflict, are thought to begin to enhance volatility at all time scales and also reinforced the co-movement between the commodity and the foreign exchange market (e.g., Almansour et al., 2024; Zhou et al., 2024). The main disturbed trait, which is observed with the help of analysis, appears as an asymmetric feature. This discovery implies that WTI is a significant producer of risk in net, which imposes significant pressure on the Chinese yuan (e.g., Mo et al., 2024; Ning & Xu, 2024; Zeng et al., 2022). The high level of sensitivity to these external shocks is caused by the fact that China is one of the biggest oil importers in the world economy, and by the fact that over the past decades, the oil markets have become highly financialized (Chen et al., 2022; Wang et al., 2021). The vulnerability of the yuan was also made worse by internal economic forces that were caused by domestic policies, in particular, the strict Zero-COVID policy (Almansour et al., 2024; Ling & Cao, 2023). Additionally, the mismatch in the currency denomination in the global oil prices, which are in USD, and the domestic financial system, which is in CNY, represents a direct pathway of volatility transmission (e.g., Ma & Yang, 2024; Zeng et al., 2022). Such shifting lead-lag processes predetermine systemic risks and emphasize the increased relevance of yuan internationalization as one of the possible defenses against these external forces (Singh et al., 2025; Umar et al., 2023).

4.1 Robustness Analysis Results

In addition to coherence and phase difference analyses, CWT Correlation and CWTC causality analyses were also used to check the robustness of the results. To prove statistical significance, this research employs bootstrap-based surrogate data significance testing as developed by Cazelles et al. (2008), since CWT surrogate tests might produce misleading results if the analysis excludes important exogenous variables. Overall, robustness analysis also validates the findings that oil and yuan volatility spillover information flow has a transient and polytomious nature.

The robustness checks, presented in Fig. 2, validate the transient and event-driven nature of the WTI-CNY spillover transmission uncovered by the coherence and phase difference analysis. For example, wavelet correlation results (panel c) show that the co-movement between these two markets with phases across time is not fixed; it moves with periods of global turmoil, sometimes positive and, at other times, negative. Finally, the wavelet causality tests (panels a and b) also support these results: a two-way spillover effect is common. Notably, these findings affirm the complex two-way relationship between the interaction where WTI largely passes the risk to the CNY, although at important times the vice versa may occur as domestic shocks in China may also affect the global oil prices.

The causal analysis of the interdependence between oil and yuan helps in the proper detection of the spillover effect, especially in a dynamic global context. To this end, the robustness analysis highly supports the presence of a dynamic and bivariate volatility spillover between the oil and the Yuan. The results of this research always point that volatility in oil and Yuan markets has a reciprocal relationship in both directions, which is in information and shock transmission. Another discovery made by the wavelet causality/correlation analysis is that the nature and the extent of co-movement are highly fluid and oscillate either way on both positive and negative directions, depending on the global and idiosyncratic shocks. The significant world events of the COVID-19 period, the Russian Ukrainian War, and the Zero-COVID policy of China have influenced transactional volatility transmission with tightening and deepening spillover effects at these critical times. This correspondence to the dynamics of events confirms the strength of the most important findings.

5 Conclusion

The oil-currency nexus is critical on account of the co-movements manifested by various oil price shocks and currency market shocks. The study sought to investigate the polytomic spillover effect between crude oil prices and the Yuan over the period 2020–2025, with data in daily frequency being analyzed in both the time and frequency domains. By applying a comprehensive strategy consisting of continuous wavelet transform-based coherence, correlation, and causality methods, novel insights into this complicated relationship are offered in this research. The findings support that a sophisticated heterogeneous spillover effect exists, which is very much time- and frequency-dependent between oil and yuan due to the financialization of oil. For oil-importing countries, oil prices and exchange rates can be mutual determinants, especially in speculative price movements. The empirical data show that causal interactions and propagation mechanisms are subject to temporal heterogeneity with regard to their character and directionality.

The results, therefore, have relevant short-term policy implications to the worldwide financial mechanism, specifically, the complex spillover dependency between the prices of crude oil and the Chinese yuan over the turbulent period 2020 2025. Changes in oil prices affect the value of currencies significantly, and this dependence has been enhanced by such significant events of 2020–2025 as the global pandemic and geopolitical conflicts (Almansour et al., 2024; Singh et al., 2025; Zhou et al., 2024). The growing volatility and speculative nature of the oil markets and the high

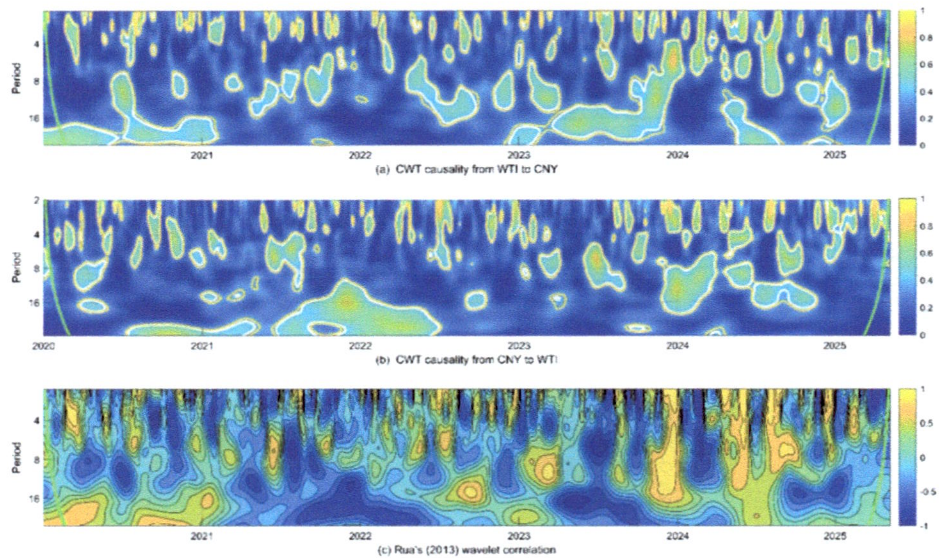

Fig. 2 WTI—CNY CWT Causality and correlation results. *Notes* The plots illustrate CWT-based causality evolution observed between oil price and yuan exchange rates. The color scheme signifies the intensity of the causal transmission. The x-axis indicates years, while y-axis displays the period (the inverse of frequency), also expressed in days. The white (yellow) contour lines represent the 5% (10%) significance level, which was established through 1000 simulations of surrogate AR (1) processes under the null of statistical insignificance, adhering to the methodology outlined by Cazelles et al. (2008)

dependence of China on imported crude oil create a missing link to ensure that the market trends are carefully monitored to relatively reduce the negative effects on the economy. This study confirms that there is a bi-spillover relationship between variables, thus advancing and narrowing down existing literature (Li & Chen, 2023; Mo et al., 2024; Zhou et al., 2024). The reciprocal connection is compounded in times of a high level of uncertainty, thus emphasizing the necessity of responsive risk-management policies. The major policy suggestions based on the literature are sophisticated real-time shock-monitoring strategies, which enable a flexible and proactive monetary response, which will contain short-term shock spreading and decrease portfolio risk (Asadi et al., 2022; He et al., 2025; Wang et al., 2021). The players in the market can also use them to take risks and manage their portfolio efficiency.

The results of this research are practically important to the short-term traders and speculators of the spread, particularly the risk management and portfolio diversification. It is necessary to have a full picture regarding the magnitude and direction of spillovers between the oil and foreign-exchange markets. Variable spillover changes between two or more time scales affect the stability of the portfolio and risk exposure. Our findings explain why the short-term correlation between the spillover effects in the dynamics between oil and currency markets can be significantly volatile, thus potentially hindering the possibilities of diversification, given that commodity trading has recently gained prominence as a mainstream investment vehicle because of its diversification benefits. As a result, during turbulent times, correlations become stronger, and the oil-CNY-weighted portfolio segments are unlikely to provide significant risk mitigation. Hence, while developing a portfolio, these structural transformations fostering market stability should be taken into account along with the aggregate loss during market stresses. While portfolio optimization is being undertaken, greater importance has to be attached to these market changes, promoting stability, accompanied by total loss during market stresses. trading of oil or through the exchanges, market intermediaries always find it natural to match strategies with respective risk profiles. Future scholars might expand their methods to analyze spillover impacts among different assets, regions, and global markets, which would significantly advance risk management research and offer a foundation for researchers, investors, and policymakers to develop robust strategies to mitigate contagion effects.

References

Aguiar-Conraria, L., Martins, M. M., & Soares, M. J. (2012). The yield curve and the macroeconomy across time and frequencies. *Journal of Economic Dynamics and Control, 36*(12), 1950–1970.

Aguiar-Conraria, L., Martins, M. M., & Soares, M. J. (2018). Estimating the Taylor rule in the time-frequency domain. *Journal of Macroeconomics, 57*, 122–137.

Ahmad, W., Sehgal, S., & Bhanumurthy, N. R. (2013). Eurozone crisis and BRIICKS stock markets: Contagion or market interdependence? *Economic Modelling, 33*, 209–225.

Alam, M. S., Shahzad, S. J. H., & Ferrer, R. (2019). Causal flows between oil and forex markets using high-frequency data: Asymmetries from good and bad volatility. *Energy Economics, 84*, Article 104513.
Albulescu, C. T., Goyeau, D., & Tiwari, A. K. (2017). Co-movements and contagion between international stock index futures markets. *Empirical Economics, 52*(4), 1529–1568.
Almansour, B. Y., Shojaei, S. A., & Elkrghli, S. (2024). Examining market synchronicity: Spillover connectedness among commodity markets and exchange rates during crisis periods. *Edelweiss Applied Science and Technology, 8*(5), 1322–1347.
Arouri, M. E. H., Lahiani, A., & Nguyen, D. K. (2011). Return and volatility transmission between world oil prices and stock markets of the GCC countries. *Economic Modelling, 28*(4), 1815–1825.
Asadi, M., Roubaud, D., & Tiwari, A. K. (2022). Volatility spillovers amid crude oil, natural gas, coal, stock, and currency markets in the US and China based on time and frequency domain connectedness. *Energy Economics, 109*, Article 105961.
Baur, D. G., & Lucey, B. M. (2010). Is gold a hedge or a safe haven? An analysis of stocks, bonds and gold. *Financial Review, 45*(2), 217–229.
Cazelles, B., Chavez, M., Berteaux, D., Ménard, F., Vik, J. O., Jenouvrier, S., & Stenseth, N. C. (2008). Wavelet analysis of ecological time series. *Oecologia, 156*(2), 287–304.
Chen, L., Wen, F., Li, W., Yin, H., & Zhao, L. (2022). Extreme risk spillover of the oil, exchange rate to Chinese stock market: Evidence from implied volatility indexes. *Energy Economics, 107*, Article 105857.
Czudaj, R. L. (2019). Crude oil futures trading and uncertainty. *Energy Economics, 80*, 793–811.
Flavin, T. J., & Sheenan, L. (2015). The role of US subprime mortgage-backed assets in propagating the crisis: Contagion or interdependence? *The North American Journal of Economics and Finance, 34*, 167–186.
Forbes, K. J., & Rigobon, R. (2002). No contagion, only interdependence: Measuring stock market comovements. *The Journal of Finance, 57*(5), 2223–2261.
Gulko, L. (2002). Decoupling. *The Journal of Portfolio Management, 28*(3), 59–66.
Hameed, Z., Shafi, K., & Nadeem, A. (2021). Volatility spillover effect between oil prices and foreign exchange markets. *Energy Strategy Reviews, 38*, Article 100712.
He, S., Cheng, Z., Wang, W., & Luo, Z. (2025). What drives currency connectedness? Evidence from the BRICS currencies. *Applied Economics, 57*(1), 67–85.
Jammazi, R. (2012). Cross dynamics of oil-stock interactions: A redundant wavelet analysis. *Energy, 44*(1), 750–777.
Jung, R. C., & Maderitsch, R. (2014). Structural breaks in volatility spillovers between international financial markets: Contagion or mere interdependence? *Journal of Banking & Finance, 47*, 331–342.
Khalfaoui, R., Boutahar, M., & Boubaker, H. (2015). Analyzing volatility spillovers and hedging between oil and stock markets: Evidence from wavelet analysis. *Energy Economics, 49*, 540–549.
Li, Y., & Chen, J. (2023). Estimating the effect of international crude oil prices on RMB exchange rate with two-way fluctuation spillover. *PLOS One, 18*(10), Article e0292615.
Ling, M., & Cao, G. (2023). Analysis of risk spillover and asymmetry between three crude oil markets and Chinese financial markets. *Fluctuation and Noise Letters, 22*(3), 2350017.
Ma, Z., & Yang, L. (2024). Revisiting the "pure" oil-exchange co-movement from a time-domain perspective. *The Singapore Economic Review, 69*(1), 183–202.
Mensi, W., Aslan, A., Vo, X. V., & Kang, S. H. (2023). Time-frequency spillovers and connectedness between precious metals, oil futures and financial markets: Hedge and safe haven implications. *International Review of Economics & Finance, 83*, 219–232.
Mo, B., Zeng, H., Meng, J., & Ding, S. (2024). The connectedness between uncertainty and exchange rates of oil import countries: New evidence from time and frequency perspective. *Resources Policy, 88*, Article 104398.
Ning, C., & Xu, D. (2024). Extreme comovements and downside/upside risk spillovers between oil prices and exchange rates. *Macroeconomic Dynamics, 29*, Article e53.

Olayeni, O. R. (2016). Causality in continuous wavelet transform without spectral matrix factorization: Theory and application. *Computational Economics, 47*(3), 321–340.

Opoku, R. T., Adam, A. M., Isshaq, Z. M., & Owusu Junior, P. (2023). Time-varying connectedness and contagion between commodity prices and exchange rate in Sub-Saharan Africa. *Cogent Economics & Finance, 11*(2), 2237714.

Reboredo, J. C., & Rivera-Castro, M. A. (2013). A wavelet decomposition approach to crude oil price and exchange rate dependence. *Economic Modelling, 32*, 42–57.

Rua, A. (2013). Worldwide synchronization since the nineteenth century: A wavelet-based view. *Applied Economics Letters, 20*(8), 773–776.

Sarathkumara, S. M. N. N., Samarakoon, S. M. R. K., & Pradhan, R. P. (2025). Navigating financial interconnectivity: Analyzing oil, exchange rates and US market influences on Asia-Pacific equities using the time-varying parameter vector autoregressive connectedness approach. *Journal of Economic Studies*. https://doi.org/10.1108/JES-10-2024-0674

Singh, S., Singh, M., & Attri, S. (2025). Mapping stock market dynamics: A tripartite neural network approach using modified grid search for stock market prediction. *Expert Systems with Applications, 278*, Article 127243.

Su, J. B., & Kao, Y. S. (2022). How does the crisis of the COVID-19 pandemic affect the interactions between the stock, oil, gold, currency, and cryptocurrency markets? *Frontiers in Public Health, 10*, Article 933264.

Tiwari, A. K., Dar, A. B., & Bhanja, N. (2013a). Oil price and exchange rates: A wavelet based analysis for India. *Economic Modelling, 31*, 414–422.

Tiwari, A. K., Mutascu, M. I., & Albulescu, C. T. (2013b). The influence of the international oil prices on the real effective exchange rate in Romania in a wavelet transform framework. *Energy Economics, 40*, 714–733.

Umar, Z., Aziz, M. I. A., Zaremba, A., & Tran, D. K. (2023). Modelling dynamic connectedness between oil price shocks and exchange rates in ASEAN+ 3 economies. *Applied Economics, 55*(23), 2676–2693.

Wang, H., Yuan, Y., & Wang, T. (2021). The dynamics of cross-boundary fire—Financial contagion between the oil and stock markets. *Journal of Futures Markets, 41*(10), 1655–1673.

Yang, L., Cai, X. J., Zhang, H., & Hamori, S. (2016). Interdependence of foreign exchange markets: A wavelet coherence analysis. *Economic Modelling, 55*, 6–14.

Zeng, H., Ahmed, A. D., Lu, R., & Dai, N. (2022). Dependence and spillover among oil market, China's stock market and exchange rate: New evidence from the Vine-Copula-CoVaR and VAR-BEKK-GARCH frameworks. *Heliyon, 8*(11), Article e11737.

Zhou, D., Liu, X., & Tang, C. (2024). Does the international oil market interact with China's financial market? New evidence from time-varying higher moments. *The North American Journal of Economics and Finance, 74*, Article 102192.

Digital and Financial Transformation in Energy Trade: The Role of Blockchain and Artificial Intelligence

Hülya Er and Lamia Guseniova

Abstract Financial technologies, developed alongside digitalisation, improve in policy frameworks, risk management, investment strategies, and financial decision-making processes in energy trade and markets. This study shows that the life-changing potential of innovative solutions such as blockchain and artificial intelligence in the energy-finance ecosystem to boost automation, and cuts costs and risks. Smart contracts, peer-to-peer trading, and data-driven forecasting have the potential advance renewable energy investments in line with global policy objectives. Similarly, digital change can build up the link between the energy and finance sectors, supporting sustainable growth through green bonds, blockchain, and AI decision-making mechanisms. The research discusses the opportunities and risks of these technologies and provides strategic insights for actors and policymakers in energy markets, also contributing an innovative perspective to the energy-finance literature.

Keywords Energy finance · Financial innovation · Sustainable finance · Blockchain · Artificial intelligence

1 Introduction

Nowadays the businesses face increasing competition, costs, and risks, making digital change in organisational activities (Minyue & XiuE, 2024). This trend is evident in energy markets (European Commission, 2025a). The oil and gas sector, one of the fundamental sub-sectors of the energy markets, is driving companies to reduce

H. Er (✉)
Bolu Vocational School, Department of Finance, Banking and Insurance, Bolu Abant İzzet Baysal University, Bolu, Türkiye
e-mail: hulyaer@ibu.edu.tr

L. Guseniova
The Faculty of Management Science and Engineering, Nanjing University of Aeronautics and Astronautics, Nanjing, China
e-mail: lamiaguseinova@nuaa.edu.cn

A. Akusta and M. Gün (eds.), *Financial Frontiers in Energy Markets*, Contributions to Finance and Accounting, https://doi.org/10.1007/978-3-032-16738-5_15

costs and digitalise as increasing supply alternatives and slowing demand growth are driving down prices (Gezdur & Bhattacharjya, 2017).

Since the beginning of the twenty-first century, global energy markets have witnessed radical changes due to climate change, uncertainties created by the 2008 crisis, and regional-political risks (Zhang & Ji, 2019). As society development from traditional methods to digital solutions, energy systems become smarter, and sustainable, new generation technologies such as artificial intelligence, cloud computing, and blockchain accelerate this change (European Commission, 2025a). In addition, digitalisation is effective in the energy value chain from production to consumption (European Commission, 2025b), information technologies and human capital stand out as key elements in the sustainable energy sector (Kuzmin et al., 2024).

Energy is a fundamental input in economic systems. Oil prices are considered to be driven by the balance of supply and demand in international markets (Zhang, 2018: 1687). And today the energy sector is a multidimensional structure that includes not only oil and gas but also renewable energy, energy grids, and battery storage (Liu & Li, 2022). The energy market, especially renewable energy, carries high volatility and risks similar to financial markets (Tekani et al., 2025). And also diversification of the production portfolio is important in energy planning (DeLlano-Paz et al., 2016).

Due to technological progress and the impact of climate change, investments in energy markets are increasing in clean technologies. According to the Energy Technology Perspectives 2024 report, clean technology production investments increased by 50% in 2023, reaching $235 billion. Current policy projects total clean technology trade to reach $575 billion by 2035, approximately 50% more than the current value of global natural gas trade (International Energy Agency, 2024). These data indicate that interest in financial technologies and next-generation solutions in energy trading is increasing and that these areas may play a more important role in the future.

The European Commission's 2022 action plan for the digitalisation of the energy system aims to strengthen consumers' control over energy, increase clarity through information technology, and secure the cybersecurity of energy networks (European Commission, 2025b). The European Union considers this plan a strategic tool to achieve its 2030 and 2050 climate targets, linking it to the Green Deal and Energy Union objectives. Digitalisation facilitates the integration of renewable energy, supports flexible market mechanisms, and accelerates to distributed energy through the active role of Distribution System Operators (DSOs) (European Commission, 2025a). It is evaluate that these developments can create a solid basis for investment strategies' predictability in energy markets.

The literature proves the connection between energy prices and financial markets, as well as the investment and funding choices made by energy companies, including carbon and green finance (Goldstein et al., 2023; Manta et al., 2025). To give the importance of energy and climate change, this study is vital for both researchers and policymakers, making energy finance a significant field of research (Zhang, 2018: 1687). Li (2023) points out that financing is essential for progress in the energy sector into renewable energy sources.

Two critical technologies, the future of the energy sector: blockchain and artificial intelligence (Hua et al., 2022), help decrease carbon emissions and energy security by optimising energy usage (European Commission, 2025a). While blockchain verifies, artificial intelligence can create practical solutions to issues in the energy sector through intelligent optimisation and decision-making support (Hua et al., 2022).

Given global environmental challenges and the importance of energy, policymakers and investors are focusing on energy finance (Zhang, 2018). This study shows the impact of financial innovation, blockchain, and artificial intelligence on energy trading. It provides examples of the contributions of financial technology startups to the energy sector and digitalisation, and determining the opportunities and challenges of the energy sector's digitalisation process.

2 Digitalisation and Financial Change in Energy Markets

Digitalisation plays a significant role in the development of the energy change production, distribution, and trading processes in the energy sector through innovative business models (Facchinetti & Sulzer, 2016). Businesses and public-private institutions are gaining cost advantages by developing new business models and regulatory strategies, and this development requires policymakers to consider their role in national energy security and system planning (World Economic Forum, 2016). For example, in Russia, digitalisation in the energy sector has been observed to increase business management processes (Samylovskaya et al., 2022: 1). In current energy systems are inadequate in terms of transparency, traceability and security, and due to their centralised and fragmented structures, they can be open to manipulation and dependent on a single point of failure (Ahmad et al., 2022). In this context, distributed energy resources (e.g., rooftop panels, microturbines) and demand management are becoming more important. Digitalisation strengthens supply security with these resources, while heat pumps, LED lighting, smart devices, and electric vehicle charging reduce costs and facilitate efficient use of resources (World Economic Forum, 2016).

The European Commission supports the digital change in the energy sector with its "Strategic Roadmap for Digitalisation and Artificial Intelligence in the Energy Sector," which it plans to publish in 2026. This roadmap includes measures for reform in buildings and industry, integrating increased energy consumption, and strengthening cybersecurity in energy networks (European Commission, 2025b).

Prioritising equity, inclusiveness, and human development are also at the heart of energy development. Fossil fuels, which account for 80% of the global energy supply combating the climate crisis in energy development. This change is financing mechanisms to increase renewable energy production (UNDP, 2025).

Renewable energy (RE) sources are becoming of the utmost environmental importance (Sharma et al., 2020). In this case, renewable natural resources like solar, wind, geothermal, and hydropower serve as the foundation for generating renewable energy (Sharma et al., 2020; Next Move Strategy Consulting, 2025). The RE is also supported by this combination of population and urbanisation pressures, decreasing technological costs, and the need for energy supply security (Statista, 2025).

Nowadays the climate change also increases the demand for renewable energy and reduces greenhouse gas emissions (Zhang, 2018), showing that digitalisation is making significant contributions to this process (European Commission, 2025a). Digitalisation offers a rapid and cost-effective solution to speed up this energy sector (UNDP, 2025) and gives the advantage to renewable energy technologies, builds up their use at lower costs compared to fossil fuels (Sharma et al., 2020).

As the following clean energy, it has reached a historic threshold, exceeding 40% of global electricity production in 2024. Record growth in solar energy is also increasing, after fossil fuel production and emissions continue to rise again, reason to high demand triggering heat waves (Ember, 2025). The important thing is that renewable and clean energy sources are becoming evident, particularly in developing economies, and this is leading to the establishment of new targets in this area. It shows that necessitates large-scale investments in new infrastructure (Alsagr & Hemmen, 2021).

More than 140 countries, including the US, China, India, Japan, and the EU, are expected to strengthen their carbon neutrality targets with formal commitments by the end of 2025. Various policy tools, such as production-linked incentives, clean energy auctions, RE mandates, and carbon pricing implemented to support these goals (Next Move Strategy Consulting, 2025). In recent years, RE technologies have been rapidly expanding globally. Global RE consumption is expected to reach 114 exajoules by 2030 (Statista, 2025), and the market size is expected to increase from US$856.08 billion in 2021 to US$2,025.94 billion in 2030, representing a 9.6% compound annual growth rate (Next Move Strategy Consulting, 2025).

According to the World Economic Forum's Fostering Effective Energy Change 2025 report, sustainability is the strongest and most stable area of the past decade. Gradual progress was made between 2016 and 2022. The post-COVID-19 economic recovery in 2023 increased fossil fuel use, causing a temporary setback. In 2024 and 2025, thanks to a record increase in RE investments and decreasing emissions intensity in significant economies, sustainability scores rose again, with a 1.2% increase recorded in 2025 (World Economic Forum, 2025). In line with these trends, Table 1 shows comparative regional sustainability performances within the scope of the Energy Transition Index (ETI) for 2025.

Table 1 presents regional sustainability performance gaps and the factors influencing these gaps (investment levels, policy frameworks, and technological capacity).

Emerging technologies such as artificial intelligence, data centers, electric vehicles, and heat pumps are among the main drivers of the increase in global energy demand (Ember, 2025). These developments require greater consideration of new applications such as big data and AI in the energy finance literature. The rapid growth of green bond markets (Zhang, 2018) highlights the need for more comprehensive analysis of the risk-return profiles of RE assets by integrating financial technology (FinTech) into decision-making processes (Tekani et al., 2025; Zhang, 2018).

To decrease renewable energy costs and supportive policy environments through the use of technology shows the digital improvement in the energy sector, the role of finance in investment processes in the energy sector is important (Krupa et al.,

Table 1 ETI regional sustainability outlook

Area	2025 average score	10-Year trend (%)	Strengths and challenges
Developed Economies	57.6	+ 14.6	Despite the increase in clean energy, high emissions and energy consumption persist in steel, cement, petrochemicals and aviation
Developing Asia	55.5	−0.7	While there has been a partial recovery in emissions, coal dependence and the low share of clean energy remain problems
Developing Europe	58.2	+ 3.6	Despite advances in energy efficiency and clean energy use, coal and methane emissions remain obstacles in some countries
Latin America and the Caribbean	62.8	+ 3.0	Although hydropower offers advantages, limited diversification poses long-term risks
Middle East, North Africa, and Pakistan	39.5	+ 3.3	Despite the rapid growth of clean energy, fossil fuel dependency continues
Sub-Saharan Africa	62.8	+ 2.5	Low per capita emissions and high potential. Lack of investment limits the share of clean energy

Source World Economic Forum (2025: 30). edited by the authors

2019). It is important to address the impact of blockchain and artificial intelligence on energy trade and finance.

2.1 *Blockchain in Energy Trading and Finance*

Blockchain technology organizes data in a decentralized manner and is primarily used in P2P trading platforms and applied within the Bitcoin framework in 2009 (Shahinzadeh et al., 2022: 241). This technology has since automated payment procedures. It ensures secure and transparent access to shared data and ledgers (Al Shareef et al., 2024: 1). Its fixed records against cyber threats and fraud raise transaction security (Rane et al., 2023). Blockchain technology presents considerable prospects in energy trading, improves trade reliability and minimising security risks (Yahaya et al., 2020). It also reduces costs in energy markets (Junaidi et al., 2023) and provides stability in energy markets (Jiang et al., 2025).

The role of blockchain technology provides processes like shipment tracking and invoice in automation (Ahmad et al., 2022). Pilot projects initiated in 2018 showed that digitalisation can lead to a 30% cut in processing times and 5–10% in costs. Gazprom Neft noted that digitalisation improved 10–15%, while Vygon Consulting mentioned that blockchain technology has the potential to lower costs by as much as 10% (Musienko, 2023).

Blockchain technology offers significant opportunities for developing an environmentally friendly and sustainable Internet of Things (IoT) ecosystem in energy systems, financial markets, e-governance, and smart cities. It supports RE production and consumption through secure and transparent transactions and contributes to overcoming the challenges facing the IoT (Sharma et al., 2020). Yahaya et al. (2020) developed a blockchain-based local energy market in a small community with many solar panels, reducing electricity costs by 28.5–65.2% with dynamic pricing and a home energy management system, and demonstrated that smart contract-based trading is resilient to vulnerabilities. Strepparava et al. (2022) tested the blockchain-based local energy market in Southern Switzerland and found it feasible with low resource consumption, but stated that it was limited at the meter level due to memory constraints. Hua et al. (2020) state that a blockchain-based peer-to-peer model increases energy exports and carbon savings by driving consumer behavior with low-carbon incentives and outperforms centralized trading methods. Lv (2023) examines the opportunities (investment, employment, energy security) and obstacles (high costs, political and social resistance) presented by this transition, emphasizing the importance of its economic benefits. He also notes that blockchain strengthens market transparency, supports RE integration, and can contribute to a sustainable energy environment.

Table 2 summarizes blockchain-based projects in the energy sector.

Table 2 shows that blockchain technology has a wide range of applications in the energy sector, from financial transactions to carbon tracking. Accordingly, R3 Corda

Table 2 Blockchain-Based projects in the energy sector

Project / Company	Year	Activity description	Source
R3 Corda/ Ethereum	2024	Blockchain for RE trading, cost reduction and 70% subsidy with 30% (VGF) support*	Khare and Bhatia (2024)
Blockchain Power	2024	A blockchain-based platform developed for the secure sharing of solar energy data has increased efficiency to 93%, and confirmation time has decreased from 4.5 s to 2.5 s	Karthi et al. (2024)
Net Zero Company	2024	Support for blockchain-based certification, emission monitoring, and financing of biochar-based carbon removal projects	Net Zero Company (2024)
C + Charge	2025	Blockchain platform that earns carbon credits for electric vehicle charging	C + Charge (2025)
Growthpoint and Fuel Switch (South Africa)	2025	Blockchain-based REC exchange in Africa enables transparent, real-time energy trading with IoT and AI	Energy Capital and Power (2025)

Source Adapted by the authors based on literature articles and online data. * Viability Gap Funding (VGF) is a mechanism that provides public subsidies to increase the viability of commercially unattractive projects

provides cost and financing support to businesses and consumers, while Blockchain Power and Net Zero Company offer transparency in data sharing.C + Charge provides carbon credits to electric vehicle users, while Growthpoint and Fuel Switch support renewable energy trading.

2.2 *Artificial Intelligence in Energy Trading and Finance*

In recent years, the energy sector has increased its use of artificial intelligence (AI). Its ability to reduce costs in renewable energy, analyse large, complex datasets (Al Shareef et al., 2024), and improve energy efficiency, clean fuels, and smart grids (World Economic Forum, 2025; Zhao et al., 2024). Studies show that AI algorithms can decrease costs more than traditional methods by predicting energy use within smart grids (Yang, 2024).

AI models provide energy investors with a chance to optimise portfolio management, improve forecasts of supply chain disruptions, and better handle fluctuations in prices (Onukwulu et al., 2025: 48). The integration of AI into energy finance can increase efficiency by improving real-time data analysis, risk assessment, and decision-making processes (Rane et al., 2023). AI models supported by big data and digital technologies increase system reliability and efficiency by predicting energy usage and resource allocation (Li et al., 2023).

Although AI provides automation, rapid decision-making and flexibility in power systems, it requires strong data management and technical compliance for effective and safe use (Hua et al., 2022: 10). AI can be used for optimization of RE systems and their integration into national power grids (Al Shareef et al., 2024: 14). Szczepaniuk and Szczepaniuk (2023) state that AI algorithms have provided significant improvements in production, distribution, storage, consumption and trade processes, but several research challenges remain in practice. Park and Kim (2024) state that AI has made significant contributions to the energy sector in areas such as power consumption, wind energy, and building management. Zhao et al. (2024) emphasize that AI research and development should be supported by subsidies and investments, large-scale RE projects focused on green AI should be encouraged, and international cooperation should be strengthened. Awogbemi et al. (2024) state that when ethical, regulatory, and human resource issues are overcome, AI and digitalization can make significant contributions to SDG 7 (accessible, reliable, sustainable, and modern energy for all) by 2030, and that infrastructure modernization, increasing data capacity, and collaborative innovation are important for this. Talaat et al. (2024) demonstrate that AI-based methods provide high accuracy for mitigating supply-demand imbalances in wind energy. Tian et al. (2024) demonstrate that declines in AI investments and reductions in climate policy uncertainty in China have significant impacts on RE development.

Table 3 summarizes AI-based projects implemented in the energy sector.

Table 3 AI-Based projects in the energy sector

Company / Project	Year	Field of activity	Source
Astro (Y Combinator)	2024	Using AI models, it identifies the most efficient grid connections, develops projects, and sells them to major energy companies. It aims to provide profitable opportunities for the 2,000 GW of generation the US needs by 2035	Astro (2025)
Climetric	2024	The platform aims to reduce energy consumption in buildings by up to 30% by optimizing HVAC systems with Edge AI	Climetric (2024)
Tibo Energy	2024	AI-based energy management simplifies renewable resource integration, reducing costs by up to 30%	Tibo Energy (2024)
Octopus Energy / Kraken Tech	2025	Kraken, an AI-based energy management platform, optimizes consumption, grid balancing, and customer solutions with advanced data analytics and machine learning	Octopus Energy (2025)
Crusoe Energy Systems	2025	It represents the first phase of the 'Stargate Project', building an $11.6 billion AI data center for OpenAI in Texas	Romburgh (2025)

Source Adapted by the authors based on literature articles and online data

Table 3 shows that AI-based energy projects offer significant benefits not only in terms of technical ability but also financial sustainability. Astro provides profitable analytics for large-scale production, Climetric and Tibo Energy cut costs and strengthen companies' financial resilience. Octopus Energy or Kraken Tech improve operational systems and customer solutions, while Crusoe Energy Systems demonstrates the strategic role of AI in energy financing with multi-billion dollar investments.

Distributed energy systems offer significant opportunities for RE integration but face challenges, resource shortages, high costs, and regulatory hurdles. Their sustainability can be strengthened through AI-powered generation forecasting, energy storage solutions, favorable regulations, and financial incentives (Nadeem et al., 2023). AI-powered analytics identify market patterns by processing large data sets and optimise energy trading strategies with high accuracy (Onukwulu et al., 2025: 48).

3 New Financial Models and Policy Approaches in Energy Transformation

The Paris Agreement encourages RE to cut fossil fuels to keep global temperature rise below 2 °C, aims for zero-carbon solutions to cover most emissions by 2030, and supports technology development and transfer in this direction (UNFCC, 2015). The European Green Deal is a comprehensive plan that aims to reduce emissions by 55% by 2030 and achieve climate neutrality by 2050, integrating energy, industry, agriculture, and environmental policies to encourage clean energy and technology investments (European Commission, 2019).

In the digital era, the financial sector is moving towards responsible practices, focusing on climate initiatives and the circular economy. Fintech advancements, resource management, and support funding for sustainable projects. The finance (DeFi), built on blockchain, enables rapid capital movement, while AI-powered analytics prioritise investments with substantial effects (Manta et al., 2025). The European Union is promoting energy digitalisation through initiatives like Horizon projects such as PARITY, OneNet, BRIGHT, and REDREAM, which can improve data management, resilience, and the integration of renewable energy sources (European Commission, 2025a).

AI and blockchain-based FinTech solutions reduce fraud risk by strengthening investor confidence through real-time data analysis and risk management (Rane et al., 2023). This change is a significant obstacle, such as a lack of qualified workforce, technical infrastructure deficiencies, and cybersecurity threats (Samylovskaya et al., 2022). The Companies which are overcome these obstacles integrate these technologies to achieve a competitive advantage and sustainable growth in the rapidly digitalising energy sector (Onukwulu et al., 2025).

Blockchain improves the clarity of green investments and environmental effects and tracking funding (Tamminedi, 2024). Green bonds support projects focused on infrastructure and carbon (Goldstein et al., 2023; Manta et al., 2025). Services like Lightency leverage blockchain technology to provide investors with environmental impact and attractive return opportunities by making renewable energy production and consumption transparent (Lightency, 2023). The National University of Singapore's S$940 million green bond and its collaboration with Northern Trust on blockchain-based reporting illustrate its commitment to responsible green financing (National University of Singapore, 2024).

It is important to lower carbon usage, as global electricity access increased from 84% in 2010 to 92% in 2023, attaining SDG7 necessitates significant investment in developing countries (United Nations, 2025).

Well-known geopolitical risks play an important role in this global change (Alsagr & Hemmen, 2021), and environmental degradation and regulatory uncertainties limit RE investments (Zhao et al., 2023). On the other hand, environmental policies, technological advances, and economic globalisation support this process (Sun et al., 2024). Energy change should be supported by financial incentives and smart urban solutions (United Nations, 2025). The risk and cost-return balance is affected by geopolitical and market factors, as well as investment costs (Tekani et al., 2025).

4 Conclusion

New-generation technologies emerging from digitalisation play a significant role in policy frameworks, risk management, investment strategies, and financial decision-making processes in energy trading and markets. Policymakers such as the Paris Agreement and the European Green Deal are green bonds of innovative tools for financing renewable energy investments. Digitalisation in the energy sector demonstrates that blockchain and AI-based projects cut costs and optimise customer solutions, and provide credit opportunities in a secure environment. For future, policies targeting the implementation of these technologies and shows that it should be prioritised.

By emphasizing the importance of regional disparities and local solutions, this study demonstrates that digital transformation can offer significant opportunities for sustainable growth and a low-carbon future, and these findings highlight the need for further research on long-term market stability and potential inequalities, and the importance of developing adaptive strategies for policymakers, investors, and energy sector stakeholders. The careful and strategic application of these technologies in the energy and finance ecosystem can be considered as a lever that both reduces risks and provides long-term competitive advantage to achieve goals.

Based on the findings, we recommend that policymakers support the integration of financial technologies and the expansion of green financing instruments to accelerate the digital development in energy markets. Future studies could focus on examining the impact of these technologies on energy financing through regional comparisons.

References

Ahmad, R. W., Salah, K., Jayaraman, R., Yaqoob, I., & Omar, M. (2022). Blockchain in oil and gas industry: Applications, challenges, and future trends. *Technology in Society, 68*, Article 101941. https://doi.org/10.1016/j.techsoc.2022.101941

Al Shareef, A. M., Seçkiner, S., Eid, B., & Abumeteir, H. (2024). Integration of blockchain with artificial intelligence technologies in the energy sector: A systematic review. *Frontiers in Energy Research, 12*(1377950), 1–26. https://doi.org/10.3389/fenrg.2024.1377950

Alsagr, N., & Hemmen, S. van. (2021). The impact of financial development and geopolitical risk on renewable energy consumption: evidence from emerging markets. *Environmental Science and Pollution Research, 28*, 25906–25919. https://doi.org/10.1007/s11356-021-12447-2

Astro. (2025). The world's first AI energy developer. Y Combinator. Retrieved September 7, 2025, from https://www.ycombinator.com/companies/astro

Awogbemi, O., Von Kallon, D. V., & Kumar, K. S. (2024). Contributions of artificial intelligence and digitization in achieving clean and affordable energy. *Intelligent Systems with Applications, 22*, Article 200389.

Climetric. (2024). The AI for HVAC optimization. Retrieved September 7, 2025, from https://www.climetric.ai

C+Charge. (2025). C +Charge—EV charging crypto fueled. Retrieved September 7, 2025, from https://c-charge.io

DeLlano-Paz, F., Martínez Fernandez, P., & Soares, I. (2016). Addressing 2030 EU policy framework for energy and climate: Cost, risk and energy security issues. *Energy, 115*, 1347–1360. https://doi.org/10.1016/j.energy.2016.01.068

Ember. (2025). Global electricity review 2025. (8 April 2025)Lead authors: Euan Graham & Nicolas Fulghum; Other author: Katye Altieri. Ember Climate. Retrieved September 2, 2025, from https://ember-energy.org/app/uploads/2025/04/Report-Global-Electricity-Review-2025.pdf

Energy Capital & Power. (2025, August 22). South Africa's growthpoint, fuel switch to launch blockchain green energy trading. Retrieved September 7, 2025, from https://energycapitalpower.com/south-africas-growthpoint-fuel-switch-to-launch-blockchain-green-energy-trading/

European Commission. (2019). The European green deal striving to be the first climate-neutral continent. Retrieved September 8, 2025, from https://commission.europa.eu/strategy-and-policy/priorities-2019-2024/european-green-deal_en

European Commission. (2025a). A green, efficient and affordable energy system fit for the future. Publications Office of the European Union. Retrieved September 3, 2025, from https://cordis.europa.eu/article/id/449270-a-green-efficient-and-affordable-energy-system-fit-for-the-future

European Commission. (2025b). Digitalisation of the energy system. *Energy, Climate change, Environment*. Retrieved September 3, 2025, from https://energy.ec.europa.eu/topics/eus-energy-system/digitalisation-energy-system_en

Facchinetti, E., & Sulzer, S. (2016). General business model patterns for local energy management concepts. *Frontiers in Energy Research, 4*(7), 1–12. https://doi.org/10.3389/fenrg.2016.00007

Gezdur, A., & Bhattacharjya, J. (2017). Digitization in the oil and gas industry: Challenges and opportunities for supply chain partners. In L. Camarinha-Matos, H. Afsarmanesh & R. Fornasiero (Eds.), *Collaboration in a data-rich world. PRO-VE 2017. IFIP advances in information and communication technology* (vol 506. pp. 97–103). Springer International Publishing. https://doi.org/10.1007/978-3-319-65151-4_9

Goldstein, J. A., Sastry, G., Musser, M., DiResta, R., Gentzel, M., & Sedova, K. (2023). Generative language models and automated influence operations: Emerging threats and potential mitigations. arXiv preprint arXiv:2301.04246, 1.

Hua, W., Chen, Y., Qadrdan, M., Jiang, J., Sun, H., & Wu, J. (2022). Applications of blockchain and artificial intelligence technologies for enabling prosumers in smart grids: A review. *Renewable and Sustainable Energy Reviews, 161*(112308), 1–13. https://doi.org/10.1016/j.rser.2022.112308

Hua, W., Jiang, J., Sun, H., & Wu, J. (2020). A blockchain based peer-to-peer trading framework integrating energy and carbon markets. *Applied Energy, 279*, Article 115539. https://doi.org/10.1016/j.apenergy.2020.115539

International Energy Agency. (2024). Energy technology perspectives 2024. IEA. Retrieved September 2, 2025, from https://iea.blob.core.windows.net/assets/25e2dab4-fe00-4e97-81e8-8f900ad5a0b6/EnergyTechnologyPerspectives2024.pdf

Jiang, T., Luo, H., Yang, K., Sun, G., Yu, H., Huang, Q., & Vasilakos, A. V. (2025). Blockchain for energy market: A comprehensive survey. *Sustainable Energy, Grids and Networks, 41*, Article 101614. https://doi.org/10.1016/j.segan.2024.101614

Junaidi, N., Abdullah, M. P., Alharbi, B., & Shaaban, M. (2023). Blockchain-based management of demand response in electric energy grids: A systematic review. *Energy Reports, 9*, 5075–5100. https://doi.org/10.1016/j.egyr.2023.04.020

Karthi, V., Revathi, S., Kumaraswamy, R., Anthonisamy, A., & Ramkumar, A. (2024). Blockchain empowered solar energy trading: A decentralized grid integration revolution. *Electric Power Components and Systems*, 1–19. https://doi.org/10.1080/15325008.2024.2316250

Khare, V., & Bhatia, M. (2024). Renewable energy trading: Assessment by blockchain. *Cleaner Energy Systems, 8*, Article 100119.

Krupa, J., Poudineh, R., & Harvey, L. D. D. (2019). Renewable electricity finance in the resource-rich countries of the Middle East and North Africa: A case study on the gulf cooperation council. *Energy, 166*, 1047–1062. https://doi.org/10.1016/j.energy.2018.10.106

Kuzmin, E., Vlasov, M., Strielkowski, W., Faminskaya, M., & Kharchenko, K. (2024). Digitalization of the energy sector in its transition towards renewable energy: A role of ICT and human capital. *Energy Strategy Reviews, 53*, Article 101418. https://doi.org/10.1016/j.esr.2024.101418

Li, B. (2023). The role of financial markets in the energy transition: An analysis of investment trends and opportunities in renewable energy and clean technology. *Environmental Science and Pollution Research, 30*(43), 97948–97964. https://doi.org/10.1007/s11356-023-29014-6

Li, J., Herdem, M. S., Nathwani, J., & Wen, J. Z. (2023). Methods and applications for artificial intelligence, big data, internet of things, and blockchain in smart energy management. *Energy and AI, 11*, Article 100208. https://doi.org/10.1016/j.egyai.2022.100208

Lightency. (2023). Lightency Documentation. 9 Avril, 2023. Retrieved September 6, 2025, from https://documentation.lightency.io

Liu, J., & Li, D. (2022). Research advances in energy investment risk management—A bibliometric perspective. *American Journal of Industrial and Business Management, 12*(06), 1125–1144. https://doi.org/10.4236/ajibm.2022.126060

Lv, Y. (2023). Transitioning to sustainable energy: Opportunities, challenges, and the potential of blockchain technology. *Frontiers in Energy Research, 11*, 1–20. https://doi.org/10.3389/fenrg.2023.1258044

Manta, O., Vasile, V., & Rusu, E. (2025). Banking transformation through fintech and the integration of artificial intelligence in payments. *FinTech, 4*(2), 13.

Minyue, B., & XiuE, Y. (2024). Asset risk assessment and management of large-scale electricity enterprises under the concept of financial sharing. *Frontiers in Energy Research, 12*(1430562), 1–12. https://doi.org/10.3389/fenrg.2024.1430562

Musienko, Y. (2023). How to use blockchain in oil and gas industry? (February 13, 2023). Retrieved September 3, 2025, from https://merehead.com/blog/use-blockchain-oil-gas-industry/

Nadeem, T. B., Siddiqui, M., Khalid, M., & Asif, M. (2023). Distributed energy systems: A review of classification, technologies, applications, and policies. *Energy Strategy Reviews, 48*, Article 101096. https://doi.org/10.1016/j.esr.2023.101096

National University of Singapore. (2024). Green finance. *Nus Sustainability*. Retrieved September 6, 2025, from https://sustainability.nus.edu.sg/campus/green-finance/

Net Zero Company. (2024). Blockchain. Net Zero Company. Retrieved September 6, 2025, https://netzerocompany.org/blockchain

Next Move Strategy Consulting. (2025). Renewable energy market by energy source, ownership & business model, technology, and end user—Global opportunity analysis and industry forecast, 2022–2030. (21 July 2025). (Report Code: EP509). NextMSC. Retrieved September 3, 2025, from https://nextmsc.com/report/renewable-energy-market

Octopus Energy. (2025). Octopus Energy Group overview, Kraken Tech. Retrieved September 6, 2025, from https://octopusenergy.group/kraken-technologies

Onukwulu, E. C., Fiemotongha, J. E., Igwe, A. N., & Ewim, C. (2025). The role of Blockchain and AI in the future of energy trading: A technological perspective on transforming the oil & gas industry by 2025. *International Journal of Advanced Multidisciplinary Research and Studies, 5*(2), 48–65. https://doi.org/10.62225/2583049x.2025.5.2.3809

Park, C., & Kim, M. (2024). Utilization and challenges of artificial intelligence in the energy sector. *Energy & Environment, 1–20.* https://doi.org/10.1177/0958305X241258795

Rane, N., Choudhary, S., & Rane, J. (2023). Blockchain and Artificial Intelligence (AI) integration for revolutionizing security and transparency in finance. *SSRN Electronic Journal*, 4644253. https://doi.org/10.2139/ssrn.4644253

Romburgh, M. van. (2025, May 21). Startup crusoe nets $11.6B in fresh financing for massive new Openai Data Center. *Crunchbase News*. Retrieved September 7, 2025, from https://news.crunchbase.com/ai/startup-crusoe-financing-openai-data-center-texas/

Samylovskaya, E., Makhovikov, A., Lutonin, A., Medvedev, D., & Kudryavtseva, R. E. (2022). Digital technologies in arctic oil and gas resources extraction: Global trends and Russian experience. *Resources, 11*(3), 1–30. https://doi.org/10.3390/resources11030029

Shahinzadeh, H., Zanjani, S. M., Moradi, J., Fayaz-Dastgerdi, M. H., Yaici, W., & Benbouzid, M. (2022). The transition toward merging big data analytics, IoT, and artificial intelligence with blockchain in transactive energy markets. *IEEE Global Energy Conference, GEC, 2022*, 241–246. https://doi.org/10.1109/GEC55014.2022.9986604

Sharma, P. K., Kumar, N., & Park, J. H. (2020). Blockchain technology toward green IoT: Opportunities and challenges. *IEEE Network, 34*(4), 263–269. https://doi.org/10.1109/MNET.001.1900526

Statista. (2025). Global renewable energy industry—Statistics & facts. Retrieved September 1, 2025, from https://www.statista.com/topics/2608/global-renewable-energy-industry/#topicOverview

Strepparava, D., Nespoli, L., Kapassa, E., Touloupou, M., Katelaris, L., & Medici, V. (2022). Deployment and analysis of a blockchain-based local energy market. *Energy Reports, 8*, 99–113. https://doi.org/10.1016/j.egyr.2021.11.283

Sun, X., Xueyang, W., Ahmad, M., & Chen, J. (2024). Contributing to SDG7: Assessing the role of geopolitical risk, environmental degradation, technological progress, and environmental taxes. *Journal of Cleaner Production, 443*, Article 141185. https://doi.org/10.1016/j.jclepro.2024.141185

Szczepaniuk, H., & Szczepaniuk, E. K. (2023). Applications of artificial intelligence algorithms in the energy sector. *Energies, 16*(1), 347. https://doi.org/10.3390/en16010347

Talaat, F. M., Kabeel, A. E., & Shaban, W. M. (2024). The role of utilizing artificial intelligence and renewable energy in reaching sustainable development goals. *Renewable Energy, 235*, Article 121311.

Tamminedi, V. (2024, Jul-Dec). Dlt-Enabled green finance: Building the future of sustainable investment. *Journal of Research In Computer Applications and Information Technology (IJRCAIT), 7*(2), 2308–2317. https://doi.org/10.5281/zenodo.14511307

Tekani, D. V., Shi, J., & Grebel, H. (2025). Managing renewable energy resources using equity-market risk tools—The efficient frontiers. *Energy Efficiency, 18*(57), 1–10. https://doi.org/10.1007/s12053-025-10350-0

Tian, L., Li, X., Lee, C. W., & Spulbăr, C. (2024). Investigating the asymmetric impact of artificial intelligence on renewable energy under climate policy uncertainty. *Energy Economics, 137*, Article 107809.

Tibo Energy. (2024). Tibo energy software take control of your energy. Predict. Optimise. Act. Retrieved September 7, 2025, from https://tibo.energy

United Nations. (2025). The sustainable development goals report (2025). Retrieved September 8, 2025, from https://unstats.un.org/sdgs/report/2025/The-Sustainable-Development-Goals-Report-2025.pdf

United Nations Development Programme (UNDP). (2025). (February 3, 2025). What is the sustainable energy transition and why is it key to tackling climate change? UNDP Climate Promise. Retrieved September 3, 2025, from https://climatepromise.undp.org/news-and-stories/what-sustainable-energy-transition-and-why-it-key-tackling-climate-change

UNFCC. (2015). United Nations Climate Change, The Paris agreement what is the Paris agreement? Retrieved September 8, 2025, from https://unfccc.int/process-and-meetings/the-paris-agreement

World Economic Forum. (2016, Mar 2). What does digital mean for the future of energy?. *World Economic Forum*. Retrieved September 3, 2025, from https://www.weforum.org/stories/2016/03/perspective-distributed-digital-and-demand-side-energy-technology-implications-for-energy-security/

World Economic Forum. (2025, June). Fostering Effective Energy Transition 2025. *Insight Report*. Retrieved September 3, 2025, from https://reports.weforum.org/docs/WEF_Fostering_Effective_Energy_Transition_2025.pdf

Yahaya, A. S., Javaid, N., Alzahrani, F. A., Rehman, A., Ullah, I., Shahid, A., & Shafiq, M. (2020). Blockchain based sustainable local energy trading considering home energy management and demurrage mechanism. *Sustainability, 12*(3385), 1–28. https://doi.org/10.3390/SU12083385

Yang, J. (2024). Energy cost forecasting and financial strategy optimization in smart grids via ensemble algorithm. *Frontiers in Energy Research, 12*(1353312), 1–18. https://doi.org/10.3389/fenrg.2024.1353312

Zhang, D. (2018). Energy finance: Background, concept, and recent developments. *Emerging Markets Finance and Trade, 54*(8), 1687–1692. https://doi.org/10.1080/1540496X.2018.1466524

Zhang, D., & Ji, Q. (2019). Energy finance: Frontiers and future development. *Energy Economics, 83*, 290–292. https://doi.org/10.1016/j.eneco.2019.07.003

Zhao, Z., Gozgor, G., Lau, M. C. K., Mahalik, M. K., Patel, G., & Khalfaoui, R. (2023). The impact of geopolitical risks on renewable energy demand in OECD countries. *Energy Economics, 122*, Article 106700. https://doi.org/10.1016/j.eneco.2023.106700

Zhao, Q., Wang, L., Stan, S. E., & Mirza, N. (2024). Can artificial intelligence help accelerate the transition to renewable energy? *Energy Economics, 134*, Article 107584.

Oil Bubbles and Cryptocurrency Returns: Evidence from Clean and Dirty Assets

Ibrahim Yagli, Ozkan Haykir, and Gokce Avbaz

Abstract The study analyzes the effect of speculative bubbles in oil prices on cryptocurrency returns, with special attention to the heterogeneity among clean and dirty cryptocurrencies. The DS-LPPLS model is employed to detect positive and negative bubble episodes in WTI oil prices. Findings obtained from daily data collected from July 2018 to June 2025 show that oil prices exhibited both negative and positive bubble characteristics and that these price bubbles significantly increased cryptocurrency returns, with negative bubble periods having the strongest effects. Regarding the consensus mechanism, the results reveal that clean cryptocurrencies benefit consistently from oil price bubbles, implying that they could serve as a green hedge during negative bubbles. On the contrary, dirty cryptocurrencies respond more strongly to negative bubbles, owing to their reliance on energy-intensive mining processes. These findings offer fresh perspectives on the relationship between energy and cryptocurrency markets, with significant implications for investors, policymakers, and sustainable finance debates.

Keywords Oil bubbles · DS-LPPLS · Cryptocurrency market · Energy-finance nexus

---

I. Yagli (✉)
The Faculty of Economics and Administrative Sciences, Nevsehir Hacı Bektas Veli University, Nevşehir, Türkiye
e-mail: ibrahimyagli@nevsehir.edu.tr

O. Haykir · G. Avbaz
The Faculty of Economics and Administrative Sciences, Nigde Omer Halisdemir University, Niğde, Türkiye
e-mail: ohaykir@ohu.edu.tr

G. Avbaz
e-mail: gokceavbaz@ohu.edu.tr

A. Akusta and M. Gün (eds.), *Financial Frontiers in Energy Markets*, Contributions to Finance and Accounting, https://doi.org/10.1007/978-3-032-16738-5_16

1 Introduction

The energy sector is still one of the most crucial industries in the global economy given the increasing global population accompanied by industrialization, urbanization, and technological progress. The sector grew by 2.2% in 2024, significantly greater than the yearly average of 1.3% recorded between 2013 and 2023. The energy sector encompasses a wide range of sources, including renewable energy sources like solar, wind, and biomass, as well as fossil fuels such as oil and natural gas. Even though renewable, clean energy sources increase their share in the global energy demand, fossil fuels, especially oil, still have the greatest share in energy produced (International Energy Agency, 2025).

Oil prices have fluctuated significantly in the past quarter-century due to economic and geopolitical developments as well as supply-related issues. Global oil prices increased sharply following the Gulf War in 1990 before plummeting in the late 1990s due to the Asian financial crisis. Oil prices started to climb again in the 2000s as a result of increased energy demand from China and other emerging economies. However, oil prices have declined sharply in 2008 due to the global financial crisis. The Arab Spring and geopolitical concerns in the Middle East have also increased oil price volatility throughout the 2010s. However, the surge in US shale oil production and OPEC's production policies between 2014 and 2016 have resulted in dramatic price decreases. In 2020, oil prices fell to historically rare negative levels as a result of declining demand due to the COVID-19 pandemic. Even though the recovery process began in the following period, oil prices have remained at moderate levels. Furthermore, several factors including energy transition, renewable energy regulations, geopolitical conflicts like the war between Russia and Ukraine, and US tariffs have continued to cause changes in oil prices in recent years.

Given its share in the energy produced globally and its highly volatile nature, the effect of oil prices on numerous micro and macro-factors has been analysed for a long time. The pioneer studies have addressed the impact of oil price shocks on macroeconomic issues, including economic growth, inflation, and unemployment (Choi et al., 2018; Kocaaslan, 2019; Mohaddes & Pesaran, 2017). A further strand of the literature has concentrated on the impact of oil price shocks on stock market performance. A substantial number of studies within this group have examined stock market performance from an aggregate perspective (Apergis & Miller, 2009; Kilian & Park, 2009; Wang et al., 2013). Another stream of the literature has analysed the impact of oil price changes on the renewable energy prices (Geng et al., 2021; Reboredo, 2015). Recent papers address the impact of crude oil prices on cryptocurrency returns, given that oil is considered an input used for crypto mining (Symitsi & Chalvatzis, 2018). For instance, Yin et al. (2021) investigated the effect of oil price shocks on the cryptocurrency market and showed that oil price shocks could appear to be a major source of concern for the cryptocurrency market. Jareño et al. (2021) also revealed that interdependence among oil and cryptocurrencies has strengthened during periods of economic instability. Naeem et al. (2023), on the other hand, detected a linear relationship between oil and cryptocurrencies under normal and bullish environments.

There are also a few studies analysing determinants of oil prices (Kilian & Park, 2009; Kruse & Wegener, 2020; Wang & Sun, 2017) and bubble behaviours in oil prices (Balcilar et al., 2014; Khan et al., 2021; Su et al., 2017; Zhang & Yao, 2016). The conclusions drawn from these studies show that oil prices occasionally display bubble behaviour, and this behaviour can last for extended periods of time. Price bubbles in oil markets affect not only the energy sector but also financial markets since excessive speculative activity during bubble periods changes investor behaviour and risk perception, which, in turn, shapes capital flows to various asset classes. In this regard, it is expected that oil price bubbles may affect cryptocurrency prices as highly speculative financial assets. Nevertheless, to the best of our knowledge, there is no study examining the impact of oil bubbles on cryptocurrency returns. In this context, the study aims to investigate speculative bubbles in oil prices and ascertain the impact of these bubbles on cryptocurrency returns.

The study attempts to contribute to the literature on three fronts. First, even though a lot of research has been done to understand the interconnections between energy commodities and other financial assets, including cryptocurrencies; these studies have focused on absolute prices rather than price bubbles. Price bubbles correspond to large price changes, resulting in the price of assets exceeding their intrinsic value. Although price bubbles resemble large price fluctuations, they have distinct characteristics. Large price fluctuations have a fundamental basis, whereas price bubbles are usually fuelled by speculation. Besides, large price movements are typically short-lived, while speculative bubbles are relatively longer-term since they are sustained by investors' expectations of further price increases rather than fundamentals.

Second, studies analysing speculative bubbles have focused on positive bubbles in general. However, bubbles can be positive as well as negative. Given the level of oil prices following the COVID-19 pandemic, the study employs the Log Periodic Power Law Singularity (LPPLS) Model which can capture both negative and positive bubbles. In this regard, the primary aim of the study is to explore the asymmetric effects of positive and negative oil price bubbles on cryptocurrency returns.

Third, following the Bitcoin invention in 2008, plenty of cryptocurrencies have been introduced, and the cryptocurrency market has become one of the most active investment areas over the past decade. Nevertheless, not all cryptocurrencies share the same characteristics. For example, proof of work (PoW)[1] based cryptocurrencies, including Bitcoin and Ethereum, are considered as dirty assets since they consume substantial amounts of electricity in the mining and transaction process. On the other hand, proof of stake (PoS)[2] based cryptocurrencies such as Ripple, Cardano, and Theta are based on more energy-efficient consensus mechanisms; therefore, they are referred to as clean cryptocurrencies. Therefore, we expect that bubbles in oil

[1] PoW is a consensus model in which participants solve complex computational puzzles to validate transactions and add new blocks to the blockchain.

[2] PoS is alternative settlement mechanism that employs randomly chosen validators to confirm transactions and generate new blocks, thereby it lowers the demand for processing resources.

prices have different impacts on cryptocurrencies based on their energy usage, as they consume different amounts of energy in the mining and transaction process.

The rest of the paper is structured as follows. The literature is reviewed in Sect. 2, the data are introduced in Sect. 3, the methodological framework and empirical findings are provided in Sect. 4, and finally results and policy discussions are discussed in Sect. 5.

2 Literature Review

Energy commodities have been the subject of finance literature ever since the Industrial Revolution. As a primary energy source, oil has played an important role in economic and political activities in the setting of energy markets. Fluctuations in oil prices observed particularly in the period following the 1973 oil crisis brought bubble discussions to the fore (Sornette et al., 2009; Su et al., 2017). Empirical studies have examined bubble behaviour in oil prices using various methods and pointed to bubble formations in different periods. Balcilar et al. (2014), for instance, identified multiple bubbles in the WTI and Brent markets, while Gronwald (2016) detected periodic, temporary bubbles in WTI prices. More recent analyses also reveal bubble formations in oil and other energy markets, particularly during the 2007–2008 period (Khan et al., 2021, 2022). On the other hand, some studies have reported periods of negative bubbles in oil markets. Fantazzini (2016), for example, points out the 2014–2015 period, while Gharib et al. (2021) document the COVID-19 period in this context. These findings enable us to better understand the financial bubble phenomenon and bubble dynamics in energy markets.

Besides the studies aiming at bubble dynamics in oil prices, another strand of the literature has focused on understanding the linkages between oil bubbles and financial assets. Studies examining the interactions between oil and capital markets highlight that volatility in energy prices has significant and economically meaningful implications for market volatility. Zhang and He (2021), for example, employed a multivariate stochastic volatility-based spillover analysis to investigate the dynamics among oil, gold, Bitcoin, and major stock indices and found that oil exhibits the strongest correlation with stocks. Similarly, Bâra et al. (2024) analysed interconnections between oil, the S&P 500, and Bitcoin volatility using various GARCH models, and determined that oil volatility generates substantial risk channels for stocks through macroeconomic, financial, and social mechanisms. Furthermore, Gherghina et al. (2024) demonstrated that the interconnectedness between the energy index and stock markets intensifies during crisis periods by applying the Diebold-Yilmaz spillover index and Granger causality tests.

There is also a subgroup of research in the literature focusing on the relationship between oil and cryptocurrency markets. These studies have generally centered on Bitcoin's roles as a hedge, safe haven, and portfolio diversification tool. Selmi et al. (2018), for instance, tested the protection and diversification performance of oil, gold, and Bitcoin against oil-related shocks and found that both Bitcoin and gold could provide portfolio protection depending on timing and market conditions. Das et al. (2020) also evaluated Bitcoin's safe haven performance against oil-related uncertainties using GARCH and quantile regression, and showed that Bitcoin is not a superior hedge instrument compared to traditional assets. Wang et al. (2023) also tested whether Bitcoin and gold were safe havens for oil by applying three different spillover measures during the COVID 19 period; they reported that Bitcoin's safe haven effect was weak and short-term. These findings reveal that while Bitcoin may exhibit protective characteristics under certain conditions, it has limitations when compared to the relative stability and safe-haven function provided by gold.

In addition to studies examining Bitcoin's relationship with oil from a safe haven and hedge perspective, another prominent subgroup in the literature focuses on propagation, volatility, and causality dynamics, particularly the asymmetric interactions that emerge during crisis periods. Okorie and Lin (2020), for example, identified both bidirectional and unidirectional volatility spillover among oil and various cryptocurrencies. Li et al. (2022) also examined risk spillover across Bitcoin and oil during extreme events using the extreme Granger causality approach and found strong and time-varying causality relationships based on the size and direction of shocks. These results indicate that correlation and financial contagion strengthen, particularly during crisis periods. Similarly, Naeem et al. (2023) reported that fluctuations in oil demand, particularly in bear markets, have a significant impact on cryptocurrency returns. These findings suggest that the propagation mechanisms between oil and cryptocurrency interactions are heterogeneous, and therefore, uniform assumptions may be insufficient in risk management applications.

Another stream of the literature focuses on the role of oil prices in the predictability of cryptocurrency returns. Salisu et al. (2023), for instance, examined the effect of oil on predicting Bitcoin's volatility by adopting an in-sample/out-of-sample estimation framework and detected statistically significant evidence that oil price increases reduce Bitcoin volatility. Gkillas et al. (2022) analysed the interaction between the high-order moments of crude oil, gold, and Bitcoin using high-frequency data and showed that risk assessments would be incomplete if these three markets were not modelled together. These findings reveal that oil is a critical variable for cryptocurrency markets not only through direct propagation mechanisms but also in terms of volatility prediction and modelling. While the literature predominantly focuses on the effects of oil on Bitcoin, some studies draw attention to the repercussions of Bitcoin on energy markets from an opposite perspective. In the context of bubbles and speculative effects, Kaabia et al. (2020) examined the effects of speculative bubbles in Bitcoin on different crude oil markets using the Bayesian Shrinkage VAR approach and revealed that Bitcoin-induced shocks can affect oil markets.

Overall, although the interconnections between oil prices and other financial assets have been studied, the impact of oil bubbles on the cryptocurrency market has received less attention. The study aims to fulfil this gap in the literature.

3 Data

The present study has three objectives: (i) to detect the presence of speculative bubbles in WTI oil prices, distinguishing explicitly between positive and negative bubbles, (ii) to examine the contemporaneous impact of oil price bubbles on the returns of cryptocurrencies, and (iii) to investigate whether this relationship differs across types of crypto assets, with particular attention to the distinction between clean and dirty cryptocurrencies. The datasets come from several sources. To detect the speculative bubble on oil prices, the daily West-Texas-Intermediate (WTI)-Cushing, Oklahoma crude oil price is retrieved from the Federal Reserve Bank of St. Louis. Daily price, volume, and market capitalization of each cryptocurrency are obtained from coinmarketcap.com. The Chicago Board Options Exchange (CBOE) Volatility Index (VIX) is also downloaded from the Federal Reserve Bank of St. Louis. The sample period spans between July 1, 2018, and June 30, 2025. Following Chen et al. (2024), the sample comprises of 35 cryptocurrencies.[3] They use several criteria to construct the sample. First, to maximize the time span of the analysis. Second, the sample incorporates cryptocurrencies with heterogeneous market capitalizations, rather than relying on market-cap rankings. The dataset contains 35 cryptocurrencies, categorized into clean and dirty groups based on Chen et al. (2024). The dirty group encompasses ten cryptocurrencies (BCH, Bitcoin, Bytecoin, Digibyte, Dogecoin, Ethereum, Ethereum Classic, Litecoin, Monero, and Zcash), whereas the other twenty-five cryptocurrencies (0x, BAT, BNB, BitShares, Cardano, Chainlink, Dash, Decentraland, EOS, IOTA, Lisk, Loopring, Nem, Neo, Ontology, Qtum, Steem, Stellar, Tezos, Theta, TRON, Vechain, Waves, XRP, and Zilliqa) are considered as clean assets.

To accurately determine linkages between oil price bubbles and cryptocurrency returns, several control variables are incorporated. Volatility is a key determinant of asset returns and risk premia in finance. Accordingly, the Garman–Klass (1980) volatility estimator is used to measure daily price variability as a volatility proxy. The Garman-Klass measure gains attention in recent papers (Enoksen et al., 2020; Fiszeder et al., 2019). Second, the logarithm of dollar trading volume serves as a proxy for liquidity, consistent with the literature showing that higher trading activity reduces transaction costs and improves price discovery (Amihud, 2002; Gervais et al., 2001). Third, size, as calculated by taking the logarithm of market capitalization, is included since smaller assets tend to earn higher average returns due to risk or mispricing, as documented in the traditional equity size effect (Banz, 1981) and extended to cryptocurrencies (Liu et al., 2020). Fourth, the one-day lagged return is added to account for short-term autocorrelation or mean reversion effects (Pham et al., 2024). Finally, the VIX index is included as a measure of global risk sentiment, given its well-established role as the fear index in financial markets (Anamika et al., 2023).

Table 1 presents the descriptive statistics of variables for the entire period. The average daily cryptocurrency return is close to zero, with considerable variation. Returns are nearly symmetric, although they display very high kurtosis, reflecting

---

[3] Chen et al. (2024) use 37 cryptocurrencies, but we could not find the data for two cryptocurrencies in our sample period so we exclude those two cryptocurrencies.

Table 1 Descriptive statistics

Variable	N	Mean	Std. Dev	Skewness	Kurtosis	p1	p95
Return	62,241	−0.001	0.063	−0.062	59.882	−0.166	0.085
Oil Price	62,241	68.196	17.226	−0.075	3.499	25.030	97.730
Volatility	62,241	0.047	0.046	10.371	226.445	0.009	0.110
Liquidity	62,241	0.193	2.525	213.012	48,482.640	0.001	0.710
Size	62,241	20.912	2.248	0.581	3.729	15.598	25.237
VIX	62,241	20.193	7.721	2.601	15.088	12.000	32.640

Notes The descriptive statistics consist of cryptocurrency return, oil price, volatility as measured using Garman-Klass daily price range, liquidity as measured using the logarithm of dollar volume, and the VIX index

Table 2 Correlation analysis

	Return	Oil Price	Volatility	Liquidity	Size	VIX
Return	1					
Oil Price	−0.035	1				
Volatility	−0.038	−0.053	1			
Liquidity	0.010	−0.031	0.029	1		
Size	0.023	0.138	−0.102	−0.005	1	
VIX	−0.033	−0.256	0.083	0.035	−0.033	1

Notes The correlation analysis consists of cryptocurrency return, oil price, volatility as measured using the Garman-Klass daily price range, liquidity as measured using the logarithm of dollar volume, and the VIX index

the fat-tailed nature of crypto markets. Oil prices average around $68 per barrel. Volatility measure averages 0.047, showing substantial skewness and kurtosis, highlighting extreme volatility episodes. Liquidity has a mean of 0.193 but exhibits high dispersion, consistent with the heterogeneous nature of trading activity across cryptocurrencies.

Table 2 reports the correlation coefficients among the variables. The findings indicate that none of the variables exhibit high correlations. As anticipated, both volatility and the VIX index are negatively correlated with cryptocurrency returns. In contrast, size and liquidity display positive correlations with returns.

4 Empirical Results

Analyses are implemented in three steps. First, positive and negative bubble periods in oil prices are identified using the DS-LPPLS model. Second, the impact of oil price explosivity on cryptocurrency returns is examined. Finally, the study analyses whether the effect varies across clean and dirty cryptocurrencies.

Price explosivity is commonly defined as a situation where an asset price diverges from its intrinsic value (Brunnermeier, 2016). Importantly, such bubbles are not merely short-lived mispricing but rather periods characterized by persistent and accelerating price increases (Brunnermeier, 2016). In the literature, two popular approaches are commonly used for detecting bubbles in financial assets. The first approach detects the speculative bubble using right-tailed unit root tests, as proposed by Phillips et al. (2015). The second approach uses the LPPLS model, initially proposed by Johansen et al. (2000) and extended to the DS-LPPLS framework by Filimonov and Sornette (2013). Although the PSY approach is statistically effective in detecting episodes of explosiveness, it is unable to differentiate between positive bubbles and negative bubbles. The DS-LPPLS model has been selected as the methodological framework since the purpose of this study is to investigate whether cryptocurrencies react heterogeneously to positive and negative oil price bubbles.

The detection of a speculative bubble is based on the LPPLS model, which assumes that the logarithm of price dynamics can be approximated by a finite-time singularity with oscillatory components. Let *p(t)* represent the price of the asset at time *t*, and defines $x(t) = lnp(t)$. Under the LPPLS hypothesis, the expected log-price is as follows:

$$x(t) = A + B(t_c - t)^m + C(t_c - t)^m \cos(\omega \ln(t_c - t) - \varphi) \tag{1}$$

where A is a baseline constant, B captures the power-law curvature, C and φ determine the amplitude and phase of oscillations, ω is the log-frequency, and m is the power-law exponent restricted to $0 < m < 1$. The critical time *(tc)* represents the theoretical termination of the bubble, which can correspond either to a crash or to a regime change.

Re-parameterization of the oscillatory term with $C_1 = Ccos\varphi$ and $C_2 = Csin\varphi$ yields

$$\begin{aligned} x(t) = A + B(t_c - t)^m + C_1(t_c - t)^m \cos[\omega \ln(t_c - t)] + \\ C_2(t_c - t)^m \sin[\omega \ln(t_c - t)] \end{aligned} \tag{2}$$

z

Figure 1 depicts the results of the DS-LPPLS model for the WTI oil price. The positive and negative price explosivity is detected when the test statistics surpass the 95% level of critical value. The dashed blue lines indicate periods of positive bubbles, while orange lines denote negative bubble episodes. Overall, positive bubbles appear more frequently than negative bubbles during the sample period.

The second aim of the article is to determine whether price explosivity in oil prices has an immediate impact on cryptocurrency returns. To achieve the second aim of the paper, fixed-effect panel regression analysis is employed. The model is as follows:

$$\begin{aligned} Return_{i,t} = \alpha_i + \beta_1 Bubble_t + \beta_2 Return_{i,t-1} + \beta_3 Volatility_{i,t} + \\ \beta_4 Liquidity_{i,t} + \beta_5 Size_{i,t} + \beta_6 VIX_t + \varepsilon_{i,t} \end{aligned} \tag{3}$$

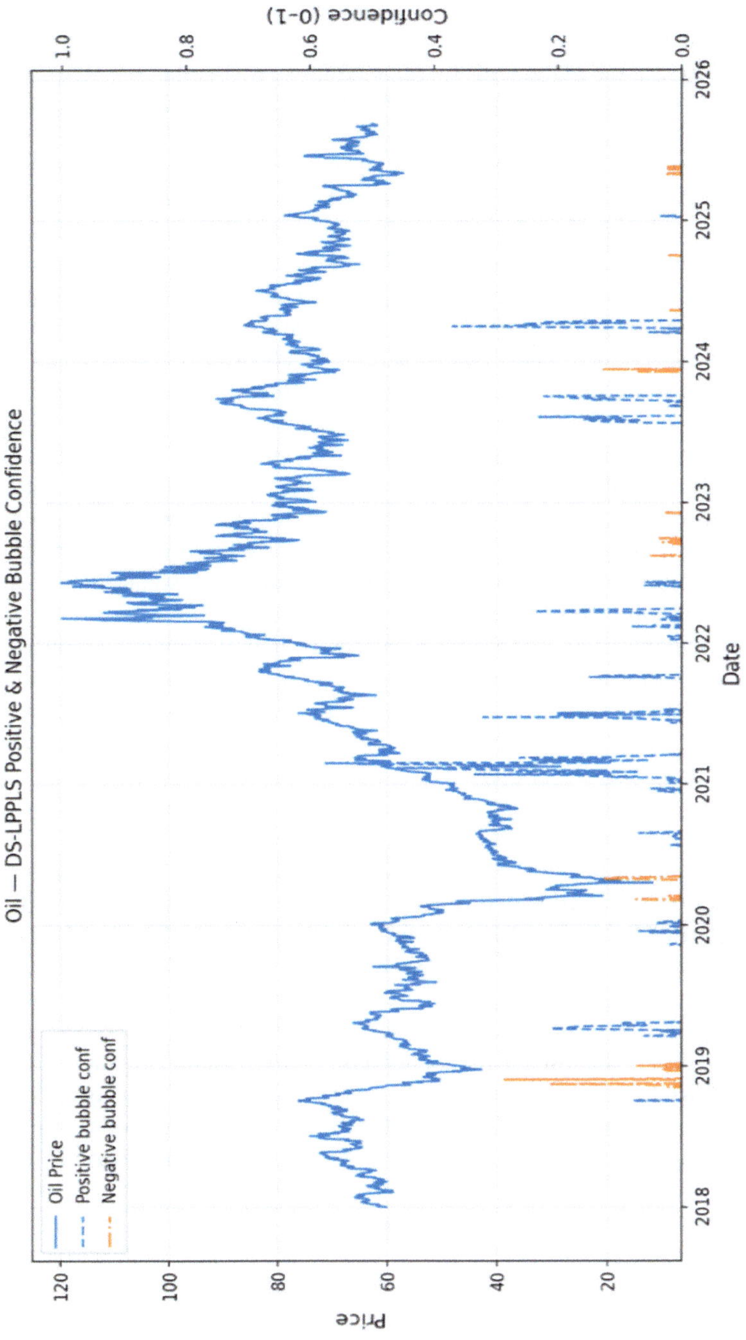

Fig. 1 Oil Price Bubble using DS-LPPLS Model

where $Return_{i,t}$ is the cryptocurrency return i on day t, α_i captures the cryptocurrency-specific fixed effect, $Bubble_t$ is the DS-LPPLS bubble indicator that gets 1 if there is a bubble and zero otherwise. $Return_{i,t-1}$ is the one-day lagged return of each cryptocurrency, $Volatility_{i,t}$ is the Garman-Klass price range volatility measure, $Liquidity_{i,t}$ and $Size_{i,t}$ are the logarithm of dollar volume and market capitalization, respectively, whereas VIX_t denotes the CBOE volatility index.

Table 3 presents the empirical findings of the panel fixed effects regressions specified in Eq. (3), estimated separately for the total, positive, and negative bubble indicators. Across all specifications, the bubble variable is positive and highly significant. This indicates that the presence of bubble episodes in oil prices is associated with higher cryptocurrency returns. The magnitude is slightly stronger for negative bubbles compared to positive bubbles. The coefficients imply that during negative bubble episodes, cryptocurrency returns increase by about 70 basis points per day, while the effect is around 50 basis points per day during positive bubble episodes. The coefficients of the one-day lagged return are negative and statistically significant, consistent with the short-term reversal dynamic in cryptocurrency returns. The coefficients of size imply that larger cryptocurrencies yield higher returns. By contrast, VIX is negative and statistically significant, suggesting that a rise in global risk reduces cryptocurrency returns. Volatility and liquidity are statistically insignificant, indicating that these factors do not significantly contribute to the explanation of daily return variations within this framework.

The last aim of the study is to examine whether the impact of oil price explosivity varies between clean and dirty cryptocurrencies. Dirty cryptocurrencies are those based on the PoW algorithm, which requires intensive electricity use for mining and transaction validation, thereby imposing significant environmental costs. By contrast, clean cryptocurrencies rely on more energy-efficient mechanisms that substantially reduce energy consumption (Chen et al., 2024). The study implements a framework in Eq. (3) separately for clean and dirty cryptocurrencies.

Table 4 presents the results of clean and dirty cryptocurrencies. In both groups, oil price bubbles are associated with higher returns. Panel A presents similar results as the full sample in Table 3, since there are more clean cryptocurrencies (25 coins) than dirty cryptocurrencies (10 coins) in our sample. The coefficients imply that during negative bubble episodes, cryptocurrency returns increase by about 60 basis points per day, while the effect is around 50 basis points per day in the positive bubble episodes. The results suggest that during periods of energy market turbulence, environmentally friendly cryptocurrencies that are less dependent on electricity-intensive mining are perceived as more sustainable, thereby becoming attractive to investors as a potential "green hedge". In contrast, the results of dirty cryptocurrencies differ between positive and negative bubbles. The results indicate that negative bubbles are linked to higher returns. The coefficients imply that during negative bubble episodes, cryptocurrency returns increase by about 80 basis points per day, while during positive bubble episodes, the effect is around 40 basis points per day, but it is insignificant (very close to the 10% threshold of significance). A plausible explanation is that falling energy prices reduce the mining and transaction costs of electricity-intensive cryptocurrencies such as Bitcoin, making them relatively more profitable and thereby

Table 3 Main analysis

Dep. Var.: Return	Bubble (All)	Bubble (Positive only)	Bubble (Negative only)
Bubble	0.006[a] (0.000)	0.005[a] (0.000)	0.007[a] (0.000)
$Return_{t-1}$	−0.080[a] (0.008)	−0.081[a] (0.008)	−0.080[a] (0.008)
Volatility	−0.050 (0.113)	−0.050 (0.113)	−0.049 (0.127)
Liquidity	0.0002 (0.180)	0.0002 (0.181)	0.0002 (0.184)
Size	0.002[a] (0.002)	0.002[a] (0.002)	0.002[a] (0.001)
VIX	−0.0003[a] (0.000)	−0.0003[a] (0.000)	−0.0003[a] (0.000)
Constant	−0.028[a] (0.008)	−0.0027[a] (0.008)	−0.030[a] (0.005)
N	48,947	48,947	48,947
R-squared	0.230	0.230	0.227
F-statistics	61.71[a] (0.000)	48.70[a] (0.000)	106.58[a] (0.000)

Notes All regressions are estimated using panel fixed effects, and robust standard errors are employed to account for potential heteroscedasticity. P values are shown in parentheses. a, b, and c signify at the 1%, 5%, and 10% levels, respectively

attracting speculative demand. At the same time, the significance of volatility and liquidity in the dirty cryptocurrencies suggests that these coins are more exposed to trading frictions and risk.

Table 4 Main analysis—Clean vs. Dirty cryptocurrencies

Panel A: Clean cryptocurrencies

Dep. Var.: Return	Bubble (All)	Bubble (Positive only)	Bubble (Negative only)
Bubble	0.006[a] (0.000)	0.005[a] (0.000)	0.006[a] (0.000)
$Return_{t-1}$	−0.052[a] (0.000)	−0.052[a] (0.000)	−0.052[a] (0.000)
Volatility	−0.020 (0.517)	−0.021 (0.512)	−0.018 (0.563)
Liquidity	0.0002 (0.133)	0.0002 (0.134)	0.0002 (0.140)
Size	0.001[b] (0.011)	0.001[b] (0.012)	0.002[a] (0.007)
VIX	−0.0003[a] (0.000)	−0.0003[a] (0.000)	−0.0003[a] (0.000)
Constant	−0.023[b] (0.039)	−0.023[b] (0.042)	−0.026[b] (0.026)
N	34,957	34,957	34,957
R-squared	0.143	0.143	0.146
F-statistics	57.27[a] (0.000)	48.87[a] (0.000)	90.61[a] (0.000)

Panel B: Dirty Cryptocurrencies

Dep. Var.: Return	Bubble (All)	Bubble (Positive only)	Bubble (Negative only)
Bubble	0.005[a] (0.008)	0.004[c] (0.099)	0.008[b] (0.014)
$Return_{t-1}$	−0.134[c] (0.050)	−0.134[b] (0.049)	−0.134[c] (0.050)
Volatility	−0.081[c] (0.057)	−0.081[c] (0.057)	−0.080[c] (0.059)
Liquidity	0.011[c] (0.058)	0.011[c] (0.057)	0.011[c] (0.055)
Size	0.003[a] (0.007)	0.003[a] (0.008)	0.003[a] (0.007)
VIX	−0.0004[b] (0.011)	−0.0003[b] (0.014)	−0.0004[b] (0.010)
Constant	−0.053[b] (0.010)	−0.053[b] (0.010)	−0.059[a] (0.009)
N	13,990	13,990	13,990

(continued)

Table 4 (continued)

Panel A: Clean cryptocurrencies			
Dep. Var.: Return	Bubble (All)	Bubble (Positive only)	Bubble (Negative only)
R-squared	0.509	0.509	0.505
F-statistics	227.03[a] (0.000)	61.48[a] (0.000)	29.23[a] (0.000)

Notes Panel A shows the clean cryptocurrency analysis, while Panel B reports the dirty cryptocurrency analysis. All regressions are estimated using panel fixed effects, and robust standard errors are employed to account for potential heteroscedasticity. P values are shown in parentheses. a, b, and c signify at the 1%, 5%, and 10% levels, respectively

5 Conclusion

The rapid development of cryptocurrencies and their increasing integrations with global financial and commodity markets have attracted growing academic and policy interest. Among the potential connections, the interaction of energy markets, particularly oil, and cryptocurrencies has emerged as an important research area. Oil prices, often characterized by speculative bubbles, play an important role in shaping investors' risk perceptions, liquidity preferences, and portfolio allocations. In addition, cryptocurrencies show varying sensitivity to energy-related developments based on their consensus mechanism. More precisely, cryptocurrencies that adopt energy-intensive proof-of-work processes may be heavily influenced by energy market changes, whereas clean cryptocurrencies that use proof-of-stake protocols may be robust to energy-related issues. In this respect, understanding how speculative dynamics in oil prices affect two types of cryptocurrencies is critical for both investors looking for diversification strategies and policymakers concerned with financial stability and environmental sustainability.

In this regard, this study aims to extend the literature on oil-cryptocurrency linkages by focusing on the role of oil price bubbles and their asymmetric effects on clean and dirty cryptocurrency returns. Using the DS-LPPLS model to determine positive and negative bubble episodes in WTI oil prices and a panel fixed effects framework to estimate the impact of bubbles on return, the study presents several novel findings. First, it documents multiple episodes of price bubbles in oil markets between 2018 and 2025, with positive bubbles occurring more frequently than negative ones. The empirical analysis also shows that cryptocurrency returns respond positively to both positive and negative oil price bubbles. The magnitude of this effect is economically meaningful, with returns increasing by approximately 50 basis points during positive bubbles and 70 basis points during negative bubbles, indicating the importance of speculative dynamics in oil prices as a driver of cryptocurrency performance. Second, it reveals that the overall results are largely driven by clean cryptocurrencies when splitting the sample into clean and dirty cryptocurrencies. Clean cryptocurrencies benefit during both positive and negative oil price bubbles, consistent with the view that investors may treat them as attractive alternatives or "green hedge" assets in periods of energy-related uncertainty. Third, dirty cryptocurrencies, while also exhibiting positive returns during oil price bubbles, display a somewhat different dynamic. Their returns are more sensitive to negative bubble episodes and to traditional risk factors such as volatility, liquidity, and VIX. This pattern suggests that dirty cryptocurrencies are more tightly linked to energy markets, both in perception and in practice, due to their electricity-intensive mechanisms.

These findings suggest several significant implications. For investors, recognizing the presence of oil price bubbles can improve portfolio allocation strategies in the cryptocurrency market. Clean cryptocurrencies may serve as a partial hedge during oil market turmoil; on the other hand, dirty cryptocurrencies may appear to amplify exposures to energy-related risks. From the perspective of policymakers, the results demonstrate the financial spillovers from oil prices into the cryptocurrency market. The environmental externalities associated with dirty cryptocurrencies also highlight the importance of ongoing regulatory debates on sustainable finance and green digital transitions.

Overall, this study investigates how speculative bubbles in oil prices affect cryptocurrency returns, offering a novel contribution by revealing the asymmetric response of clean and dirty cryptocurrencies. Nevertheless, the study has several limitations that require additional investigation. First, the analysis focuses primarily on WTI oil prices. Second, even though the classification of cryptocurrencies as clean and dirty coins based on the consensus mechanism is standard in the literature, this procedure may not completely reflect emerging technical transitions such as hybrid models. Therefore, broadening the scope to include additional commodities such as natural gas, coal, or renewable energy indices could provide a more complete picture regarding the interaction energy market with the cryptocurrency market. Furthermore, refining the classification of clean and dirty cryptocurrencies to account for evolving technological innovations would enhance the accuracy of comparisons and provide deeper insights into how sustainability-oriented technological shifts affect cryptocurrency returns.

References

Amihud, Y. (2002). Illiquidity and stock returns: Cross-section and time-series effects. *Journal of Financial Markets, 5*(1), 31–56. https://doi.org/10.1016/S1386-4181(01)00024-6

Anamika, Chakraborty, M., & Subramaniam, S. (2023). Does sentiment impact cryptocurrency? *Journal of Behavioral Finance, 24*(2), 202–218. https://doi.org/10.1080/15427560.2021.1950723

Apergis, N., & Miller, S. M. (2009). Do structural oil-market shocks affect stock prices? *Energy Economics, 31*(4), 569–575. https://doi.org/10.1016/j.eneco.2009.03.001

Balcilar, M., Ozdemir, Z. A., & Yetkiner, H. (2014). Are there really bubbles in oil prices? *Physica A: Statistical Mechanics and Its Applications, 416*, 631–638. https://doi.org/10.1016/j.physa.2014.09.020

Banz, R. W. (1981). The relationship between return and market value of common stocks. *Journal of Financial Economics, 9*(1), 3–18. https://doi.org/10.1016/0304-405X(81)90018-0

Bâra, A., Georgescu, I. A., Oprea, S. V., & Cristescu, M. P. (2024). Exploring the dynamics of Brent crude oil, S&P 500 and Bitcoin prices amid economic instability. *IEEE Access, 12*, 31366–31385. https://doi.org/10.1109/ACCESS.2024.3370029

Brunnermeier, M. K. (2016). Bubbles. In Cheah, G. (Eds.), *Banking crises*. Palgrave Macmillan.

Chen, Y., Zhang, L., & Bouri, E. (2024). Co-bubble transmission across clean and dirty cryptocurrencies: Network and portfolio analysis. *Journal of International Money and Finance*, 145. https://doi.org/10.1016/j.jimonfin.2024.103108

Choi, S., Furceri, D., Loungani, P., Mishra, S., & Poplawski-Ribeiro, M. (2018). Oil prices and inflation dynamics: Evidence from advanced and developing economies. *Journal of International Money and Finance, 82*, 71–96. https://doi.org/10.1016/j.jimonfin.2017.12.004

Das, D., Le Roux, C. L., Jana, R. K., & Dutta, A. (2020). Does Bitcoin hedge crude oil implied volatility and structural shocks? A comparison with gold, commodity and the US Dollar. *Finance Research Letters, 36*, Article 101335. https://doi.org/10.1016/j.frl.2019.101335

Enoksen, F., A., Landsnes, C., J., Lučivjanska, K., & Molnar, P. (2020). Understanding risk of bubbles in cryptocurrencies. *Journal of Economic Behavior and Organization, 176*, 129–144. https://doi.org/10.1016/j.jebo.2020.05.005

Fantazzini, D. (2016). The oil price crash in 2014/15: Was there a (negative) financial bubble? *Energy Policy, 96*, 383–396. https://doi.org/10.1016/j.enpol.2016.06.020

Filimonov, V., & Sornette, D. (2013). A stable and robust calibration scheme of the log-periodic power law model. *Physica a: Statistical Mechanics and Its Applications, 392*(17), 3698–3707. https://doi.org/10.1016/j.physa.2013.04.012

Fiszeder, P., Fałdzinski, M., & Molnar, P. (2019). Range-based DCC models for covariance and value-at-risk forecasting. *Journal of Empirical Finance, 54*, 58–76. https://doi.org/10.1016/j.jempfin.2019.08.004

Garman, M., B., and Klass, & M.J. (1980). On the estimation of security price volatilities from historical data. *Journal of Business, 53*(1), 67–78.

Geng, J. B., Liu, C., Ji, Q., & Zhang, D. (2021). Do oil price changes really matter for clean energy returns? *Renewable and Sustainable Energy Reviews, 150*, Article 111429. https://doi.org/10.1016/j.rser.2021.111429

Gervais, S., Kaniel, R., & Mingelgrin, D. H. (2001). The high-volume return premium. *Journal of Finance, 56*, 877–919. https://doi.org/10.1111/0022-1082.00349

Gharib, C., Mefteh-Wali, S., Serret, V., & Jabeur, S. B. (2021). Impact of COVID-19 pandemic on crude oil prices: Evidence from econophysics approach. *Resources Policy, 74*, Article 102392. https://doi.org/10.1016/j.resourpol.2021.102392

Gherghina, S. C., Armeanu, D. S., Andrei, J. V., & Joldes, C. C. (2024). Spillover connectedness between cryptocurrency and energy sector: An empirical investigation under asymmetric exogenous shocks of health and geopolitical crisis and uncertainties. *Journal of the Knowledge Economy, 15*(4), 16454–16510. https://doi.org/10.1007/s13132-024-01773-8

Gkillas, K., Bouri, E., Gupta, R., & Roubaud, D. (2022). Spillovers in higher-order moments of crude oil, gold, and Bitcoin. *The Quarterly Review of Economics and Finance, 84*, 398–406. https://doi.org/10.1016/j.qref.2020.08.004

Gronwald, M. (2016). Explosive oil prices. *Energy Economics, 60*, 1–5. https://doi.org/10.1016/j.eneco.2016.09.012

International Energy Agency (2025), Global Energy Review 2025. https://iea.blob.core.windows.net/assets/5b169aa1-bc88-4c96-b828-aaa50406ba80/GlobalEnergyReview2025.pdf

Jareño, F., González, M. D. L. O., López, R., & Ramos, A. R. (2021). Cryptocurrencies and oil price shocks: A NARDL analysis in the COVID-19 pandemic. *Resources Policy, 74*, Article 102281. https://doi.org/10.1016/j.resourpol.2021.102281

Johansen, A., Ledoit, O., & Sornette, D. (2000). Crashes as critical points. *International Journal of Theoretical and Applied Finance, 3*(02), 219–255. https://doi.org/10.1142/S0219024900000115

Kaabia, O., Abid, I., Guesmi, K., & Sahut, J. M. (2020). How do Bitcoin price fluctuations affect crude oil markets? *Management & Prospective, 37*(1), 47–60. https://doi.org/10.3917/g2000.371.0047

Khan, K., Su, C. W., Umar, M., & Yue, X. G. (2021). Do crude oil price bubbles occur? *Resources Policy, 71*, Article 101936. https://doi.org/10.1016/j.resourpol.2020.101936

Khan, K., Su, C. W., & Khurshid, A. (2022). Do booms and busts identify bubbles in energy prices? *Resources Policy, 76*, Article 102556. https://doi.org/10.1016/j.resourpol.2022.102556

Kilian, L., & Park, C. (2009). The impact of oil price shocks on the US stock market. *International Economic Review, 50*(4), 1267–1287. https://doi.org/10.1111/j.1468-2354.2009.00568.x

Kocaaslan, O. K. (2019). Oil price uncertainty and unemployment. *Energy Economics, 81*, 577–583. https://doi.org/10.1016/j.eneco.2019.04.021

Kruse, R., & Wegener, C. (2020). Time-varying persistence in real oil prices and its determinant. *Energy Economics, 85*, Article 104328. https://doi.org/10.1016/j.eneco.2019.02.020

Li, D., Hong, Y., Wang, L., Xu, P., & Pan, Z. (2022). Extreme risk transmission among bitcoin and crude oil markets. *Resources Policy, 77*, Article 102761. https://doi.org/10.1016/j.resourpol.2022.102761

Liu, W., Liang, X., & Cui, G. (2020). Common risk factors in the returns on cryptocurrencies. *Economic Modelling, 86*, 299–305. https://doi.org/10.1016/j.econmod.2019.09.035

Mohaddes, K., & Pesaran, M. H. (2017). Oil prices and the global economy: Is it different this time around? *Energy Economics, 65*, 315–325. https://doi.org/10.1016/j.eneco.2017.05.011

Naeem, M. A., Karim, S., Abrar, A., Yarovaya, L., & Shah, A. A. (2023). Non-linear relationship between oil and cryptocurrencies: Evidence from returns and shocks. *International Review of Financial Analysis, 89*, Article 102769. https://doi.org/10.1016/j.irfa.2023.102769

Okorie, D. I., & Lin, B. (2020). Crude oil price and cryptocurrencies: Evidence of volatility connectedness and hedging strategy. *Energy Economics, 87*, Article 104703. https://doi.org/10.1016/j.eneco.2020.104703

Pham, H., Tran, T.N.D., Nguyen, N.T.T., & Duong, K.D.(2024). The reversal in the cryptocurrency market before and during the Covid-19 pandemic: Does investor attention matter? *Plos One, 19*(11). https://doi.org/10.1371/journal.pone.0304377

Phillips, P. C. B., Shi, S., & Yu, J. (2015). Testing for multiple bubbles: Limit theory of real-time detectors. *International Economic Review, 56*(4), 1079–1134. https://doi.org/10.1111/iere.12131

Reboredo, J. C. (2015). Is there dependence and systemic risk between oil and renewable energy stock prices? *Energy Economics, 48*, 32–45. https://doi.org/10.1016/j.eneco.2014.12.009

Salisu, A. A., Ndako, U. B., & Vo, X. V. (2023). Oil price and the Bitcoin market. *Resources Policy, 82*, Article 103437. https://doi.org/10.1016/j.resourpol.2023.103437

Selmi, R., Mensi, W., Hammoudeh, S., & Bouoiyour, J. (2018). Is Bitcoin a hedge, a safe haven or a diversifier for oil price movements? A comparison with gold. *Energy Economics, 74*, 787–801. https://doi.org/10.1016/j.eneco.2018.07.007

Sornette, D., Woodard, R., & Zhou, W.-X. (2009). The 2006–2008 oil bubble: Evidence of speculation, and prediction. *Physica a: Statistical Mechanics and Its Applications, 388*(8), 1571–1576. https://doi.org/10.1016/j.physa.2009.01.011

Su, C. W., Li, Z. Z., Chang, H. L., & Lobonţ, O. R. (2017). When will occur the crude oil bubbles? *Energy Policy, 102*, 1–6. https://doi.org/10.1016/j.enpol.2016.12.006

Symitsi, E., & Chalvatzis, K. J. (2018). Return, volatility and shock spillovers of Bitcoin with energy and technology companies. *Economics Letters, 170*, 127–130. https://doi.org/10.1016/j.econlet.2018.06.012

Wang, Q., & Sun, X. (2017). Crude oil price: Demand, supply, economic activity, economic policy uncertainty and wars–From the perspective of Structural Equation Modelling (SEM). *Energy, 133*, 483–490. https://doi.org/10.1016/j.energy.2017.05.147

Wang, Q., Wei, Y., Zhang, Y., & Liu, Y. (2023). Evaluating the safe-haven abilities of bitcoin and gold for crude oil market: Evidence during the COVID-19 pandemic. *Evaluation Review, 47*(3), 391–432. https://doi.org/10.1177/0193841X221141812

Wang, Y., Wu, C., & Yang, L. (2013). Oil price shocks and stock market activities: Evidence from oil-importing and oil-exporting countries. *Journal of Comparative Economics, 41*(4), 1220–1239. https://doi.org/10.1016/j.jce.2012.12.004

Yin, L., Nie, J., & Han, L. (2021). Understanding cryptocurrency volatility: The role of oil market shocks. *International Review of Economics & Finance, 72*, 233–253. https://doi.org/10.1016/j.iref.2020.11.013

Zhang, J., & He, Q. Z. (2021). Dynamic cross-market volatility spillover based on MSV model: Evidence from Bitcoin, gold, crude oil, and stock markets. *Complexity, 2021*, 9912418. https://doi.org/10.1155/2021/9912418

Zhang, Y. J., & Yao, T. (2016). Interpreting the movement of oil prices: Driven by fundamentals or bubbles? *Economic Modelling, 55*, 226–240. https://doi.org/10.1016/j.econmod.2016.02.016

Electricity Futures Markets in Transition: Liberalization, Risk, and Decarbonization

Öykü Yücel

Abstract This chapter presents the challenges and improvements in electricity futures markets from the perspectives of global market liberalization and the ongoing decarbonization of the power sector. Originally designed to hedge against price volatility in competitive electricity systems, electricity futures have evolved into key instruments for investment planning, price discovery, and comprehensive risk management. The transition to low-carbon energy, marked by a surge in variable renewable energy (VRE), has introduced new volatility patterns across temporal and spatial dimensions—necessitating advancements in forecasting, locational hedging, and weather-contingent financial contracts. Decarbonization has also reshaped the structure of financial instruments: formal carbon pricing mechanisms and the growth of green finance have driven the emergence of carbon-linked and sustainability-driven derivatives. These instruments help connect financial risk management with climate goals, strengthening the dual financial and environmental role of electricity futures markets. In doing so, futures markets can actively shape the path toward more resilient, net-zero electricity systems.

Keywords Financial markets and institutions · Financial modelling · International finance · Electricity futures markets · Decarbonization

1 Introduction

The liberalization of electricity markets has changed how electricity is produced, priced, and traded. Earlier, vertically integrated utilities worked under regulated systems with prices set by authorities. In such settings, there was little reason to use market-based hedging tools. As markets began to open, competition increased and so did exposure to price and volume risks. Some liberalized structures existed before the 1990s, but the more developed electricity markets—such as those in the United

Ö. Yücel (✉)
The Faculty of Economics and Administrative Sciences, OSTİM Technical University, Ankara, Turkey
e-mail: oyku.yucel@ostimteknik.edu.tr

A. Akusta and M. Gün (eds.), *Financial Frontiers in Energy Markets*, Contributions to Finance and Accounting, https://doi.org/10.1007/978-3-032-16738-5_17

States and Europe—took shape during that decade. It was also then that electricity derivatives, including futures contracts, started to emerge. These instruments offered new ways to manage uncertainty and to plan investments, though their effectiveness varied across markets (Fanelli et al., 2016; Pindyck, 2001). Electricity, unlike many other traded commodities, cannot be stored. Its prices can change sharply within very short periods. These features may make electricity markets suitable for derivatives trading and hedging that can resemble arbitrage. Futures markets can allow generators, retailers, and large consumers to secure prices for future delivery. In this way, they may reduce exposure to unpredictable spot prices. Futures markets can help with price discovery and bring together expectations about the future, though their importance differs across markets (Kallabis et al., 2016). Electricity futures have also gained new roles as countries work toward decarbonization. More wind and solar power mean more variability in supply. This creates a need for tools that help manage risk and stabilize cash flows (Pavlik et al., 2025). Electricity futures are not only for speculation or hedging. They have become part of how the energy system adapts to change. This chapter looks at how electricity futures developed, how they are designed, and what purposes they serve. It draws on examples from NYMEX, EEX, and BMW. The discussion also touches on how these instruments have changed with decarbonization and what this might mean for investment and policy.

2 The Emergence of Electricity Futures Markets

The liberalization of electricity markets brought a shift in how price risk, investment, and market expectations were managed. Before deregulation, most electricity systems were vertically integrated monopolies and were regulated by the public sector (Woo et al., 2006). Price signals were set by administrative means and there was little room for risk hedging or financial innovation. The wave of liberalization during the 1990s tore the sector apart into distinct generation, transmission, and retail entities, creating competitive spot markets, thereby allowing for electricity derivatives (De Hauteclocque, 2013).

The first institutional electricity futures contracts were launched by NYMEX in 1996. Nord Pool, EEX, and PJM Interconnection all established futures contracts shortly thereafter. In the early years, there was serious scepticism on the part of traders to engage due to the non-storability and extreme volatility in electricity, as well as the still esoteric and uncertain nature of the electricity derivative products available. There was sufficient appetite, however, for standardized products on a monthly and quarterly base-load basis (Conejo et al., 2010). Nord Pool had a particularly transformational effect, in that it integrated trading in derivatives contracts with its public day-ahead and intraday spot markets, thereby giving valuable price reference signals to its derivatives contracts and was a harbinger of reforms to come in much of the rest of the Nordic, and to some extent, the Western European markets The renown of these exchanges and their methods for trading and establishing prices helped to bring institutional legitimacy and adopted both physically-settled and financially-settled contracts, which expanded and diversified the market from being primarily utility participants to include traders, retailers, and industrial consumers (Fanelli et al., 2016).

Electricity futures can serve several purposes, most often hedging, arbitrage, and price discovery. Generators will take short contracts to lock in future revenue, while consumers and retailers will take long contracts to hedge their cost of procurement. By engaging in arbitrage of differences between forward and spot prices, speculators help create market liquidity, which in turn creates additional market efficiency. While futures prices provide short-term trading opportunities, they also provide a way of observing aggregated forward-looking information that candidates' investment decision-making is associated with generation and infrastructure (Pindyck, 2001).

Following the advent of electricity futures, there was considerable diversity in type of standardized futures product, including base-load contracts that provide for the delivery of an amount of electricity 24 h per day or peak-load products that are models of what happens during high-demand periods for electricity that could include delivery periods by the hour and different quantities ranging from daily to annual delivery (Wang et al., 2024). The current futures landscape includes contracts that are financially settled in reference to spot prices or indices based on a hub, all of which allow an open marketplace and trading without the need for physical delivery (Fanelli et al., 2016).

More recently, researchers have provided empirical evidence that the formation of futures prices is increasingly shaped by regulatory and macroeconomic influences, particularly within the European experience. Kallabis et al. (2016) observed within their analysis of EEX data that long-term electricity futures curves reflected expectations regarding carbon pricing and renewable energy penetration. Moreover, a cluster of researchers can assess the structural dynamics of these complex markets through machine learning models. Zhu et al. (2024) developed a hybrid forecasting model that integrates CEEMDAN, fuzzy entropy, PSO-optimized random forest, ELM, LSTM, and ARIMA, and found that it produced notably better accuracy in carbon price prediction compared to conventional time-series models.

At the same time, new technologies related to grid-connected flexibility assets, such as battery energy storage systems (BESS) and virtual power plants (VPP), are challenging the assumption that electricity cannot be stored in time-based markets. These technologies allow for time-based arbitrage, help decrease volatility in spot prices, and should strengthen the hedging capability of futures instruments. Spodniak and Bertsch (2020) analyse whether electricity futures markets in multiple countries provide price signals that reward flexible and dispatchable generation capacity, finding that such technologies are generally undervalued despite their importance for system reliability.

3 Market Deepening and Integration

3.1 Diversity of Participants

Electricity markets did not begin as the complex systems we see today. Their evolution came in waves, each bringing new actors and new intentions. In the early years of electricity futures, participation was narrow. Most activity came from familiar players such as utilities, independent power producers (IPPs), and large industrial users. For this group, futures were not about speculation but survival. They needed a way to manage risk. Generators often sold contracts to secure future income, while retailers and consumers bought them to guard against price swings in the volatile spot market (Daskalakis et al., 2015).

Over time, the landscape changed. As trading volumes grew and markets matured, financial institutions began to take notice. Hedge funds, investment banks, and asset managers entered with different motives and a different rhythm. Their focus was not the physical flow of power but the price movements themselves. They looked for arbitrage, for patterns, for moments of inefficiency that could be turned into profit. With their entry came faster trading and new tools—quantitative models, algorithmic systems, real-time analytics—that reshaped the pace and texture of the market.

It is often said that these developments improved liquidity and price discovery. That may be true in part, but the picture is not entirely clear. Some observers argue that the influx of financial players detached prices from physical realities, creating a market that felt efficient on paper but less connected to the actual flow of electricity (Hendershott et al., 2011). Others believe that this was simply an inevitable step in the market's evolution toward maturity. Either way, by the time the dust settled, electricity trading had become faster, more aggressive, and far more intricate than before.

It may be no coincidence that major commodity traders such as Vitol and Trafigura have turned their attention to electricity futures. In seeking balance and diversification, they have begun to treat power as just another leg in their global trading portfolios. Their methods rely on cross-commodity strategies that exploit price relationships—known as spark and dark spreads—linking electricity to natural gas or coal (Pirrong, 2015). These spreads can reveal hidden value across connected markets, though the results are not always predictable. Still, the entry of such players seems to have given electricity futures a stronger presence within multi-asset portfolios, and possibly a more speculative edge as well.

A newer wave of participants is coming from an unexpected direction. Technology giants like Google, Amazon, and Microsoft have started to appear in these markets, though for different reasons. Their involvement is tied less to trading profits and more to the pursuit of sustainability goals. Through instruments such as virtual power purchase agreements (vPPAs), they aim to secure renewable power for their operations and stabilize future energy costs (Feng et al., 2024). This blending of financial hedging and environmental strategy may mark an emerging phase in market development—one where electricity futures begin to carry both financial and moral weight.

Still, the implications are not entirely straightforward. Sustainability frameworks such as the EU Sustainable Finance Taxonomy are pushing firms to align procurement with green finance principles, which can strengthen accountability but also narrow flexibility. Some researchers note that companies increasingly view electricity exposure not just as a financial liability but as a component of ESG performance (Zhang, 2025). Yet this shift raises questions. When risk management becomes intertwined with reputation, can market signals remain clear?

Price volatility now seems to carry two identities: a financial risk to hedge and a public measure of environmental intent. It is an interesting tension. On one hand, the deepening financialization of sustainability could draw capital and innovation into clean energy markets. On the other, it may also open the door to distortion—where speculation overpowers substance and futures drift away from the realities of physical power supply. The challenge for regulators will be to walk that fine line between oversight and innovation, keeping markets efficient without draining them of their purpose (Jørgensen & Ma, 2025).

3.2 Regional Integration

The regional integration of electricity markets has gathered pace in recent years. Progress has been uneven, yet the overall direction seems clear: cross-border cooperation is deepening, and with it, the liquidity of electricity futures markets. As more countries open their systems to competition—especially those with a growing share of VRE the case for regional coordination has become difficult to ignore. Integrated markets tend to promise better operational efficiency and broader participation. They may also create stronger and more transparent price signals, though the extent of these benefits still varies across jurisdictions (Zachmann et al., 2024).

In Europe, the European Network of Transmission System Operators for Electricity (ENTSO-E) has been a central force behind this shift. Through its coordination efforts, it has supported the development of the Target Model, which aims to align day-ahead, intraday, and balancing markets. The launch of the Cross-Border Intraday Market Project (XBID) in 2018 marked an important step in this process. By enabling continuous trading up to one hour before delivery across EU member states, XBID made it possible for traders to adjust positions as new information on demand or weather emerged (Kath, 2019).

This feature has particular value in systems with high renewable penetration, where forecast errors can lead to costly imbalances and inefficient dispatch. It is believed that XBID's flexibility has improved short-term hedging opportunities, allowing participants to better match financial positions to real-time conditions and limit price exposure (Miliarakis & Tsakanikas, 2025). In this sense, temporal integration—tightening the link between physical delivery and financial settlement—seems to have strengthened both market responsiveness and confidence.

Still, questions remain. Greater integration can also expose national systems to external shocks and complicate regulatory oversight. Spatial granularity is improving, yet many regions are only beginning to experiment with contracts that reflect locational risk. The process remains incomplete, and perhaps inevitably so. Electricity, unlike other commodities, moves through a network that is both physical and political. For this reason, regional integration should be seen less as a finished project than as a living process, shaped by negotiation, adjustment, and, at times, contention across Europe's interconnected grids.

In U.S. markets like PJM and ERCOT, locational marginal pricing (LMP) has allowed for the development of nodal and zonal futures contracts based on localized clearing prices. These instruments enable hedging for spatial basis risk—price differences arising from grid congestion or bottleneck limitations (Wang et al., 2020).

In Europe, similar geographically aligned futures can be found at the European Energy Exchange (EEX) and at Nord Pool, but they are specifically designed for national and sub-national bidding zones. Zonal contracts reflect tangible through-variable parameters affecting renewable output for individual locations or groups of locations, demand profiles, and interconnection capacity, which can strengthen risk management and investment planning (UKERC, 2025). With the increasing electrification of many economic activities, as well as the need for cross-border balancing among interconnected systems, zonal alignment will continue to be relevant. Financial transmission rights (FTRs) and congestion revenue rights (CRRs), which hedge congestion-based price differentials, can also facilitate these developments (Kristiansen, 2005). These instruments promote a more efficient use of grid capacity. At the same time, they shift the economic risk of congestion to market participants, making the cost of limited transmission capacity part of investment decisions.

4 The Decarbonization Era and Its Impacts on Futures Markets

Global decarbonization has added new complexity to electricity markets. The shift from fossil fuels to renewables is not only changing how power is produced but also how it is priced and traded. Electricity futures, once used mainly for hedging, now play a structural role in reshaping the energy sector itself.

This change stems from more than policy. It reflects political commitments, rapid advances in technology, and investors' growing concern with climate risk. Decarbonization, it seems, is not just an energy shift but an economic and institutional one as well.

Where market liberalization once aimed at efficiency and competition, the decarbonization phase leans toward system transformation. The large-scale use of variable renewable energy (VRE), the phaseout of coal and gas, and the rise of carbon pricing all bring new uncertainties. Futures markets must adapt to these shifting fundamentals and the broader influence of environmental regulation (Mai et al., 2012). As

VRE grows, price volatility widens. Futures markets are increasingly used for long-term hedging and to signal where clean energy investment may flow. Yet the alignment between carbon pricing and sustainable finance remains uneven. It is possible that future instruments themselves will evolve—linking financial performance more closely to emission trends and the pace of decarbonization.

4.1 Volatility from Variable Renewables

The shift toward a low-carbon energy system seems to be reshaping electricity markets in ways that reach well beyond technology alone. Climate policy, public pressure, and rapid innovation are all part of the story, though their influence differs across regions. What stands out most is the rise of VRE—wind and solar in particular—which has begun to alter both how electricity is produced and how it is traded.

Because these sources depend on the weather, they cannot be dispatched on command as fossil-fuel plants can. This simple fact adds new layers of uncertainty to markets already known for volatility. Prices may swing more sharply, forecasts can lose precision, and familiar hedging tools often prove less reliable than before. It is believed that futures markets, once focused mainly on fuel and demand, now must also grapple with less predictable factors: weather conditions, forecast errors, and the fluctuating output of renewables. In short, the move to cleaner power brings not only environmental gains but a different rhythm of risk—one that market participants are still learning to price, predict, and, at times, live with.

Unlike thermal power plants, which can respond quickly to market signals, VRE sources follow meteorological patterns that are outside human control. Their generation output can change sharply within minutes or hours, and their average capacity factors remain lower than those of coal or gas plants. At the same time, the marginal cost of producing electricity from wind or solar is very close to zero. Together, these features tend to push wholesale prices downward, especially when renewable output is high (Gökgöz & Yücel, 2025). These extreme impacts distort the merit-order curve and threaten the economic viability of flexible and dispatchable assets. Certain authors, for example, Fanelli et al. (2016), conclude that this new generation environment introduces regime-dependent volatility, whereby prices are no longer predominantly driven by demand-side shocks or fuel prices, but rather stochastic changes in solar irradiance and wind speeds. Therefore, traditional pricing models based on autoregressive processes or constant volatility have ceased to adequately describe the conditions of the market. Rather, seasonal and path dependency stochastic models have been created to acknowledge cyclical and weather-dependent features of electricity prices when under high-VRE modes. Empirical evidence demonstrates the changes from Germany, a frontrunner in the uptake of VRE. Utilizing data from German spot and futures markets and the Heath-Jarrow-Morton (HJM) framework coupled with jump-diffusion models, it has been observed by several researchers that intraday volatility can be pronounced, particularly in the solar ramp-up and ramp-down periods (Fanelli et al., 2016). Price changes frequently show asymmetric spikes, a higher level of kurtosis, and fat tails. These characteristics can result in not only a deviated forecasting of the short-term period but can also impact the risk-neutral pricing of the futures contracts.

Because futures products are settled against realized spot prices, the growing share of VRE introduces a degree of basis risk between futures and spot markets. This is especially evident when futures contracts reference system-average prices, while actual generation is unevenly distributed across regions. For example, strong wind output in northern Germany may lower prices locally, whereas southern load centres can face higher spot prices due to network congestion or limited VRE capacity. Such spatial differences call for a reassessment of hedging strategies and highlight the potential value of nodal or zonal futures contracts that better reflect locational risk (Lucia & Torró, 2011).

Forecast uncertainty related to VRE offers another source of complexity. Although the accuracy of wind and solar forecasts has improved dramatically thanks to numerical weather prediction models and machine learning, errors exist and become more pronounced as we get closer to real-time, adding incrementally to balancing costs and increasing the volatility of intra-day and real markets. Fluctuations in renewable output are now leaving clear traces along the electricity futures curve. Traders tend to read these patterns as signs of widening risk premiums, especially when markets are most exposed to swings in wind or solar generation (Kulakova & Zielb, 2021). It also seems that carbon prices often move with the weather. Research by Daskalakis et al. (2015) suggests that meteorological variability can shift both carbon and electricity prices at once, sometimes distorting forward curves and reducing the accuracy of hedging.

If that link continues to strengthen, the design of electricity futures may need to change. Contracts built for older, fuel-based systems no longer capture the risks that matter most. Weather has become a market variable. It is possible that futures will need to include new layers—derivatives tied to solar radiation, wind capacity, or even temperature—that can help manage uncertainty in renewable forecasting. Some exchanges are already experimenting with hybrid products that connect renewable generation to environmental certificates, such as guarantees of origin (Wimmers & Madlener, 2024).

Volatility from renewables is not purely a problem. It might be an opening. Financial markets, after all, have long turned uncertainty into tradable value. Instruments such as volatility futures or contracts linked to renewable intermittency could bring new liquidity and attract a different class of investors. Still, there are risks. Greater complexity may invite speculation and weaken the link between financial and physical markets. Yet, if carefully managed, these same innovations could also support more flexible capacity—storage, batteries, and demand response—that the grid will likely need as decarbonization accelerates.

5 New Instruments: Green Derivatives and Carbon Futures

The turn toward low-carbon electricity is beginning to leave its mark on financial markets. One of the clearest places to see this is in electricity derivatives. As climate rules tighten and renewables take up more space on the grid, traditional futures contracts are slowly changing character. They now carry traces of environmental value and carbon risk, reflecting how producers and consumers alike are learning to navigate the costs attached to their own emissions (Hoque et al., 2024).

Much of this shift is linked to carbon pricing systems such as emissions trading schemes. These markets—well established in the European Union and increasingly active in China—allow firms to hedge against the rising cost of carbon compliance. Utilities and large industrial emitters have become regular players, using carbon futures to manage exposure and plan long-term investments in cleaner technologies. In some situations, carbon hedges are placed alongside energy hedges, creating a kind of dual layer of protection against both fuel and emissions price swings (Daskalakis et al., 2015).

It appears that markets are slowly weaving carbon costs into broader asset decisions. Portfolio strategies now balance two moving targets: the volatility of fuel prices and the uncertainty of carbon prices. This dual-hedging approach may not be universal, and its effectiveness remains open to debate, yet it suggests an emerging view that financial and environmental risks can no longer be managed in isolation.

Empirical research supports that carbon prices and electricity prices are becoming more integrated. Chu et al. (2025) find the development of more co-movement in emissions trading market over time, and emissions prices explain most of the variation in European electricity futures prices—suggesting that carbon prices play a role in the formation of electricity prices and therefore require new risk management models with emissions as a variable. Financial innovation goes beyond compliance markets. In voluntary carbon markets (VCMs), carbon credits from nature-based or technological removal projects are being packaged with renewable electricity through structured contracts. Emerging products, like carbon-intensity-indexed forwards, adjust price to reflect the generator's marginal emissions rate to create dynamic instruments built around environmental performance (Buse, 2024). At the same time, green futures contracts linked to certified renewable electricity have recently gained notoriety. To draw distinctions from tradable futures, these contracts will have a pricing structure similar to traditional futures, but include criteria based on environmental eligibility. This allows sustainable, renewable electricity to be integrated into ESG-focused capital flows or directly related to sustainable procurement.

6 Challenges to Hedging and Policy Coordination

While electricity markets are changing in response to climate obligations, traditional financial means of transferring risk are increasing in difficulty and stress due to typical uncertainties, regulatory unpredictability, and new types of misalignments between contract design and exposure in the actual marketplace.

One of the most enduring hedging contradictions in electricity futures markets is the growing degree of basis risk. Basis risk, in a generally stable market, is the separation between the price movement of the hedging instrument and that of the underlying exposure, a general mismatch. To mitigate basis risk, standardization and historical correlation allow for manageable basis risk in a stable market (Deng & Oren, 2006). However, structural fragmentation of price signals in space and time is now an established product of commercializing variable renewable energy (VRE), decentralized generation facilities, and different demand characteristics. All of which introduce new transmitter risks in determining future nodal locations for hedging.

The shift to electric transport, heating, and industry is changing how electricity demand behaves. These changes come with decarbonization and make demand harder to predict. Short-term hedging becomes more important, while long-term forecasts are less reliable. This creates a need for new ways to hedge, maybe through models that can work across different time scales and respond to real-time changes in the market. At the same time, forward markets are facing more regulatory and political risk. Governments keep adjusting their net-zero targets, emission caps, and renewable support schemes (Onabowale, 2024). These policy shifts affect how the market works and how futures prices are formed.

Carbon pricing adds another layer of risk for market participants. It can come through trading schemes, taxes, or other policy tools. Firms now face uncertainty in both fuel costs and emissions outcomes. Carbon prices also move a lot, shaped by markets and politics. This makes hedging harder, especially across different rules and regimes (Daskalakis et al., 2015).

Green finance taxonomies add another layer of complexity. The EU Sustainable Finance Taxonomy is one example. Such frameworks can change which hedging instruments count as eligible in ESG-focused portfolios. Instruments that fall outside these rules may face higher costs or lower liquidity (PSF, 2025). Differences in national energy policies, even within the EU, also make cross-border hedging and market integration more difficult. Although platforms like the European Energy Exchange (EEX) and ENTSO-E have successfully promoted the integration of electricity spot and intraday market coupling, forward markets continue to reflect a fragmented regulatory context. Different capacity remuneration approaches, grid fee designs, and decarbonization paths all lead to different futures market depths, volatilities, and contract designs.

7 Futures Electricity Market in Türkiye

The advancement of the Turkish electricity market in the last 20 years is notable, culminating in the launch of organized financial trading markets, with the Power Futures Market (VEP) being arguably the most significant innovation. The development of the VEP was a critical part of Türkiye's energy deregulation program, initiated to provide long-term price visibility, establish risk mitigation mechanisms for electricity market participants, and promote investment in an emerging landscape of volatility and deregulation. The VEP was launched officially in June 2021 under the governance of Energy Exchange Istanbul (EPİAŞ) in conjunction with existing short-term market mechanisms (e.g., the Day Ahead Market and Intraday Market), completing Türkiye's electricity market design with a new financial forward structure (PwC Türkiye, 2023).

The Power Futures Market is a notable institutional achievement that aligns Türkiye's market structure with more advanced liberalized economies. Futures contracts in the VEP are to be financially settled (i.e., not delivered physically), based on the market-clearing prices developed by EPİAŞ's Day Ahead Market, and are utilized by market actors simply as hedging mechanisms for short-term price volatility. Futures contracts cover various lengths of time (i.e. monthly, quarterly, annually) and are standardized regarding capacity and settlement procedure. At present, each futures contract covers a "baseload" product of 1 MW per hour (i.e. 24 h for the length of the contract). Settlement of these contracts occurs through Takasbank, which also provides risk management via margining and default funds (Çatak, 2022). The justification for establishing the power futures market derives from the nature of the highly volatile electricity price environment in Türkiye. The domestic prices are influenced by widely varying structural and external inputs for a multitude of issues, such as dependency on natural gas imports, exchange rate fluctuations, and inconsistent renewables generation, which all can shift based on changes to the weather. Since the established domestic generation capacity is made up of more than 50% natural gas and coal generation, imports are subject to complex exposure to risks that abound. Furthermore, the energy procurement contracts often use foreign currency as the denominated currency to transact and increase the risks for the market participants as they must now account for currency fluctuations as well. The futures market can manage price risks within this complicated framework, managing exposure and allowing producers, suppliers, and large-scale consumers to remove price risks by contracting in advance an expectation on their future business through pre-defined financial settlements, with the intention of stabilizing their expectations of revenue and costs (Ocakoğlu & Tolga, 2018).

In terms of structure, the product format and basic concepts align with accepted international practices and standards. The futures market has struggled to seek and maintain significant trading volumes and scale since its inception. For instance, the VEP has only found a fraction of activity from mostly state-owned or vertically integrated energy companies, with little broker and investment fund activity recorded thus far to support, enhance, or increase participation and trading volumes in the market.

Low liquidity remains a primary concern for the VEP for viable price discovery to happen, and the market is not useful for engaging speculation or arb-mode business. The VEP product offering has also thus far been very limited, focusing only on baseload futures contracts and with no resource-specific contracts or future peak load contracts as products common in other competitive and liquid power futures markets. However, in 2022, calendar year products were made available, which was an important step towards satisfying longer-term financial planning and risk management needs for utilities and large consumers (PwC Türkiye, 2023).

The design and operational aspects of the Turkish futures market have been determined by economic aspects, but have also been influenced by regulatory phenomena. Together, the Energy Market Regulatory Authority (EMRA) and EPİAŞ have designed a legal and technical framework aimed at providing depth and transparency to the market. Governments have sometimes stepped in with price caps or floor rules in wholesale markets. These moves can weaken trust and make people less willing to trade (Çelikkol & Köse, 2015). It shows the tension between market liberalization and the need to keep power affordable, especially when prices rise or currencies fall.

8 Conclusion

Electricity futures markets have developed from instruments for financial risk management to critical infrastructures for contemporary electricity systems. When originally developed for hedging against spot price volatility in liberalized markets, electricity futures and derivatives are now used for coordinating investments, long-term planning, and as a regulatory benchmarking tool. Public and private exchanges such as NYMEX, EEX, and Nord Pool have facilitated this change by establishing transparent, standardized, financially settled products for use by utility firms, industrial consumers, and financial organizations (Fanelli et al., 2016; Lucia & Torró, 2011).

Within the current context of global decarbonization, the future of electricity futures, derivatives, and other financial products as established and accepted infrastructures is clearly improving. The advent of electric power systems with increasingly high shares of variable renewable energy means there will be a need for forward markets to provide certainty with revenue expectations for capital-intensive investments. Futures contracting can address this uncertainty, much of it associated with weather-dependent generation and changes to policies, and will enable market actors (e.g., consumers, generators, financial intermediaries) to participate confidently in the energy transition (Wimmers & Madlener, 2024). Furthermore, forward prices are beginning to reflect environmental regulations, carbon pricing mechanisms, and anticipated regulations, and therefore offer market actors a significant mechanism for coupling market performance with environmental objectives.

Throughout many emerging economies, significant hurdles, such as liquidity constraints, regulatory instability, and limited financial literacy, inhibit the full potential of the application of futures markets. However, even within mature electricity systems, barriers remain in establishing green contracts, managing regulatory interventions, and earning sufficient trust in the market-based formation of baseline prices. To conclude, electricity futures markets are far more than financial overlays to physical electricity markets; they represent institutionalized mechanisms for linking short-run market behaviour with long-run policy outcomes. Their continuing relevance and durability depend on how effectively 'decarbonization forms' are integrated, evolving generation portfolios are managed, and preferred reliability in market price signals are achieved amidst a complicated global energy system.

References

Buse, J. (2024). *Sustainable aviation fuels: Transitioning towards green aviation.* CRC Press.

Chu, W., Fan, L., & Zhou, P. (2025). Examining the interactions of carbon, electricity, and natural gas markets. *Frontiers of Engineering Management*, 1–15. https://doi.org/10.1007/s42524-025-4077-3

Conejo, A. J., Carrión, M., & Morales, J. M. (2010). *Decision making under uncertainty in electricity markets* (Vol. 1, pp. 376–384). Springer.

Çatak, Ç. (2022). Energy derivatives—An analysis of the Turkish electricity market. *International Journal of Economic and Administrative Studies, 35*, 17–30. https://doi.org/10.18092/ulikidince.930399

Çelikkol, H., & Köse, F. (2015). SWOT analysis of Turkish energy market in the context of electricity market. *Copernican Journal of Finance & Accounting, 4*(2), 27–41. https://doi.org/10.12775/CJFA.2015.014

Daskalakis, G., Symeonidis, L., & Markellos, R. N. (2015). Electricity futures prices in an emissions constrained economy: Evidence from European power markets. *The Energy Journal, 36*(3), 73–92. https://doi.org/10.5547/01956574.36.3.gdas

De Hauteclocque, A. (2013). *Market building through antitrust: Long-term contract regulation in EU electricity markets.* Edward Elgar Publishing.

Deng, S. J., & Oren, S. S. (2006). Electricity derivatives and risk management. *Energy, 31*(6–7), 940–953. https://doi.org/10.1016/j.energy.2005.02.015

Fanelli, V., Maddalena, L., & Musti, S. (2016). Modelling electricity futures prices using seasonal path-dependent volatility. *Applied Energy, 173*, 92–102. https://doi.org/10.1016/j.apenergy.2016.04.003

Feng, H., Zhang, Y., Lan, Z., Wang, K., Wang, Y., Chen, S., & Feng, C. (2024). Developing China's electricity financial market: Strategic design of financial derivatives for risk management and market stability. *Energies, 17*(23), 5854. https://doi.org/10.3390/en17235854

Gökgöz, F., & Yücel, Ö. (2025). Measuring the long-term impact of wind, run-of-river, solar renewable energy alternatives on market clearing prices. *Renewable Energy, 241*, Article 122292. https://doi.org/10.1016/j.renene.2024.122292

Hendershott, T., Jones, C. M., & Menkveld, A. J. (2011). Does algorithmic trading improve liquidity? *The Journal of Finance, 66*(1), 1–33. https://doi.org/10.1111/j.1540-6261.2010.01624.x

Hoque, M. E., Kabir Hassan, M., & Pezzo, L. (2024). Managing risk and reaping rewards: Climate-change futures as a game-changer for energy futures markets. *Journal of Futures Markets, 44*(8), 1338–1356. https://doi.org/10.1002/fut.22513

Jørgensen, B. N., & Ma, Z. G. (2025). Regulating AI in the energy sector: A scoping review of EU laws, challenges, and global perspectives. *Energies, 18*(9), 2359. https://doi.org/10.3390/en18092359

Kallabis, T., Pape, C., & Weber, C. (2016). The plunge in German electricity futures prices–analysis using a parsimonious fundamental model. *Energy Policy, 95*, 280–290. https://doi.org/10.1016/j.enpol.2016.04.025

Kath, C. (2019). Modeling intraday markets under the new advances of the cross-border intraday project (XBID): Evidence from the German intraday market. *Energies, 12*(22), 4339. https://doi.org/10.3390/en12224339

Kristiansen, T. (2005). Markets for financial transmission rights. *Energy Studies Review, 13*(1).

Kulakova, S., & Zielb, F. (2021). The impact of renewable energy forecasts on intraday electricity prices. *Economics of Energy & Environmental Policy, 10*(1), 79–104. https://doi.org/10.5547/2160-5890.10.1.skul

Lucia, J. J., & Torró, H. (2011). On the risk premium in Nordic electricity futures prices. *International Review of Economics & Finance, 20*(4), 750–763. https://doi.org/10.1016/j.iref.2011.02.005

Mai, T., Sandor, D., Wiser, R., & Schneider, T. (2012). *Renewable electricity futures study. executive summary* (No. NREL/TP-6A20-52409-ES). National Renewable Energy Lab.

Miliarakis, S., & Tsakanikas, A. (2025). An empirical assessment of market liquidity in Greece's continuous intraday market in the target model's first 24 months. *SSRN 5270619*. https://doi.org/10.2139/ssrn.5270619

Ocakoğlu, K. O., & Tolga, A. C. (2018). *Effective trading in Turkish electricity market: Hedging with options*. Proceedings of the World Congress on Engineering 2018, London, UK.

Onabowale, O. (2024). Energy policy and sustainable finance: Navigating the future of renewable energy and energy markets. *World Journal of Advanced Research and Reviews, 25*, 2235–2252. https://doi.org/10.30574/wjarr.2025.25.1.0319

Pavlík, M., Kurimský, F., & Ševc, K. (2025). Renewable energy and price stability: An analysis of volatility and market shifts in the european electricity sector (2015–2025). *Applied Sciences, 15*(12), 6397. https://doi.org/10.3390/app15126397

Pindyck, R. S. (2001). The dynamics of commodity spot and futures markets: A primer. *The Energy Journal, 22*(3), 1–29.

Pirrong, C. (2015). The economics of commodity trading firms: Abridged version. *Trafigura*. https://www.trafigura.com/media/k4ocz3zq/2015_trafigura_economics_of_commodity_trading_firms_abridged_en.pdf

Platform on Sustainable Finance. (2025). Background report on the use of derivatives under the SFDR and EU Taxonomy. *European Commission*. https://finance.ec.europa.eu/document/download/95dd9888-256e-44d3-979f-70cf6694fde7_en

PwC Türkiye. (2023, September). Overview of the Turkish electricity market. PricewaterhouseCoopers Türkiye.

Spodniak, P., & Bertsch, V. (2020). Is flexible and dispatchable generation capacity rewarded in electricity futures markets? A multinational impact analysis. *Energy, 196*, 117050. https://doi.org/10.1016/j.eneco.2024.107438

UK Energy Research Centre. (2025). *Zonal pricing, volume risk, and the 2030 clean power target*. https://d2e1qxpsswcpgz.cloudfront.net/uploads/2025/03/Zonal-Pricing-Volume-Risk-and-the-2030-Clean-Power-Target-final.pdf

Wang, Y., Shi, E., Xu, Y., Hu, J., & Feng, C. (2024). Short-Term electricity futures investment strategies for power producers based on multi-agent deep reinforcement learning. *Energies, 17*(21), 5350. https://doi.org/10.3390/en17215350

Wang, Y., Yang, Z., Yu, J., & Fang, X. (2020). Revisit the electricity price formulation: A formal definition, proofs, and examples. *Energy, 200*, Article 117542. https://doi.org/10.1016/j.energy.2020.117542

Wimmers, A., & Madlener, R. (2024). The European market for guarantees of origin for green electricity: A scenario-based evaluation of trading under uncertainty. *Energies, 17*(1), 104. https://doi.org/10.3390/en17010104

Woo, C. K., King, M., Tishler, A., & Chow, L. C. H. (2006). Costs of electricity deregulation. *Energy, 31*(6–7), 747–768. https://doi.org/10.1016/j.energy.2005.03.002

Zachmann, G., Batlle, C., Beaude, F., Maurer, C., Morawiecka, M., & Roques, F. (2024). *Unity in power, power in unity: Why the EU needs more integrated electricity markets* (No. 03/2024). Bruegel Policy Brief.

Zhang, L. (2025). The correlation between ESG, financial performance and systemic risk: Evidence from Shanghai and Shenzhen listed electric power enterprises. *Frontiers in Environmental Science, 13*, 1507151. https://doi.org/10.3389/fenvs.2025.1507151

Zhu, Y., Chen, Y., Hua, Q., Wang, J., Guo, Y., Li, Z., Ma, J., & Wei, Q. (2024). A hybrid model for carbon price forecasting based on improved feature extraction and non-linear integration. *Mathematics, 12*(10), 1428. https://doi.org/10.3390/math12101428

Policy and Transformation Strategies to Combat Energy Poverty

Cengiz Çağrı Kabakci, Çağatay Orçun, and Erhan Demireli

Abstract As the concept of energy poverty has gained increasing scholarly attention in recent years, particularly in connection with climate change debates, access to electricity, clean cooking facilities, and essential energy services is now widely recognized as a fundamental prerequisite for sustainable development and social justice, highlighting the need for an energy-justice-oriented development model that balances social, environmental, and economic objectives. Regional manifestations of energy poverty differ markedly, emerging from infrastructural deficits and biomass dependence in developing countries, while in developed economies it is primarily driven by high energy costs and inefficient housing. Measurement approaches range from simple expenditure-based metrics, such as the 10 percent rule, to multidimensional indices including the MEPI and CEPI, which incorporate health, housing quality, and social vulnerability. Effective mitigation requires a phased policy strategy encompassing short-term financial support, medium-term energy-efficiency investments, and long-term structural reforms.

Keyword Energy poverty · Energy justice · Sustainable development

1 Introduction

In this century, sustainability, resolving the climate change problem, and poverty reduction are among the most important objectives on the global agenda. When these goals are examined at their core, they mainly emphasize the importance of "reliable access to energy and ensuring this access is sustainable." Energy is not only a matter of production, but also a prerequisite for individual access to essential amenities such as heating, lighting, clean water, and healthcare. Therefore, inadequate access

C. Ç. Kabakci · Ç. Orçun · E. Demireli (✉)
Faculty of Economics and Administrative Sciences, Department of Business Administration, Dokuz Eylul University, Izmir, Turkey
e-mail: erhan.demireli@deu.edu.tr

C. Ç. Kabakci
e-mail: cagri.kabakci@deu.edu.tr

A. Akusta and M. Gün (eds.), *Financial Frontiers in Energy Markets*, Contributions to Finance and Accounting, https://doi.org/10.1007/978-3-032-16738-5_18

to energy and the inability to meet energy needs are considered more than just a technical problem; they are also a profound dimension of poverty. This reality facing humanity is conceptually defined as "energy poverty."

The first definitions of energy poverty appeared in socio-political studies conducted in the UK. Boardman (1991) first used the concept as "the inability of households to afford the energy services necessary for adequate heating. " This definition, developed by Boardman (1991), was expanded in the literature to include electricity and clean cooking services, leading to a multidimensional understanding of energy poverty, which has gained acceptance on the global agenda (Bouzarovski & Petrova, 2015).

While energy poverty can be conceptually explained in the literature, significant challenges arise regarding its quantification. One of the main reasons for this is the geographically diverse perception of energy poverty. While developing countries associate energy poverty with inadequate infrastructure, a key component of energy dissipation, in developed countries, this assessment is replaced by quantitative issues such as excessive increases in energy consumption costs, heat loss in residences, and the inability to meet energy costs due to low income (Sovacool, 2012). These assessments, linked to the level of development, have traditionally framed energy poverty in developing countries through concepts such as fuel dependency, the health impacts of biomass use, and time losses. However, when energy poverty is considered more comprehensively, it rests on a triangular pillar: energy access, affordability, and efficiency.

Access: Refers to the availability of energy resources,
Affordability: The share of energy expenditures in household income,
Efficiency: The measure of how effectively energy is used.

These different approaches developed in the literature arise from geographic and geopolitical reasons and the extent of energy poverty. Energy poverty refers to a socio-economic concept different from the traditionally defined "poverty" for high-income households that need to spend a significant portion of their income on energy services. Within the concept of poverty, energy poverty, in essence, underlines that individuals do not directly consume energy, encompassing not only poverty in terms of energy services, but also that they need energy in every aspect of their lives to alleviate the deprivation created by poverty and support socio-economic development (Manga, 2020). As a result of this limitation, the terms "fuel poverty" and "energy poverty" have become interchangeable in the literature. Fuel poverty: While Boardman (1991) defined it as the situation where a household cannot afford sufficient energy services with 10% of its income, Foster et al. (2000) considered it the situation where energy consumption levels are insufficient to meet basic energy needs. In fact, to clarify the differences between the concepts, the relationship between fuel cost and income was redefined to quantify fuel poverty. When measuring fuel poverty, the size and type of the dwelling and the average fuel cost are considered as the determining factors for cost adequacy. For the measurement of fuel poverty, the average remaining amount after housing expenses is considered the determining factor for the household's total income (Ateş & Polat, 2023; Hills, 2012).

Despite all this, energy poverty is defined as the inability to access adequate, high-quality, reliable, and environmentally friendly energy services necessary for economic and social development (Emeç et al., 2015; Reddy et al., 2000; UNDP, 2000). Energy poverty is the inadequate access to modern energy sources that are cleaner than conventional (Al-Tal et al., 2021; Şahin & Algül, 2025). In other words, energy poverty refers to the inability of individuals to provide sufficient energy at affordable prices in their homes (Pye et al., 2015).

According to 2023 data from the International Energy Agency (IEA), approximately 675 million people worldwide lack access to electricity, a significant decrease from 1.2 billion in 2010. However, energy inaccessibility remains a chronic problem despite this progress, particularly in Sub-Saharan Africa (IEA, 2023). Energy poverty should be considered a multifaceted problem created by high-energy appliances and inefficient buildings.

Energy poverty is not solely an economic issue; it can also arise from several structural factors. For example, when technical, social, and demographic variables are considered together, the multidimensional nature of energy poverty can be better understood. Indeed, energy production and consumption are interconnected with the environment and impact global climate change (Munasinghe, 2002). Policies that include energy efficiency investments, access to clean energy, energy price regulations, and targeted social assistance should be considered to eradicate energy poverty.

2 Energy Poverty and Related Concepts

2.1 Income Poverty

The positive impact of energy consumption on economic growth will result in increasing labor demand, wages, and household income. This, in turn, will increase household income through economic growth, facilitating access to social services such as better education and healthcare. Furthermore, individual access to energy can also impact well-being. Therefore, it can be argued that the share of energy consumption in income inequality can be explained within the framework of energy poverty. It should also be noted that access to energy will reduce individual living standards and reinforce income inequality. Full individual access to education and healthcare will also lead to increased human capital and access to higher income levels (Aghaei & Lin Lawell, 2022; Arı, 2022; Nkomo, 2007).

2.2 Energy Justice

The concept of energy injustice is linked to environmental justice and climate struggles. Environmental justice is an approach that addresses the sources of global inequalities caused by environmental problems arising from industrialization and development, as well as their solutions (Kılıç & Tok, 2014). Climate justice, by considering the impacts of climate change on low-income and vulnerable communities, ensures that these communities have a voice in climate-related debates. The concept of energy justice is built upon the bureaucratic and economic aspects of environmental and climate justice. Meeting increasing energy demand through fossil-based systems is the most significant factor fueling energy injustice. The energy phenomenon is evaluated globally through industry, trade, and economy, rather than fundamentally meeting human needs. In this regard, energy injustice's fundamental causes and consequences are systemic inefficiency, disregard for human rights, lack of access to equitable and accessible energy, and climate change (Baş & Demirtaş, 2022).

2.3 Health and Well-Being

The healthcare and energy sectors interact significantly, and the diversity of energy sources can have significant environmental impacts. These impacts can affect the health of humans and all other living beings, leading to significant health problems. Fossil fuels, which are widely used today, can cause major health problems such as heart disease, respiratory illnesses, and other health conditions. Moreover, the diverse use of energy sources can lead to global consequences such as climate change. Therefore, the choice of energy sources can affect all living things. Furthermore, energy use is a prerequisite for the continuity of services provided in the healthcare sector. Energy consumption enables the use of medical technological devices and ensures access to sustainable and uninterrupted healthcare services. All of this demonstrates an undeniable relationship between the healthcare sector and the energy sector. In recent years, using clean energy has been encouraged to address these negative impacts, and the understanding that choosing clean energy will eliminate the problems associated with conventional energy sources has been acknowledged (Aygün et al., 2025).

2.4 Educational Inequality

Energy poverty and educational inequality are concepts with multiple interconnections. In households experiencing energy poverty, inadequate lighting and heating in study environments lead to ineffective learning in low-income areas. Furthermore, the inevitable integration of digital technologies in education demonstrates that the lack of consistent electricity and internet access exacerbates educational inequality. The share of energy expenditures in total household income can limit resources available for educational materials and supporting learning tools, thereby contributing to the reflection of socioeconomic disparities in educational attainment. Therefore, the concept of energy poverty is linked to improved living conditions and can directly impact access to education and equal opportunities, contributing to the perpetuation of the cycle of poverty across generations.

2.5 *Housing and Energy Efficiency*

Housing's qualitative characteristics and energy efficiency are among the primary determinants of energy poverty. Insulation properties, the effectiveness and suitability of heating systems, and the efficiency of preferred energy technologies directly affect households' energy use preferences and energy costs. Low energy efficiency in housing requires greater energy consumption to maintain the same standard of living, further exacerbating energy poverty for low-income groups. Particularly in developing countries, where housing stocks lack quality insulation and inadequate and unsustainable energy efficiency investments are among the most significant obstacles to eradicating energy poverty. Therefore, increasing residential energy efficiency is becoming a critical strategy for combating energy poverty for environmental sustainability and social policy.

3 Gender and Energy Poverty

In countries with free market economies, the volatility in energy prices significantly impacts energy poverty through its social dimension. In particular, in countries with high current account deficits and externally dependent economies, the volatility in exchange rates is directly reflected in energy prices. From a societal perspective, improving economic, social, and environmental conditions and providing comprehensive energy services is a fundamental need for all humanity today and in the future. Furthermore, society expects these services to be provided globally in the most accessible, cost-effective, reliable, and environmentally friendly manner possible (Öcal & Başarslan-Arslan, 2022).

The concept of gender is directly linked to society's expectations of different genders and the roles they assume. According to this concept, society assigns different duties and responsibilities to women and men, distributing expectations disproportionately between them. Furthermore, at the societal level, it is observed that the elderly, immigrants, and women experience energy poverty more rapidly and more intensely (Butler, 2022). Today, energy poverty is no longer merely a technical problem but has become a gender justice issue. Especially in rural areas, women shoulder almost the entire burden of collecting fuel, creating both a loss of time and health concerns. Women's lower share of income distribution and their higher share of home care work increase their likelihood of becoming "energy poor."

Energy poverty, the inadequate access to energy to meet basic needs, can disrupt or even prevent activities expected to be carried out at home. In such a situation, women responsible for essential household activities can be considered the social segment most exposed to energy poverty due to the imbalance in energy supply and demand. Therefore, the gender-based breakdown in energy poverty is more likely associated with women than men (Koyuncu Hışım, 2025). Rising energy prices increase budgetary pressure when household incomes are low. Women, responsible for managing household expenses and consumption, are the most affected by this pressure. High energy bills not only lead women to cut back on essential expenses such as education, healthcare, and food, but also exacerbate gender-based poverty. Deepening energy poverty leads to the foregoing of education, particularly for girls, and the need to spend more time on household chores (collecting firewood, heating water, etc.), thus reintroducing gender-based inequality and creating disparity in opportunities. In addition, energy poverty at the gender level may even cause women to face negative health problems, both physically and mentally.

From another perspective, access to energy enables women to take a more active role in income-generating activities, while energy poverty limits their economic independence. The decline in women's participation in the labor market and employment due to energy poverty further perpetuates gender inequalities. Access to energy services enables women to engage in small-scale production, agricultural activities, or home-based entrepreneurship. Conversely, women's participation in paid and income-generating work will be limited, and their productivity and participation in household roles will be insufficient.

Considering women as a relatively high-priority group in energy access within the framework of an energy justice approach is increasingly important in social policy development. In other words, women's participation in the formulation and implementation of energy policies is strategically important for ensuring that energy justice is reflected in consumption and decision-making processes. It increases the effectiveness of the fight against energy poverty and creates a significant transformation in eliminating gender inequality.

4 Climate Change—Energy Poverty Relationship

The intertwined relationship between climate change and energy poverty constitutes one of the most pressing global challenges, often conceptualized as the "energy justice triad" alongside energy security (McCauley, 2017). This nexus is fundamentally bidirectional: on one hand, energy poverty exacerbates climate change as constrained low-income groups are forced to rely on carbon-intensive and inefficient energy sources. Conversely, climate change mitigation policies—such as poorly designed low-carbon policies—can inadvertently worsen energy poverty by increasing costs, creating new forms of deprivation, and deepening existing energy inequalities. Analysis of European energy transitions, for example by the EVALUATE project (Bouzarovski, 2018), reveals that a lack of coordination between climate and social policies frequently overlooks low-income households in energy efficiency investments, perpetuating issues like poor insulation and high bills. Therefore, effective energy policy must simultaneously integrate environmental sustainability and social equity under the crucial framework of energy justice.

5 Measuring Energy Poverty: Indicators, Controversies, and Methodological Limitations

Measuring energy poverty is among the most controversial topics in academic literature and policymaking. The concept of energy poverty itself has varying definitions across contexts, while the indicators and methods used to measure it vary significantly across countries, regions, and time periods. This complicates the comparability of policies to reduce energy poverty and sometimes leads to misleading results (Bouzarovski, 2018).

As mentioned above, measurement efforts began with the concept of "fuel poverty," which was similar to energy poverty. During this period, the focus was on the ability of households to heat their homes adequately. Since the 1990s, the concept has expanded and been redefined to include access to energy services (cooking, lighting, communication, and transportation) (Boardman, 1991; McCauley, 2017). Today, energy poverty is considered a multidimensional phenomenon, and its measurement incorporates economic, social, technological, and environmental factors.

5.1 One-Dimensional Economic Indicators

The oldest and most common methods for measuring energy poverty have been approached based on economic indicators. These primarily focus on the relationship between household energy expenditures and income levels. The relevant indicators are presented below:

10% Indicator

Developed in the UK in the 1980s, this method predicts that a household is considered energy poor if it spends more than 10% of its total income on energy expenditures (Boardman, 1991). This method has been widely used in Europe for a long time. Its advantage is that it is easy to calculate and understand. However, its disadvantage is that it can produce misleading results when energy prices, income levels, and climate conditions in different countries are not taken into account. For example, even if a household living in cold climates has the same income level as a household living in temperate regions, their energy expenditures can differ significantly (Bouzarovski, 2018).

Low Income High Cost (LIHC) Indicator

The LIHC approach, developed in the UK in 2012, aimed to overcome the limitations of the 10% indicator (Hills, 2012). Accordingly, two conditions are required to be considered energy poor:

- Household income being below the median (Median refers to the value in the middle of a distribution, with half the population below and half above it. In energy poverty studies where income and expenditure inequalities are evident, the median value provides a more reliable measure than the mean.)
- Energy expenditures are above the median value.

This approach offers a more precise assessment by considering both rather than a measure focused solely on income or expenditure. However, the LIHC is also open to criticism. The discrepancy between median income and expenditure values, particularly in non-European contexts, limits the indicator's applicability (Butler, 2022). The median represents the value in the middle of a distribution, with half the population below and half above it. In energy poverty studies with prominent income and expenditure inequalities, the median value provides a more reliable measure than the mean.

Double Median Indicator (2 M)

Another method used to measure energy poverty is to consider households as energy poor if their energy expenditure is more than twice the median expenditure. This approach is useful in identifying overburden issues. However, contextual differences limit its use internationally (Guruswamy, 2015).

5.2 *Multidimensional Indicators*

Income and expenditure metrics alone fail to capture the multidimensional nature of energy poverty. Therefore, modern indices integrate economic indicators with factors like access, housing quality, and social/environmental vulnerability.

Boardman Approach and Housing Quality

Boardman (1991) asserted that energy poverty measurement must consider a dwelling's physical characteristics and efficiency, not just expenditure. UK studies highlighted that factors like insulation and energy technologies are critical to household costs. This led European countries to include housing-based indicators (e.g., poor insulation, single-pane windows) in official definitions. However, since these indicators often rely on qualitative data, they pose a challenge for objective cross-country comparisons (Butler, 2022).

Multidimensional Energy Poverty Index (MEPI)

The Multidimensional Energy Poverty Index (MEPI) is the most well-known example of multidimensional measurement. Developed under the leadership of UNDP, MEPI measures energy poverty not only on income level but also on access to basic energy services (Nussbaumer et al., 2012).

The Multidimensional Energy Poverty Index (MEPI) assesses energy deprivation across five fundamental areas: Lighting (access to electricity); Cooking (utilizing clean fuels or technology); Cooling/Heating (the thermal comfort capacity of a residence); Access to Information (availability of devices like TV, radio, and telephone); and Education/Health Linkages (the measured impact of energy shortages on essential basic services).

The MEPI has the advantage of conceptualizing energy poverty through energy services, not just income. However, its drawback is its high data requirements. The lack of microdata on health, education, and energy access, particularly in low-income countries, limits the index's applicability (Nalule, 2019).

Comprehensive Energy Poverty Index (CEPI)

Another method gaining increasing attention in the literature is the Comprehensive Energy Poverty Index (CEPI). This index attempts to integrate some dimensions that the MEPI does not cover (e.g., household health indicators, environmental sustainability) (Okushima, 2016).

The Comprehensive Energy Poverty Index (CEPI) offers a holistic measurement by integrating a household's economic burden (income/expenditure balance) and access to essential services like electrification and clean cooking technologies, alongside structural factors such as housing conditions (insulation and building quality), the resultant health effects (respiratory issues and indoor air quality), and the broader social dimension related to energy deprivation leading to social exclusion.

The CEPI's advantage is that it conceptualizes energy poverty as a multidimensional "well-being deficit." However, its most significant limitation is the uncertainty surrounding how to weight different dimensions. The literature notes that weights are often arbitrary, and results vary from country to country (Rubio-Bellido & Solís-Guzmán, 2022).

5.3 *Health and Social Dimension-Focused Indicators*

In measuring energy poverty, economic and access indicators, as well as social impacts are becoming increasingly important. Indicators focused on health and social dimensions originated in Europe and have since been used globally.

Thermal Comfort and Health Indicators

One of Europe's most frequently used indicators is the rate of "not being able to heat one's home adequately." This data, published regularly by Eurostat, reflects a dimension of energy poverty directly linked to health (Bouzarovski, 2018).

Cold homes can cause respiratory illnesses, cardiovascular problems, and psychological stress. Butler (2022) argues that the "cold house syndrome" seen in low-income households should be included in measurement methods.

Indoor Air Quality and Clean Cooking Technologies

Energy poverty is often measured by cooking technologies based on biomass use. According to data from the World Health Organization, 2.5 billion people worldwide still use traditional biomass (wood, dung, and coal). This situation causes serious health problems and is considered one of the main indicators of energy poverty (Simcock et al., 2018).

From a measurement perspective, "access to clean cooking technology" is critical in multidimensional indices such as the MEPI and CEPI. However, access to clean technologies (LPG, electric cooking appliances) remains limited in rural areas, leading to significant geographic variation in measurement (Nalule, 2019).

Social Exclusion and Quality of Life

Energy poverty is not only the inability to meet physical needs; it is also a matter of social exclusion. Limited access to electricity also limits social participation through a lack of access to information (TV, internet). Guruswamy (2015) considers energy poverty internationally a "violation of basic human rights" and states that measurement tools should reflect this dimension.

Butler (2022) emphasizes that the social dimensions of energy poverty are still underrepresented in measurement methods, and that particularly vulnerable groups such as the elderly, people with disabilities, and migrants remain invisible.

5.4 Methodological Limitations

Both unidimensional and multidimensional indicators lack cross-country comparability. The fact that the same threshold value (e.g., 10%) has different meanings in different countries creates serious methodological problems (Bouzarovski, 2018). The lack of reliable household surveys, especially in less developed countries, reduces the applicability of indices such as MEPI and CEPI (Nalule, 2019). In most countries, expenditure-based approaches, such as the 10% indicator, are limited by the reliability of household income and consumption data. Households with the same income level experience differing outcomes due to variations in energy prices and climate conditions, as evidenced by the dissimilar meaning of the 10% threshold in Spain versus Finland. These single-figure methods also fail to account for structural factors like energy efficiency and housing quality, while multidimensional indices such as MEPI and CEPI face the significant methodological challenge of the weighting problem (Okushima, 2016).

Energy poverty is not constant; it is susceptible to seasonal fluctuations. The need for heating in winter and cooling in summer exacerbates energy poverty differently in different regions. However, most measurements are based on annual data and do not reflect these fluctuations (Simcock et al., 2018).

Bouzarovski (2018) and Simcock et al. (2018) state that defining energy poverty solely on the income-expenditure axis is "overly reductionist" and leaves out social and technological dimensions.

Traditional indicators are often calculated based on the "average household." This approach obscures the specific needs of vulnerable groups such as the elderly, people with disabilities, immigrants, and women (Butler, 2022). For example, heating deprivation leads to fatal health consequences for the elderly, while the digital divide in education is even more critical for children. Energy prices, consumption patterns, infrastructure quality, and income levels vary across countries. Therefore, the comparative power of international indices remains limited (McCauley, 2017). Furthermore, most official statistics do not include parameters such as energy efficiency and social impacts.

Recently, a point of increasing discussion is the need to align existing measurement tools with climate change, digitalization, and energy transitions. Digitalization of energy consumption enables more detailed household-level data. Data collected through smart meters can be used to measure energy poverty in real time (Simcock et al., 2018). However, this approach also raises data privacy and ethical concerns.

The effects of climate change (e.g., increasing heat waves) are redefining energy poverty. In the future, measurements should take into account not only the "heating need" but also the "cooling need" (Butler, 2022). In this context, "thermal stress indicators" is proposed as a new dimension in measuring energy poverty.

McCauley (2017) and Bouzarovski (2018) recommend that the measurement of energy poverty be more closely aligned with the energy justice literature. This approach would include physical access and indicators such as democratic participation, access to renewable energy, and billing fairness. Butler (2022) and Guruswamy

(2015) emphasize the need to integrate social science methods (qualitative research, ethnographies, community-based studies) into the measurement. This would make the subjective experiences of individuals suffering from energy poverty more visible.

6 Policy Recommendations and Strategic Roadmap

Energy is a concept that is at the center of sustainable development as well as the provision of basic services such as health and education (Nalule, 2018). Ensuring that societies have access to energy and meeting their energy-based needs is a critical component in achieving their well-being (Bouzarovski & Petrova, 2015). Energy poverty, defined by Reddy (2000) as the lack of sufficient options to access adequate, affordable, reliable, high-quality and environmentally friendly energy services to support economic and human development, is a set of problems that cannot be limited to just the lack of infrastructure. The most common problems arise from low-income households that try to cover high energy costs with a large percentage of their income. In addition, there are high energy-consuming devices, inefficient buildings and household-specific energy needs (Öcal & Başarslan-Arslan, 2022).

6.1 Evaluation of Current Policies in the Context of Energy Poverty

Energy policies generally focus on macro-level objectives such as economic growth, energy security, and carbon emission reduction. However, this focus often overshadows social justice-based dimensions such as access to energy, addressing social inequalities, and protecting vulnerable groups (Butler, 2022).

In this context, to accurately assess the impact of existing policies, the concept and analysis must first be clarified. As previously mentioned, single-dimensional indicators (e.g., the threshold for allocating more than 10% of income to energy) can be context-insensitive, so multidimensional indices that track dimensions such as housing quality, health, and financial hardship are increasingly being proposed. Factors such as demographic structure, household life cycle, and urban-rural segregation reinforce the distributional character of energy poverty; therefore, targeting and instrument selection should incorporate these contextual variables.

Evaluation is also related to how the tools used are implemented over time. For example, in the short term, measures such as utility bill subsidies, debt deferrals/freezes, and power outage bans, while implemented for groups exposed to energy poverty, are insufficient, even if they support the process. In another example, medium and long-term housing efficiency investments (insulation, heating/cooling system improvements, etc.) can provide lasting cost reductions and health/comfort gains.

However, current financial constraints at the micro (household) and macro (country) levels prevent these investments from being realized.

The key factors determining success in combating energy poverty are correctly defining the problem, setting targets, developing various intervention tools, and designing these policies in a way that is appropriate for society (Rubio-Bellido & Solís-Guzmán, 2022). This emerges as a multi-layered process.

6.2 Strategic Intervention Areas: Short, Medium, and Long-Term Goals

Solving energy poverty and ensuring sustainable access to energy across societies requires policies distributed across different timeframes. Within this framework, the goal should be to first meet urgent needs in the short term (0–2 years), then ensure transformation in the medium term (2–5 years), and then ensure sustainability of the transformation in the long term (5 + years) (Bouzarovski, 2018).

Solutions to meet the urgent needs of groups experiencing or facing energy poverty can be considered short-term interventions. In this context, providing them with utility bill support can significantly reduce energy costs. Additionally, measures such as debt deferral and bill freezing for these groups may be effective in the short term. Power outages could be prohibited during specific periods of the year (e.g., very cold or very hot days) to increase the energy security of vulnerable groups (Charlier & Legendre, 2023). Furthermore, energy literacy training could be provided to these groups to change their consumption habits.

The primary medium-term goal is to transform energy poverty toward energy justice. The first action is to increase energy efficiency in areas where energy-poor groups live. Urban renewal activities in these areas should target physical infrastructure and equitable access to energy. Furthermore, building renovations can reduce energy consumption while improving user health and comfort (Bardazzi & Pazienza, 2023).

Long-term interventions must be taken to develop structural and lasting solutions to energy poverty and make the process sustainable. In this context, energy poverty must first be clearly integrated into national energy, housing, and development strategies (Bouzarovski, 2018). To implement this holistic approach, it is crucial to increase the governance capacity of public institutions, actively involve local governments in decision-making processes, and establish data-based decision support systems (Guruswamy, 2015). Finally, a long-term transformation is only possible through public awareness. In this context, increasing energy literacy, incorporating energy justice-based content into educational curricula, and disseminating community-based innovative practices will trigger a cultural shift in the fight against energy poverty.

6.3 Successful Policy Implementations

While policies and practices used to combat energy poverty vary depending on countries' socioeconomic structures and capacities, they ultimately represent successful examples. As seen in the Table 1, renewable energy solutions, community-based participation, energy efficiency investments, support mechanisms, and other common themes are among these policies and practices.

Table 1 Successful country implementations

Country	Policy/Practice name	Application summary	Success and impact factor
Bangladesh	Solar Home Systems	Providing basic electricity access to rural areas with solar-powered microsystems	Reaching over 4 million households, reducing external dependency Groh et al. (2023)
United Kingdom	Warm Front Program	Support for insulation and efficient heating for low-income households	Support for approximately 2 million households; bills reduced by up to 20% Bouzarovski (2018)
Bulgaria	Energy Subsidy	Invoice support	Direct aid was provided to poor households. Bouzarovski (2018)
China	Rural Electrification, Energy Transition	Transforming from coal to clean energy	Nearly 100% electrification Bouzarovski (2018)
France	Treve Hivernale, Medical Supports and FSL Fund	Prohibition of winter power outages, health-based energy assistance, and local debt support	Protecting vulnerable households, improving quality of life through health-based subsidies Charlier and Legendre (2023)
South Africa	Free Basic Electricity	Providing a certain energy quota free of charge	Preventive measures to reduce inequalities in energy access Simcock et al. (2018)
Spain	Bono Social	Discounts on electricity bills for low-income households	The number of households covered by social protection increased by 15% annually Bouzarovski (2018)
Chile	Heater Replacement Program	Replacing old heating systems with environmentally friendly models	Improvement in air quality and reduction in energy costs Velasco Herrejón et al. (2024)
Türkiye	Social Assistance	Electricity Consumption Support	Direct support to low-income households Rubio-Bellido and Solís-Guzmán (2022)
Jordan	Solar Energy Investments	Solar rooftop projects	Effects on reducing fossil dependency Butler (2022)

7 The Economic Dimension of Energy Justice

The economic dimension of energy justice is not limited to ensuring access to energy; it also requires that this access be economically sustainable, equitable, and inclusive. The high share of energy expenditures in income, particularly among low-income groups, reveals the structural dimensions of energy poverty (Bouzarovski & Petrova, 2015: 32). In this context, the economic dimension of energy justice includes policy axes such as reducing income inequalities, restructuring energy subsidies, and developing alternative financing models (Sovacool et al., 2017).

7.1 Cost of Energy Access and Income Inequality

Energy poverty refers to households' inadequate physical and economic access to energy. The high share of energy expenditures in the total income of low-income households can lead to difficulties in meeting basic needs in some cases (Öcal & Başarslan-Arslan, 2022). However, for high-income households with similar energy expenditures, the situation may appear insignificant. Consequently, energy poverty emerges as a concept directly linked to income inequality (Bouzarovski & Petrova, 2015). Furthermore, differing energy investment policies across countries exacerbate this situation. Countries where energy-related infrastructure investments are concentrated in high-income regions are particularly exemplified by this situation (Groh et al., 2023).

Consequently, considering energy poverty across different income groups together is crucial in the context of energy justice. Ensuring equal access to energy services for low-income groups is crucial not only for establishing social justice but also for achieving sustainable development.

7.2 Energy Subsidies and Equitable Distribution

Energy subsidies are considered an important tool for reducing energy access costs for households, particularly in low-income areas. For this tool to be effective in reducing energy poverty, its targeting, type, and distribution mechanisms must be carefully determined. If subsidies are applied to the general consumer, higher-income groups may benefit more from this support, which could weaken the corrective effect of subsidies on income distribution (Coady et al., 2015). A study by Coady et al. (2015) emphasizes that policies directly targeting low-income groups are more successful in terms of both cost-effectiveness and equity.

Ultimately, energy subsidies both financially support low-income households and reduce economic inequalities. This will be possible by considering disparities between income groups and directing resources to the most vulnerable.

7.3 Innovative Financing Approaches for Energy Access

The inadequacy of subsidies and tariff discounts in addressing energy poverty has paved the way for the emergence of innovative financing approaches. In this context, energy cooperatives, microfinance programs, and green bonds are among the prominent tools (Bauwens et al., 2016; Sovacool & Dworkin, 2015).

Energy cooperatives are defined as non-profit organizations based on democratic governance principles that enable local communities to participate directly in energy production and consumption processes. These cooperatives play a significant role, particularly in the dissemination of renewable energy technologies. By strengthening the participation of individuals and communities in the energy system, they reduce energy costs and contribute to the development of energy democracy. In terms of energy access, they enhance energy supply security in disadvantaged or rural areas through on-site production and consumption models, create local employment opportunities, and reduce external dependency (Wierling et al., 2018).

Microfinance stands out as a key tool in alleviating energy poverty by facilitating access to modern energy services for low-income households. These financial mechanisms offer favorable credit and savings opportunities, particularly for the acquisition of renewable energy technologies (such as solar power systems), helping households overcome high initial costs. Microfinance channels increase access to energy, resulting in long-term reductions in energy costs, support for income-generating activities, and an improved quality of life. Particularly in rural or off-grid areas, energy solutions provided through microfinance strengthen energy supply security and foster social inclusion, thereby facilitating a transformation process aligned with the Sustainable Development Goals (Manko & Watkins, 2022).

Green bonds are important capital market instruments designed in line with environmental sustainability principles, particularly used to finance renewable energy and energy access projects. These bonds offer investors the opportunity to directly fund projects that generate environmental benefits, while providing issuers with a long-term, relatively low-cost source of financing. From an energy access perspective, green bonds contribute to scaling up investments such as solar and wind power plants, strengthening energy transmission infrastructure, microgrids, and off-grid solutions. In this respect, they enhance supply security, particularly in regions where energy poverty is prevalent. They also reduce the financing gap for projects by encouraging public-private sector collaboration and accelerating the energy transition, which is aligned with the Sustainable Development Goals (Lucchetta, 2025).

In this regard, innovative financing tools such as energy cooperatives, microfinance programs, and green bonds contribute to the development of holistic and sustainable solutions to energy poverty by facilitating access to capital and increasing participation and ownership at the local level.

8 Transformational Strategies to Solve Energy Poverty

Ensuring equity in energy access is possible not only by providing temporary solutions to existing problems, but also by developing and implementing strategies that identify and eliminate the underlying causes of these problems. These strategies can be defined as long-term, holistic interventions that combine financial, technological, and social dimensions (Bouzarovski, 2018; Simcock et al., 2018).

While policies addressing energy poverty often offer short-term solutions, lasting progress can only be achieved through innovative policies that center on energy justice. Prominent approaches in this context include ensuring access to energy as a fundamental human right, protecting disadvantaged groups against the impacts of climate change, and reducing social inequalities (Guruswamy, 2015; Rubio-Bellido & Solís-Guzmán, 2022).

Innovative policies should also include aligning energy infrastructures with renewable and low-carbon technologies, strengthening local capacities, and expanding community-based models. Such an approach not only increases energy supply security but also reduces income inequalities and supports the more active participation of vulnerable groups in social life (Butler, 2022; Groh et al., 2023).

For innovative strategies to be effectively implemented, policy and implementation models must be compatible, inclusive, and complementary at both the local and global levels. Considering the structural causes of energy poverty, the socioeconomic conditions of countries, and the differences in existing energy infrastructures, multi-scalar and multi-actor governance models emerge as a key approach (Bouzarovski, 2018; Simcock et al., 2018).

Locally developed policies should aim not only to alleviate energy poverty through short-term support but also to create lasting solutions that strengthen social equity and align with climate goals. A powerful example of this approach is the European Union's "Just Transition Mechanism" program. This mechanism aims to increase economic diversification in regions dependent on fossil fuels, encourage investments in renewable energy, and prevent job losses during the energy transition (Rubio-Bellido & Solís-Guzmán, 2022). Similarly, national programs supporting energy efficiency investments in areas with high concentrations of low-income households not only reduce household energy expenditures but also produce tangible improvements in health, quality of life, and comfort (Butler, 2022).

Global collaborations play a critical role in alleviating energy poverty through financing, technology transfer, and capacity building. For example, in South Africa, the transition of coal-fired regions to renewable energy was supported by international funds, gradually replacing coal demand with renewable energy sources (Guruswamy, 2015). Similarly, in Bangladesh, the "Solar Home Systems" program, supported by microfinance mechanisms, brought solar-powered solutions to rural areas, providing electricity access to more than four million households and reducing energy poverty, as well as significantly reducing the country's external dependence (Groh et al., 2023).

Eradicating energy poverty and ensuring the sustainability of policies in this area is only possible with practical strategies and supporting implementation tools. To achieve this, it is necessary to accurately identify the key factors hindering the success of existing policies. Simcock et al. (2018) list the following obstacles: the mismatch between macroeconomic objectives and socially equitable development, lack of coordination between government units, insufficient financial resources of local governments, limitations in technical and human resource capacity, and the inability to accurately and consistently identify households experiencing energy poverty.

Policy tools used to overcome these obstacles can be considered in three main dimensions: financial, technological, and social. Financial tools include models such as microfinance programs, energy cooperatives, and green bonds. These mechanisms contribute to reducing long-term energy costs by facilitating access to renewable energy sources, particularly for low-income households. Technological tools include innovations such as the development of renewable energy infrastructure, the establishment of microgrids, solutions that increase energy efficiency, and intelligent metering systems. Social tools, on the other hand, focus on increasing energy literacy, conducting awareness campaigns, and transforming energy consumption habits through community-based projects.

Planning these three dimensions with a holistic approach and implementing them in coordination will go beyond short-term relief in the fight against energy poverty, enabling the creation of lasting, equitable, and sustainable solutions.

9 General Evaluation

Eliminating energy poverty in favor of disadvantaged groups and ensuring and sustaining energy justice in the long term depends on monitoring and analyzing all processes. The monitoring process involves regularly collecting data on the area. Examples of monitoring data include the rate of household access to energy, the share of household energy expenditures in total expenditures, and the rate of renewable energy resource use. The evaluation process involves analyzing the data obtained and comparing the outcomes with the expected results of existing policies. Conducting monitoring and evaluation processes with a holistic approach contributes to the sustained and effective fight against energy poverty by ensuring the continuous improvement of policies and practices.

Within this framework, monitoring and evaluation steps should not focus solely on output indicators such as the number of households reached; they should work with a multidimensional set of indicators that include both outcomes (reduced energy load, fewer outages, improved heating/cooling comfort) and impact (health, well-being, education). They should include household energy expenditure as a percentage of income, the ratio of overdue bills/debts, the number and duration of energy outages, and notifications of heating/cooling inadequacy; heat loss measures related to housing efficiency and consumption intensity; and equity dimensions such as energy-related health complaints, gender, aging, and immigration. Furthermore, the results should be shared with the public to ensure public awareness and participation in the process.

Finally, the monitoring and evaluation mechanism should be structured as a continuous learning cycle. This clarifies inter-institutional responsibilities, collects and analyzes data in a standardized format at regular intervals (e.g., every 1, 3, 6 months, or annually), and shares the results with the public. Goals can be redefined through feedback channels. In this context, support can be redesigned to benefit disadvantaged groups, for example, or productivity investments can be restructured. Thus, the monitoring and evaluation process provides clear answers not only to questions like "What did we do?" but also to questions like "What worked? What can we improve?", permanently strengthening the impact of the policy on the ground.

References

Aghaei, M., & Lin Lawell, C. Y. C. (2022). Energy, economic growth, inequality, and poverty in Iran. *The Singapore Economic Review, 67*(02), 733–754. https://doi.org/10.1142/s0217590820500198

Al-Tal, R., Murshed, M., Ahmad, P., Alfar, A. J. K., Bassim, M., Elheddad, M., & Mahmood, H. (2021). The non-linear effects of energy efficiency gains on the incidence of energy poverty. *Sustainability, 13*(19), 1–20. https://doi.org/10.3390/su131911055

Arı, A. (2022). The relationship between income inequality and energy consumption: Evidence from Turkey. *Manisa Celal Bayar University Journal of Social Sciences, 20*(2), 236–244. https://doi.org/10.18026/cbayarsos.1056051

Ateş, B. & Atay Polat, M. (2023). The effects of energy poverty and renewable energy use on environmental degradation. *Hitit Journal of Social Sciences, 16*(2), 290–315. https://doi.org/10.17218/hititsbd.1265226

Aygün, S., Onaran, S., & Altun, U. (2025). Analysis of studies on the relationship between health and energy using content analysis method. *Çukurova University Social Sciences Institute Journal, 34*(1), 118–133. https://doi.org/10.35379/cusosbil.1434304

Bardazzi, R., & Pazienza, M. G. (Eds.). (2023). *Vulnerable households in the energy transition: Energy poverty, demographics and policies.* Springer. https://doi.org/10.1007/978-3-031-35684-1

Baş, B., & Demirtaş, I. (2022). A view of energy cooperatives from the framework of energy justice. *Journal of Recycling Economy & Sustainability Policy, 1*(1), 18–26.

Bauwens, T., Gotchev, B., & Holstenkamp, L. (2016). What drives the development of community energy in Europe? The case of wind power cooperatives. *Energy Research & Social Science, 13*, 136–147. https://doi.org/10.1016/j.erss.2015.12.016

Boardman, B. (1991). *Fuel poverty: From cold homes to affordable warmth.* Belhaven Press.

Bouzarovski, S. (2018). Energy poverty: (Dis)assembling Europe's infrastructural divide. *Palgrave Macmillan.* https://doi.org/10.1007/978-3-319-69299-9

Bouzarovski, S., & Petrova, S. (2015). A global perspective on domestic energy deprivation: Overcoming the energy poverty–fuel poverty binary. *Energy Research & Social Science, 10*, 31–40. https://doi.org/10.1016/j.erss.2015.06.007

Butler, C. (2022). Energy poverty, practice, and policy. *Springer Nature.* https://doi.org/10.1007/978-3-030-99432-7_6

Charlier, D., & Legendre, B. (2023). Energy poverty and health pathologies: An empirical study on the French case. In R. Bardazzi & M. G. Pazienza (Eds.), *Vulnerable households in the energy transition* (pp. 59–75). Springer. https://doi.org/10.1007/978-3-031-35684-1_4

Coady, D., Parry, I. W. H., Sears, L., & Shang, B. (2015). How large are global energy subsidies? *IMF Working Papers, 15*(105). https://doi.org/10.5089/9781513532196.001

Emeç, H., Altay, A., Aslanpay, E., & Özdemir, M. O. (2015). Energy poverty and energy choice profile in Turkey. *Finans Politik Ve Ekonomik Yorumlar, 608*, 9–21.

Foster, V., Tre, J.-P., & Wodon, Q. (2000). Energy prices, energy efficiency, and fuel poverty. *World Bank*. http://info.worldbank.org/etools/docs/voddocs/240/502/Gua_price.pdf

Groh, S., Van der Straeten, J., Lasch, B. E., Gershenson, D., Leal Filho, W., & Kammen, D. M. (2023). Decentralized solutions for developing economies: Addressing energy poverty through innovation. *Springer*. https://doi.org/10.1007/978-3-319-15964-5

Guruswamy, L. (2015). International energy and poverty: The emerging contours. *Routledge*. https://doi.org/10.4324/9781315762203

Hills, J. (2012). *Getting the measure of fuel poverty: Final report of the fuel poverty review*. Crown Copyright. https://sticerd.lse.ac.uk/dps/case/cr/casereport72

Kılıç, S., & Tok, N. (2014). From the traditional understandings of justice to environmentalist justice. *International Journal of Alanya Faculty of Business, 6*(3), 213–228.

Koyuncu Hışım, B. (2025). A general evaluation on examining nexus of gender, energy and poverty. *Artvin Çoruh University International Journal of Social Sciences, 11*(1), 12–26. https://doi.org/10.22466/acusbd.1594055

Lucchetta, M. (2025). *Civil rights and green bonds: Advancing energy equity*. Advance online publication. https://doi.org/10.2139/ssrn.5309552

Manga, M. (2020). The relationship between energy poverty and economic growth. *Bulletin of Economic Theory and Analysis, 5*(2), 101–114. https://doi.org/10.25229/beta.812850

Manko, K., & Watkins, T. A. (2022). Microfinance and SDG 7: Financial impact channels for mitigating energy poverty. *Development in Practice, 32*(8), 1036–1048. https://doi.org/10.1080/09614524.2020.1863338

McCauley, D. (2017). Energy justice: Re-balancing the trilemma of security, poverty and climate change. *Palgrave Macmillan*. https://doi.org/10.1007/978-3-319-62494-5

Munasinghe, M. (2002). The sustainomics trans-disciplinary meta-framework for making development more sustainable: Applications to energy issues. *International Journal of Sustainable Development, 5*(1–2), 125–182. https://doi.org/10.1504/IJSD.2002.002563

Nalule, V. (2018). *Energy poverty and access challenges in Sub-Saharan Africa: The role of regional organizations in overcoming the problem* (Doctoral dissertation). University of Dundee.

Nalule, V. R. (2019). Energy poverty and access challenges in Sub-Saharan Africa: The role of regionalism. *Palgrave Macmillan*. https://doi.org/10.1007/978-3-319-95402-8

Nkomo, J. C. (2007). Energy use, poverty and development in the SADC. *Journal of Energy in Southern Africa, 18*(3), 10–17. https://doi.org/10.17159/2413-3051/2007/v18i3a3385

Nussbaumer, P., Bazilian, M., & Modi, V. (2012). Measuring energy poverty: Focusing on what matters. *Renewable and Sustainable Energy Reviews, 16*(1), 231–243. https://doi.org/10.1016/j.rser.2011.07.150

Öcal, A. T., & Başarslan-Arslan, T. (2022). Focusing on energy poverty in the world: Issues and policiesç. *İnsan ve İnsan, 9*(33), 15–32. https://doi.org/10.29224/insanveinsan.1099470

Okushima, S. (2016). Measuring energy poverty in Japan, 2004–2013. *Energy Policy, 98*, 557–564. https://doi.org/10.1016/j.enpol.2016.09.005

Pye, S., Dobbins, A., Baffert, C., Brajković, J., Deane, P., & De Miglio, R. (2015). Addressing energy poverty and vulnerable consumers in the energy sector across the EU. *L'europe En Formation, 378*(4), 64–89. https://doi.org/10.3917/eufor.378.0064

Reddy, A. K., Annecke, W., Blok, K., Bloom, D., Boardman, B., Eberhard, A., & Ramakrishna, J. (2000). Energy and social issues. In *World energy assessment* (pp. 39–60). UNDP.

Rubio-Bellido, C., & Solís-Guzmán, J. (2022). Energy poverty alleviation: New approaches and contexts. *Springer*. https://doi.org/10.1007/978-3-030-91084-6

Şahin, G., & Algül, Y. (2025). Examining the link between clean energy poverty and climate policies in the scope of OPEC countries. *Journal of Abant Social Sciences, 25*(1), 593–617. https://doi.org/10.11616/asbi.1585892

Simcock, N., Thomson, H., Petrova, S., & Bouzarovski, S. (Eds.). (2018). *Energy poverty and vulnerability: A global perspective*. Routledge. https://doi.org/10.4324/9781315231518

Sovacool, B. K. (2012). The political economy of energy poverty: A review of key challenges. *Energy for Sustainable Development, 16*(3), 272–282. https://doi.org/10.1016/j.esd.2012.05.006

Sovacool, B. K., Burke, M., Baker, L., Kotikalapudi, C. K., & Wlokas, H. (2017). New frontiers and conceptual frameworks for energy justice. *Energy Policy, 105*, 677–691. https://doi.org/10.1016/j.enpol.2017.03.005

Sovacool, B. K., & Dworkin, M. H. (2015). Energy justice: Conceptual insights and practical applications. *Applied Energy, 142*, 435–444. https://doi.org/10.1016/j.apenergy.2015.01.002

UNDP. (2000). *World energy assessment: Energy and the challenge of sustainability*. UNDP.

Velasco-Herrejón, P., Lennon, B., & Dunphy, N. P. (Eds.). (2024). *Living with energy poverty: Perspectives from the Global North and South*. Routledge. https://doi.org/10.4324/9781003408536

Wierling, A., Schwanitz, V. J., Zeiß, J. P., Bout, C., Candelise, C., Gilcrease, W., & Gregg, J. S. (2018). Statistical evidence on the role of energy cooperatives for the energy transition in European countries. *Sustainability, 10*(9), 3339. https://doi.org/10.3390/su10093339

MIX
Papier aus verantwortungsvollen Quellen
Paper from responsible sources
FSC® C105338

If you have any concerns about our products,
you can contact us on
ProductSafety@springernature.com

In case Publisher is established outside the EU,
the EU authorized representative is:
Springer Nature Customer Service Center GmbH
Europaplatz 3, 69115 Heidelberg, Germany

Printed by Libri Plureos GmbH
in Hamburg, Germany